Anti-Semitism and British Gothic Literature

Other publications by this author

BRAM STOKER'S DRACULA: Sucking Through the Century, 1897–1997 (*editor*)

Anti-Semitism and British Gothic Literature

Carol Margaret Davison
Assistant Professor
University of Windsor
Ontario
Canada

First published 2004 by
PALGRAVE MACMILLAN
Houndmills, Basingstoke, Hampshire RG21 6XS and
175 Fifth Avenue, New York, N.Y. 10010
Companies and representatives throughout the world

PALGRAVE MACMILLAN is the global academic imprint of the Palgrave
Macmillan division of St. Martin's Press, LLC and of Palgrave Macmillan Ltd.
Macmillan® is a registered trademark in the United States, United Kingdom
and other countries. Palgrave is a registered trademark in the European
Union and other countries.

ISBN 0–333–92951–9 hardback

This book is printed on paper suitable for recycling and made from fully
managed and sustained forest sources.

A catalogue record for this book is available from the British Library.

Library of Congress Cataloging-in-Publication Data
Davison, Carol Margaret.
    Anti-Semitism and British gothic literature / Carol Margaret Davison.
        p. cm.
    Includes bibliographical references and index.
    ISBN 0–333–92951–9
        1. Horror tales, English – History and criticism. 2. Gothic revival (Literature) –
Great Britain. 3. Antisemitism – Great Britain. 4. Wandering Jew in literature.
5. Antisemitism in literature. 6. Jews in literature. I. Title.

PR830.T3D385 2004
823'.08738—dc22   2004043618

10   9   8   7   6   5   4   3   2   1
13 12 11 10 09 08 07 06 05 04

Printed and bound in Great Britain by
Antony Rowe Ltd, Chippenham and Eastbourne

For my precious parents, my castle keep,
And Keeper and Katmandu, gargoyles extraordinaire

Contents

Preface and Acknowledgements   viii

Introduction: The Nation and the Spectral
Wandering Jew   1

1 The Contested Enlightenment, the
   Contested Castle   15

2 The Primal Scene: The Skeleton in Britain's Closet   34

3 Cabalistic Conspiracies and the Crypto-Jew   55

4 The Rise of the Vampiric Wandering Jew: A
   Sinister German–English Co-Production   87

5 Britain, Vampire Empire: Fin-de-Siècle Fears and
   Bram Stoker's *Dracula*   120

6 Afterword: Pathological Projection and the Nazi Nightmare   158

Notes   166

Works Cited   200

Index   218

Preface and Acknowledgements

Like the demonic Wandering Jew in Gothic literature who constitutes my focus here, this study in cultural pathology has had various incarnations. It began life as a doctoral dissertation written under the extremely astute and rigorous guidance of Maggie Kilgour at McGill University whose own very provocative work, *The Rise of the Gothic Novel* (Routledge, 1995), sparked my interest at a time when I barely even knew what 'Gothic' meant. She was vital to the genesis and presentation of these ideas, the oversights of which are entirely mine, and I am forever thankful for her ongoing support. Dr Kilgour has my 'undying' respect and admiration for re-teaching me the meaning of caution and precision, and especially for expertly preparing me in early 1998 for that terrifying primal scene in every academic's professional life – the doctoral defence.

My tremendous thanks are also due to numerous others at McGill – Michael Bristol for his thorough examination of this dissertation at a very early stage, and Gary Wihl, David Hensley, Tess O'Toole, Josef Schmidt, and Eugene Orenstein, whose perceptive questions and comments during and subsequent to my doctoral defence were invaluable to what has been, due to pressing practical issues and serious health difficulties, a fairly lengthy revisionary process.

Profound thanks are especially due to two friends and fellow Gothicists – Marie Mulvey-Roberts, whose early encouragement as my external dissertation examiner opened the door for me at Palgrave Macmillan, and William Hughes, whose insatiable thirst for all things *Dracula*-related is a source of constant amazement. Their assiduous comments have helped me reconceptualize components of this project and saved me, in numerous instances, from possible embarrassment.

I would also like to thank Concordia University's Part Time Faculty Association for several substantial awards for research in Romania, Ireland, Philadelphia, and New York while this project was in its early stages. For his crucial role in helping me to acquire this funding and his consistently provocative questions and invaluable suggestions during many lengthy and exciting discussions over the years, I am eternally grateful to G. David Sheps, former Chair of English at Concordia University in Montreal. If this book makes any valuable contribution whatsoever to the field of Gothic Studies, it is a result of his unflagging encouragement and incalculable influence. As my bibliography attests, I also stand on the shoulders of hundreds of other dedicated and disciplined scholars in related fields without whose bold investigations this study would not have been possible.

Special thanks are also due to Helen Smailes, the Assistant Keeper of British Art at the National Gallery of Scotland, who very graciously provided me with contemporary commentaries about William Fettes Douglas's painting, *The Spell*, which was first presented at the Royal Scottish Academy Exhibition in 1864 and a detail of which graces this study's cover. Ms. Smailes also facilitated the permissions process. This painting is one of thousands of cultural artifacts that attest to the deeply entrenched association between the Jews and magical/secret societies in the European consciousness. The two gentlemen engaged in invoking spirits possess traditionally Jewish physiognomies, but what is particularly striking is the very telling inscription on the wall of the Star of David instead of a pentagram, a traditional occult symbol. This image of the alchemist Jew also captures his traditional ambivalent semiotics: depending on one's perspective, he may be regarded as dreadfully atavistic or treacherously progressive.

Various editors at Macmillan are also due my thanks – Charmian Hearne, Emily Rosser, and Paula Kennedy – for their great patience, timely reminders, and helpful advice regarding manuscript requirements. I am also grateful to Kate McCrone, former Dean of Arts at the University of Windsor, who granted me the necessary course release over the 2002–03 academic year that enabled my revisions, and to Susan Wendt-Hildebrandt at the University of Windsor for some linguistic clarification. I am also deeply indebted to the various Interlibrary Loan Departments at Concordia University (Montreal), the University of Toronto at Scarborough, and the University of Windsor, and to Dima Ayoub who provided some research assistance. Corey Evan Thompson is also due my thanks for his very astute proofreading and verification of the bibliographic data. Finally, I am especially grateful to this book's extremely patient and assiduous project manager, Veena Krishnan, for her detailed attention to the text in every aspect.

On a more personal note, I am, as always, indebted to my loving and supportive family for instilling in me a sense of passion for knowledge and pride in hard work and, on a more pragmatic note, helping me out financially and otherwise during the last leg of my doctorate. Their unconditional love and encouragement, in both sickness and health, has helped me to prepare this manuscript, as it merited, for its final resting place.

Introduction: The Nation and the Spectral Wandering Jew

> Among the living nations of the earth the Jews are as a nation long since dead … [A]fter the Jewish people had ceased to exist as an actual state, as a political entity, they could nevertheless not submit to total annihilation – they lived on spiritually as a nation. The world saw in this people the uncanny form of one of the dead walking among the living. The ghostlike apparition of a living corpse, of a people without unity or organization, without land or other bonds of unity, no longer alive, and yet walking among the living – this spectral form without precedence in history, unlike anything that preceded or followed it, could [not] but strangely affect the imagination of the nations. And if the fear of ghosts is something inborn, and has a certain justification in the psychic life of mankind, why be surprised at the effect produced by this dead but still living nation?
>
> A fear of the Jewish ghost has passed down the generations and the centuries. First a breeder of prejudice … it culminated in Judeophobia … a variety of demonopathy with the distinction that it is not peculiar to particular races but is common to the whole of mankind, and that this ghost is not disembodied like other ghosts but partakes of flesh and blood, must endure pain inflicted by the fearful mob who imagines itself endangered.
>
> (Pinsker: 163)

Leo Pinsker's famous 1882 essay promoting Zionism entitled 'Auto-Emancipation' identifies the key elements of the present study – national identity and belonging, the principal trope of the undying and uncanny Wandering Jew spectre who haunts European nations, and the Jewish Question, which Michael Ragussis rightly characterizes as plural and incorporating 'a variety of Jewish questions (religious, legal, racial, and so on)' ('Secret': 298). With the Enlightenment era genre of British Gothic fiction as its principal domain of focus, this study engages with the related questions

1

of why, in what ways, and with what implications, the legendary Wandering Jew, Ahasuerus, haunts modern Britain in the eighteenth and nineteenth centuries. This infamous, transgressive antichrist, associated with what Edgar Rosenberg has called 'the Ur-crime of the Crucifixion' (27), was cursed to immortality until the Millennium for mocking Christ as he carried the cross to Calvary.[1] In that instance, he figuratively assumed the cross as an ambivalent representative of 'a deicide nation ... on whose redemption the fate of mankind' was said to hang (Fisch: 15).[2] He has since been repeatedly crucified for his Original Sin (Horkheimer and Adorno: 49–50).

In the European worldview, wandering is the 'master image of Jewish identity' (Freedman, *Temple*: 25) and the Wandering Jew has been, as Pinsker's essay attests, the figure through which feelings about the Jewish Question have been most popularly articulated in Europe since the establishment of the Spanish Inquisition (Poliakov: 352, Rose: 27, Susan Shapiro: 63, 66). It was then, when Jewish refugees were literally dispersed throughout Europe, having been expelled from Spain, that this legend emerged. Notably, it arrived on British soil in the early seventeenth century, virtually concurrent with the Jews' readmission to England.[3] With its lens focused on the nation of Britain, *Anti-Semitism and British Gothic Literature* illustrates how this ontologically slippery emblem of the Jewish Question (Freedman, *Temple*: 39) speaks, often in compelling and cryptic ways, to the vexed issue of national identity in its various ideological dimensions – religious, political, economic, moral, ethnic/racial, and sexual.

To adapt the memorable, opening pronouncement of Karl Marx's 1848 'Manifesto of the Communist Party', if a spectre may be said to haunt modern Europe, prior to, during, and even after the advent of Communism, that spectre is the nationless Wandering Jew. Indeed, given the anti-Semitic statements enunciated in Marx's 1843 essay 'On the Jewish Question' where the Jew is characterized as a recalcitrant Mammonist whose values have tainted and enslaved the age (34), he may even be identified as the repressed spectre in the 'Manifesto'. In the broader domain of the European imaginary, he is more semiotically elastic. Exemplifying the traditional ambivalence Bryan Cheyette calls 'semitic discourse' (*Constructions*: 8), the anti-Semite's Jew is both the longstanding emblem of social mobility and the capitalism that Marx so vehemently despised, and the representative promoter, among its detractors, of the communism that Marx so ardently espoused.[4] Although the ideological associations of the ghostlike Wandering Jew may vary from one historical and national context to another, one certainty remains: wherever he appears – in popular and sectarian pamphlets, literature, or folklore – the question of the nature and parameters of European national identity, as constituted by various commercial, religious, and social practices and values, is raised. Moreover, as Michael Ragussis has astutely noted and illustrated, 'the figure of the Jew was used in British fiction to mediate the definitions of different European national identities: France's emancipation of the Jews during the revolution and Spain's persecution of the Jews during the Inquisition were set beside the conduct of Protestant England' (*Figures*: 175–6). What Ragussis fails to note, however, and what I argue here is that the Wandering Jew's engagement with these questions saw its inception and development in the pages of Gothic fiction. Notably, the fictional Wandering Jew performed a similar, albeit more negative, role in relation to the establishment of national identity in other European countries. As regards Germany, Paul Lawrence Rose relates that 'For nineteenth-century Germans, so unsure of their own "Germanness", the Jewish Question was ultimately the German Question. It was, in effect, another way of asking "What is German?" and receiving the satisfying answer–"whatever is not Jewish"' (41). A similar situation existed in late eighteenth-century France. With regard to the Jewish emancipation debate in that country in the 1790s, Eugene Weber has unequivocally asserted that 'the Jewish question was a *Jewish* question' of interest only to Jews (8). Drawing attention to the negligible numbers of Jews in France, Gary Kates has persuasively countered Weber's claim. In his view, 'Non-Jews chose to address this issue because the emancipation debate was not really about the Jews at all. Since there were so few Jews in France, and since they played little role in the Revolution, they were easily turned into symbols of something else ... The debate over Jewish emancipation was thus a debate over what it meant to be a French citizen' (109).

The present study, guided by James Shapiro's compelling statement that 'the English turned to Jewish questions in order to answer English ones' (1), makes similar allegations about the British case. While I would add the proviso that the English did not turn to Jewish questions *exclusively* in order to answer English questions, I would reiterate David Feldman's assertion that 'conceptions of the nation were constituted and developed, in part, through the ways [British] men and women confronted the Jewish issue' (*Englishmen*: 13). As I hope to illustrate in the course of this investigation and in keeping with Frank Manuel's claim that '[i]mages of Judaism cannot be wholly divorced from Christian practice in dealing with Jews in the marketplace' (8), the figure of the Wandering Jew played an especially significant role in the ongoing cultural negotiation regarding the public 'face' of British commercialism. This debate had long featured a tension between ethics and economics. At a time when capitalism as a process of investing money in order to maximize returns was being more strictly observed (Reddy: 12) and approximating more and more to usury in the popular worldview – a form of capitalism traditionally regarded as Jewish (Weber: 271) – that debate was extended to the moral nature of different modes of capitalism.[5] Such moral distinctions intensified during this era as a 'new ideology [was being instituted that] taught how self-enrichment could be personally enhancing and socially cohesive' (Porter: 396). It is a compelling phenomenon that while the Rothschild family was becoming increasingly engaged in their uniquely multinational operations (Ferguson: xxiv) and 'the language of supernaturalism was increasingly employed to justify and universalize the characteristics of market capitalism' (Clery: 7), the vampiric Wandering Jew was on the ascent in Gothic fiction. In that singular venue, this 'figure of racial alchemy … possessing ambiguous powers to transmute or transform all that he came in touch with' (Freedman, 'Poetics': 477), came to symbolize, among other things, a spectral paper/stockmarket economy fuelled by 'ghost money' (Clery: 133), historically said to be of Jewish invention,[6] to which it was said Britain was being demonically converted. By way of a new economic/racial anti-Semitism that remained underpinned by theological anti-Semitism (Freedman, *Temple*: 59), Britons accused Jews, who had long been the focus of Christian conversion societies, of Judaizing Britain. This was but one way in which the 'transmission' of Jewishness was popularly conceived and one instance in which 'the English turned to Jewish questions in order to answer English ones' (Shapiro: 1).

James Shapiro chronicles the relevance of his guiding statement from the production of Shakespeare's *The Merchant of Venice* until 1753, the year the Jewish Naturalization Bill was decisively rejected in Britain. As such, he unwittingly issues a rejoinder to Linda Colley's historic study, *Britons* (1992), which fails to mention the Jews in relation to the development of British national identity.[7] Michael Ragussis's *Figures of Conversion: 'The Jewish Question' and English National Identity* (1995) furnishes a similar corrective. By way of his examination of a series of classic British novels ranging from Sir Walter Scott's *Ivanhoe* (1819) to Anthony Trollope's *The Way We Live Now* (1875), Ragussis elucidates how 'the Jewish Question' was frequently debated in the Victorian novel, and actually lay 'at the centre of a profound crisis in nineteenth-century English national identity' (8), which involved reconciling 'the rise of nationalism and the claims made on behalf of Jewish Emancipation' (90). Considering conversion narratives and the British mission to convert the Jews, Ragussis persuasively illustrates the vital role played by 'the rhetoric of conversion and the figure of the Jewish convert' (1) in the developing construction of British identity. In his words, conversion was 'the literary and cultural master trope by which Jewish identity … [was] represented and regulated' throughout the nineteenth century (86).

Notably, given what he suggests is the problematic dehistoricization of the Jew in Gothic fiction, a genre that frequently features the narrative ingredients of the Spanish Inquisition and the Wandering Jew, Ragussis denies the Gothic's role in addressing the Jewish Question and British national identity formation (135–6). Like works on the Inquisition by such writers as Voltaire and Diderot (Barzilay: 244), a curious phenomenon is in evidence in British Gothic fiction whereby Roman Catholic atrocities are foregrounded with little or no mention of Jewish persecution. More disconcerting, however, is the fact that in that literature the Jew is placed on par with the Inquisition, thus becoming a 'part of the stock horror equipment' (Ragussis, *Figures*: 135). His ethnicity is thus stripped away as he comes to represent homelessness and an almost metaphysical alienation (136). In the light of this treatment of the Jew, Ragussis's critique is astute. Romantic literature, under whose aegis the Gothic essentially falls in terms of its historical moment and many of its aesthetic preoccupations, did frequently and somewhat problematically attempt to universalize the Wandering Jew as a type of 'anti-bourgeois hero' (Maccoby: 254). It is notable, however, that the Wandering Jew's ethnic badge and stereotypical Jewish traits are retained, with intriguing but unsettling resonances, in his appearances within both classic Romantic works like Percy Bysshe Shelley's *The Wandering Jew* (1810) and Gothic novels like Matthew Lewis's *The Monk* (1795). Conversely, and with some fascinating implications, as the Victorian era progresses and the imperialist project proceeds, he is divested of his ethnic label and further demonized. As Edgar Rosenberg rightly observes, 'The history of Ahasuerus in the period between the appearance of Lewis's *The Monk* in 1796 and the publication of *Trilby* in 1894 is largely the story of his translation from a religious figure of whom Christ made an example for the edification of other sinners, to a black magician whose sorcery was interesting on secular grounds' (206). This radical revolution in the Wandering Jew's representation in British literature reflects a similar shift in his representation in legend.[8] Extrapolating on these observations, my investigation exposes how a latent and symbolically multifaceted vampirism detectable in this character in early Gothic works became full-blown by the Victorian fin de siècle.

Drawing upon the insights of James Shapiro and Michael Ragussis, and inserting itself historically between their respective studies, *Anti-Semitism and British Gothic Literature* focuses its attention on the cultural expression of the Jewish Question and participates in what Ragussis identifies in a 1997 Review Essay in *Victorian Studies* as the rewriting of English literary and cultural history generated by the 'rediscovery of the breadth and depth of the English interest in the Jews' ('Secret': 298). To this end, it considers a broad spectrum of canonical literary works, speculative texts, and popular materials ranging from political pamphlets to periodical illustrations. Until fairly recently, 'the dark side of British history' that involved the expression of anti-Semitism (Rubinstein, *History*: 30), has been largely ignored and trivialized in the academy (Cheyette, *Constructions*: 1). Despite being first identified as a concern and debated in England during Cromwell's government (Vital: 38), the Jewish Question has tended to remain 'an underground, half realized issue in the study of English literature and history' (Ragussis, 'Secret' 297). Edmund Silberner's 1952 pronouncement that '[t]he Jewish problem did not play a very great role in nineteenth-century England' (27) has characterized the predominant scholarly viewpoint on this subject. The issue of the very existence of a Jewish Question in England has even been the cause of some recent heated debate (Ragussis, 'Secret': 297). The examination of England's darker side continues to be controversial, provoking discussion about the accuracy of Anglo-Jewish historical studies.[9] As Bryan

Cheyette has provocatively noted with regard to the recent impassioned debates over the issue of Paul de Man's and Martin Heidegger's complicity with Nazism, academic resistance to such an examination comes at a cost. Deploying Gothic-infused rhetoric, Cheyette issues the ominous reminder that 'even in the academic community, a largely repressed European past still has the capacity to return and haunt the present' (1).

A few words should be said with regard to this controversy given its relevance to the present study. We should never lose sight of the noteworthy and ever-improving legal situation of the Jews in modern England and the creditable efforts of such nineteenth-century thinkers and activists as Richard Owen, William Hazlitt, Thomas Babington Macaulay, Daniel O'Connell, and Henry Hetherington who openly promoted Jewish emancipation in England.[10] Indeed, these progressive acts should be recognized and foregrounded as the actualization of the Enlightenment's emancipatory project and promotion of tolerance. They stand in stark contrast to the regressive and reprehensible views of such thinkers as William Cobbett who lamented publicly in 1823 in his popular column in the *Political Register* – at the same time that he was openly promoting Catholic emancipation (Schweizer and Osborne: 17) – that Jews were no longer banished from Britain or, at least, readily identifiable by way of a required badge (72). The persistence in nineteenth-century Britain of socially widespread and entrenched anti-Semitic representations, especially in the face of progressive legislation, surely warrants further and sensitive examination. It was, after all, during this period, 1830–58, that consequential debates on the subject of Jewish emancipation were occurring (Ragussis, 'Secret': 295). David Vital rightly observes that the popular *Punch* image of 'the Jew' as an 'old clothes' man, tailor, petty usurer, occasional thief, hook-nosed, pot-bellied, lisping, obsequious, unclean, alien, [and] absurd' was a 'world away from the compliments paid the Jews in the House of Commons in 1847' (185). Various questions are raised by this apparent disjunction, foremost among which involves considering the ends to which such humiliating representations were put. Michael Ragussis's injunction to consider 'why "the Jewish question" arose in England and what forms this question took' ('Secret': 297) should be heeded alongside the advice of historian David Feldman that '[w]e need to shift the initial historical question away from the problem of why men and women objected to the Jews, to the question of what they meant when they were doing so' (*Englishmen*: 14).

An even more sinister image of the Jew was fashioned and circulated in the pages of Gothic fiction. In this new Gothic economy, the traditional yoking of vampirism and Judaism may be said to have been revamped in more ideologically resonant and unsettling ways. Given this phenomenon, the joint questions of genre and cultural contexts are of special importance to my examination. As I elaborate in Chapter 1, which examines the Enlightenment and the Gothic, the literature of terror – with its 'language of panic, of anxiety, blind revulsion, and distancing sensationalism' (Malchow: 4) – is the logical territory in which to examine 'the vexed question of anti-Semitism in enlightened England' (Ragussis, 'Secret': 295). While artistic productions of all sorts played a part in consolidating a sense of national identity (Blanning: 147), the Gothic uniquely engaged with Enlightenment principles, functioning as a corrective to Enlightenment smugness and myopia. As such, as Frederick Frank has shrewdly noted, it functioned 'as a phenomenon of cultural and spiritual uncertainty and psychological self-revelation [that] deserves to be rediscovered, restudied and revaluated' (xxix). The Gothic exposes the generally repressed 'dark side' of British middle-class consciousness during an extremely transitional period that witnessed the growth of national consciousness.[11] Major transitions of the era included the increasing legitimacy of scientific technology and the birth of industrial modernization, the expansion of a 'credit economy … based on market forces' (Henderson: 40), the growth of religious scepticism, and a 'print revolution' that helped spawn the rise of the reading public (Porter: xxiv).

With reference to three principal areas of scholarship – Gothic studies, Jewish studies, and Anglo-Jewish history – this investigation is attentive to the nature and implications of the negative, distorted representations of the Wandering Jew and Jewish culture in British Gothic fiction, or what I call that genre's anti-Semitic 'spectropoetics'. I borrow this term from Jacques Derrida's *Specters of Marx: The State of the Debt, the Work of Mourning, and the New International*, which assesses Marx's rhetorical ' "spectropoetics" – his obsession with ghosts, specters and spirits'.[12] Indebted to Freudian psychoanalysis, Derrida's theory defines the spectre as 'among other things, what one imagines, what one thinks one sees and which one projects – on an imaginary screen where there is nothing to see' (100–1). While the make-up and implications of the anti-Semitic spectropoetics that form my principal concern are more specifically analysed in the pages that follow, they may be generally said to raise two related spectres – the spectre of Jewish difference and the spectre of Jewish assimilation. Both prospects are historically contingent and reflect changing social anxieties in Britain and the shifting resonances around the idea of Jewishness and fears about its 'transmission'. Extremely significant for my project is the broad historical shift from religious to racial anti-Semitism that, it is generally agreed, occurred in the eighteenth century (Garb: 22). Marked by this and the unsettling yet textured treatments of the Jewish Question in the narratives under examination, Gothic fiction functions, in my view, as nothing short of a compelling register of the changing conception of Englishness.

In essence, then, this study probes the dark underbelly of the conversion plots identified by Ragussis that chronicle the Christianization of Jews. To his credit, in his sixth and final chapter on Crypto-Jews, Ragussis identifies, in the works of Anthony Trollope, the counter-dialectic that constitutes my focus – the possible Judaization of Christian Britons. It is ironic yet significant that concurrent with the production of conversionist literature that promoted assimilation into the British nation, the British Gothic novel often manifested the terror evoked by the realization of such a process. Citing the infamous Augustus Melmotte from Trollope's 1870s satire *The Way We Live Now* as one of the most notorious representatives of such a threat, Ragussis describes such 'invaders' as 'apparently assimilated ... Englishmen, [who] in fact carry with them the threat of Judaizing England, not through religious proselytism, but through the corruption of the traditional system of values defined as English' (*Figures*: 240). Notably, Ragussis recognizes neither the origin of this Judaizing figure nor his ubiquity at the fin de siècle. In keeping with his nationally transgressive nature, this spectre resists generic containment. He inhabits realist works by Trollope and Henry James and such Gothic productions as Bram Stoker's *Dracula*[13] and George du Maurier's *Trilby*. Despite their diverse generic locations, however, these various Wandering Jew figures are semiotically consanguineous. Like their alchemist forefathers, they are figurative alchemists capable of demonically transforming people and nations. Extending Ragussis's conception of conversion as 'the literary and cultural master trope by which Jewish identity ... [was] represented and regulated' (*Figures*: 86) to its legal meaning, these characters are figuratively, and sometimes literally, guilty of conversion – 'An unauthorized assumption and exercise of the right of ownership over goods or personal chattels belonging to another, to the alteration of their condition or the exclusion of the owner's rights' (Black: 332). Ultimately, the spectre of Judaization they raise alters depending on historical moment and geographical location. Specificities aside, however, they consistently serve both to contest *and* to construct the changing conception of Englishness as it was 'envisioned variously as Protestant, Christian, freeborn, imperial, and so on' (Feldman, *Englishmen*: 11). Teresa Goddu's insights about the Gothic's role in American literature apply equally to the British case: 'while the gothic reveals what haunts the nation's narratives, it can also work to coalesce those narratives' (10). The Wandering Jew in British Gothic fiction functions, in this manner, to both strengthen and unsettle an idealized vision of Englishness. Like his fictional brethren, he is 'a shifting signifier that could be used to establish cultural, social, and religious continuity or to define historical, cultural, and religious rupture' (45). He becomes 'the charged site for underlying anxieties informing nationalist discourse, which is always trying to negotiate the challenges or disruptions caused by traditions or subcultures perceived to be particularist, alien, or ... transnational' (Anderson, 'George': 43).[14] His Jewish difference and the dreaded prospect of his assimilation always serve to bring British national identity and the values that constitute it into sharp relief. His manner of reflecting such shifting ideologies ultimately provides, as Edgar Rosenberg astutely observes, a fascinating 'footnote to the history of ideas' (10).

* * *

I begin this inquiry into the Gothic's engagement with the Jewish Question and British national identity formation in the daylight world of categories and boundaries otherwise known as the Enlightenment. The fascinating confluence of phenomena that constitutes my focus is in evidence during this highly charged and contested era of tremendous intellectual debate and social transition. This definition-obsessed period, therefore, offers a fitting departure point for unpacking some of my investigation's most significant terms—'nation', 'modernity', 'the Uncanny', and 'the Gothic'. Curiously, the concept of the Jew became an *idée fixe* among Enlightenment philosophers, many of whom heralded the advent of religious tolerance and the eradication of anti-Semitism. Based on the cultural evidence, however, it would seem that the Blood-Libelled Jew infamous throughout medieval Europe was not entirely exorcized by so-called progressive Enlightenment thinkers. Generally, a deep ambivalence prevailed in their writings that drew upon dark medieval stereotypes. These were more complexly developed during the Elizabethan era and the scientific revolution and were ultimately distilled into British Gothic fiction. The transgressive Wandering Jew in that genre became an agent of the uncanny onto whom were projected that nation's anxieties and aspirations regarding the process of modernization, which involved socio-political and commercial/imperial initiatives, technological revolution, religious scepticism, and the Enlightenment's emancipatory project. The Gothic, a symbolic form of modernity that tapped the dreams and especially the nightmares of burgeoning middle-class consciousness, became the consummate site where such feelings were registered and imaginatively negotiated.

From this ostensible era of daylight, I move into the darkness of British history in Chapter 2 in order to elucidate the complex Frankensteinian construction of the Wandering Jew. I endeavour to put the Gothic into broader historical perspective than has been done to date by illuminating that genre's outstanding debt to a longstanding Christian tradition which linked the Jew to the devil and all things anti-Christian. As David S. Katz has highlighted, 'it is the demonological, supernatural element in the early modern attitude to the Jews which renders it quite different from other forms of opposition to religious minorities and outcasts' (*Philo*: 3–4). The demonic spectral Jew had long predated the demonic spectral Catholic in the British worldview, and Gothic novelists availed themselves of the rich medieval iconography attached to 'the devil Jew' in their works. I build, therefore, on H.L. Malchow's perceptive claim that '[r]acial gothic, if not imperial gothic, has an older and deeper provenance' than the nineteenth-century fin de siècle (4), and begin to trace the provenance and semiotic make-up of the medieval bloodthirsty, usurious Jew, that 'creature of covenants and contracts' (Freedman, *Temple*: 68), from whom Gothic literature's Wandering Jew descended. Maria Edgeworth's *Harrington* (1817), a highly self-conscious apologia for its author's earlier anti-Semitic portraits, provides a springboard into this subject. *Harrington* was published virtually at the close of the classic period of British Gothic literature and, while not a Gothic novel itself, it manipulates popular Gothic conventions in order to issue a socio-political indictment. Like a transgressive Gothic protagonist, Edgeworth brazenly and shamelessly enters the closet of British middle-class consciousness to expose the dark and dirty secret of anti-Semitism and to speculate upon its psychopathology. *Harrington*'s phantasmagoric primal scene is nothing short of a Gothic gem that graphically dramatizes the bogey of the Blood Libel that continues to haunt enlightened England. This compelling yoking of the Jewish Question and the Gothic has two somewhat antithetical effects – it highlights the entrenched and resonant association between these concepts in British culture but also combines them to dismantle a litany of anti-Semitic stereotypes. *Harrington* may lay bare a problematic ambivalence at the core of British enlightened consciousness, therefore, but it fails to destroy the fatal Gothic–Jew connection.

Chapter 3 continues my genealogical work on Gothic literature's Wandering Jew and unearths, in a cross section of late eighteenth-century speculative and political texts, a complex semiotic chain forged in that genre that yokes the figure of the hyper-rational, conspiratorial Jew to the concepts of the French Revolution and secret societies. The Wandering Jew was not, I argue, the only Jewish ingredient in the Gothic novel. Indeed, if a single rubric may be applied to Gothic literature's semiotics it is 'cabalistic', a qualifier that had acquired negative political and religious meaning in Britain by the 1790s, Gothic literature's boom period. The word 'cabal' entered the English language, replete with negative connotations, during the latter half of the seventeenth century when Jews were allowed re-entry into Britain and, by the end of the eighteenth century, the word 'Cabala' had become interchangeable with the word 'Occult'. What I call the cabalistic backdrop of early Gothic fiction featured such elements as the Spanish Inquisition, conspiratorial anti-Christian secret societies (or cabals), secret sciences, the violation of familial bonds (e.g. patricide and incest), popular millenarian ideas, and the bastardization and demonic figuration of the Cabala as a dark mirror, or double, of the Christian New Testament. This complex Gothic creation was underpinned, in part, by fears that a secular-spiritual Apocalypse like the French Revolution would occur on British soil. Many felt that such a cataclysm, signalling the Last Days, would proceed from an intricate anti-Christian conspiracy. This conspiracy plot, formulated by such British and French authorities as Monsignor Barben, Edmund Burke, John Robison, and the Abbé Augustin Barruel, was widely disseminated and qualified as Gothic fiction in its own right. As E.J. Clery aptly describes it, 'the French Revolution was being written, and consumed by a paranoid British public, like a gripping romance translated from the German' (172). The preeminent storyline featured politically subversive secret societies, like the Freemasons and Rosicrucians, believed to be controlled by avaricious Jacobin-like Jews who were advancing their own socio-economic interests to the detriment of the British nation and its progress. This terror was compounded by the threat, suggested by the formation of the Great Sanhedrin in France, of Jews gaining national citizenship, thus annihilating the protective barrier between native Briton and foreign Jew. In the light of these circumstances, Gothic fiction of the 1790s staged a figurative British Inquisition that responded in dramatically imaginative ways to the dreaded prospect of Jewish Emancipation.

Chapter 4 briefly examines the influence of the German *Schauerroman* on British Gothic and brings the semiotic readings of Chapters 2 and 3 to bear on three popular works featuring the Wandering Jew – Matthew G. Lewis's *The Monk* (1795), William Godwin's *St. Leon* (1799), and Reverend Charles Robert Maturin's *Melmoth the Wanderer* (1820). According to Edgar Rosenberg, unlike the generally static literary representation of the Jew, 'each age recreates the Wandering Jew in its own image' (188). As socio-political spectres shifted, so too did the monstrous Wandering Jew who helped give them expression. It is noteworthy that in the three works I examine, the Wandering Jew is never entirely patterned after his regenerated, repentant, and benevolent legendary counterpart. Instead, he evokes incredible dread and is remarkable in that he is either represented as a vampire figure or is associated with such a figure. These portraits counter Montague Summers's observation 'that such writers as Monk Lewis … and Charles Robert Maturin … the two lords of macabre romance, … [never] sent some hideous vampire ghost ravening through their sepulchral pages' (Varma: 159). H.L. Malchow has claimed that the vampire is a latent aspect of the Wandering Jew's character. In his view, the 'popular story of the Wandering Jew, even when the Jew is presented in a favorable light, does not escape the vampire association. He cannot die, and he brings the plague' (160). To date, this aspect of the Wandering Jew's make-up has been observed in Gothic scholarship only in relation to Bram Stoker's *Dracula*. It remains unrecognized and uncharted in the period 1764–1820, popularly regarded as the classic era of Gothic fiction.

Although, due to length restrictions, I am not able to elucidate how the powerful Gothic–Jew association is retained in mid- and late-nineteenth century British political, social, and realist fiction, it is necessary to briefly delineate its persistence. There are, as I am fond of saying, numerous and notable 'Gothic closets' in the manor house of Victorian fiction. Despite what some may regard as its rather cumbersome formal elements, the Gothic made various incursions into, and underwent diverse transmutations within much Victorian literature.[15] As C.C. Barfoot has provocatively claimed, the ghost of the Gothic is in evidence in 'the best nineteenth-century fiction', where it accumulates 'at the margins threatening to oust and disturb the centre of apparent common sense reality … [and] normality' (169).[16] The vampiric Wandering Jew is one such ghost of the Gothic who haunts the established ideological and Enlightenment-grounded epistemological certainties of the realist genre. Benjamin Disraeli's 'super-Jew' Sidonia (Smith, Introduction: 11) in *Coningsby; or The New Generation* (1844), for example, may be a brilliant and strategic political thinker whose money is vital to the maintenance of British national stability, but he remains steeped in Gothic romanticism in his association with secret sciences and secret societies. Sidonia's view that the French Revolution was a great achievement (252) and his claim that 'the world is governed by very different personages from what is imagined by those who are not behind the scenes' (262–3) was undoubtedly as disconcerting to many Britons as was Disraeli's later suggestion in *Lord George Bentinck: A Political Biography* (1852) that Britain's cultural, political, and legal foundations were indebted to what he termed 'the Semitic principle' (496) and were essentially Jewish in nature.

Many dialogued with Disraeli in relation to what they regarded as an unsettling assessment. Matthew Arnold, for example, conceptualized 'Hellenism' and 'Hebraism' in *Culture and Anarchy* (1869), equating the latter with duty and work. The racial ideology underpinning his ethnically inflected terminology was rendered transparent, however, when what he deemed the 'triumph of Hebraism' (108) was blamed for 'the commercial immorality in our serious middle-class' (133). While Arnold concurred with Disraeli that the 'Semitic principle' had the upper hand in British society, Arnold deemed this lamentable as opposed to worthy of celebration. Following Arnold, Anthony Trollope crafted a more insulting commentary on Disraeli's theory in his indictment of Britain's Judaization in *The Way We Live Now* (1875). The religiously indeterminate Melmotte is a sinister and Mammonistic Crypto-Wandering Jew who stages a British invasion two decades prior to Count Dracula. Although Trollope suggests that Britain's Judaization was well underway prior to Melmotte's arrival, the problem as Trollope identifies it, is unarguably Christian Britain's demonic conversion to what he characterizes as 'Jewish' values.

Finally, George Eliot's *Daniel Deronda* (1876) may work in the tradition of Edgeworth's *Harrington* as a corrective to established anti-Semitic stereotypes but her narrative nonetheless retains traditional Gothic conventions and prejudices relating to this character. Daniel's developmental trajectory from benighted self-estrangement to self-enlightenment adheres to that of the traditional Gothic character. In a unique revision of the Crypto-Jew narrative, Eliot's Crypto-Jew long remains Crypto, especially to himself. While the vampire motif is displaced, in part, onto Gwendolen's Christian husband Henleigh Mallinger Grandcourt, it remains associated with several prominent Jewish characters, including Mirah's abusive father Lapidoth, the novel's various commercially active Jews, and especially those characters who deny their racial associations. In response to his question, 'What is the citizenship of him who walks among a people he has no hearty kindred and fellowship with, and has lost the sense of brotherhood with his own race?', Mordecai, Eliot's primary Jewish mouthpiece, states:

> It is a charter of selfish ambition and rivalry in low greed. He is an *alien in spirit*, whatever he may be in form; *he sucks the blood of mankind*, he *is not a man*. Sharing in no love, sharing in no subjection of the soul, he mocks at all. (587; emphasis added)

Eliot may, as Bryan Cheyette suggests, construct Jewish nationalism as 'an "ideal" for the "English nation" to follow' (*Constructions*: 271), however, her proto-Zionist novel ironically and problematically embraces a racialist theory and fails to forge any positive role for the Jew in Britain. At its conclusion, Daniel contemplates a political vocation and is poised to depart England for 'the East to become better acquainted with the condition of … [his] race in various countries there' (*Daniel*: 875). The persistent relevance of the Jewish Question in Britain into the 1880s is attested to by the very public and lengthy debate over Jewish patriotism between Rabbi Herman Adler and History Professor Goldwin Smith in the pages of *The Nineteenth Century* between 1878 and 1882. The Gothic Jew association is retained in Smith's resuscitation of medieval anti-Semitic stereotypes and such descriptions of Jewish lawyers as 'legal vampire[s]' ('Jews': 695).

These developments all feed into Bram Stoker's *Dracula*, a morality tale about money and empire which enacts the culmination in the Gothic Wandering Jew's development. Count Dracula may be of another order in this tradition given his unidentified Jewishness and literal vampirism, but he is nonetheless a blood brother to the imperialist Disraeli who generated grave anxiety in Britain throughout the 1870s. This new order of vampiric Wandering Jew gives expression to Britain's intense Judaization fears in their various dimensions at the fin de siècle. With an eye to contextualizing these anxieties, Chapter 5 provides an overview of the changing face of the Jewish Question between the 1840s and 1890s in the light of developments relating to British nationalism, capitalism, and imperialism. It then undertakes a detailed reading of Bram Stoker's *Dracula* in the light of these developments and a cross section of fin-de-siècle preoccupations and anxieties as expressed in numerous cultural, literary, and medical texts – including mass-scale Jewish immigration, the Jack the Ripper murders, the New Woman phenomenon, the syphilis epidemic, the public exposure of homosexual activity, and 'the prospect of imperial and racial decline' (Arata, *Fictions*: 112). What is especially compelling about Stoker's novel is its registration of terrors relating both to Jewish assimilation and the resistance to assimilation while, albeit unconsciously, sometimes blurring the boundaries between British imperialism/ gentlemen and vampirism.

The persistence of the vampiric Wandering Jew tradition is briefly considered in my Afterword where I transgress the official historic and national parameters of this study. I conclude by coming full circle to Germany where the hugely influential *Schauerroman* was forged in the 1790s. More specifically, I turn my attention to the subject of early twentieth-century German Expressionist cinema. As Fred Botting has noted, the cinema has especially 'perpetuated distinctly Gothic figures' in this century (*Gothic*: 13). Two Nazi propaganda films from 1940 produced to promote and justify Hitler's Final Solution to exterminate the Jews – Fritz Hippler's *Der Ewige Jude* (*The Eternal Jew*) and Veit Harlan's *Jud Süss* – supply the focus of my conclusion. These distorted and disturbing creations provide ample evidence of the longstanding association between the Jew and the Gothic and the deep entrenchment of anti-Semitic spectropoetics in the European consciousness. They lend support to the reiterated claim that anti-Semitism 'ends in persecution... [and] is a discourse that intends harm' (Julius: 11). Toni Morrison's eloquent acceptance speech for the 1993 Nobel Prize for Literature perhaps best characterizes its vampiric and oppressive nature. In her words:

> Oppressive language does more than represent violence; it is violence; does more than represent the limits of knowledge; it limits knowledge... *It is the language that drinks blood*, laps vulnerabilities, tucks *its fascist boots* under crinolines of respectability and patriotism as it moves relentlessly toward the bottom line and the bottomed-out mind. (16, emphasis added)

Ultimately, the Holocaust provided irrefutable testimony that Gothic literature's anti-Semitic spectropoetics, as distilled into German Expressionist cinema and Nazi propaganda films, were not only oppressive and persistent but also fatally profound in their consequences. This central nightmarish event in twentieth-century history and Morrison's portrait of the language that precipitated it, expose the ultimate truth about the Nazi's 'Final Solution'. In tandem with the Jewish Question, which 'cannot easily or simply be put to rest, but continues to haunt our discourses of self, of other, of nation, of religion, of identity, and identification' (Shapiro, 'Uncanny': 75), anti-Semitism is a disturbing revenant that has been variously repressed and expressed throughout history (LaCapra: 189). Despite the fact that '[d]efining a modern British nation was and is a difficult, evolving, and varied task' (Weinbrot: 408), anti-Semitism has remained a consistent and readily adaptable component in British identity construction. Indeed, it has been the real vampire that has birthed demons by projecting its macabre tendencies onto the Jew.

1
The Contested Enlightenment, the Contested Castle

> ... in an important sense a nation is also a symbolic community which creates powerful – and often pathological – allegiances to a cultural ideal
>
> (Evans 1)

The Contested Enlightenment

In order to begin to understand both the Wandering Jew's role in relation to British national identity formation in Gothic fiction, and the Gothic's role as the consummate genre within which that identity and the anti-Semitic spectropoetics that I have identified are expressed, it is imperative to return to the birthplace of secular European nationalism[1] and the Gothic genre – namely, the Enlightenment. This complex intellectual epoch marked 'a new era in Jewish–Christian relations' (Barzilay: 260) and functioned as the matrix of the intellectual, social, and cultural developments central to this study. To describe the Enlightenment as a hugely contentious domain in recent scholarship is, perhaps, to understate the case. As Roy Porter has astutely observed, 'Enlightenment historiography has been distorted by hindsight, and remains unashamedly *parti pris*': while progressives have long celebrated Enlightenment *philosophes* for articulating and promoting the Rights of Man, right-wing scholars have indicted the same thinkers for providing the ideological fuel for the Terror (xx). A tendency to demonize the Enlightenment has, Porter rightly notes, characterized most recent scholarship. 'It has become,' he comments, 'almost *de rigueur* to paint the Enlightenment black' (xx). Many scholars have uncritically adopted Michel Foucault's claims that the Enlightenment's driving logic was to control and dominate rather than to emancipate ('What': 37), resulting, Porter fails to observe, in such politically incompatible bedfellows as the Abbé Barruel and Max Horkheimer. Deeming these recent postmodern studies 'wilfully lopsided' (xxi), Porter encourages us, 'the Enlightenment's children', to take

15

a 'nuanced view' (xxii) of what was not, he reminds us, a 'monolithic project' (xxi). Porter's suggestion that the positive and revolutionary developments of the Enlightenment have been grossly ignored in recent scholarship is indisputable. His insights regarding the ideologically driven tendency to distort the Enlightenment should also be applauded. In the light of these problems, a more nuanced analysis of the Enlightenment and of 'the relationship between modernity and the Jews' (Feldman, 'Was': 177) is certainly overdue. That being said, however, it is undeniable that certain problematic, often repressed, propensities that run counter to the Enlightenment's purported drives are undeniably present in Enlightenment thought. In this regard, the representation of the Jew provides a compelling case in point.

Secular national identity was, ironically, cast in the crucible of the Enlightenment, an ostensibly international phenomenon (O'Brien: 19–20) that endorsed 'a European culture that could at moments transcend national borders' (Jacob, *Living*: 9). Indeed, as David Simpson has noted, the Enlightenment was, among other things, preoccupied with defining national character (41). Recent scholarship has begun to identify the vital role played by the Jewish Question in both this process and in formulating the various discourses we often group together under the rubric of Enlightenment' (Hess: 83). The evidence suggests that an antagonistic 'enemy within', like the Jew, was a prerequisite for fostering nationalist sentiment (Finzi: 12, Newman: 57). According to Jonathan Freedman, the preeminence of the Jewish Question in such debates was attributable, in part, to the growing presence of Jews in European society. The Jew functioned as 'the limit case of the categories the Enlightenment sought to valorize: the state, reason, and the innate rights of man' (*Temple*: 37). In many instances, 'establishing the nature of Jewish difference and its proper place in the culture of the West became one crucial way for those categories to be shaped, articulated, defined, and sharpened' (*Temple*: 37).

In both Germany and France, the Jewish Question became an *idée fixe* among a broad spectrum of Enlightenment philosophers. In fact, the period witnesses a proliferation of documents featuring the transgressive, 'international' Wandering Jew who exemplifies the uncontainability of the Jewish people and resists both containment and conversion (Poliakov: 352).[2] Immanuel Kant, for example, promoted an image of Rabbinic Judaism as obscurantist, authoritarian, and fossilized and, in private correspondence, voiced the opinion that the Jews were 'social vampires' who were harmful to civil society due to their resistance to assimilation (Manuel: 286; Robertson, 'Jewish': 25). Similarly, both Voltairean theists and Holbachian atheists promoted 'a monster image of Judaism' in France (Manuel: 193) that, from the 1770s onwards, was featured in discussions about the nature of citizenship (Schechter: 87). In such debates, the figure of the Jew epitomized the anti-citizen (Hess: 84), an ironic association as it was an excommunicated Sephardic Jew, Baruch Spinoza – the man Conor Cruise O'Brien deems the best candidate for the title 'Father of the Enlightenment' (20) – who, on the basis of the Old Testament, first formulated 'the concept of nationalism in general terms' (21) in his 'deified nation' doctrine outlined in the *Tractatus Theologico-Politicus* (1670). It is noteworthy, however, that Spinoza promoted mutual tolerance between the Christian and the Jew in that document.

Notably, Enlightenment thinkers tended to speak out of both sides of their mouths when it came to the Jews, a fact that goes some way towards explaining why the Enlightenment is now regarded as an 'overdetermined symbolic battleground for modern scholarship, an intellectual field that has been appropriated both as an emancipatory movement that marks the very antithesis of anti-Semitism and as an essential moment in the rise of those forms of anti-Semitism that led to the Nazi Holocaust' (Hess: 83). While Enlightenment thinkers generally promoted 'arguments for the toleration of diverse religions on the basis of their shared ethical principles' (Robertson, *German-Jewish*: viii), and 'rejected the idea of religious persecution' (Hampson: 252), they frequently and disconcertingly portrayed the Jews as they had done since the Medieval period – namely, in an extremely libellous fashion. According to Arthur Hertzberg, 'throughout the eighteenth century an important anti-Jewish element could always be found among the new thinkers, even as they were arguing for tolerance for all opinions' (29). To a disturbing degree, the anti-Semitic spirit of Luther lived on in 'the Enlightenment's intolerance of Judaism' (Manuel: 289). In his article 'Juifs' in the *Dictionnaire Philosophique*, Voltaire denounced 'the Old Testament Jews for massacring their enemies, denies them any philosophy, art, or learning, complains of their material conception of the soul, and charges them with cannibalism, bestiality, and human sacrifice' (Robertson, *'Jewish'*: 22–3). Taken as a whole, the Enlightenment portrait of the Jews is one of a 'profoundly anomalous' (Vital: 32), 'savage' (Manuel: 291), and ' "backward" people' (Vital: 34) wedded to the past[3] and an irrational, fanatical, and 'superstitious' belief system.[4] In the face of such entrenched views, Moses Mendelssohn, a pioneer of German *Aufklärung*, could not successfully establish Judaism as a rational religion and thus enable Jews full participation in civic society. In the new demonology of the secular religion of nationalism, the Jews were nothing short of a veritable 'problem for modernity' (Anderson, 'George': 42). In a rapidly secularizing Europe, they were 'the epitome of incongruity: a non-national nation … [that] cast a shadow on the fundamental principle of modern European order: that nationhood is the essence of human destiny' (Bauman: 153).

What was to be done in the face of such an anomaly? The solution seemed self-evident: for their own good, the Jews had to be brought into the modern age. To this end, they had to be subjected to a radical and rapid civilizing process. Indeed, in the light of their purportedly atavistic nature, they seemed 'the perfect test case for revolutionary principles of the regeneration and moral transformation of both individuals and the French nation as a whole' (Hess: 84). As part of this new experiment, they were granted full civil rights by the National Assembly in France in 1791, causing some to remark that 'Enlightenment rationalism and the forces of modernity... "emancipated" even the Jews' (Cheyette, *Constructions*: 9). While this event caused some European thinkers to associate Jews with the dangerously progressive ideas of the Enlightenment,[5] a more complex and questionable agenda underpinned it. In the eyes of various scholars, the old theological project of conversion gave way to a new secular and 'proto-totalitarian' drive (Vital: 32) to 'save' the Jews by way of national assimilation. This new mode of conversion, which entailed the annihilation of Judaism (Poliakov: 226), went hand-in-glove with a new obsession 'with the social, economic, and political behavior of individual Jews or Jewish collectives' (Manuel: 292), and was founded upon the conviction that the 'only good Jew was an invisible Jew. The other, the visible Jew, was an obscene creature, indecent' (Finkielkraut: 66). Emancipation amounted, for the Jews, to 'a flawed bargain in which... [they] gained their freedom as citizens by effacing their identity as Jews' (Feldman, 'Was': 175). In the words of London's current Chief Rabbi, Professor Jonathan Sacks, the Enlightenment and the French Revolution were the sites of all contemporary anxieties about Jewish identity, unity, and continuity, for they 'presented European Jews with a messianic promise and a demonic reality' (Sacks). Indeed, as the popular social reaction to the changes promoted by such legislation attest, anti-Semitism was not eradicated during the Enlightenment. Rather, it was exacerbated as the threat to annihilate traditional exclusionary barriers generated tremendous social anxiety and a reactionary backlash (Vital: 166). While, as Zygmunt Bauman has noted, Christian dominance was affirmed by way of the demand for assimilation, assimilated Jews were given no guarantee of 'an unambiguous acceptance by modern states and societies' (Feldman, 'Was': 175). In the new secular religion of nationalism, anti-Semitism was reconceptualized as racial, a development that rendered Jewish national assimilation a logical impossibility (Poliakov: 352). This European phenomenon is perhaps best exemplified in the German case and reflected in the representation of the Wandering Jew. According to Paul Lawrence Rose, that figure's epithet, *ewige*, shifted from referring to 'the eternally unending character of Ahasverus's punishment' to 'those guiltful traits that were commonly regarded as eternally stamped on the Jewish national character and demanded redemption' (24).

It can surely be no coincidence that the period in which efforts were being made to legally emancipate the Jews also witnessed 'an intensification of thought about communal racial origins' (Newman: 115). Similar preoccupations were in evidence before the establishment of the Spanish Inquisition when the prospect of Jewish assimilation threatened the Spaniard's ability to define himself in contrast to the Jew, that nation's foremost 'Other'. The spectre of Judaization, adhering to a type of 'logic of contagion', became more pervasive and threatening in these instances because the Jew was 'invisible, unlocatable, and, thus, uncontainable' (Shapiro, 'Uncanny': 65). Ironically, as Alain Finkielkraut notes, it was precisely this invisibility of the Jew that most threatened European communities – 'The more they hid their Jewishness, the more terrifying they became to others' (69). No personal history better captures this truth than that of Joseph Süss Oppenheimer, known as 'Jud Süss', who was put in charge of the state's finances in Vienna by the Duke of Württemberg in 1734. While in that office, Oppenheimer 'dressed like a nobleman, professed deism, and immersed himself in secular culture'. Subsequent to the Duke's death, Oppenheimer was arrested and executed (Robertson, *Jewish*: 18). As would again occur two centuries later in Nazi Germany, assimilation came at a disastrously heavy cost.

Despite the fact that England's Jews did not experience the ongoing persecution of their continental brethren (Katz, 'Marginalization': 60), similar phenomena occurred in that country in relation to the question of emancipation. While it was 'the governing elite who first equate[d] Englishness with non-Jewishness' (Richmond: 56) during the medieval period when the Jews were expelled from England, this equation became more broadly socially entrenched by the eighteenth century, 'one of the most formative periods in the making of the modern world and – not accidentally – in the forging of British identity' (Colley, *Britons*: 7). Frank Felsenstein has persuasively argued that the increasing visibility of the Wandering Jew in eighteenth-century British popular culture 'owed as much to the novelty of the readmission of actual Jews into the country as to the ancient roots of the legend itself' (62). In terms of his role in a variety of English discourses, however, it was as if the Jew had never left the country. As Colin Richmond has shrewdly remarked, while the 'Jews disappeared from England in 1290; "the Jew" did not' (56). Bernard Glassman has illustrated, further to this, that the *number* of actual Jews in Britain mattered little to the creation and dissemination of anti-Semitic ideas. As was the case in revolutionary France (Kates: 109), their small numbers did not 'prevent the Jew[s] from becoming symbolically central' to various British debates (Hutson: 226–7). Indeed, the figure of the Jew had been used to address the ethical nature of English commercial practices since at least the late sixteenth century. First promoted in Christopher Marlowe's *The Jew of Malta* (1590), this role was consolidated in William Shakespeare's creation of Shylock in *The Merchant of Venice* (1596–97). With the shift piloted by the Enlightenment from *homo civilis* to *homo economicus*, 'which involved the rationalization of selfishness and self-interest as enlightened ideology' (Porter: 396), he retained a principal yet increasingly complex role. In keeping with his association with the most current and controversial questions, therefore, the imaginary Jew became the charged site for various anxieties relating to national identity during the Enlightenment.

Although there were only approximately 8000 Jews in Britain in 1800 (Cohen: 62), the community was growing. Discussions about extending them the rights of citizenship elicited a predominantly negative outcry from the British public. While serious debates about Jewish emancipation would only take place in the Victorian era, and Jews would be granted full legal emancipation in 1858 (Roth, *History*: 333), an important piece of eighteenth-century legislation relating to the Jewish population provides some sense of popular British attitudes. As I discuss at greater length in Chapter 2, the popular response to the Jewish Naturalization Bill of 1753, whose provisions would have facilitated the naturalization of foreign Jews, was resoundingly negative (Rubin: 37). As was the case in France, rationalist works and Enlightenment-inspired polemics were also, significantly, marked by anti-Semitic sentiments and semiotics. The English Deists, for example, launched a 'many-pronged attack on Judaism' (Manuel: 175) that portrayed that faith as carnal and material (186) and repudiated its claim to having introduced monotheism (177). Perhaps most injurious was the Deists' allegation that Judaism was a type of pagan, savage, unspiritual belief system that engaged in necrolatry, the worship of dead things (178).

As in France, the Jew in British Enlightenment discourse is often positioned as the pre-eminent anti-citizen by writers on both sides of the political spectrum. In Thomas Paine's *The Rights of Man* (1791–92), for example, the Jews are aligned with the aristocracy[6] as a degenerate, monstrous, and archaic group whose power, generally maintained by tyranny and injustice, is deemed to be on the wane in an increasingly enlightened Britain (42–3). In true Enlightenment fashion, Paine presents a paradoxical treatment of the Jews: an indisputably anti-Semitic portrait is promoted alongside recommendations to practice religious tolerance while ensuring the strict separation of Church and state. In the latter instance, however, Paine also indirectly undermines Judaism by indicting 'national religions' – into which category Judaism was regularly placed – as political conspiracies. In his words, they are 'either political craft or the remains of the Pagan system, when every nation had its separate and particular deity' (194). Paine happily anticipates the passing of these outmoded, primitive theocracies.

In Edmund Burke's rhetorically strategic, alarmist, and Gothic[7] *Reflections on the Revolution in France* (1790), an ideologically curious Frankenstein monster is assembled in the form of the 'degenerate' (45), democratic (18), and revolutionary Jew (29). In a fascinating semiotic sleight of hand designed to terrorize – a specialty that he later, ironically, attributes to the Jacobins in his *Letters on a Regicide Peace* (1795–97) – Burke conflates the concepts of Judaism and Revolution to the point, as one scholar notes, where his argument seems 'rather more consistently anti-Semitic than antiphilosophes' (Simpson: 57). Richard Price's sermon in support of the French Revolution, to which Burke's *Reflections* responds, was delivered to the Revolution Society in London that was located in the old Jewish ghetto. On the basis of this spurious association between Britain's pro-Jacobins and the Jews, Burke punctuates his *Reflections* with joint allusions to 'the Old Jewry' and 'the Revolution Society' (Burke: 12, 15, 29). France has been Judaized, Burke urgently declares (254), and this treacherous national conversion will only intensify in the next generation. In keeping with the popular dynamic in Gothic fiction whereby the sins of the fathers are visited upon the sons, the new nobility, he prophesies, 'will resemble the artificers and clowns, and money-jobbers, usurers, and Jews, who will be always their fellows, sometimes their masters' (46). Recognizing a national threat in the increasing influence of these speculators – indeed, 'a conspiracy to create a paper-money despotism' ultimately destructive to healthy commerce (Pocock, *Virtue*: 200) – Burke proposes to export Britain's disrespectable Jews to France. There, those 'house-breakers, and receivers of stolen goods, and forgers' (Burke: 254) – may 'fill the new episcopal thrones' (255) and unite with other materialistic and speculative 'Jews and [stock]jobbers' (52) who, for their 'lust of unhallowed lucre' (148), have converted France into a gaming-table (189). Working from an ideal of political economy 'founded on an assumed identity of interests between a managerial landed aristocracy and a system of public credit, in which rentier investment in government stock stimulated commercial prosperity, political stability, and national and imperial power' (Pocock, *Virtue*: 195), Burke castigates landless Jews and their speculating brethren as a revolutionary menace to rational liberty.

The uncanny Wandering Jew

While a more detailed portrait and interpretation of the alien, anti-citizen Jew in Britain is developed in the following pages, the examples from Paine and Burke provide significant evidence that this spectre was not restricted to continental Europe. I would like to suggest further, however, in the light of the prevalent semiotic pattern involving the spectral, nationless Wandering Jew, that he was at the centre of a significant ideological development during the Enlightenment. As the parameters of Western European national identity were being debated and the prospect of Jewish assimilation was being broached, he became an agent of the uncanny. Such an argument is in keeping with Terry Castle's 'ambitious claim' (9) in her introduction to *The Female Thermometer: Eighteenth-Century Culture and the Invention of the Uncanny*, that the uncanny has a history and that, more specifically, this phenomenon first became a part of human experience during the Enlightenment (7). Reading Sigmund Freud's 'magnificent, troubling, and inspired' (3) essay, 'The Uncanny' (1919), as a type of 'historical allegory' relating to the eighteenth century (9), Castle concludes that 'the aggressively rationalist imperatives of ... [that] epoch – also produced, like a kind of toxic side effect a new human experience of strangeness, anxiety, bafflement, and intellectual impasse' (8). In a theory that echoes Friedrich Nietzsche's statement in

The Will to Power that 'Whoever pushes rationality forward also restores new strength to the opposite power, mysticism and folly of all kinds' (qtd. in Sagan: 1), Castle maintains that a compelling and tormenting dialectic resides at the core of this intellectual era whereby 'the more we seek enlightenment, the more alienating our world becomes; the more we seek to free ourselves, Houdini-like, from the coils of superstition, mystery, and magic, the more tightly, paradoxically, the uncanny holds us in its grip' (15).

In these claims, Castle admittedly joins the 'phalanx of historians and social theorists from E.P. Thompson to Michel Foucault' (6) and Eli Sagan who have revealed a dark side to an age that heralded the end of tyranny and obscurantism. Reason, they maintain, may actually be tyrannical, and appeals to reason may be 'used "instrumentally": to control and dominate rather than to emancipate' (Castle: 6). One of the offshoots of such tyranny, according to Castle, comes in the form of a haunting. In the figure of the uncanny, we encounter something, in Freud's words, 'secretly familiar and old-established in the mind...which has become alienated from it only through the process of repression' (247). Bringing Freud's definition to bear on the Enlightenment, Castle suggests that we are a culture haunted since the Enlightenment by pre-Enlightenment ideas and belief systems. In effect, they form a historical equivalent of the 'infantile stage' that we are ambivalent about having surmounted. In fact, according to Freud's theory, we have never entirely managed to surmount it.

Building on the insights of Freud and Castle, the driving claim of *Anti-Semitism and British Gothic Literature* is that the Wandering Jew in British Gothic fiction functions as a compelling agent of the uncanny upon whom are projected ambivalent feelings about modernity and the modernization process. In order to dismantle this figure's various ideological investments within the British Gothic tradition over the course of a century, this study urges a historicist approach to the uncanny and a semiotically aware examination of cultural history. As such, it is attentive to Robert Mighall's censuring of what he describes as 'the ahistorical loop of psychological Gothic criticism' and his reminder that:

> [t]he Gothic is a process, not an essence; a rhetoric rather than a store of universal symbols; an attitude to the past and the present, not a free-floating fantasy world. Epochs, institutions, places, and people are Gothicized, have the Gothic thrust upon them. That which is Gothicized depends on history and the stories it needs to tell itself. (xxv)

Contrary to Mighall's repeated denunciatory remarks in his introduction to *A Geography of Victorian Gothic Fiction*, however, most recent Gothic scholarship deploying psychoanalysis does pay heed to socio-historical and cultural contexts. Mighall's denial of this fact is, rather curiously and ironically, matched by a denial of his own psychoanalytic propensities. His aforementioned claim that the Gothic is 'thrust upon' various epochs, institutions, places, and people, for example, shares distinct connections with the psychoanalytic process of projection. Bypassing that tangential issue, I would piggyback on his claims and suggest that, in the form of the Wandering Jew, the Gothic is 'thrust upon' Jews beginning in the late eighteenth century. While a historicist examination of the specific projections relating to this figure will be undertaken in the course of this study, a few words need be said about his role in the projection process itself. Pinsker's epigraph to my Introduction and a preponderance of other statements by a broad spectrum of scholars over the past century identify a vital link between the Jewish Other and the European psyche. The trope of the Jew as an uncanny or ghostlike figure is especially evident in cultural criticism. Tamar Garb has asserted, for example, that the Jew has long 'haunted the Gentile imagination', functioning alternately as its [Western Christian culture's] conscience, its alter ego, its abject, its Other' (20), and Bryan Cheyette has described the figure of the Jew as 'deeply embedded in the unconscious' (3). Both draw upon earlier claims, such as Leslie Fiedler's pronouncements in his famous 1949 essay 'What Can We Do About Fagin?', that the Jew is a type of Jungian archetype that emanated from the British collective unconscious. In Fiedler's more precise words, 'he [the Jew] is the Usurer, the Jew with the Knife, the Jew as Beast. A compulsive image, he haunts the English imagination; a creature of fear and guilt, he exists before and beneath written literature, an archetype inhabiting the collective unconscious of the English-speaking peoples' (412–13).

The historicization of the uncanny – and by extension, this uncanny ghostly archetype – is one of my central objectives. Complexities consistently arise in unpacking the significance of this apparently unchanging 'estranged self', this fleshly embodiment of the wandering signifier 'Jew' that, like that signifier, may simultaneously represent various and sometimes contradictory values and meanings. For example, this figure often blurs the boundary between the old and new orders and occupies a variety of dispositions and temporal positions – anti-, pro-, pre-, proto-, and hyper-[8] – towards enlightened modernity and modernization. In an era that, rather significantly, witnessed the birth of nostalgia and in a cultural by-product of antiquarianism (the Gothic novel) that tends to evoke a 'nostalgia for the past' and attacks 'a dehumanising modern world' (Kilgour, *Rise*: 12),[9] the Wandering Jew could function as a dreaded reminder of a benighted, superstitious past or a harbinger of technological advancement, mass literacy,[10] hyper-rationalism, and dreaded, unstoppable change. In his international aspect, he could also tap the mixed fears and desires relating to the international drives of the Enlightenment 'movement'. Although the Wandering Jew thus upheld the longstanding association in a variety of European discourses between the Jews and ambivalence (Bauman: 141), a deeply problematic tradition that remains discernible in present-day cultural theory,[11] he was consistently negatively characterized.

That the ambivalently positioned Wandering Jew, a dark double to Enlightenment Britain, should make his first literary appearance in the pages of Gothic fiction is entirely appropriate given that genre's function as a barometer of the sometimes contradictory currents of the Enlightenment era. Castle's claim that the Enlightenment, the historical moment of the uncanny's invention, remains 'a sort of specter in ... [Freud's] argument' (14) is granted further support by the fact that Freud chose a Gothic text – E.T.A. Hoffmann's 'The Sandman' – as his study's principal example. Before considering why that genre functions as the consummate literary site for both Freud's examination and mine, it should also be noted that Hoffmann's story – and, by extension, Freud's essay – is marked by a significant repression[12] that attests to the vexed Jewish-Enlightenment connection I have described. Coppelius, the mysterious figure who terrifies Nathanael from youth to adulthood and generates that tale's uncanny moments, possesses many of the trademark attributes of the stereotypical Jew and Wandering Jew. This conspiratorial shape-shifter initially appears as an 'old advocate' (88), a professional occupation often associated with the people of the book. Further to this, he possesses 'a large beaky nose' (88), engages in costly 'secret alchemical experiments' (94), and is 'a sinister monster, particularly hostile to children' (94). The image of Nathanael's father in front of the fireplace with Coppelius holding 'strange instruments' and 'a pair of red-hot tongs' is a haunting one that raises the spectre of the Blood Libel while combining the longstanding images of the Jew as dreaded devil and castrating, murderous father. Nathanael's insistence that his father's face was contorted into the 'repulsive mask of a fiend' so that he 'looked like Coppelius' during the incident (90) speaks stereotypical volumes. The issue of Coppelius's national identity is also repeatedly and significantly raised throughout the story. While we are initially informed that he is 'a German, though not an honest one' (96), this national shape-shifter later reappears as Coppola, a Piedmontese barometer-seller in league with the physicist Spalanzani (105–6). His involvement with the secret sciences, long regarded as a Jewish domain, serves further to entrench the connection as does his name, which derives from the Italian word *coppo* meaning eye socket (403, n. 88). While this is the key to Coppola's terror – Nathanael believes Coppola wants to remove his eyes (90) – Jews had a longstanding belief in, and were said to possess, the *mal'occhio* or evil eye, which caused misfortune to its victims. In fact, the German word for evil eye – *Judenblick* – was directly associated with the Jews and, more specifically, the 'look' of the Jew (Pick, 'Powers': 116). Certainly, when Coppola arrives in the town at story's end and heads, rather notably, 'directly for the market-place' where he witnesses Nathanael's suicide, it is suggested that his gaze actually helps to effect that tragic conclusion (118).

While I would reject as preposterous the suggestion that any of Freud's essays are, themselves, works of Gothic fiction,[13] I would maintain that

Freud intuits two fundamental things about that genre in 'The Uncanny': first, that the Gothic gave pronounced and graphic expression to the subject of psychic and socio-political repression and, second, that the figure of the Jew, sometimes featured within its pages, was a powerful and uncanny spectre that had long haunted the European consciousness and remained notably prevalent in the age of reason.[14] In fact, it is as if Freud, albeit unconsciously, moved beyond the ostensible agenda of 'The Uncanny' of furnishing a 'modest contribution' on the aesthetics of terror (219), to unearthing and exposing a compelling primal scene in Christian European consciousness. In this instance, I think it fair to say that he had his finger firmly placed on a pulse detectable over several centuries throughout Europe. The weird nightmare-scapes of German Expressionist Cinema, populated by a variety of grotesque and mysterious Jews, that were subsequently imported into Nazi propaganda cinema, are cousin to those found in various eighteenth-century European Gothic texts – the British Gothic novel, the French *roman noir*, and the German *Schauerroman*.

The 'Contested Castle': The Gothic, modernity, and the Nation

Returning my critical sights to the matrix out of which the late-eighteenth century British Gothic emerged, writers of that era had witnessed, in the French Revolution and Terror, the resulting fall-out of the tyranny of reason and the repression of the passions. Despite the fact that the driving principles behind that Revolution derived largely from rationalist Enlightenment philosophies, nightmarishly visceral and memorable transmutations occurred between the 1780s and 1794: 'cosmopolitanism became conquering nationalism, pacifism became militarism, tolerance became fanaticism, [and] liberty became Terror' (Baczko: 667). The pivotal dynamic of repression and revolution that lay behind those events was registered, albeit in displaced and sometimes cryptic ways, in the pages of British Gothic literature. Indeed, it seems fair to say that the spectre of that Revolution and the questions it generated about political economy, religion and spiritual reality, illegitimate and legitimate authority, the dangerous potential of mass literacy, individual rights and social responsibilities, and socio-political repression and its impact on the individual, continued to haunt Britons well into the nineteenth century. Certainly, British Gothic fiction of that era in its multifarious manifestations seems to be, like the protagonists who populate its pages, haunted by that Revolution's irrepressible ghosts. It may be said that this era of hyper-rationalism that 'could explain everything, but understand nothing' (Blanning: 129) is especially haunted by the ghost of Hamlet's father. Hamlet's slightly revised words in the face of that spectre offer the timely reminder that 'there are more things in heaven and earth…than are dreamt of in… [Enlightenment] philosophy' (Shakespeare, *Hamlet* I.v: 166–7).

In its further articulation of desires and fears related to the Industrial Revolution, the Gothic novel qualifies as a 'symbolic form of modernity' whose various and sometimes contradictory ideological engagements have rendered it a 'contested castle'.[15] In his controversial 1987 study, *The Way of the World: The Bildungsroman in European Culture*, Franco Moretti argues that 'Virtually without notice, in the dreams and nightmares of the so-called "double revolution" [Industrial and French], Europe plunges into modernity, but without possessing a *culture* of modernity'. In his opinion, the Bildungsroman responded to that need and became *the* 'symbolic form of modernity' (5). It is my contention, however, that the Gothic may also lay claim to this title as it gave expression to the repressed dreams and, more notably, the nightmares of the Enlightenment. Past and present commentators lend me support in their recognition that the Gothic novel was a crucial product of Europe's double revolution. According to the Marquis de Sade in his 'Reflections on the Novel' (1800), for example, the Gothic was a predictable and even necessary cultural development given the violent events of the late eighteenth century (109). In his words, it was 'the inevitable outcome of the revolutionary upheavals experienced throughout the whole of Europe', one conceived to rival the Revolution's horrors (109). More recently, E.J. Clery describes the Gothic as both 'a symptom and reflection on the modern' (9), and Robert Miles deems it 'an epiphenomena (*sic*) of modernity, a monstrous dramatisation of its conflicts' (Rev.: 119). Indeed, it may best be described as a singular creation of the Enlightenment's 'print revolution' (Porter: xxiv) and its 'mission to modernize' (xxii).

The arts in general have been necessary to the establishment of 'that common culture without which no nation-state can survive' (Blanning: 147). Much has been written, to date, about the novel's role as 'a socio-symbolic message' (Jameson: 141) vital to social formation and the consolidation of a sense of national identity. In the perceptive words of Timothy Brennan, 'Nation states are imaginary constructs that depend for their existence on an apparatus of cultural fictions in which imaginative literature plays a decisive role. And the rise of European nationalism coincides especially with one form of literature – the novel' (49). Patrick Brantlinger has expanded upon this idea in his suggestion that 'the development of the modern nation-state and that of the novel were not just simultaneous occurrences, but in some sense codeterminant' ('Nations': 255). *Anti-Semitism and British Gothic Literature* maintains that the Gothic also employed unique strategies and conventions to create and consolidate a national cultural sensibility. Especially in its secondary, more political phase in the 1790s, it engaged with the revolutionary events of the eighteenth-century fin de siècle. This genre did not, however, simply *reflect* those cataclysmic events. It responded to them in what David Punter describes as 'a very intense, if displaced' manner (*Literature*: 62) in a bid to caution against and promote certain national propensities.[16] As Maggie Kilgour has illustrated, the Gothic played an 'important part in the development of both political and literary nationalism' by 'recovering a *native* English literary tradition' that placed Shakespeare at its foundation (*Rise*: 13); however, it also became part of 'the battery of discursive and representational practices which define, legitimate, or valorize a specific nation-state or individuals as members of a nation-state' (During: 138). A developing sense of national identity may be discerned in the figurative contests, return of the repressed episodes, and exclusionary, purification rituals staged in the Gothic. These serve to identify and either endorse or reject certain values.

Although regarded at its worst until fairly recently by literary critics as 'an embarrassing and pervasive disease *destructive* to national culture and social fabric' (Gamer, *Romanticism*: 8; emphasis added), the British Gothic novel functioned as a singular and *constructive* mediating site in the ongoing debates about national identity in an increasingly secular age. These long-standing prejudices and misreadings have resulted, as Robert Miles recently observed, in the subject of nationalism and the Gothic being a 'much over-looked issue' (*Gothic*: ix). Indeed, several studies have made only minimally successful forays into exploring the question of the Gothic's vital and often constructive role in national identity formation on both sides of the Atlantic. Cannon Schmitt's 1997 study *Alien Nation: Nineteenth-Century Gothic Fictions and English Nationality* is, to my knowledge, the first critical study to claim for Gothic literature an important role in the construction of British national identity. While Schmitt's work highlights the profound xenophobia at the core of Gothic fiction, his primary argument that the besieged female in those narratives stands in for a besieged nation state is fairly simplistic and, as such, often more problematic than illuminating. Among other flaws, this driving claim downplays and even totally denies the presence and operation of the Female Gothic in the narratives under study. Despite Schmitt's reiteration of his principal claim that 'the English nation is defined primarily against that which it is not – against an anti- or alien nation' in the Gothic (164), he consistently resists any discussion or description of the nature and changing face of British nationalism over the course of a century – between the publication of Ann Radcliffe's *The Italian* in 1797 and Bram Stoker's *Dracula* in 1897.

Teresa Goddu's *Gothic America: Narrative, History, and Nation*, published in the same year as Schmitt's study, turns its attention to American Gothic fiction, yet its insights remain applicable to the British case. It is noteworthy in this regard that both British and American Gothic literature saw their genesis in the 1790s when the 'double revolutions' to which Moretti makes reference were occurring. Goddu may be guilty on the joint counts of denying her tremendous critical debts and distorting the American Gothic tradition,[17] but her study perceptively diagnoses that genre's apparently oppositional tendencies of disrupting 'the dream world of national myth with the nightmares of history' and consolidating national myths and values (10). Most recently, Toni Wein's *British Identities, Heroic Nationalisms, and the Gothic Novel, 1764–1824* (2002) advances the thesis that 'the Gothic novel figures a nationalist community through its imagining of a hero' (8) whose principal attributes are 'masculinity, hygiene, and citizenship' (10). In her view, '[t]o read the Gothic as always or only concerned with its villains does the novels and their audiences a disservice' (9). While Wein's act of shifting focus to the hero sheds a certain light on the make-up of British national identity, she would do well to consider that opposition is imperative to the creation of national identity: heroes and villains, dreams and nightmares are inextricably connected in Gothic fiction and, in fact, necessary one unto the other in the figuration of a nationalist community.

In the wake of these varied studies of Gothic literature and the nation, I would contend that the Wandering Jew is a particularly exemplary figure upon which to focus my critical lens. Always cloaked in mystery and increasingly figured as a villain, the Wandering Jew does help to establish, generally by way of contrast, the image of the ideal Briton as characterized by 'masculinity, hygiene and citizenship'. Certain energies and ideas, however, cannot be entirely reined in. While this anti-citizen enables the consolidation of this ideal, he also contests it, thus assuming the role of what Jay Salisbury has playfully and adeptly described as the Wandering *Jeu*. Located 'between old and new orders' (53), he signals 'a movement away from older structures of meaning and ways of knowing and into an encounter with the moment of epistemological uncertainty' (46).[18] Salisbury cites episodes featuring the Wandering Jew in Matthew Lewis's *The Monk* and Charles Robert Maturin's *Melmoth the Wanderer* – two texts that I examine in closer detail in Chapter 4 – as exemplifying 'moments when belief is suspended or has collapsed into despair' (46). Although Salisbury's claims shed some light on the Wandering Jew's vexed and vexing role in romantic narratives, they are unfortunately marked by a tendency prevalent in Romantic literary scholarship to deny the Wandering Jew's religious affiliation and position him as an Everyman.[19] Contrary to Salisbury's assertion that all wanderers in both Gothic and Romantic literature haunt epistemological certainties (46) and the implication that the Wandering Jew's ethnicity bears no significance, I would assert that this Gothic terrorist haunts Enlightenment certainties *in very ethnically specific ways*: while his wandering implies an internationalism that transcends racial and national boundaries, he nonetheless remains a Wandering *Jew*. In the minor sequence in which he appears in *The Monk*, for example, he calls rationalism into question by way, in part, of his association with magic and alchemy. Simultaneously, in the very assertion of his existence combined with his unnatural longevity, he upholds fundamental Christian religious certainties about the Crucifixion and the Millennium.

Despite the fact that religious belief was fast 'becoming a matter of private judgement' during the Enlightenment (Porter: 99), and that nationalism increasingly and unofficially functioned as a powerful and 'secular alternative to religion' (Blanning: 145), the 'Enlightenment in Britain took place within, rather than against, Protestantism' (Porter: 99). Indeed, as Linda Colley suggests, the major identifying feature of British national identity in the second half of the eighteenth century was Protestantism, which was conceptualized as a union of Reason and Religion. According to Roy Porter, the 'enlightened' held that '[r]eligion, ... must be rational, as befitted the mind of God and the nature of man' (100). Although, as Michael Wheeler has argued, 'for many critics in the modern, mainly secular western world, religion in historical literature is something of an embarrassment' (*Heaven*: 2), several scholars have considered the significance of religious issues in Gothic fiction over the course of the last half century. Mary Muriel Tarr (1946), Irene Bostrom (1962), Joel Porte (1974), and Victor Sage (1988) have affirmed that that genre's terror is 'usually at bottom theological' (Porte: 45) and that its rhetoric 'is demonstrably theological in character' (Sage: xvi). Directly or indirectly, these critics have opposed Montague Summers' 1928 declaration that 'it is folly to trace any "anti-Roman [Catholic] feeling" in the Gothic novel' as these authors 'employed abbots and convents ... because such properties were exotic, ... mysterious, and capable of the highest romantic treatment' (*Gothic* xviii). They have eloquently exposed the Gothic genre, in its equation of Catholicism with barbarism, 'monkish superstition,' and 'priestcraft' (Tarr: 18), as responding to 'the campaign for Catholic Emancipation from the 1770s onward until ... the Emancipation Act of 1829' (Sage: 28–9). Adopting Freudian lenses in relation to these works, Joel Porte has also interpreted them as forceful 'religious drama[s] [conveying] the dark rites of sin, guilt, and damnation' (45) where British Gothic writers have simply displaced Protestant fears onto Catholics and Catholic settings. Especially in their representations of such figures as Faust, Cain, Prometheus, and the Wandering Jew, these Gothic writers, Porte maintains, produced 'fable[s] of inexpiable guilt and unremitting punishment – in which ... [they] saw an image of their own condition and fate' (50).

While several exemplary studies exist that focus on the figure of the Jew in Bram Stoker's *Dracula* and other Victorian fin-de-siècle texts,[20] an exploration of the Jewish Question as a component of the theological terror in the Gothic has yet to be undertaken in any systematic way. Porte's elision of the Wandering Jew's religious identity provides yet another case in point regarding this oversight. When the Wandering Jew's Jewishness is foregrounded, however, the Gothic is revealed to enact, on one level, a dramatic and often violent type of family romance about Christian Britain's religious inheritance. This romance about religious filiation is in keeping with the Gothic's preoccupation with 'the issues of succession and inheritance' (Kilgour, *Rise*: 18), and features a Jewish father and a Catholic mother ('Mother Church'). It is deeply and ambivalently marked by self-righteousness and guilt, for the Jews 'were the representations of the Old Religion, against which Christianity had rebelled, and there was a feeling of bad conscience about them. The Jews were Father-figures, and rebellion against the father is never a straightforward expression of hatred' (Maccoby: 239). The figuration of the Jew as 'the bad father' (Cohn, *Protocols*: 86) or 'symbolic father-in-law, a cruel and unwilling parent to whom disobedience is a virtue' (Fiedler, 'What': 414) was an established European idea. Roy Porter notably references an atavistic Judaism with a demonic paternalist deity as the point of contrast in his claim that the 'Enlightenment in Britain took place within, rather than against, Protestantism' (99): 'Rejecting the bogeyman of a vengeful Jehovah blasting wicked sinners, enlightened divines instated a more optimistic (pelagian) theology, proclaiming the benevolence of the Supreme Being and man's capacity to fulfil his duties through his God-given faculties, the chief of these being reason, that candle of the Lord' (100). A certain guilt generally accompanies the rejection of this Jewish bogeyman, however, for although the Christian son may, on one hand, insist on his difference from and superiority to his Jewish father, the nagging doubt remains that they may be dreadfully similar. During such exemplary uncanny episodes in the Gothic, the vampiric Wandering Jew is revealed to be a buried aspect of the Christian self. Although he is generally condemned and frequently exorcized in that tradition, this 'Other' is also exposed as 'Brother' – or 'Father' as the case may be. At his most treacherous, this Jewish figure threatens to enact a ritual to restore a primal unity by way of consuming his Christian offspring, an act that annihilates that offspring's autonomy. Despite his semiotic transformation in the face of socio-cultural change and the concurrent shifts in the nature of anti-Semitism, this theological relationship remains fundamental (Freedman, *Temple*: 59, Poliakov: 397).

Joel Porte's displacement theory may be fruitfully brought to bear on the bad conscience associated with the Wandering Jew. In its treatment of that figure, British Gothic fiction may be said to be extremely self-reflexive on at least two major counts: it both displaces disagreeable national propensities on to him and registers authorial concerns regarding engagement with the Gothic, an increasingly lucrative yet contentious and disparaged genre that 'played a significant part in late eighteenth-century debates over the moral dangers of reading' (Kilgour, *Rise*: 6). While a nationalist community was imagined in the Gothic, as Toni Wein has argued, in the form of a hero characterized by 'masculinity, hygiene, and citizenship' (10), a spectre was simultaneously conjured up that dramatically clarified all that Britons considered anathema to their national sensibility. The Jews had long been deemed the 'colonizers for progress' (Horkheimer and Adorno: 175). They became, by the Victorian fin de siècle, as Bryan Cheyette has accurately commented, 'a dark double of Empire' antithetical to the ' "civilizing" Imperial [British] Race' (*Constructions*: 92). Ironically, however, in the form of the mesmerizing Wandering Jew, an international, Mammonistic, magician-scientist, and accursed criminal, Britain also projected its own demonic self-image as an increasingly imperialist, scientifically industrial, and aggressively missionary nation.

In its treatment of the Wandering Jew, British Gothic literature also gave expression to otherwise repressed anxieties relating to the prospect of Jewish assimilation. During a period when narratives of conversion and conversionist societies were advocating the assimilation of the Jews, Gothic novels sometimes played out the terror of such a prospect. In true projectionist style, it is the Wandering Jews in these texts, and not the Christians, who resist assimilation. Unlike the uncanny moments, therefore, where the demonic is revealed to be domestic and the 'Other' revealed to be 'Brother', a corollary exists in the Gothic where the successfully 'invasive' Crypto-Jewish 'Brother' is exposed to be a sinister 'Other' who wishes to convert his national host. Slavoj Žižek notably and unwittingly describes this manifestation of the Gothic uncanny specifically in relation to anti-Semitism. The anti-Semite's Jew is compared to the alien body snatchers in the well known 1950's film *Invasion of the Body Snatchers* where

> an invasion of creatures from outer space [who] assume human shape – they look exactly like human beings, they have all their properties, but *in some sense this makes them all the more uncannily strange*. This problem is the same as anti-Semitism (and for that reason *Invasion of the Body Snatchers* can be read as a metaphor for McCarthyite anti-Communism in the fifties): Jews are "like us"; it is difficult to recognize them, to determine at the level of positive reality that surplus, *that evasive feature*, which differentiates them from all other people. (89; emphasis added)

The fear Žižek describes is essentially one of reverse colonization where the chameleonic Crypto-Jew with a nationally subversive agenda successfully mimics Britons. As Jay Geller has commented, especially since the nineteenth century fin de siècle, '[t]alent in the mimetic arts was as much a signifier of the … Jew as the badge had been the visible mark in [the] medieval period' (30). Despite their historic distance, both cases actually convey the same idea: the Jew is unassimilable either religiously or nationally. The resistance to assimilation, in short, is *on the Jew's part* and not the Christian's. This accusation of unassimilability has a lengthy history as does the strategy of yoking it to the motif of consumption, which involves the issue of individual autonomy. As Maggie Kilgour explains, 'To accuse a minority that resists assimilation into the body politic of that body's own desire for total incorporation is a recurring tactic: during the Middle Ages the Jews were accused of cannibalism, after the Reformation the Catholics were, and Christ has continually been accused of being the head of a Jewish cannibal sect' (*From*: 5). British Gothic literature's vampiric Wandering Jew is subject to an extension of such medieval anti-Semitic accusations. Radically resistant to assimilation by way of religious conversion, his draining and infectious bite poses the threat of spiritual conversion to vampirism and the literal assimilation of the Christian son by way of physical consumption.

The concept of originality, 'the artistic counterpart to individualism', which was beginning to emerge as a value in the late eighteenth century (Kilgour, *Rise*: 21), was also carried over to the self-reflexive projection process involving the vampiric Wandering Jew and Gothic novelists. Through him, they registered desires and anxieties regarding their involvement with a genre that frequently engaged in narrative mimicry. While the Wandering Jew's role as a Cabalist is discussed more fully in Chapter 3, it · may be argued that the Gothic novelist desired that figure's supernatural conjuring powers. As Robert Irwin has so aptly phrased it, 'Cabalism is literary occultism par excellence. The Cabalist and the novelist are jointly committed to the magical creation of a world through the manipulation of words' (6). Gothic novelists projected onto the Wandering Jew, therefore, their yearning to become mesmerizing literary Cabalists. Writerly anxieties were also expressed, however, in relation to the Wandering Jew and the brazenly unoriginal Gothic novel, which was significantly preoccupied with doubles and doubling. David Punter has perceptively described the Gothic as a 'para-site' in its relation to mainstream culture ('Introduction': 3). Indeed, it is parasitic on at least two counts: 'it feed[s] off the literary remains of previous Gothics' (Frank: xii) and upon a 'wide range of literary sources out of which it emerges and from which it never fully disentangles itself' (Kilgour, *Rise*: 4). Curiously and compellingly, the Gothic is, therefore, remarkably like the parasitic Wandering Jew often featured in its pages. Further to this, it is as transgressive as that lawless figure, having invaded other high-cultural forms in the late eighteenth and early nineteenth centuries (Gamer: 12). 'The gothic seems', as Maggie Kilgour has remarked, 'a puzzling contradiction, denounced and now celebrated for its radical imaginative lawlessness' (*Rise*: 10). The endless, labyrinthine Chinese Box style structure of the Gothic and its treatment of 'fantasised transcendences' (Punter, *Gothic*: 10) also mirror the Wandering Jew's unnatural longevity. According to the most popular version of the legend, every time he reaches the age of one hundred, he 'is seized by a sickness culminating in a trance, from which he emerges once again as a man of thirty – the age he was when Jesus suffered' (Railo: 191). His increasing association with Gothic literature's vampire is virtually predictable given this make-up.

Finally, the Gothic novelist is also like the Mammonistic Wandering Jew in that s/he is often commercially driven and aware. Many Gothic works published between 1764 and 1824 were 'written for purely monetary motives' (Frank: xxix). Jonathan Freedman has intriguingly interpreted the Victorian novel's 'increasing concern with Jews [as] ... the product of a crisis of self-definition posed for writers engaging with the increasing mass market for fiction in mid- to late nineteenth century' (*Temple*: 9). The Jew 'figured their own experience in a mature capitalist economy', one characterized according to Freedman by ambivalent feelings of shame and pleasure (*Temple*: 10). This character served 'as the embodiment of ... [the ambivalent] new affective possibilities in the brave new world of the marketplace' (*Temple*: 10). Freedman's provocative insights may be rewardingly extended to the character of the Wandering Jew and the genre of the Gothic novel. That the Wandering Jews are frequently extremely literate in that genre and in possession of esoteric knowledge that may prove lucrative (such as the philosopher's stone and the *elixir vitae*) is especially noteworthy in this regard. This association combines the popular conceptions of the Jews as both the 'People of the Book' and monetary magicians. Thus is the ideologically charged figure of the Jew invested by the authors' conscious and unconscious fears and desires about their personal propensities and the influence of their Gothic productions on a national readership. As the figure of the Wandering Jew, however, is usually employed in that genre to identify and promote an ethical mode of capitalism, its sometimes self-consciously didactic authors may also regard themselves as engaged in maintaining the social welfare. Freedman's speculative theory about this character should be expanded, therefore, given this complex role.

As I have tried to suggest in this chapter, however, the Wandering Jew's significance extends well beyond commercial issues. During the formidably transitional Enlightenment era, the Wandering Jew became a highly charged figure positioned at anxious crossroads between such seemingly incompatible ideas as magic and science,[21] superstition and reason, religion and nationalism, and mercantilism and speculative capitalism. This abject figure that does not 'respect borders, positions, rules' and 'disturbs identity, system, [and] order' (Kristeva: 4), thus came to emblematize numerous Jewish Questions and to voice that nation's anxieties regarding modernization in its various facets, her socio-political propensities, and the Enlightenment's emancipatory project. It is to a detailed examination of the complex historic semiotic construction of this titillating yet terrifying character that I turn in the next two chapters.

2
The Primal Scene: The Skeleton in Britain's Closet

[Y]ou are influenced by the darkest superstitions of the darkest ages that ever existed in this country. It is this feeling that has been kept out of this debate; indeed, that has been kept secret in yourselves – enlightened as you are – and that is unknowingly influencing you as it is influencing others abroad. – Benjamin Disraeli 1847, Debate on Jewish Emancipation.

(*Hansard's* 95:1329)

If there exists a cure for Judeophobia, the age-old malady of Christianity, it lies not in the suppression of symptoms but in their exposure to the light.

(Manuel: 1)

Published just several years before the traditionally acknowledged termination of the classic British Gothic period, Maria Edgeworth's 1817 novel *Harrington* may seem an unusual and even illogical point of departure for a study of the Jewish Question in Gothic fiction. What *Harrington* is singular in providing, however, is a remarkably self-conscious exploration from early nineteenth-century England of the psychopathology of anti-Semitism. Conceived as 'an act of reparation' for Edgeworth's previous and numerous anti-Semitic literary portraits (Ragussis, *Figures*: 62)[1] – the most famous of which are Sir Kit's nameless Jewish wife, his 'stiff-necked Israelite' (31) in *Castle Rackrent* (1800) and the eerily inhuman, Shylockean coachmaker-creditor Mordicai in *The Absentee* (1811)[2] – *Harrington* features an unsettlingly plentiful storehouse of anti-Semitic stereotypes. As Susan Manly has noted, *Harrington* 'powerfully represents the unselfconscious anti-semitism of its mid-eighteenth-century Londoners' ('Introductory': xxvi). It also furnishes, with an eye to their dismantling, a sense of the nature, prevalence, and entrenchment of such stereotypes in early nineteenth-century England. While Gothic fiction's Wandering Jew does not appear in all of his full-fledged and demonic glory, that 'Jew whom Christians most abominate'

34

(*Harrington*: 95) is frequently invoked by way of pejorative name-calling.[3] Further to this, many of the ingredients of his graphic Gothic portrait are present in the novel's memorable and fascinating primal scene. *Harrington* functions as the ideal springboard into this study, therefore, as it allows privileged, albeit mediated, access to a generally tabooed closet in British middle-class consciousness. It thus facilitates an investigation of both the provenance of Gothic fiction's Wandering Jew, a character literally centuries in the making, and the cabalistic semiotics associated with him.

Harrington also furnishes an exemplary jumping-off point for this study as it attests to the entrenched and resonant association between the Jew and the Gothic in British culture. By 'Gothic' I am referring to more than simply the sense of dread attached to the Jew, a dread that is especially evoked by way of the medieval Blood Libel in the novel's primal scene. What is particularly noteworthy about *Harrington* is the fact that Edgeworth, an author adept in various modes of Gothic, as *Castle Rackrent* and 'Angelina' (*Moral Tales*) testify, chose this genre, heretofore frequently employed by British authors to *construct* a singular image of the dreaded Jew, to *destroy* this figure by exposing its fictionality, thus indicting anti-Semitism. Faced with numerous generic options, Edgeworth elected to deploy the Gothic in order to produce a cautionary tale about intolerance and the English national sensibility. Given its unique engagement with personal and national histories, and its deep-rooted anxieties about the alterity of personal identity and the instability of national boundaries, the Gothic was an especially judicious choice.

What is also noteworthy about Edgeworth's Gothic strategies is the fact that she produces a self-reflexive meditation on the uses and abuses of the Gothic in *Harrington*. As such, Edgeworth's novel complies with some of the ideological precepts behind the anti-Gothic vogue of the early nineteenth century which included works like Sarah Green's *Romance Readers and Romance Writers* (1810), Jane Austen's *Northanger Abbey* (1818), and Thomas Love Peacock's *Nightmare Abbey* (1818). *Harrington* is not a purely anti-Gothic novel for it is not an exaggerated imitation of that form replete with characters who are burlesque equivalents of those featured in the Gothic. It does, however, reformulate the female-quixote theme popular in those narratives in order to convey a sophisticated and sobering message about two related issues – real and imaginary terrors, and the power of representation. Central to this commentary is the figure of Harrington who is, tragically, not alone in believing that the dreadful fictions relating to Jews are truths. Misreading is represented as a national problem, and the fact that Harrington is socialized into his anti-Semitic belief system makes *Harrington* a socio-political indictment. While Edgeworth's novel highlights the power of representations in general, it censures the abuse of such influence. *Harrington* may not constitute an act of reparation on Edgeworth's part for her Gothic literary productions, but it certainly advances an intriguing retrospective meditation on those earlier works.

Notably, discussion of the role of the Gothic in *Harrington* has been surprisingly absent from critical assessments to date. Concurrent with the rise of scholarship examining the socio-historical and cultural construction of British national identity, there has been renewed critical interest in this novel in recent years. Michael Ragussis employs *Harrington* to illustrate both the ongoing negotiation throughout the nineteenth century between British national identity and Jewish Emancipation, and the oppressively powerful nature of conversion as 'the literary and cultural master trope by which Jewish identity is represented and regulated' (*Figures*: 86). Susan Manly similarly classifies *Harrington* as 'an interrogation of Englishness and English liberties' ('Burke': 154) that 'reflects on Burke's *Reflections*' (153) and exposes the complicity of British print culture and xenophobic politics in fostering anti-Semitism. Most recently, Neville Hoad has provided a deconstructive reading of the 'class and gender textual economies' (128) at work in *Harrington*'s engagement with issues of 'national incorporation and exclusion' (122). As illuminating as such critical readings have been, especially with regard to the issue of national identity formation, they fail to recognize that the Gothic is key to Edgeworth's interrogation strategy. Hoad is the only reader, in fact, who even addresses the issue of genre, and he characterizes *Harrington* as providing a 'weird mix of modes', namely 'a confession, a fairy-tale and proto-psycho-analytic cure' (122). While I would suggest that these various critical assessments would be enriched, generally, by a consideration of Edgeworth's generic choice, I would argue more specifically that Ragussis's insightful identification and interpretation of the 'return of the repressed' dynamic in *Harrington* would be especially enhanced by this approach.

The 'return of the repressed' dynamic resides at the very core of Gothic fiction, and is most commonly manifested in the form of a 'fear of historical reversion; that is, of the nagging possibility that the despotisms buried by the modern age may prove to be yet undead' (Baldick, *Oxford*: xxi). As such, the joint questions of personal and national improvement are a generic preoccupation, and the signature Radcliffean narrative dynamic of gradual enlightenment facilitated by rationalism and Christianity (figured as a rational and national religion), is a standard structuring principle. Collapsing English national history into the personal history of its eponymous narrator and his developmental trajectory from a benighted attitude towards the Jews to one of enlightened tolerance and respect, *Harrington* identifies the primary fear in its narrator's possible regression. This horrifying prospect is of concern not only to Harrington, but to his prospective 'Jewish' wife Berenice (who is later revealed to be Christian) and father-in-law, Mr Montenero, a benevolent and wealthy refugee from the Spanish

Inquisition. Harrington explicitly expresses concern about this possible regression in the early stages of their friendship:

> ...I thought I saw in Mr. Montenero's, and still more in the timid countenance of his daughter, a fear that I might relapse; and that *these early prepossessions, which were so difficult, scarcely possible, completely to conquer,* might recur. I promised myself that I should soon convince them they were mistaken, if they had formed any such notion. (102)

This concern is entirely warranted given the relationship between Harrington's development and British history with its irrepressible anti-Semitism. Thus does Edgeworth innovatively manipulate the 'return of the repressed' dynamic to signify both the idea of the return of generational and national pasts upon presents and the tyrannical return of earlier stages of selfhood in personal histories.

England's regression into anti-Semitic prejudice is consistently figured in relation to Spain, a national site of obscurantism and arrested development where the Inquisition remained in operation until 15 July 1834 (Bostrom: 159; Roth, *Spanish*: 267), almost two decades after *Harrington*'s publication. Spain and the Spanish Inquisition are popular features in British Gothic fiction for reasons that are more intensely examined in the following chapter. For the present examination, it should be noted that Edgeworth follows in the footsteps of established Gothic tradition when she repeatedly raises what I will call the spectre of Spain throughout *Harrington*. This includes numerous references to the Inquisition and an explicit invocation, anticipating the invasion scare narratives of the Victorian fin de siècle, of national invasion by way of the sixteenth-century Armada. She strategically employs the powerful Gothic techniques of unsettling the boundary between what I call 'Other' and 'Brother', and staging the incursions of pasts upon presents to conduct a narrative Inquisition into the integrity of English liberty and tolerance. In the process, she repeatedly intimates England's likeness to Spain. As in *Caleb Williams* (1794) and *St. Leon* (1799), where William Godwin suggests that traces of inquisitorial, tyrannical despotism are also in evidence in late eighteenth-century Britain's penal and legal systems,[4] Edgeworth's no-holds-barred exposé of England's anti-Semitic past frequently blurs the boundary between historic barbarism and present-day Enlightenment. Her reluctance to provide details of the Inquisition or of what Jacob circumspectly describes as Mr Montenero's 'difficulties' with it (99), implies the unspeakability of its horrors. Spain, however, is not shown to possess a monopoly on anti-Semitism: England's ostensible *past* is graphically exposed and revealed to be undead. Indeed, anti-Semitic attitudes are irrepressibly alive and thriving despite Harrington's early beliefs to the contrary.

Narrated in retrospect in 1778,[5] Harrington's story conveys how he long maintained that anti-Semitic prejudice was 'confined to the vulgar, ... the ill-educated and the ill-informed' (85). Nowhere is Harrington's hopeful insistence that British anti-Semitism is but an archaic memory more plainly expressed than in the novel's compelling primal scene, which chronicles the young boy's initial traumatic encounter with the Old Clothes Man, Simon the Jew. Michael Ragussis notes how this episode functions as 'an early Romantic harbinger of Freud' and registers 'the pathogenic effect of a critical scene of childhood' (*Figures*: 65). It is also, however, a classic Gothic scene rife with Gothic atmospherics and is intriguingly situated within that tradition: it is highly reminiscent of the opening scene in E.T.A. Hoffman's 'The Sandman', published just a year earlier,[6] and anticipates the openings of various Victorian Gothic works like Charlotte Brontë's *Jane Eyre* (1847) and Charles Dickens's *Great Expectations* (1860–61). Mesmerized by the sight of Simon, a 'mysterious old man with a long white beard and a dark visage, ... holding a great bag slung over one shoulder' (2), the vulnerable and semi-conscious Harrington is readily furnished by his terrorist nursemaid Fowler with the anti-Semitic lenses through which to read him. Despite possessing what Harrington notes is a 'good-natured countenance' (2) and what he later describes as an 'inoffensive hand' (6), Simon is irrevocably transformed when Fowler threatens the young boy, who refuses to go to bed, that Simon will come and take him away in his 'great bag' (2). Harrington is understandably 'struck with terror' by this suggestion and imagines the bag to contain the 'mangled limbs of children' (4).[7] This horrifying thought is thereafter magnified by various Blood Libel tales related by Fowler over the course of eighteen months, representing the Jews as a treacherously blood-thirsty nation with a particularly perverse and literal taste for children. Speaking mysteriously, Fowler exploits the longstanding 'culturally powerful association between the Jew and the act of consumption' (Freedman, *Temple*: 85), and relates stories about Jews who abduct children 'for the purpose of killing, crucifying, and sacrificing them at their secret feasts and midnight abominations' (3). An anti-Semitic version of the popular Sweeney Todd story involving a Parisian Jew who sells pork pies made of the flesh of little children holds a particularly dreadful power (3). Thus is this young and vulnerable child reduced for the duration to the status of a Female Gothic heroine, his home converted into what he describes as a 'prison-house' (5). More ironically and strategically, however, he is placed in the position of persecuted victim, a position generally occupied by the Jews in England.

Harrington's subsequent commentary about these events, some twenty years later, betrays his persistent naiveté and optimism about British progress. Considering the period since his childhood in the 1750s, he concludes:

> In our enlightened days, and in the present improved state of education, it may appear incredible that any nursery-maid could be so wicked as to relate, or any child of six years old so foolish as to credit such tales; but I am speaking of what happened many years ago; nursery-maids and

children, I believe, are very different now from what they were then; and in further proof of the progress of human knowledge and reason, we may recollect that many of these very stories of the Jews, which we now hold too preposterous for the infant and the nursery-maid to credit, were some centuries ago universally believed by the English nation, and had furnished more than one of our kings with pretexts for extortion and massacres. (3–4)

These statements about British progress are subsequently exposed as ironic. In sometimes unwitting disclosures, Harrington reveals the grotesque anti-Semitic worldviews of such individuals as his friend's aristocratic mother, Lady de Brantefield, and his own father, a Member of Parliament whose first memorable political act during Harrington's childhood is to oppose the 1753 Jewish Naturalization Bill. Thus does Edgeworth portray anti-Semitism as an equal opportunity prejudice that extends far beyond Harrington's maidservant Fowler in the novel's opening primal scene. England's benighted anti-Semitic past, represented by that primal scene which compresses the notorious and multifaceted Blood Libel, continues to haunt her purportedly enlightened present. Harrington is, likewise, a decidedly haunted man fearful of regression into an infantile sensibility. As the complex semiotics of that primal scene are as vital to the provenance of the Wandering Jew in British Gothic fiction as they are to Edgeworth's subversion strategies in *Harrington*, I turn now to a semiotically focused overview of the Blood Libel.

The benighted Blood Libel

Given what Joshua Trachtenberg has so brilliantly delineated as the long-standing representation of the Jew as devil in the worldview of medieval Christian Europe,[8] it was almost inevitable that this figure would be pressed into service centuries later as a vital spectre in the Gothic genre. Most of the taboos at the core of that genre – such as incest, fratricide, miscegenation, and castration – involve blood in either a literal or a figurative sense (as in the concept of blood money, or familial or 'racial' blood-ties), and had long been associated with the Jew, the primary anti-Christian 'Other' in the European worldview. Since 'medieval Christendom did not distinguish between the religious and social realms as we do today, its theology became law and social policy. Hence, the Jews came to be seen not only as a religious Other but as a socially and economically disruptive figure as well' (Gregg: 171).

The Blood Libel condenses these various anti-Christian associations. By way of it, Jews were accused of desecrating the Host and of murdering 'non-Jews so their blood could be used ... [for] the Passover seder', the prolongation of life (Trachtenberg: 215), and other purposes (Friedman, 'Edge': 52).[9] That the Blood Libel was generally said to involve children, society's most vulnerable and valuable members, magnified the reprehensible nature of this crime.[10] It was thus perceived as a threat to both the family and the nation. It is significant that the 'first recorded Blood Libel in medieval Europe took place at Norwich [England] in 1144' (Efron: 34). As this alleged ritual sacrifice of William of Norwich in 1144 and that of Hugh of Lincoln in 1254 attest,[11] Jews in medieval Britain were, first and foremost, labelled Christ-killers who delighted in mocking the Passion. While Jews were officially expelled from Britain in the year 1290 for their 'persistence in practising usury in direct contravention of the *Statutum de Judeismo* of 1275' (Mundill: 255), the expulsion was popularly understood to be punishment for 'their notorious Crimes; as, poysoning of wels, counterfeiting of coins, falsifying of seals, and crucifying of Christian children, with other villainies' (James Howell, qtd in David Katz, *The Jews*: 191).[12]

Other taboo blood-related activities attributed to the Jews in medieval Britain included incest, cannibalism, ritual circumcision, and male menstruation. As this list attests, Christians often distorted Jewish cultural and religious practices in blasphemous ways. Jewish endogamy was misrepresented as incest (a violation of blood relations in the Christian world-view), and kosher practices involving ritual slaughter were demonized as cannibalistic, against the directive outlined in Genesis 9.4 that Noah and his descendants should not consume 'flesh with the life thereof which is the blood thereof'. In some instances, Jewish religious practices were represented as a macabre parody of Christian religious practices. While Christians were portrayed as participating in spiritually enlightened Masses, Jews were said to engage in satanic Black Masses where they cavorted with the devil and engaged in macabre rituals.

As it involved blood and bloodsucking,[13] the Jewish rite of circumcision spoke to a variety of Christian fears. It also subtended the popular Christian portrait of the Jews as a materialistic, flesh-bound nation divorced from the spiritual world and divine love. Although Paul was himself circumcised and had circumcised others (Shapiro, *Shakespeare*: 117), his remarks on this Jewish practice, once he became a Christian convert, called Jewish identity into question and implied that that nation was spiritually myopic. Aware that this rite was based on a tradition expressly referred to in Deuteronomy 10.16 and 30.6, which read, 'Circumcise the foreskin of your heart,' and 'The Lord thy God will circumcise thine heart', Paul wrote, 'He is not a Jew which is one outward, neither is that circumcision, which is outward in the flesh. But he is a Jew which is one within, and the circumcision is of the heart, in the spirit, not in the letter, whose praise is not of men, but of God' (Shapiro, *Shakespeare*: 118). Central to Paul's statements was the idea of Jews as the people of the Book and the Law bound to the literal, material world, and blind to the realm of the spiritual and the figurative. The *adversus judaeos* literature of the early Christian era 'argued that Hebrew Scripture proved that the Jews had demonstrated in numerous instances their incapacity to serve as the guardians of sacred Scripture – by misreading it, mistranslating it, even mutilating it' (Ragussis, *Figures*: 81).

Whether or not the distinguishing 'mark' of circumcision drew parallels in medieval times with the mark of Cain remains a matter for speculation. There is 'a long history of describing the male Jew as having been born circumcised' (Gilman, *Freud*: 52), however, and Theodor Reik, one of Freud's early supporters, does consider the possibility of the Cain-circumcision connection in 1919. In his argument 'that the origin of circumcision lay in the self-mutilation of Cain as his punishment for an act of incest' (85), Reik actually combines anti-Semitic stereotypes. As this sign of Jewish difference was considered to be, as Sander Gilman has noted, a deceptively 'hidden' mark of membership in 'the secret [Jewish] race' (*Jew's*: 18), the Medieval Church saw fit to impose a more visible mark of Cain on the Jews. The Fourth Lateran Council, called by Innocent III in 1215, instituted 'a distinctive Jewish garb' and a badge that were mandatory attire for all members of the Jewish community (Trachtenberg: 116). Several surviving illustrations of Satan wearing a Jew badge (Trachtenberg, frontispiece) – including one in which Satan is shown participating in 'Jewish financial transactions' (195) – are a disturbing testament to the popular idea of the Jew as devil, 'a staple of medieval anti-Judaism' (Gregg: 195). Furthermore, Trachtenberg relates how this badge was regarded as a type of mark of Cain worn by a demonic, nationless brotherhood: 'with a little ingenuity the Jew badge may be explained altogether as a sign of the Jews' allegiance to the devil, as medieval versifiers ultimately get around to doing' (26).

England was the first European nation to adopt the Jew badge in 1218 (Glassman: 16), a move that seemed intended to safeguard that country from a group it regarded as conspiratorial and, effectively, in league with the devil. As Saul Friedländer has written:

> The Christian phantasm of a Jewish plot against the Christian community may itself have been a revival of the pagan notion that the Jews were enemies of humanity acting in secret against the rest of the world. According to popular medieval Christian legend, 'a secret rabbinical synod convened periodically from all over Europe to determine which community was in turn to commit ritual murder'. (84)

The popular view of the Jews as a criminal and conspiratorial nation of Christ-killers with indelibly bloodied hands, coloured all subsequent libels against them. This attitude had, in large part, derived from the story of Cain. Frank Felsenstein explains the origins of this association in his book, *Anti-Semitic Stereotypes*:

> From Genesis, the story of Cain, 'cursed from the earth' (4:11) for the murder of Abel, his brother, helped promote the belief that not only he,

but also the people of the Old Testament, should in later ages be 'a fugitive and a vagabond in the earth' (4:14). Significantly, the slain figure of Abel had been 'a keeper of sheep' (4:2), offering unto God the firstling of the flock, in symbolic terms prefiguring the sacrificial role of Christ in the New Testament. Christian typologists descried no obstacle in forging parallels between Abel's treatment at the hand of Cain and the treatment of Christ by the Jews. (59)

An association is, in fact, clearly forged in the Oberammergau Passion Play between Cain and Judas. In its juxtaposition of scenes from the New Testament and tableaux from the Old, it suggests that Cain's murder of Abel foreshadowed Judas's betrayal of Jesus (Moncure: 71).

Reverend Sabine Baring-Gould has also observed that the legend of the Wandering Jew 'has been taken as a crystallisation of the odyssey of the descendants of Cain, wandering over the earth with the brand of a brother's blood as their curse' (25). The conception of the Jews as a lupine nation guilty of slaughtering the lamb of God is also implied in the Wandering Jew legend given Ahasuerus's failure to aid Christ on the road to Calvary. That exile's rejection of Christ represents the ultimate blood-related violation and, like Cain's bloody fratricide, it is penalized by nationlessness and eternal wandering. Cain is, as Hyam Maccoby aptly phrases it, 'condemned to life' (241). As Cain's subsequent coupling with 'his wife' must have involved incest either with his mother, Eve, or an unmentioned and unnamed sister, his association with the Jews is further established in the medieval world-view. According to that framework, Cain was the father of monsters and since the Jews were believed to be his descendants, they were deemed to be abominations of humanity. A final significant point of contact linking Cain and the Wandering Jew involves the former's mark which ensured that no one would kill Cain and deliver him from his punishment. In a tradition that appears to have begun in Spain, the Wandering Jew is similarly indelibly inscribed. He is usually portrayed with a flaming cross on his brow (Railo: 193), the manner in which he appears in Matthew Lewis's *The Monk*.

In what is perhaps the most absurd Blood Libel claim, namely that Jewish men menstruated four times a year,[14] an obvious attempt is made to undermine the Jewish nation by characterizing it as effeminate. This libel, however, has other deep-seated religious implications. As Lawrence Osborne has noted, it was 'the thirteenth-century anatomist Thomas de Cantimpré [who] wrote the first "scientific" account of this bloody and improbable phenomenon, and supplied the sensational theory that it was a sign of the Father's curse by way of punishment for their denial of Christ' (129). Like most 'curses' associated with the Jew – de Cantimpré also mentions hemorrhoids (Trachtenberg: 148)[15] – this one involves blood and originated at the Crucifixion, an event which Christians perceived as the Jewish 'Fall' from

God's grace. For both Eve and the Jew, therefore, the 'curse' (menstruation) was one form of retribution for transgressing divine law.

Given the renown of these literally bloody myths, it should come as no surprise that, as Joshua Trachtenberg has so aptly demonstrated, 'English literature [has] regularly described the Jews as "bloudie" ' (125). The popular and perverse knife-wielding Jew featured in medieval religious drama who took pleasure in acts of 'torture, crucifixion and rape' (Rubin: 53), is the principal ancestor of most Jewish literary characters. This thirteenth-century Judas figure, with his signature 'bloody' red beard and heavy money bags (Felsenstein: 31), maintained the connection between blood and money which was vital to the story of Christ's betrayal. This 'apostle of the cash nexus' (Rosenberg: 97) also anticipated Shakespeare's infamous usurer, Shylock, who so ardently pursued his pound of flesh. The blood-money theme may be significantly reconfigured in the latter representation – Judas gains money in exchange for Christ's blood while Shylock seeks flesh in compensation for 'lost' money – but the Jewish nation is portrayed in both instances as spiritually benighted, money-hungry, and bloodthirsty. Antonio's friend, Gratiano, articulates this popular anti-Semitic image when he describes Shylock's desires as 'wolvish, bloody, starv'd and ravenous' (IV.i.: 137–8). Notably, Shylock lends credence to this stereotype when he announces to his daughter, after accepting an invitation to dine with Bassanio, that he will 'go in hate, to feed upon / The prodigal Christian' (II.v.: 14–15).

This notion of the Jews as bloodthirsty was especially employed in popular representations of their economic activity. Although they engaged in a variety of commercial activities, Jews were particularly associated with moneylending,[16] an activity for which Christians were excommunicated in the Middle Ages as it was perceived as a threat to the commonwealth (Mergenthal: 320; *Confutation*: 25). James Shapiro explains that the discourse around usury in Britain incorporated the notion of cannibalism:

William Prynne … [a Puritan zealot of the seventeenth century] quoting from the Tudor chronicler John Speed, writes that 'by their cruel usuries' the Jews have 'eaten' the English 'people to the bones'. Moreover, exorbitant moneylending was often referred to as 'biting' usury, and the elision of Jews as economic exploiters and literal devourers of Christian flesh was easily made. This may in part be explained by the philological determination of Elizabethan writers on usury, whose Hebrew was good enough to know that the biblical word for lending at interest, *neshech*, also meant 'to bite'. (110)

This 'biting' image gave a sense of immediacy to Jewish usury by effectively linking the personal and the political: the act of 'biting' the body was linked to that of putting the economic bite on the body politic.[17] It was perhaps this metaphor that underpinned the popular and grotesque act of the dentition of the Jews in the early Middle Ages. In a disturbing act of displacement, King John and subsequent English rulers of the House of Plantagenet punished wealthy, 'usurious' Jews by extorting large sums of money from them. The bloody process of dentition, which involved removing one of the Jewish victim's teeth every day until he handed over a stipulated sum (Brewer: 681), was a popular extortion method.[18]

It would seem that the figuration of the Jew as canine and lupine (in possession of fang-like canine teeth) was bound up with this economic reading of the Blood Libel. Shylock, Shakespeare's 'wolvish' (IV.i.: 137), 'currish Jew' (IV.i.: 292), cautions Antonio that since he regards Shylock as a 'cut-throat dog' (I.iii.: 111), he should 'beware ... [his] fangs' (III.iii.: 6–7).[19] This lupine association is again forged, specifically with reference to possible inter-marriage between Jews and Christians, in the 1715 *Confutation*. According to its anonymous author, 'as Nature will not allow Sheep to Associate with Wolves, no more will the Law of the Gospel allow Christians to Associate or Intermix with Jews' (25).[20] A similar canine image is promoted by John Calvin who labelled the Jews 'dogs' (Manuel: 49), and by Martin Luther who called them 'bloodhounds' (10). It is further suggested in a German illustration of a Jew hung upside down between dogs with cut throats, a popular and gruesome method of execution for Jews accused of the Blood Libel. As R. Po-chia Hsia explains, this manner of execution 'mimicked a reversed Crucifixion: Christ was crucified between two thieves' (28). This image of the 'fanging' Jew is also evoked in a curious 1640 British publication entitled *The Wandering-Jew, Telling Fortunes to English-men*. This work relates how an extortionist who comes to hear his fortune told by the Wandering Jew (actually an English Christian in disguise), informs his fortune-teller that he (the extortionist) is also a Jew for he 'fang[s] ... Citizen[s]' (36).

In this seventeenth-century image of the 'fanging' Jew and the popular libel which maintained that Jews consumed human blood as 'they believe[d] that the sacrifice of an innocent life ... [would] prolong their own lives' (Trachtenberg: 215), one may discern, without much effort, an emerging vampire motif. As H.L. Malchow has argued, 'There was always a metaphoric vampirism in the traditional image of the Jew as usurer, as bloodsucker' (160). Luther's description in 1543 of the usurious Jews 'suck[ing] the marrow from our bones' (61) perhaps suggests cannibalism more than vampirism, but in an earlier passage in that treatise he describes the Jews as 'thirst[ing] for Christian blood' (58). A passage in the 1715 *Confutation* provides a further example of this popular 'Jew as financial vampire' motif in its allusion to the Jews 'drain[ing] all Christian Countries of their Coin' (34). The popular medieval view of the Jews as an infectious nation of poisoners responsible for the great plagues of the period (Walker: 472) also shares much with vampire folklore which figures vampirism as a type of infectious disease. Indeed, it is highly significant that the appearance of vampirism in folklore coincided with serious outbreaks of plague throughout Europe (Marigny: 24, 61), and that two of the most significant early descriptions of a 'bloodsucking corpse' (*cadaver sanguisugus*) appear in two twelfth-century British chronicles composed in Latin (24). Jews and vampires, both considered to be accursed agents of the devil, were similarly demonized in medieval anti-Christian symbolism.

The complex, multifaceted Jewish Blood Libel may be said to have subsequently 'infected' many of the popular demonic figures in Gothic literature. As I illustrate in the following chapter, this intricate process involved the Jewish theosophical tradition known as the Cabala which became synonymous with magic during the early Renaissance (Trachtenberg: 77). Since that period, secret societies were popularly conceived to be socially subversive, power-hungry cabals whose doctrines were founded upon the Cabala. Given this connection, it is not surprising that the Faust story, for example, has a Jewish connection. As Trachtenberg relates, the 'earliest German version of ... [that] legend pits a Jew against the devil to whose wiles ... the Jew succumbs' (23). The warning against anti-Christian activities is explicit: 'Thus can the devil lead into error the minds of those whose hearts do not cleave to God's word' (23).

Although Faust is not represented as a Jew in later versions of that drama, Faustian figures in Gothic literature seem tarred with the brush of the Jewish Blood Libel. In such tales as Adalbert von Chamisso's *Peter Schlemihl* (1813), which presents a Jewish Faustian character,[21] the reader encounters the popular image of the Jew as a gambling, Faustian, secret society magician who wilfully exchanges his soul for material gain. As I explain in Chapter 5, Count Dracula also falls into this category. Moreover, the infernal equation of Jew and devil is retained in subsequent versions of the Faust legend in the form of the seductive Mephistopheles.[22] Trachtenberg astutely notes that 'Satan's semitic features are often emphasized with grotesque exaggeration ... [and] Mephistopheles is usually swarthy, hook-nosed, [and] curly-headed' (26). In his unique study *Money, Language, and Thought: Literary and Philosophic Economies from the Medieval to the Modern Era*, Marc Shell suggests a vampiric dimension to the Faust legend when he describes Mephistopheles as a 'vampyric (*sic*) devil' who 'does not care what kind of paper is used ... [as long as] Faust sign[s] (*unterzeichen) in blood*' (88; emphasis added).[23] As with much anti-Semitic lore, a blasphemous version of established Jewish law seems to be at work. In this instance, the Jewish ritual of circumcision, which signifies a covenant with God, is parodied. According to Joshua Trachtenberg, 'until recent times it was still believed in parts of Europe that the pact with the devil must be written in Jewish blood' (141).[24]

*   *   *

As this mini-portrait of the Blood Libel attests, Britons developed, over the course of centuries, a rich and complex storehouse of anti-Semitic propaganda. The Blood Libel yoked together the charges of deicide, usury, and miscegenation, to create a crowning image of a race of avaricious, vengeful, and bloodthirsty criminals guilty of various national transgressions – theological, economic, racial, and sexual. Distilled in terms of the blood motif, the single charge against them would read: The Jews, after spilling Christ's blood, continued to suck the blood of the British nation and threaten its purity with their degenerate, diseased blood and strange bloody rituals. Edgeworth's structural strategy in *Harrington* involves dismantling and subverting these hateful stories, and revealing their true nature as nightmarish British fabrications and projections *that actually promoted the spilling of Jewish blood*. As Leslie Fiedler reminds us in his essay on Fagin, 'It is impossible to forget that men have died of ... [the Blood Libel] myth' ('What': 418). *Harrington* issues a clarion call to an amnesiac nation that has repressed the damaging truth about its own criminal anti-Semitic past and remains blind to the fatal dynamic between anti-Semitic representations and real Jews. In short, in Edgeworth's extremely capable hands, the category 'Literature of Terror' assumes radical new meaning and greater perspective is urged regarding the notion of 'pleasurable terror'. Notably, conventions and strategies of the Gothic, the established literature of terror, are vital in advancing her agenda.

Harrington's primal scene makes clear that the folly, danger, and impact of anti-Semitic representations, conveyed orally, in print, and by way of the visual arts, are the principal targets of this very self-reflexive narrative. Michael Ragussis has noted that Edgeworth's 'point of departure is to acknowledge "the indisputable authority of *printed books*" and thereby to formulate the question of Jewish identity as a question of the *representation* of the Jew' (*Figures*: 58). It would seem, however, given the tremendous impact of Fowler's oral tales, with which Harrington is terrorized for 18 months, that various forms of representation come under Edgeworth's fire. Ignorance, he states clearly, is key to his deception. 'The less I understood', he says, 'the more I believed' (3). Formal education exacerbates rather than diminishes the problem. Once literate, he notes that all of the books to which he is introduced – including Edgeworth's own anachronistically cited *Moral Tales for Young People* (1801) – represent Jews in negative ways. Harrington rather lamely adds that he does not mean to suggest that anti-Semitism 'was the serious intention of these authors' (16). Intended or not, however, the violent effects are shown to be the same. These various representations – particularly of Shylock and the Wandering Jew – engender anti-Semitic actions. As Daniel Jonah Goldhagen reminds us, anti-Semitism 'is always *abstract* in its conceptualization and its source (being divorced from actual Jews), and always concrete and *real* in its effects' (35). Old Simon's son, Jacob, is a chief target throughout. Notably, he can find no safe haven even outside of England as the English carry their prejudices with them: the same schoolboys who abuse him as a child continue this persecution into adulthood after he removes to Gibraltar to undertake trade in the jewellery business and they are stationed there as soldiers (97). Time and again, Edgeworth's meditation on anti-Semitic representations lends force to Richard Cumberland's contentious comment that 'the odious character of Shylock has brought little less persecution upon us poor scattered sons of Abraham, than the Inquisition itself' (*Observer*: 267).

In the face of such debilitating and socialized anti-Semitism, *Harrington* aims to enlighten its readers by exposing Britain's prejudicial *mis*education system and divesting the Jew of his seemingly inalienable sense of dread. In a strategic effort to remove England from the figurative and literal dark ages and its 'prison-house' of ignorance (4–5), Edgeworth stages a sustained and multidimensional battle of representations. She shamelessly reveals both Britain's true history in relation to the Jews, and the Blood Libel's actual nature as a libel. Two Gothic-style paintings featured in the novel that effectively and graphically represent 'the sins of the British fathers' are key in Edgeworth's arsenal – 'Sir Josseline [de Mowbray] going to the Holy Land' (54) and 'The Dentition of the Jew' (126). Especially in that both depict actual *historic* horrors, they undermine the primal scene with its *fictitious* horrors. Harrington is introduced to the haunting 'Sir Josseline' image when he is still a child. In a scene that re-positions the Gothic in relation to anti-Semitism as opposed to the Jew, this 'antique wonder' is situated in the suitably Gothic 'tapestry chamber' at the Brantefield Priory, the ancient family seat of his manipulative and anti-Semitic friend Mowbray (54). It depicts Mowbray's ancestor, Sir Josseline, standing 'in complete armour, pointing to a horrid figure of a prostrate Jew, on whose naked back an executioner, with uplifted whip, was prepared to inflict stripes for some shocking crime' (54). Harrington explains how the 'horrible effect' of this graphic image of the 'bastinadoed Jew' (117) is intensified by the distorted proportions of the two human figures: 'Sir Josseline stood miraculously tall, and the Jew, crouching, supplicating, sprawling, was the most distorted, squalid, figure eyes ever beheld or imagination could conceive' (56). Harrington is equally horrified when he is later apprised of another painting, 'The Dentition of the Jew', which Mowbray wishes to purchase as a companion piece to the Sir Josseline painting (128). In the words of that wily and shameless anti-Semite, that work illustrates 'the drawing the teeth of the Jew, by order of some one of our most merciful lords the kings – John, Richard, or Edward' (126).

Unlike Harrington's traumatic encounter with Old Simon, which only continues to haunt him unconsciously (181), the effect of the 'Sir Josseline' painting is consciously retained well into adulthood. When Mowbray deliberately mentions it in the presence of Mr Montenero as they tour the Tower of London, Harrington is physically unsettled and shudders with horror (116). This episode in the Tower is one of the novel's most ideologically sedimented sequences engaging a revised version of the female-quixote theme and the question of the power of representations. In response to Harrington's nervous excitement over the pleasures of fictitious terror and 'the nature and power of the early association of ideas' as described by the poet and physician, Mark Akenside, Mr Montenero advises gaining a clearer perspective on the idea of terror. He remarks that they can appreciate the pleasures of the imagination at some other time and then points out 'the patterns of the Spanish instruments of torture, with which her politic majesty Queen Elizabeth frightened her subjects into courage sufficient to repel all the invaders on board the invincible armada' (117). Mr Montenero's intentions are to highlight two sets of disjunctions – first, that between pleasurable, imaginative terror and real terror and, second, that between tolerant, enlightened England and barbaric, benighted Spain. His claim is ironic, however, given Edgeworth's driving agenda of indicting Britain as a place where the heretical Harrington feels himself to be 'on the rack' when he considers his parents' anti-Semitism (121). Spain and England are not, she repeatedly suggests, as different as many Britons would like to think. This idea is compounded by the fact, perhaps even unknown to Edgeworth, that the Tower is not only the site of various historic atrocities but of the greatest massacre of Jews in British history.[25]

The terror associated with the Spanish Inquisition may be unrepresentable and ineffable, but Edgeworth brazenly details British acts of anti-Semitism in relation to Spain and the Spanish Inquisition. The Gothic manifests a deep anxiety about the permeability of boundaries and Edgeworth adopts its techniques initially to unsettle national boundaries and, thereafter, to fashion a national ideal. The depiction of Sir Josseline and the 'bastinadoed Jew' (117) compresses the three principal sets of divisions that Edgeworth destabilizes throughout the novel: England/Spain, gentleman/criminal, Christian/Jew. That painting may be set in the Holy Land, but it portrays brutal and unholy unChristian behaviour and intimates forced conversion. The specific reference to the Jewish man in that painting as 'bastinadoed' – a type of physical torture associated with the Spanish, as the word suggests – further forges the connection between Christian Britain and Inquisitorial Spain. The purported Christian and gentlemanly Sir Josseline, despite the reference to the Jew's 'shocking crime' (54), functions as the actual criminal caught virtually bloody-handed as his 'executioner' abuses the Jew. Bloody crimes generally attributed to the Jews, are depicted, therefore, as enacted by Christians while the bastinadoed Jew's alleged 'shocking crime' remains, significantly, unspecified and substantiated in the novel. The 'Dentition' image represents yet another act of bloody cruelty that reinforces the idea of Christian criminality. Mr Montenero's act of purchasing the latter work at auction and burning it in a type of 'auto da fè' (133) neatly subverts the brutal ceremony accompanying the final sentence imposed on heretics by the Spanish Inquisition. This act also serves, in Montenero's eloquent words, as a symbolic purgation of 'every record of cruelty and intolerance' and all 'feelings of hatred and vengeance between Jews and Christians!' (133). Perhaps most importantly, its destruction is also timely as it deters it 'from being [reproduced and] seen and sold in every print-shop in London' (133). Mr Montenero, like his creator, recognizes the tremendous power of circulating print and is actively engaged in disrupting the cycle of violence it can engender.

It is especially by way of the character of Montenero, who is specifically counterpointed to the Christian Lord Mowbray, that Edgeworth destabilizes the established division between English Christian gentleman and Jewish criminal. Superficially, Montenero adheres to the Wandering Jew stereotype as he is extremely well travelled and well known. He is starkly contrasted to that figure, however, in that he is esteemed rather than dreaded. At the gathering to destroy the 'Dentition' image, the reader is informed that he 'stood high in the estimation of every individual in the company, all of whom had known him intimately at different times of his life, and in different countries' (130). This international nature is magnified by his racial indeterminacy, upon which Harrington comments during their initial encounter: 'From his figure, he might have been thought a Spaniard – from his complexion, an East Indian; but he had a peculiar cast of countenance, which seemed not to belong to either nation' (81). In keeping with Edgeworth's positive conceptualization of the Wandering Jew as a cosmopolitan gentleman, Mr Montenero is not, however, morally indeterminate. Indeed, the reader is informed that in any country, he would be immediately identifiable as a gentleman. According to Harrington, 'He had that indescribable air, which, independently of the fashion of the day, or the mode of any particular country, distinguishes a gentleman – dignified, courteous, and free from affectation' (81).

Harrington's extremely favourable initial impression of Montenero is subsequently borne out in both his actions and their discussions. Especially with regard to his religious tolerance and magnanimity of spirit, Montenero is presented in opposition to Harrington's own intolerant, anti-Semitic father. Indeed, in his guidance of and concern for the young Briton, Montenero effectively assumes the role of Harrington's surrogate father (Manly, 'Burke': 162), a relationship signalled in Montenero's final address to Harrington where he explicitly calls him 'son' (260). Montenero's boundless generosity of spirit is matched by an equally boundless material generosity. After the costly anti-Catholic Gordon Riots, for example, he acts as an enlightened paternalist who saves both Harrington's father and Baldwin's Bank from bankruptcy. In this instance, in the words of a clerk at Baldwin's, Montenero, 'a foreigner, and a stranger to the house' proves in deed to be a 'high-bred gentleman' (217). The alien Jew thus acts in the manner of a true British citizen. As such, he counters the established Gothic stereotype of the nationally parasitic Jew promoted by both the Blood Libel and Harrington's father who warns that Montenero will turn out to be 'an adventurer' whose 'foreign clutches' will threaten Harrington's 'good English fortune' (45). Precisely the opposite occurs. Lady de Brantefield's maligning of Jews as 'those who have sacrificed' (200) is likewise subverted. Ironically and significantly, Montenero nobly acts to provide that Lady with protection during the Gordon Riots, thus undermining her equally offensive and ultimately unsupported assertion that 'no Jew ever was or ever will be a gentleman. I am sure our family, since the time of Sir Josseline, have had reason enough to know that' (127). Like the bastinadoed Jew's alleged and nameless 'shocking crime' (54), the so-called 'reasons' for this statement are never provided. The implication is that the longstanding animosity that has survived generations is baseless and irrational.

In what may be criticized as a simplistic reversal of established stereotypes, Edgeworth ascribes the stereotypical traits of the heartless, mercenary, conspiratorial, and chameleonic Gothic Jew to the ostensible English gentleman, Lord Mowbray. Intriguingly, Mowbray is as mercenary and heartless as such Gothic villains as Walpole's Manfred in *The Castle of Otranto* and Radcliffe's Montoni in *The Mysteries of Udolpho*. This greedy gambler fails to honour his debts (168) and disinherits himself through gambling (168) and extravagant expenditures related, he claims, to his passion for an actress (146). Desperate in the face of his impoverished situation, he declares that he will even convert for a Jewess (146), and thus sets about to wed Berenice, Mr Montenero's financially well-endowed daughter. In this enterprise, however, Mowbray falls into the category of men 'who could be induced to sacrifice religious and principle to interest or passion', exactly the type of man whom Berenice is 'determined never to marry' (255). In his chameleonic powers and mastery of artifice, he assumes the stereotypical role of theatrical Jew. Mowbray is, as Harrington informs the reader, 'a perfect Proteus when he wished to please' (160). Such a figure is notoriously without fixed allegiances beyond the self, and the height of Mowbray's self-interested theatricality is reached with his dastardly and elaborate conspiracy, in conjunction with Harrington's dreaded nursemaid Fowler, to deter Harrington from marrying Berenice. In exchange for assistance in enabling her daughter's marriage to a wealthy apothecary (246), Fowler becomes embroiled, under Mowbray's expert direction, in a dramatic plot which promotes a false impression of Harrington as severely mentally unstable and thus a poor matrimonial candidate. The former nursemaid and adept storyteller proves, rather unsurprisingly, to be 'a good actress' (248). Mowbray's sudden death in a duel signals Edgeworth's attitude on the subject, as does the concluding marriage between Harrington and Berenice where it is revealed that no religious impediment actually exists. Berenice is, like the mother who bore her, a Protestant (254), and perhaps more importantly, as Montenero proudly informs Harrington, she is the '[d]aughter of an English gentleman of good family, who accompanied one of your ambassadors to Spain' (254). Ironically, given *Harrington*'s powerful exposure of such good English families, this genealogy should be a cause for concern.

In keeping with the traditional Female Gothic plot to which *Harrington* in part adheres, the virtue that serves to overcome the ritual tests of terror associated with love and intimacy is rewarded with marriage. Like many marriage conclusions in nineteenth-century fiction, however, Edgeworth's is critically controversial. According to Michael Ragussis, for example, while many anti-Semitic stereotypes are dismantled in *Harrington*, the conclusion 'satisfies the requirements of Christian ideology, [but] ultimately fails the Jewish reader' (*Figures*: 80). This dénouement provides further evidence, in Ragussis's view, that both the real and the imaginary Jew are always haunted by conversion, 'the literary and cultural master trope by which Jewish identity is represented and repudiated' (86). In the revelation that Berenice is actually a Protestant, Edgeworth arrives at a compromise solution in the form of what Ragussis calls a 'figurative conversion' (80). She is ultimately unable, therefore, to divest her narrative of the tyrannical conversion plot. Susan Manly advances an alternate reading to Ragussis's, however, lauding Edgeworth for using a conventional marriage plot for progressive ends ('Burke': 163). In its act of heralding an era of greater tolerance in England, *Harrington*'s romance plot is in Manly's view, at the service of a liberal message.

Harrington's conclusion is as vexed as Edgeworth's overall narrative agenda. It is certainly overshadowed, as Ragussis suggests, by the oppressive convention of the conversion plot where Christianity assumes the dominant position. In this regard, *Harrington* does indeed fail the Jewish reader. Readers' expectations are thwarted, however, in this regard as the anticipated and traditional stumbling-block to marital union is altered from the issue of religious difference to attitude towards religious difference. As the articulate Mr Montenero explains, Berenice is extremely specific and rigorous regarding her criteria for the selection of a husband:

> My daughter was determined never to marry any man who could be induced to sacrifice religion and principle to interest or to passion. She was equally determined never to marry any man whose want of the spirit of toleration, whose prejudices against the Jews, might interfere with the filial affection she feels for her father – though he be a Jew. (255)

In the light of what Edgeworth has represented as contemporary English attitudes towards the Jews, the young Harrington is an extremely rare specimen. Notably, he has undergone a *literal* conversion in attitude. On this front, the multidimensionality of Edgeworth's conversion plot must be recognized. In keeping with her structural strategy of revising stereotypes, Edgeworth subverts the traditional conversion plot dynamic. In *Harrington*, it is the Christians who must convert – and several do. Harrington's Christian parents, for example, also experience a dramatic and literal conversion in their attitudes towards the Jews. As such, they stand in for the ideal readers targeted by Edgeworth's novel, which was significantly and comically characterized by Thomas Babington Macaulay as a Judaizing text that would readily – given the representation of the generous and merciful figure of Mr Montenero – convert Christians into Jews (Ragussis, *Figures*: 87). A symbolic exchange is, therefore, made at narrative's end, one that revises the conclusion of Shakespeare's *The Merchant of Venice*: in exchange for such tolerance, Mr Montenero will forego both his daughter and his ducats.[26]

Harrington's classic marriage dénouement may also be read symbolically. It marks the culmination in the developmental trajectory in Harrington's consciousness from paralysing and debilitating primal scene generated by fear of the alien Other to symbolic union with that Other. On one hand, the fact that the Other (Jew) is revealed to be the same as the self (Christian) suggests a common humanity that diffuses fear of difference and the hostility it commonly engenders. While Edgeworth may dissatisfy the Jewish reader with this conclusion, she does not fail the Gothic reader. *Harrington's* plot dynamic charts a psychic transformation from benightedness to Enlightenment that adheres to the traditional Gothic ritual dynamic of rationally exposing and exorcizing dark personal and national secrets, 'the sins of the fathers'. Mr Montenero essentially informs Harrington that he has disrupted this violent cycle when they discuss the possibility of his forgiving Fowler for her conspiratorial labours. As Montenero explains, 'you have given proofs that your matured reason and your humanity have been able to control and master your imagination and your antipathies' (259). The 'dictates of pure reason and enlightened philanthropy' were earlier at work when Harrington aided a fainting Berenice during their first encounter at the dramatic presentation of *The Merchant of Venice* (92). The bogey of the Gothic Jew and its power to terrorize is thus successfully deconstructed and the paternal spectre of Harrington's historical namesake, James Harrington, figuratively defeated. This seventeenth-century British political philosopher, like Edgeworth's eponymous hero, ran the gamut in his views about Jews and Jewish culture. While he may have been 'particularly interested in Jewish history as one of the sources of archetypes for a model commonwealth', as Susan Manly has noted ('Introductory': xxxii), he nonetheless promoted an image of the Jews as nationally parasitic. As I explain further in the following chapter, Harrington's 1659 treatise *The Art of Lawgiving* ascribes sinister conspiratorial intrigues to the Jews, an unassimilable group for whom he devises a solution in his 1656 work, *The Commonwealth of Oceana* (1656). In James Harrington's words, 'To receive the *Jews* after any other manner into a commonwealth, were to maim it: for they of all nations never incorporat, but taking up the room of a limb, are of no use or office to the body, *while they suck the nourishment which would sustain a natural and useful member*' (*Commonwealth* 33; emphasis added). Edgeworth's Harrington lays such vile ideas to rest. Rendered in terms of the novel's Spanish motif, England figuratively declares victory at *Harrington's* conclusion over her Spanish propensities, a battle intimated throughout by way of reference to such English-Spanish engagements as the riot at Gibraltar (94–9).

Harrington's enlightenment plot is designed to forge what Leslie Fiedler calls a 'rival myth' that dispossesses 'the ancient images of terror' associated with the Jew ('What': 418). In what appears to be a plot promoting coexistence and equality, however, Christianity does retain the dominant position and subsumes Judaism as Ragussis suggests. When actions are morally assessed, a Christian philosophy consistently provides the gauge. For example, an orange-selling Irish widow, whom Montenero has helped many times in the past, describes him as a Jew who is 'as good [as] a Christian' (195). It will clearly take some time before this culture can see beyond itself. The Jewish characters are not only repeatedly and problematically represented as model Christians, they are, as *Blackwood's* reviewer noted, 'too uniformly perfect', which throws 'a degree of suspicion over her [Edgeworth's] whole defence' (qtd. in Manly, 'Introductory': xxxiii). Other more canonical authors like George Eliot who treat the Jewish Question in a more realistic manner will encounter the same criticism in the Victorian era. Anticipating those works, *Harrington* offers up a curious representational conundrum: while it successfully combats the sinister image of the Gothic Jew, it engenders a series of equally unrealistic stereotypes that greatly undermine its goal of promoting tolerance. The characters of Jacob and Mr Montenero and his daughter are simply too idealistic while the Christian characters, with the exception of the educable Harrington, are vulgar, ignorant, and ignoble. Given this recipe, Edgeworth may be faulted for risking insulting the very readers whose attitudes she wished to reform. To be fair, however, she does gesture towards a more tolerant worldview in the novel's final exchange. Montenero's culminating act is the characteristically generous one of providing Fowler, a symbolic scapegoat who is exiled to America at novel's end,[27] 'with an asylum for the remainder of her miserable old age' after her friends and family have abandoned her (260). This persecuted Spanish Jew, therefore, expends his final energies expounding to the young Harrington a doctrine of mercy – a 'Christian precept' according to Jacob (99) – in relation to the suffering Fowler, a woman with whom he can empathize. This merciful worldview notably undermines the popular idea, expressed by Mrs Coates, that the Jews are 'both a very unsocial and a very revengeful people' (124). Harrington's father's concluding comment that Montenero's charity towards Fowler could only be the act of a good Christian is met with Berenice's significant rhetorical question, 'why not a good Jew?' (260). *Harrington* concludes, therefore, with a plea for greater tolerance as the limited equation of Christianity and goodness is called into question (260).

Edgeworth manages to expose much to the light in *Harrington* in her exploration of the figurative closets of both personal and national history and the psychopathology of anti-Semitism. Her novel is particularly realistic in its representation of the truly deep-seated, unconscious, and persistent nature of anti-Semitism. In a compelling and realistic episode after Mr Montenero enforces physical distance between Harrington and Berenice, for example, the images of Montenero and Old Simon blur in a wild phantasmagoric nightmare experienced by Harrington (181). Similarly, when Harrington believes he sees Old Simon the Jew in a Synagogue – it is later revealed to be only Fowler in disguise – he is utterly horrified (165). Despite these extremely compelling episodes, much remains shrouded in darkness with regard to the full extent of British anti-Semitism. Old Simon functions well as a powerful personal demon, but he fails to capture the formidable dread of the national threat posed by Gothic literature's Wandering Jew at the height of his powers. The complex cultural history behind that monstrous creature who memorably fleshes out the skeleton of the Blood Libel Jew, is delineated in the following chapter.

3
Cabalistic Conspiracies and the Crypto-Jew

Phantasmagoria and the French Revolution: Bogeys and 'Boney'

> All the misfortune of the modern world, if it is traced to its furthest roots, comes manifestly from the Jews, they alone made Bonaparte emperor.
>
> (Friedrich Gentz, qtd. in Poliakov: 297)

According to the Marquis de Sade, Gothic fiction was 'the inevitable outcome of the revolutionary upheavals experienced throughout the whole of Europe'. In order to compete with the cataclysmic events of the 1790s, Gothic novelists had 'to call upon the aid of hell itself' (109). While several Gothic novels in England pre-dated these upheavals, it is unarguable that two particular forms of terror in the 1790s – one historical, the other fictional – were distilled into the stuff of which British nightmares were made, thus providing this genre with an unprecedented blood transfusion. News of the notorious *Kannibalregiment* Terror in France involving the September massacres (Brinton: 177) and the cannibalistic *buveurs du sang* (Singer: 163) – as the Terrorists were referred to by their enemies – set the stage for a revitalized brand of British Gothic fiction.[1] This was combined with the popularly welcomed entry of the German terror-novel (*Schauerroman*), which blended 'political and magical ingredients' and focused on 'the activities of powerful secret societies' (Tompkins: 281). Plagued by 'domestic unrest [and] fears of invasion from abroad' (Punter, *Literature*: 61), Britain was particularly susceptible to this onslaught of terror. As E.P. Thompson relates, 'In 1797 the invasion scare was growing, armed loyal associations and volunteer corps were formed, as much against internal conspiracy as against the French.' British invasion fears gained ground in February of that year when 'the French actually made a small landing near Fishguard, on the Pembrokeshire coast' (Thompson: 180).[2] The threat of internal subversion also loomed large as radical French Republican ideas were taking hold in Britain. Pitt established spy networks, 'believing , or professing to believe, that the radical societies threatened a "whole system of insurrection...laid in the modern doctrine of the rights of man"' (Porter: 450). The trials for treason and sedition electrified the nation in the early 1790s, causing some to draw connections between British radical societies and European secret societies believed to have promoted the French Revolution.[3]

In the midst of these threats of conspiracy and invasion, British readers found a titillating outlet in the domain of Gothic literature where, as one disgruntled reader observed, terror was 'the order of the day' (Probatum Est: 227). As such, those readers chose to undertake what J.M.S. Tompkins fancifully describes as 'an exhaustive tour of the vaults'. Such a tour was, according to Tompkins, 'a natural reaction from a long period of sobriety in literature combined with revolutionary excitement and the growth of the reading habit in the lower middle classes' (221). Not everyone was amused. William Wordsworth, for example, in his second edition of the *Preface to the Lyrical Ballads* (1802) issued an excoriating attack on the Gothic. It was guilty, in his view, as were the 'great national events', including Britain's war with France, of 'blunt[ing] the discriminating powers of the mind' (254). '[T]he invaluable works of our elder writers', he wrote, 'are driven into neglect by frantic novels, sickly and stupid German tragedies, and deluges of idle and extravagant stories in verse' (254). Most twentieth-century critics have followed Wordsworth's cue and dismissed the Gothic as merely escapist. More recent critics, however, have suggested that while Gothic novelists rejected 'direct engagement with the activities of contemporary life in favour of geographically and historically remote actions and settings' (61), they favoured indirect engagement with such pressing contemporary concerns as growing urbanization and the genesis of industrial capitalism, to the persistence of English Jacobinism and the inception and maturity of working-class consciousness (E.P. Thompson: 199). Nina Auerbach's concluding comments in the introduction to *Our Vampires, Ourselves*, an examination of cinematic and literary vampires in the twentieth century, advances a similar point about the deceptive escapism of the vampire phenomenon: 'They [vampires] promise escape from our dull lives and the pressure of our times, but they matter because when properly understood, they make us see that our lives are implicated in theirs and our times are inescapable' (9).

While some consensus has been reached in recent years, therefore, regarding the Gothic's social reflexivity and relevance, the jury is still out as to its exact political nature and relationship to its socio-historic context.[4] In his study of the sociology of the modern monster, Marxist critic Franco Moretti argues that 'the literature of terror is born precisely *out of the terror of a split society*, and out of the desire to heal it' (*Signs*: 83). Michel Foucault advances a similar, partially etymologically based theory in his seminal study *Madness and Civilization*. He argues that socially defined monsters play a crucial monitory role as they warn their society about potential unethical acts and disorder (69–70). Extrapolating on the idea that literary monsters are 'most evident in periods of social, political and economic crises', Fred Botting elucidates Gothic literature's role in providing a cultural medium for an imaginative expression and resolution of social anxieties: 'Derived from the Latin *monere*, to warn, and *demonstrare*, to show or make visible, monsters stage the opposite of the audience's position and vindicate that position by making the vice and folly of the monster visible, so warning potential imitators against such monstrous actions' (*Making*: 142).

Chapter 1 has gestured towards several ways in which these theories are at play in relation to the Wandering Jew in Gothic fiction. It is compelling to note, further to this, that the bogey of the secret society, long considered to be engaged in 'actively subverting national sovereignty' (Clery: 160), is often represented in works featuring the Wandering Jew. These clandestine associations were also persistently invoked as the putative instigators of class division and tyranny in the 1790s, a period of growing class consciousness and antagonism. Although the subject of the secret society has been regarded generally by contemporary historians as 'an area of highly organised nonsense' (Roberts, *Mythology*: 1) and the argument that secret societies were responsible for political organizations and conspiracies in the 1790s has been discounted (87),[5] a few have maintained that the study of secret societies has been long overlooked (13). Many in the late eighteenth century, ranging from governmental authorities and clerics to creative artists, considered these organizations to be the control centres of anti-government conspiracies. As Marie Roberts explains, 'In the wake of the French Revolution, the secret societies were the dark spectres haunting the mass-movements of Europe. Gothic novelists had seized upon them as metaphors of terror' (*Gothic*: 59). Considering 'the Terror of the French Revolution … [to be] the most cogent example of how the "Enlightenment behaves toward things as a dictator toward men", Gothic novelists deployed the secret society as 'a paradigm for the dialectical reversal of the Enlightenment movement which had transmogrified into its own opposite' (61). They considered the secret society to be a power-hungry, terrorist organization that preached democracy while covertly practising tyranny. As the Two 'Gagging' Acts of 1795 outlawing seditious meetings and treasonable practices, and the 1799 Act banning secret and seditious societies attest, the British government also felt the threat of secret societies to be more than merely apparitional. This threat grew a thousandfold after the Irish rebellion of 1798. In its wake, reference to the Illuminati controversy especially 'obsessed the English conservative press' (Simpson: 87). What David Simpson has aptly described as a 'conspiracy-theory industry' emerged (89), linking secret societies to European political troubles in general and the French Revolution in particular.

Regardless of its actual relationship to subversive political activity, the secret society was certainly a symbolically important idea whereby socio-political anxieties were articulated. David Brion Davis has argued persuasively that the 'imagery of counter-subversion may give symbolic expression to the deepest fears and needs of a people' (6). Robert S. Levine reinforces this theory in his claim that conspiratorial discourse is 'a rhetoric of extremity' that 'more often than not manifests at its least flexible and most repressive a culture's dominant ideology – the network of beliefs, values, and, especially, fears and prejudices that help social groups to construct and make sense of their social identity and reality' (12). Just as American romances featuring countersubversion participate symbolically in the boundary-drawing necessary to that nation's ideals (6), so too do British Gothic romances spotlighting secret societies. Of particular interest in the British case is the strikingly parallel rhetoric between the Gothic and non-fictional treatments of secret societies. Although a semiotic analysis of this rhetoric remains to be undertaken, literary and cultural critics have insightfully commented on this connection. In the words of Patrick Brantlinger, for example, 'If from 1789 onward, Gothic terror often reflects revolutionary terror, nonfictional accounts of the events in France often read like Gothic romances' (*Reading*: 51). E.J. Clery concurs in her claim that, throughout the 1790s, 'the French Revolution was being written, and consumed by a paranoid British public, like a gripping romance translated from the German' (172). Rhetorical reverberations between Gothic fiction and ostensible exposés regarding secret societies bespeak, on one hand, the Gothic's close identification with its socio-historical context and its influence on that era. On the other, however, they amplify the predominant cultural value system.

A more detailed semiotic examination of the literary treatment of secret societies and countersubversion is provided in Chapter 4. It should be noted, however, that in both fictional and non-fictional works, the author/narrator assumes the role of rational, enlightened Christian exposing the benighted philosophy underpinning superstitious secret societies associated with the Gothic and Roman Catholicism. Thomas Atkinson, for example, describes his duty as a Christian minister in 1798 in *An Oblique View of the Grand Conspiracy, against Social Order; or A Candid Inquiry, tending to shew what part The Analytical, the Monthly, the Critical Reviews, and the New Annual Register, have taken in that Conspiracy* as 'attack[ing] the infidel in his strong holds of literature with the torch of manly reason in one hand, and the word of God in the other; he will thus armed soon find the enemies intrenchments imaginary like the enchanted castles of old; or transitory like the mountains which are compelled by omnipotence to flee before the strong faith of a real christian' (33). Similarly, William Hamilton Reid discredits the suggestion made by 'Infidel Societies' that 'the Light of Nature and the Revelation of the Gospel are one and the same' (71): 'Volney, for this purpose, refers me to the remains of Egyptian antiquities; I examine them, and am disappointed.

As well might the bigotted Papist appeal to the exterior and venerable appearance of some Gothic structure; which may be surveyed by the rational with a sigh, while it is worshipped by the superstitious: the former, penetrating its inmost recesses, might scrutinize the character and principles of the original occupants. The observations of the latter, would probably extend no farther than the monuments, the ramifications of the columns, the floried windows and the length of the aisles!' (71–2).

Turning to a more in-depth assessment of non-fictional accounts of the role of secret societies in the French Revolution, the year 1797 saw the appearance of both John Robison's *Proofs of a Conspiracy against all the Religions and Governments of Europe, carried on in the Secret Meetings of Free Masons, Illuminati and Reading Societies* and Abbé Augustin Barruel's five-volume work entitled *Mémoires pour servir à l'histoire du Jacobinisme*. In a work whose first edition sold out in only a few days (Simpson: 88), Robison, Professor of Natural Philosophy at Edinburgh University, produced proofs of a revolutionary conspiracy among secret societies fostered under the pretext of 'enlightening the world by the touch of philosophy and of dispelling the clouds of civil and religious superstition which keep the nations of Europe in darkness and slavery' (11). The laws of British Freemasonry stipulated that 'nothing touching religion or government shall ever be spoken of in the Lodge' (10) but, according to him, Freemasonry became corrupted after it was exported to France. There, it was infected by 'every strange and obnoxious doctrine' ranging from 'Theurgy'[6] and 'Cosmogony' to the Cabala (38). Although Robison concludes by relating how 'the good sense and sound judgements of Britons have preserved them from the absurd follies of Transmutation, of Ghost-raising, and of Magic, so that their honest hearts and their innate good dispositions have made them detest and reject the mad projects and impious doctrines of Cosmopolites, Epicurists, and Atheists' (538), he relays the sense that the 'contagion' of Freemasonry (495) remained an ever-present danger. Apart from Robison's blatant anti-French critique regarding an impending sexual revolution as the Illuminati enlisted women, the Jesuits come under special fire. According to Robison, they successfully infiltrated the Masons in the eighteenth century in attempts to re-establish the dominion of the Roman Catholic Church in England (22), and aided in the Stuarts' attempts to reinstate the Pretender as King (27, 38).

Ironically, it was a Jesuit, Abbé Augustin Barruel, 'a major contributor to the MaCarthyism (*sic*) of the 1790s' (Roberts, *British*: 89), who offered a similar 'exposé of alleged Masonic, Rosicrucian and Illuminist activities' in France. In a work that J.M. Roberts describes as a 'farrago of nonsense' (197), and E.J. Clery and Robert Miles label 'paranoiac' (249), Barruel traced 'the origins of the French Revolution from the Illuminati in Ingoldstadt to the Freemasons, philosophers and Jacobins, and then to the mobs on the street'. This 'bible of the secret science mythology' (Roberts, *Gothic*: 193) portrayed secret societies 'as precipitators of the French Revolution based on an anti-monarchical and anti-ecclesiastical conspiracy' (60). Barruel especially vilified the Illuminati, a secret society founded by Adam Weishaupt in 1775, that Barruel portrayed as a 'subversive organization committed to the "annihilation of every Empire, of all order, rank, distinction, property, and social tie"' (Roberts: 60–1). With the purported aim of achieving equality and liberty for all, this secret society actually 'stimulated *all nations* to rebellion', according to Barruel, and 'aimed at plunging them ultimately into the horrors of anarchy' (ix; emphasis added). Barruel's choice of an excerpt from Weishaupt's *Discourse for the Mysteries* as his epigraph highlighted this threat: 'Princes and Nations shall disappear from the face of the Earth... and this Revolution shall be the work of secret societies' (Clery and Miles: 249). Although proffering what has been deemed 'superficially intricate, but really over-simplified, explanations of a vast political change' (Tompkins: 284), Barruel's alarmist document managed nonetheless to find many respected English adherents (283). Not surprisingly, perhaps the most prominent among these was Edmund Burke, a friend who had welcomed Barruel when he emigrated to London after the September Massacres (Roberts, *Mythology*: 192). In a letter addressed to Barruel and dated May 1797, Burke applauded the first volume of Barruel's four-part *Mémoires* as 'admirable in every point of view, political, religious, and... philosophical'. Describing himself as 'a witness' to the truth of Barruel's claims, Burke added, 'I have known myself, personally, five of your principal conspirators, and I can undertake to say from my own certain knowledge, that so far back as the year 1773, they were busy in the plot you have so well described, and in the manner, and on the principle you have so truly represented' (Clifford, prefacing Advertisement).

   With the exception of Léon Poliakov's comprehensive study of *The History of Anti-Semitism*, the significant role played by Judaism in Barruel's popular conspiracy theories has gone unrecorded in historical accounts. Although not explicitly expressed in France until 1806, the year Napoleon created the central Jewish tribunal of the Great Sanhedrin, the conspiracy theory linking Jews to the French Revolution was an offshoot of popular medieval theories about Jewish conspiracies.[7] While there are grounds to argue that Barruel's friend, Edmund Burke, gestured towards a Jewish conspiracy theory in relation to the French Revolution in his 1790 publication, *Reflections on the Revolution in France*,[8] it was first clearly articulated and disseminated by the Abbé Barruel. It should be underlined that what he referred to as 'his ultimate revelation' did not upset any of his earlier claims; rather, it was perfectly aligned with them. Barruel may not have specifically mentioned the Jews in his *Mémoires*, but he did foreground the specifically anti-Christian nature of the Jacobinical 'sect' that, in combination with 'the Occult Masons', threatened 'God, the King, and Society' (xxiii).[9] Notably, when the *Mémoires* were first translated into English in 1798, the word 'Jacobinism' was entirely excised from the title. In its place, anti-Christianity became the focus. According to its alarmist, patriotic translator who undertook the work in order to 'serve his country' (v), *Memoirs Illustrating the Antichristian Conspiracy* delineated 'The Antichristian Conspiracy, or that of the *Sophisters of Impiety* against the God of Christianity, and against every religion and every altar, whether Protestant or Catholic, Lutheran or Calvinist, provided it be but Christian' (iv).

The longstanding holder of the title of anti-Christian religion *par excellence*,[10] Judaism was the perfect choice for a vital role in conspiracy theories about the French Revolution. In 1806, Barruel revealed his shocking discovery that Crypto-Jews – Jews posturing as New Christians – posed the primary threat to the social order. An Italian army officer had apparently apprised Barruel of this information about the Jewish designs for world rule (Katz, *Jews*: 220). Although Barruel refrained from making his ultimate revelation public in order to avoid a general massacre of the Jews that he feared might result, he informed influential members of government circles, the police, and Church officials (Poliakov: 282–3). Léon Poliakov has cogently argued that Barruel's theory was, possibly, 'the primary source of the *Protocols of the Elders of Zion*' which was originally published in Russia in the revolutionary year 1905. This work, the most notorious anti-Semitic forgery, claims to be the minutes of a conference attended by the senior leaders of world Jewry (Larsson: 9). It relates how Jews purposely spread diseases and instigate social disorder in the form of revolutions and wars in order to gain political control (9). It also maintains that Antichrist will appear in a revolutionary crisis (Hill: 179), and portrays Jews and Freemasons as co-conspirators for world domination (Poliakov: 283). Actually written by Sergei Nilus, a Russian Orthodox Christian who believed that the arrival of the Antichrist and the Apocalypse were imminent, the *Protocols* originally appeared as 'an appendix in a larger book from 1901, the title of which clearly reveals its purpose and content: *The Great in the Little: Antichrist Considered as an Imminent Political Possibility*' (Larsson: 15).

Like the *Protocols of the Elders of Zion*, Barruel's sensational hypothesis reads like Gothic fiction[11] and incorporates traditional millenarian ideas. In direct opposition to the 'idealization of Israel [that] took shape in some official French religious circles' just prior to the Revolution that helped to prepare the way for Napoleon's establishment of the Sanhedrin (Manuel: 233), Barruel blamed Jews for founding several secret societies and charged them with attempting to infiltrate the Catholic Church 'with the result that, in Italy alone, over eight hundred ecclesiastics, including a few bishops and cardinals, were actually working on their behalf. As for the conspirators' final goal, it was nothing less than to be the masters of the world, to abolish all other sects in order to make their own reign supreme, to make as many synagogues as there were Christian churches, and to reduce the remaining Christians to slavery' (Poliakov: 283). Circulation of this conspiracy theory on the heels of the formation of the Great Sanhedrin was extremely significant. As this tribunal reminded Christians of the crucifixion – the Sanhedrin made the conspiratorial deal with Judas for thirty pieces of silver (229) – it was popularly thought to be a conspiracy against the Catholic Church in France (Cohn-Sherbok: 150). A number of anti-Semitic legends were also revived along with Barruel's theory (214). Foremost among them was the legend of the Wandering Jew, which combined the subject of deicide with the issues of Jewish conversion and the Millennium.

According to Bernard McGinn in his fascinating 1994 study *Anti-Christ: Two Thousand Years of the Human Fascination with Evil*, 'The French Revolution sparked one of the most important outpourings of political apocalypticism in modern times' (242). A combination of events fed into established Christian eschatology. Millenarian ideas triggered by this cataclysmic event were further ignited by Bonaparte's establishment of the Great Sanhedrin (277–8). Thereafter, when Napoleon invaded Palestine in 1791 and called upon Jews to return there (Ragussis, *Figures*: 4), extreme, alarmist Catholic Cardinals informed him that 'once a Jewish state was established, the end of the world would occur' (Poliakov: 229–30). Despite the facts that the primary agenda of the Sanhedrin was an assimilationist one designed to convert Jews into patriotic and productive Frenchmen, and that Napoleon did eventually dissolve this body composed of 46 rabbis and 25 laymen in 1808 (Ausubel: 153), fervent millenarians increasingly associated Napoleon with the Anti-Christ.[12] Contemporary Russian newspapers, for example, gave a great deal of space to the idea of Napoleon as the Anti-Christ and the Jews' Messiah (Poliakov: 279).

Nowhere did this millenarian fervour take greater hold than in England, the 'traditional home of apocalyptic exegesis and sworn enemy of the Ogre [Napoleon]'. Further, England was the main centre of propaganda for French *émigrés* who were dedicated to acting as socio-political agitators from across the Channel (Poliakov: 281). *L'Ambigu*, their principal organ, devoted a dozen articles to the Great Sanhedrin from 1806 to 1807, and in the issue dated 20 October 1806, suggested that Napoleon was the Jews' Messiah. A month later *L'Ambigu* reported that Napoleon 'was himself a Jew'. As Poliakov relates, this latter theory explaining Napoleon's Jewish background 'must have been propagated at the time of the Egyptian campaign, since in May of 1799, a friend wrote to [German mystic and writer] Jung-Stilling...that the "man of sin" was born of adulterous intercourse between an oriental princess and an "important" Jew' (282).

As these events make clear, a demonic semiotic chain was forged in England in works like those by Robison and Barruel, linking the concepts of France, Revolution, Illuminism, Freemasonry, and Judaism. This resulted, in part, from the interpretation of contemporary events in France in the light of established Christian eschatology. Drawing upon the vital and popular millenarian idea that the Second Coming was to be preceded by the restoration of the Jews to Palestine and their conversion to Christianity (Ragussis, *Figures*: 4), or their reunion with the Anti-Christ (Gow: 9), 1790s tracts produced by highly imaginative millenarian Dissenters consistently twinned the concepts of Revelation and Revolution (Oliver: 42). Perhaps the most memorable and popularly discussed Christian millenarian of the period was the Newfoundland-born, pseudo-Messiah named Richard Brothers. In 1794 he identified England with the Ten Lost Tribes (Roth, *History*: 245),[13] and styled himself 'Nephew of the Almighty', the long-awaited descendant of David who would lead both the real Jews and those concealed among the population of Great Britain to Jerusalem (Garrett: 183). As Frank Felsenstein notes, Brothers further reconfirmed the prevalent anti-Semitic equation in Britain between Judaism and demonic France. Brothers 'publicly called upon the English to lay down their arms before the French, the agents of God's wrath against hereditary monarchy, and for King George III to resign his throne to him' (96). In 1795, Brothers was arrested on a charge of treason and ordered to be locked away in an Islington asylum.

For those writers like William Hamilton Reid who disagreed with Burke[14] and considered the French Revolution to be a repetition of the bloody English Civil War (83) – he particularly notes the fact that 'a variety of creeds circulated which discredited religious authority' during and subsequent to both events (84) – popular millenarian tracts had significant historic reverberations. Another mentally unstable preacher, John Tanny, changed his name to Jacob Israel in 1650 and declared it his purpose to bring the Jews into Judea (Matar, 'The Idea...Between': 32).[15] The anti-monarchical and millenarian Fifth Monarchy Men who supported the Rump Parliament that condemned Charles I to death in January of 1649 also regarded Revolution as an essential stage in fulfilment of Biblical millennial prophecy. One of the most radical groups of the English Civil War period, they initially supported Oliver Cromwell for they believed that 'victory over the king had marked the beginning of the Fifth Monarchy predicted in Daniel 2, during which time Christ would return to rule on earth together with the saints' (McGinn: 224).

The Jews had been, therefore, a significant component of British millenarian discourse during the Civil War period. N.I. Matar, a specialist on the restoration of the Jews in English Protestant thought, relates how they had functioned as 'an instrument in English theological aspirations' ('The Idea...1661': 119). Representing themselves as the new chosen nation, English people argued that their history was inextricably bound up with that of the Jews whom they would lead to Christ:

> ...since the Jews' conversion was associated with the second coming, then the English, in controlling the Jews' conversion, were in control of global history. By their kindness to the Jews, they would bring to realization Christ's English-sponsored second coming.
>
> (Matar, 'The Idea...Between': 33)

Fervent Christians advocated the readmission of the Jews to England in order to hasten the Millennium (Katz, *Philo-Semitism* 127; Rubin: 6) and, more importantly, to consolidate England's role as the messianic kingdom (Matar, 'The Idea ... 1661': 119). Support for the Jewish restoration to Palestine was also strong during this period but, as Matar emphasizes, 'only after the English had imposed the prospect of conversion to Christianity upon the Jews did they respond to Jews positively; they called for Jewish settlement in England or Restoration to Palestine only insofar as that served the Protestant ideals of Christian England' (118). It was believed that the latter event would grant England both a theological victory over Catholicism which had persecuted the Jews, and a military victory over the 'infidel' Turks whose Ottoman Empire was engaged in expanding its power (124–5).

Although Cromwell presented a petition at the Whitehall conference on December 4, 1655, to officially readmit 'the Jews into England ... [and make] a number of other important [religious and mercantile] concessions' (Rubin: 7), he had lost the support of the Fifth Monarchists after he dismissed the Rump Parliament in 1653. Realizing that Cromwell's 'foreign policy was aimed at commercial profit, not at the destruction of Babylon' (Hill: 121), the Fifth Monarchists concluded that the readmission of the Jews was also commercially motivated. As Abba Rubin notes, Cromwell recognized Jewish commercial services to England (6). Like Napoleon, therefore, Cromwell was a supporter of Jewish readmission for predominantly financial reasons. Realizing that Cromwell was not furthering the advance of the millennium, the Fifth Monarchists determined that he was the Anti-Christ, and they rose up against him in 1657 in an unsuccessful rebellion (McGinn: 224).[16]

With the merchants vehemently opposed to Jewish admission on both moral and financial grounds (Rubin: 7), the Whitehall conference was, unfortunately, a dress rehearsal for reaction to British legislation promoting Jewish rights during the eighteenth century. Concluding with the official position of the Jews unchanged, its only effect was, as Abba Rubin notes, to instill or reinforce anti-Semitic prejudice in England (7). In fact, texts such as Alexander Ross's 1656 work *A View of the Jewish Religion* which maintains that Judaism is an unholy, impure, and accursed religion, followed on the heels of this conference. In keeping with the popular Christian view that Judaism was an ancient and false religion that was outdated and had been justifiably overthrown, its author wrote:

> ... there is nothing to be found in their [the Jews'] pretended Worship of God, but meer hypocrisie and untruth; in the most wise and prudent of their learned Rabbins and Scribes, nothing but ignorance and extraordinary stupidity, especially in the knowledge of God and exposition of his word: Lastly, through the whole Nation [there is] nothing [to be found] but strange and fearfull obstinacy and pertinaciousnesse in all depraved course and wayes of living. (1–2)

It must be noted that Ross's anti-Semitic views were upheld by others *prior* to the Whitehall conference. For example, in a sermon entitled *The Devilish Conspiracy...by the Jewes, against the Anointed of the Lord, Christ their King* (1649), which was presented on 4 February 1649, John Warner accused the Jews of executing King Charles (Matar, 'The Idea...Between': 31). The association forged between Republicans and Jews in such works as Warner's was typical of the seventeenth century when the 'study of Hebrew, Cabala, and rabbinical sources was on the rise...[and] English Protestant sects were emulating Jewish Sabbath observance and dietary laws' (14). In his *Voyage into the Levant*, Henry Blount compared Jews to radical English Puritans saying that Jews have 'light, aerial, and fanatical brains, spirited much like our hot apocalypse men' (qtd. in Shapiro, *Shakespeare*: 35). The accusation of Judaization became a popular insult.[17] James Shapiro notes 'how convenient it became to label opponents, especially those who favored republicanism, as Judaizers' during this period (21).

As the events surrounding Cromwell and the Fifth Monarchy Men illustrate, British millenarian tracts were comprised of certain consistent elements. Moreover, in their prevalent Republican-Jewish connection, such tracts anticipate the Abbé Barruel's 'revelation' of 1806 and even mirror Gothic literature of the 1790s that frequently treated the theme of eschatology. As Rhonda Johnson Ray argues, 'The collapse of political, social, and religious foundations during the Romantic period generated a crisis literature exploring eschatological and apocalyptic themes' (2068A). That such millenarian concerns and ideas should have found their way into Gothic literature in the 1790s seems almost inevitable given the political and intellectual climate.

The fact that the Abbé Barruel could articulate the make-up of such a complex Gothic spectre in early nineteenth-century France attests to his awareness of ideas that were becoming popular in Europe. Barruel's conspiracy theory linking the Jews to the French Revolution also became popular cultural currency subsequent to that event. In his 1835 Parisian publication *Conspiration universelle du judaïsme*, for example, the Catholic apologist Renault Bécourt claimed that Jews were both responsible for the French Revolution and singlemindedly intent on world domination (qtd. in Hallman: 446). The notorious French anti-Semite Edouard Drumont, a converted Jew, also asserted in 1886 that the only group that benefited from the French Revolution were the Jews (Cohn-Sherbok: 169). Perhaps a surprising British proponent of this idea was Benjamin Disraeli who maintained that the Jews were, contrary to their natural conservatism and in retaliation for Christian tyranny, at the head of every secret society in Europe (*Lord*: 496–7). This would imply their participation in the French Revolution, which Sidonia, Disraeli's revered model of the Jewish civilized gentleman in *Coningsby*, proclaims as one of the most important 'landmarks of human action and human progress' (252).

Barruel's was no small contribution to the later European bestseller, *The Protocols of the Elders of Zion*, and he certainly helped to foster an entire sub-genre of Gothic literature featuring conspiracies and cabals. Barruel's complex and arcane Jewish bogey is rendered both more explicit and public in European socio-political thought of the late nineteenth century. His power-hungry Jewish monster especially rears its head in the popular anti-Semitic writings of the Chevalier Gougenot des Mousseaux, Dr Ehrmann, Edouard Drumont, and Alban Stolz. Indeed, claims by Stolz and Dr Ehrmann that Jews are behind all revolutions worldwide and that they infiltrated the Masons in order to achieve world domination, render the anti-Semitic spectropoetics subtending Gothic literature more explicit. Des Mousseaux's statements in his 1880 tract *Le Juif, le judaïsme et la judaïsation des peuples chrétiens* which received the blessing of Pius IX, that Jews 'continually conspire against Christians and encourage revolution' in consonance with the Talmud, a 'savage code, which combines the precepts of hatred and plunder with the doctrine of cabbalistic magic, which professes high idolatry' (Cohn-Sherbok: 168), also sheds light on another vital component of British Gothic literature – the Cabala. It is to an assessment of the misrepresentation of that esoteric tradition within the Gothic genre that I now turn.

Cabals/Cabala: secret race/secret tradition/ secret society/secret science

> When Luther excoriated Jewish superstition and magic, his real target was this newfangled Kabbalah. When a host of works on magic appeared boasting Jewish inspiration, it was this they really meant. When the attack on Jews as sorcerers increased in intensity and the Pope gave it official expression, the Christian version of Kabbalah was the cause…Paracelsus went about elaborating a scheme to create a homunculus by alchemical means with supreme assurance of its ultimate success – for had he not learned the secret from the Kabbalah? – and Schudt could proclaim confidently: 'The present-day Polish Jews are notorious masters of this art, and often make the *golem* (a homunculus), which they employ in their homes, like kobolds or house spirits, for all sorts of housework.'
>
> (Trachtenberg: 80)

Over the course of centuries, the Jews in Britain were the victims of an intricate series of anti-Semitic stereotypes that were eventually incorporated, to varying degrees and in varying forms, into British Gothic literature. In a nutshell, bastardized ideas about the Cabala in the Renaissance were integrated with medieval tales of blood libel and post-Reformation millenarian narratives about the restoration of the Jews to Palestine. Before examining the representations of the Cabala in works by Christian authors and the ends to which such depictions were put, it is important to explain briefly the nature of the Cabala. A theosophical tradition that emerged during the era that saw the birth of Christianity, Cabala signifies 'the Hidden Wisdom' (Ausubel: 139) or the 'secret tradition' (Scholem, 'Kabbalah': 493). This multifaceted system essentially engages with 'the mysteries of the hidden life of God and the relationships between the divine life on the one hand and the life of man and creation on the other' (490). There are two principal branches of the Cabala: the speculative or theoretical Cabala which involves mystical speculation, and the practical Cabala which involves an engagement with magical lore. It was the latter branch of this esoteric teaching that Christian Europe adapted for its own ends during the Renaissance. In the fifteenth and early sixteenth centuries, Giovanni Pico della Mirandola and Johann Reuchlin were the first to popularize the Cabala in Christian circles where they basically transformed these 'bogies that haunted Europe' (Manuel: 3) by way of assimilation, claiming that they actually pointed in a Christian direction (Scholem, 'Kabbalah': 643). In this manner, attempts were made to convert Jews to the dogma of the Trinity (Manuel: 143). According to Pico, 'no science can better convince us of the divinity of Jesus Christ than magic and the Kabbalah' (Scholem, 'Kabbalah': 644). Along with other Christian cabalists, Pico contended that Jewish cabalist manuscripts contained 'an arsenal of arguments for the conversion of the Jews to the dogma of the Trinity': 'Moses' hidden meaning in Old Testament prophecy was a foretelling of Christ' (Manuel: 143). Pico's attempts to represent the Cabala as pro-Christian in its essence were definitively rejected by Martin Luther. To the latter, the Cabala became 'the sign of a demonic language of enchantment' (Hsia: 135). Luther's own theological views were, ironically, labelled 'a Jewish conspiracy to destroy Christianity' (Manuel: 47).

The actual 'relationship of the Kabbalah to other 'occult sciences' such as astrology, alchemy, physiognomy, and chiromancy was slight' (Scholem, 'Kabbalah': 636),[18] but it was this minor aspect of the practical Cabala that Luther foregrounded as the mainstay of this 'secret tradition'. Although Jews did believe that knowledge of the Cabala granted supernatural powers and imparting such knowledge to Christians was under severe sanction (Manuel: 142), a defective understanding of the Cabala led to its misrepresentation as a type of superstitious system grounded in magical science. According to Nathan Ausubel, such an inadequate knowledge of the Cabala's 'literature and history made it appear a silly hodge-podge of numerological reckonings, alphabetical abracadabra, childish beliefs, dreams and superstitions fortified by magical amulets and incantations in gibberish' (139). Indeed, Christians found it easier and more desirable to assimilate the Cabala in a theosophical dress. As such, it became a prized adjunct of alchemy and astrology, and synonymous with magic (Trachtenberg: 79). This profanation by Christians of a Jewish practice was in Christian interests as it further established Judaism as an anti-Christian heresy. Raphael Patai also notes that the 'widely held belief that Jews were experts in alchemy was grist for the mills of anti-Semitic authors' until, at least, the nineteenth century (12). As alchemy and other forms of secret sciences lost status as legitimate and laudable practices, their association with Judaism was more strongly forged.

As a result of this misrepresentation, the Cabala fell into disrepute among rationalists (Ausubel: 139) and was denigrated in European universities and religious establishments (Manuel: 148). These misconceptions of this esoteric teaching were later distilled into Gothic literature, a genre that may be said to frequently feature a cabalistic backdrop of secret societies or heretical cabals that practise magical science and threaten social, political, and religious order. On the basis of an examination of eighteenth-century German and British Gothic literature, one may conclude that the word 'Cabala' had become synonymous, by that time, with the word 'Occult'.[19] This equation was present, however, since the seventeenth century when both the words 'Cabala' and 'cabal' entered the English language. Both had negative connotations, and it is significant that their genesis was concurrent with the official re-entry of the Jews into Britain. Deeming the words 'cabal' and 'Cabala' to be interchangeable at that time, the *Compact OED* defines 'cabal' jointly as the 'Jewish tradition as to the interpretation of the Old Testament' and 'a secret or private intrigue of a sinister character formed by a small body of persons' (I: 311).[20]

The *OED*'s definition of 'cabal' as a sinister form of intrigue is upheld in James Harrington's 1659 treatise *The Art of Lawgiving*. More significant, however, is the fact that this work associates such sinister intrigues with the Jews. Its second section is entitled 'The Second Book Containing the COMMONWEALTHS of the Hebrews, Namely ELOHIM, or the Commonwealth of *Israel*; and CABALA, or the Commonwealth of the *Jews*.' Therein, Harrington targets the Biblical Sanhedrin when he criticizes the 'cabalistical or Jewish commonwealth' which was 'an oligarchy, consisting of a senat and a presbytery, which not only scourg'd the apostles, but caus'd Christ to be crucify'd' (398). In an earlier work, *The Commonwealth of Oceana* (1656), published the year that Cromwell agreed to the readmission of the Jews, Harrington also discusses the Jews. He describes a utopian commonwealth called Oceana (England) located near a neighbouring island called Panopea (Ireland), and suggests that since Panopea is populated by 'a slothful and pusillanimous people' (33), Jews should be 'planted' there in their stead.[21] As Oceana would then demand 'two millions annual revenue', Harrington argues that this transplantation scheme would be the best thing for the commonwealth's purse (33). Moreover, this would provide a requisite solution to the 'problem' of having 'parasitic', unassimilable Jews living in Oceana itself. According to Harrington, 'To receive the *Jews* after any other manner into a commonwealth, were to maim it: for they of all nations never incorporat, but taking up the room of a limb, are of no use or office to the body, *while they suck the nourishment which would sustain a natural and useful member*' (33; emphasis added).

Francis Bacon's earlier rendition of an ideal commonwealth in his 1627 publication, *New Atlantis*, was also preoccupied with the role of the Jews. Further, Bacon even mentions the word 'cabala' in relation to them. Indeed, Jewish and Masonic echoes are rife throughout that treatise which was, intriguingly, later plagiarized by 'the quack John Heydon' as 'A Voyage to the Rosicrucians' (Ormsby-Lennon: 54). On an island called Bensalem (a name that sounds like Jerusalem), Bacon's observer encounters a world that seems to be regulated according to theosophical principles. In a central site on Bensalem known as Saloman's House,[22] a noble foundation 'dedicated to the study of the works and creatures of God' (276), science is regarded as the prime civilizer that will lead man to the love of God. Bacon's observer encounters a 'circumcised' Jew (283) on the island who recounts how Moses ordained the laws of the utopian land of Bensalem by way of a 'secret cabala' (283). Deeming both this idea and that about the forthcoming Messiah to be 'Jewish dreams', the observer notes that Bensalem is predominantly inhabited by Christians, but also by 'some few stirps of Jews' who are of a different breed than Jews 'in other parts … [for] they give unto our Saviour [Jesus Christ] many high attributes, and love the nation of Bensalem extremely' (283). Bacon insinuates that Jews are generally unlike these fervently nationalistic Bensalem Jews who respect Christianity. He, therefore, anticipates Harrington's view that the Jews tend not to assimilate into the nations they inhabit. In Bacon's Utopia, however, Jews are appropriated for Christian ends – they lend support to Christianity.

As these examples illustrate, the terms 'cabal' and 'Cabala' were virtually synonymous, since their entry into the English language, with the Jews and sinister secrecy. The association between the Jewish Cabala and secrecy is particularly apt given the Cabala's literal translation as 'secret wisdom'. The popular view of its Jewish creators as 'the secret race' whose primary sign of difference, circumcision, was considered to be deceptively hidden (Gilman, *Jew's*: 18) is also noteable. Moreover, the Cabala is also associated with secret societies, another suitable affiliation given that bastardized cabalistic ideas constituted the philosophical foundations of most secret societies in Europe. Finally, the Cabala was also conceived, rather appropriately, to be fundamental to any engagement with secret science. In *The Rosicrucian Enlightenment*, Frances Yates articulately argues that the Hermetic-Cabalist tradition only managed to survive within such secret societies from whence it generated the scientific revolution of the seventeenth century. With specific regard to the foundations of Rosicrucianism, Yates claims that the 'manifestos stress Cabala and Alchymia as the dominant themes in the movement' (222). Following Yates, Marie Roberts explains that

> [e]soteric sects also cultivate alternative modes of communication through secret signs, pass-words and hieroglyphics.[23] For example, the Rosicrucians blend the hermetic mysteries with those of the Cabala, a

strain of Jewish mysticism which incorporates a system of numerology. In some secret societies Cabalistic trance techniques were employed in order to induce visionary states. (*British*: 4)

While Yates and Roberts are correct in their claims that the Cabala was at the core of most European secret societies, they fail to note that the popular understanding of the Cabala was a bastardization of the original theosophy.

Marie Roberts notes, however, that Gothic literature was a crucial medium for demonizing secret societies. For example, despite the fact that the Illuminati emerged as a society with a revolutionary socio-political message that originated as a harbinger for the Enlightenment (61), they were represented in literature as an instrument of repression (6). This transformation reflected a critique of what some social thinkers perceived to be an ironic but dangerous hypocrisy lurking at the core of all secret societies. According to English journalist and diarist Henry Crabb Robinson, although the Illuminati professed themselves 'to be the arch-enemies of such obscurantists as the Jesuits, ... [they] had become ... "an Antijesuitical Jesuitism"' (Roberts: 61). Such a critique of the Illuminati suggests that they, with the best of spiritually motivated intentions, ended up adopting tyrannical measures and succumbing to materialistic gains, thus reproducing the flaws of the very order they set out to oppose. A similar sort of critique was launched in Gothic literature where the founding philosophy of the Rosicrucians was represented as materialistic rather than spiritual in its aims. While the Rosicrucians established the pursuit of the philosopher's stone and the elixir vitae as goals involving mankind's spiritual development, these aims were represented in Gothic literature as solely materialistic, as involving freedom from the physical plights of poverty, death, and old age. The *Confessio*, the second Rosicrucian manifesto published in 1615, clearly expresses the spiritual tenet that the brotherhood will be visible only to those who are chosen by God and not to those pursuing riches and knowledge in defiance of God's will. In spite of this doctrine, Rosicrucianism was consistently portrayed in eighteenth-century literature as focusing primarily on secular concerns (Roberts: 6). The Cabala was similarly demonized in the Gothic genre and, as it was regarded as the ideological basis of the most prominent secret societies, the equation between Judaism and the occult was readily forged.

Moreover, the perceived view of the Cabala's position vis-à-vis religion and science rendered it the enemy of both Christians and rationalists. Based upon a philosophy that encouraged the scientific exploration of God, cabalistic magical science was regarded as a paradoxical domain of investigation that blurred the boundary between religion and science. As the Gothic novel often intervened in the science versus faith debate which was prevalent during the Enlightenment, it was a highly suitable genre for featuring magical science. The products of magical science were also considered to be socially dangerous. In fact, they were sometimes blamed for promoting anti-Christian ideas and perpetrating the French Revolution. According to the Abbé d'Auribeau d'Hesmivy in his *Mémoires pour servir à l'histoire de la persécution française, recueillis par les ordres de Notre Très Saint-Père Pie VI*, which was published in Rome in 1794, ingenious inventions like Montgolfiers and the 'science' of mesmerism were revived in the 1790s with the intention of exposing Christ's miracles as attributable to natural causes (Poliakov: 527). D'Hesmivy's argument stands in stark contrast to Pico's claim several centuries earlier that the Cabala provided supportive evidence of Christ's existence and his miracles. The Abbé's opinion that magical science inventions were subversive and anti-Christian did, however, represent the popular religious view at the end of the Enlightenment.

Another key element in the Cabala's demonization in both the European world-view and Gothic fiction was its association with messianism. It is significant to note that messianism became a core part of the Kabbalah on the heels of the Jews' expulsion from Spain in 1492 (Scholem, 'Kabbalah': 641). The legend of the Wandering Jew was also widely disseminated at this time when it was thought that the Last Days were at hand (Gow: 16), and the Marranos, dispersed throughout Europe, were actually wandering (Poliakov: 352). Like Christian Millenarianism, Jewish messianism escalated during periods of social crisis. Many Christians equated the Jewish Messiah with the anti-Christ whose goal was world domination. This connection between Judaism and powermongering was due, as Jacob Katz has explained, to the concept of Jewish messianism (*Jews*: 218–19). Ironically, the Cabala, which desired to hurry the coming of the Messiah (Ausubel: 140), was actually regarded as heretical by many Jews. Among Christians, it was regarded as the height of anti-Christianity, a sort of dark mirror or demonic double of the New Testament. The heretical Lurianic Cabala, so called because it was disseminated throughout Europe in the late sixteenth and early seventeenth centuries by Isaac Luria and his followers who formed a group in Palestine, was particularly reflective of the New Testament in its millenarian focus (Yates: 228).

The hugely popular seventeenth-century Jewish millenarian movement known as Sabbatianism which heralded the Levantine Jew Sabbatai Zevi as the Messiah, was also grounded in mystical cabalism (Garrett: 9). It was not unusual for some cabalists to declare themselves the long awaited Jewish Messiah, and Zevi was the most famous of such Messiahs.[24] Born in Turkish Anatolia in the seventeenth century, he was bitterly denounced as an impostor and swindler by the rabbis (Blau: 142). He especially appealed, however, to the oppressed and the desperate. Great crowds of hysterical men and women, especially drawn from the ghettos of Europe, paid him homage and prepared for the day on which he would announce the beginning of the Messianic era and would lead them to the Holy Land (142). Zevi's move towards Palestine also occurred in the ominous year 1666 (Matar, 'The idea … 1661': 127). Although Zevi subsequently converted to Islam – an act which shocked Christians and Jews alike – the Jewish millenarian movement of Sabbatianism was regarded as dangerous in England for it 'challenged both New Testament doctrine and the theological legitimacy of the English state' (139). Without the proviso of conversion to Christianity, the Jewish restoration to Palestine both 'undermined Christian doctrine and made England subservient to Israel' (139).

Jewish messianism also had a connection to the secret sciences. Perhaps the most popular creation to emerge from the practical Cabala was the zombie-like figure of the Golem, a messianic being fashioned out of clay and animated by a cabalistic adept or a rabbi in order to help the Jewish community in times of crisis. The Golem is most popularly associated with the famous folk hero Rabbi Judah Loew ben Bezalel, the Maharal of Prague (Bilski: 13), who has been described in rather Gothic terms as a 'Faustian' figure (Nurbhai: 39) with 'kabbalistic proclivities' (Ruderman: 98). Sixteenth-century Prague was, of course, the great centre for Jewish Cabalism (Yates: 228) and the birthplace of several cabalistically based secret societies. Loew's miraculous Golem was apparently divinely sent in response to a dream question from Loew about how to protect the Jewish community against the Blood Libel (Goldsmith: 16).

The legend of this messianic figure is rich with Gothic possibilities. Indeed, this uncanny creature is particularly intriguing in the light of Gothic novels ranging from Mary Shelley's *Frankenstein* to Bram Stoker's *Dracula* which feature alchemy and living-dead creatures composed of inanimate or dead matter.[25] Animated by the adept's inscription of a sign – the word *emet*, meaning truth – on his forehead, the Golem often becomes an uncontrollable creation that reflects an inner tension in his creator. The reconfiguration of several key elements in his story has resulted, particularly in the realm of German expressionist cinema, in his sinister transformation into a bloodthirsty Anti-Christ figure inscribed with a mark of Cain. In this menacing form, the Golem is, unarguably, a blood brother of the vampiric Wandering Jew in Gothic literature.[26] Both are undead, uncanny creatures who blur the boundary between life and death. As Paul Wegener's demonic treatment of the Golem in his 1920 film *Der Golem: Wie er in die Welt kam* and Walter Jacobi's Anti-Semitic tract of 1941, *Golem ... Geissel der Tschechen* (*Golem ... Scourge of the Czech*) illustrate, the transmission of this tale into European society rendered it a terrifying story of Jewish powermongering.[27] By way of this figure, the Jews were portrayed as possessing the ultimate powers of controlling life and death. Gothic literature's Wandering Jew is similarly portrayed as his prolonged life is usually attributed to his demonic magical powers, powers he wields in defiance of God's natural laws. The Wandering Jew generally recognizes, however, that his prolonged existence is a curse and that he is the accursed of God.

Jewish messianism also became linked increasingly to Freemasonry across Europe (Katz, *Jews*: 219–20; Roth, *History*: 226). The roots of the statement published in 1882 in *La revue des questions historiques* that 'Judaism rules the world, and we must therefore conclude either that the Masons have become Jewish or that the Jews have become Masons' (Cohn-Sherbok: 169) finds its origins in the fact that 'the emergence of the Freemasons and the entry of Jews into European society took place almost simultaneously' (Katz, *Jews*: 8). In his compelling work, *Jews and Freemasons in Europe 1723–1939*, Jacob Katz outlines how 'a new type of Jew was emerging' in the early to mid-eighteenth century, 'one who had acquired some Western education and had adjusted his behavior to conform to the standards accepted among gentiles, to the extent that he now could aspire to full membership in their society' (2). In considering the rise of this new type of Jew, the radically changing face of traditional Europe in the eighteenth century, and the growth of Freemasonry, Katz delineates the real and imaginary links forged between Judaism and Freemasonry since the latter's inception in England in 1717.[28] Although it is true that Freemasonry, in its initial form and as it continued to develop, incorporated a fair amount of cabalistic, iconography and content (222)[29] – in fact, a reform rabbi named Gotthold Salomon 'argued that Freemasonry was more Jewish than Christian' (221) – many Masonic lodges throughout Europe, particularly in Germany, were anti-Semitic. They strictly disallowed the entry of Jewish members. As Katz notes, 'the Masonic lodges themselves not only entertained serious reservations against Jews but even gave vent to expressions of contempt for Jews and to the systematic exposition of anti-Semitic ideas' (222).[30]

Such blatant anti-Semitism did not prevail in British lodges. According to Cecil Roth, in some English Lodges Jews held high office as early as 1723 (*History*: 226). This served to establish a connection between Judaism and Freemasonry in British popular mythology as brotherhoods which challenged, and even threatened to subvert, all forms of authority. Branded as constituting 'a state within a state', both Jews and Freemasons became equally despised groups in Britain who were accused of craving world power. Particularly in the Jews' move towards social assimilation, an act which involved both the dismantling of traditional exclusionary barriers and the erasure of ethnic and class differences, they aroused nothing short of resentment, fear, and hatred.

As Jacob Katz foregrounds, the eighteenth century marked a crucial period of transition in the British Jewish community. Among other reasons, British Jews were attracted to Freemasonry at this time because it offered a key to their entry into British society. According to Katz, in 'Jewish eyes, the chief importance of Freemasonry lay in its opening a path for Jewish integration into the social environment' (216). Although the Freemasons were described in popular tracts as a state within a state, many of their members were well-respected citizens who wielded tremendous social power. Acceptance of the Jews within such a circle, therefore, did have an impact on their acceptance in society at large. It is vital to note that, in adopting what Katz refers to as the 'principle of universality [which] was the justification for most of the social transformations of the eighteenth century' (9), all specifically Jewish traditions were abandoned by Jews in favour of 'a universal value-system which they could display before all men' (216). Notably, one of the first things that European Jews abandoned was the Cabala (Scholem, *On*: 1).

Ironically, while certain segments of the Jewish population discarded the Cabala in an attempt to be assimilated more easily into Christian European society, the Jew-Cabala association was concurrently being reinforced in European cultural productions like the Gothic novel. Institutions like Freemasonry that offered and promoted democracy and assimiliation were also libelled during this time. Secret societies like Freemasonry were depicted as hotbeds of political radicalism that used terrorism as a means of control. Gothic fiction seems to have greatly influenced Robert Clifford's description of a secret society initiation in his 1798 treatise, *Application of Barruel's Memoirs of Jacobinism, to the Secret Societies of Ireland and Great Britain*. According to Clifford, the secret society candidate was subject to a type of terrorizing brainwashing process. As he describes it:

> ... the candidate was led through dark windings into a cavern, where the image of death, the mechanism of spectres, potions of blood, sepulchral lamps, subterraneous voices; every thing, in short, that can affright the imagination, and successively hurry the candidate from terror to enthusiasm, is put in action. When the candidate is worn out with fatigue, a voice dictates the following execrable oath which is sworn: 'I here break all the ties of the flesh that bind me to father, mother, brothers, sisters, wife, relations, friends, *mistresses*, kings, chiefs, benefactors; in short, to every person to whom I have promised faith, obedience, gratitude, or service. I swear to reveal to the new chief whom I acknowledge every thing that I shall have seen, done, read, heard, learned, or discovered; and even to seek after and spy into things that might otherwise escape my notice. I swear to revere the *Aqua Tophana* (a most subtle poison) as a certain, prompt, and necessary means of ridding the earth, by death or stupefaction, of those who revile the truth, or seek to wrest it from my hands.' After this the reader will not be surprised to hear of the *Black List*, on which were inscribed the names of those who gave umbrage to the Sect, and of the *Red List*, or *Blood List*; and when once a person was entered on that, it was, among the Order, held futile to flatter one's self with the hope of escaping the poisons or the assassins of the Sect. (xviii)

It was widely believed that these secret societies were increasingly controlled by Jews or Crypto-Jews who not only fervently resisted religious and national assimilation but deliberately undermined the institutions that promoted familial and national order. Suggestions are frequently made that, by way of these Cabala-based institutions[31] which were ostensibly advocating religious tolerance and political equality, powermongering Jews were engaged in the socio-political subversion of Christian Europe. It would seem that when the Cabala is mentioned in anti-secret society pamphlets published during the eighteenth-century fin de siècle, the suggestion is made that the worship of Judaism actually lies at the core of those societies. It is also intimated that secret society members are seduced by the guise of religious tolerance and are themselves unaware of the society's actual aim to 'Judaize', to convert unwitting Christians to Jewish practice and ritual.

Evidence that the cabalistic semiotics I have outlined were operative by the 1790s is provided in *The Life of Joseph Balsamo commonly called Cagliostro*, a captivating account of the life of the notorious Italian impostor. Written by one Monsignor Barben and published in Dublin in 1792 before the Abbé Barruel disseminated his Jewish conspiracy theory, this work portrays Cagliostro as a Wandering Jew-style gambler whose 'cabalistical discoveries' (69) and use of freemasonry were instrumental in his robbery of European citizens and his subversion of European governments. Claiming that he was 'born before the deluge' (62), Cagliostro is described according to established anti-Semitic stereotypes. He is also said to 'love the Jews…exceedingly'. Linking the Jews and the concept of revolution, Cagliostro heralds Judaism as 'the true religion' that will be reinstated after the French Revolution occurs (103). Described as using 'an almost Israelitish jargon' (40), and affirming that the Jews are 'the best nation in the world' (143), Cagliostro is also said to 'have a passion for wandering' (49). Barben explains, however, that this obsessive behaviour has 'peculiar advantages' for it removes him 'from his censors, his creditors, and his enemies' (49). Despite his knowledge of 'the art of making gold and of prolonging human existence' (46) – abilities often shared by Gothic literature's Wandering Jew – Cagliostro is said to be drawn to Masonry for economic reasons. He is attracted by the prospect of rich contributions from his followers (134).

Rather appropriately, the passage relating the origins of Cagliostro's magical abilities read like Gothic fiction. Explaining the significance of Cagliostro's ritual act of swearing by the names of Helios, Méné, and Tetraganimaton, Barben relates:

> In a book said to be printed at Paris in 1789; it is asserted that these… words were suggested to Cagliostro, as sacred and cabalistical expressions, by a *pretended* conjurer, who said that he was assisted by a spirit, and that this spirit was no other than the soul of a cabalistical Jew, who by means of the *magical art* had murdered his own father, before the coming of Jesus Christ. (140)

Yoking together the Cabala, imposture, and an ancient act of patricide, Barben anticipates the semiotics of much Gothic literature and Barruel's *Mémoires* (which were also published in Dublin). The Jewish Blood Libel is even vaguely alluded to when Barben describes how the Masonic initiation ritual involves removing blood from the initiate (144) who subsequently becomes, in a parody of Christian conversion, a new man on the fortieth day (145).[32] Cagliostro is even connected to the French Revolution, an event he apparently predicted in a letter written in London in 1786 (103). His revolutionary principles are especially upheld, however, in his act of establishing different Masonic lodges across Europe. These 'monstrous assemblage[s] of persons of all sects and denominations of religion' (124) include 'Jews, Calvinists, Lutherans, [and] Catholics' (138). Barben is disturbed by this inclusion of members of various religious faiths and the fact that Cagliostro extends Masonic membership to women (136). Barben disapprovingly notes that as long as Cagliostro's 'many millions' of Masonic followers (181) believe in God and the immortality of the soul, they are all regarded as equals (185). In their eradication of religious and gender differences, Cagliostro's European lodges raise the spectre of assimilation. Given Barben's claim that Cagliostro's ultimate goal is to reinstate Judaism as the official state religion after the French Revolution (103), Cagliostro's policy of religious inclusion is even more sinister.

Finally, a link is suggested in this compelling document between Cagliostro and the Anti-Christ. Events before his arrest and judgement by the holy Roman Inquisition parodically replay Christ's last days. Barben points out how in Lyons

> ... in imitation of the great founder of Christianity, he [Cagliostro] elected twelve disciples whom he named his apostles, and empowered them to preach his doctrines to all nations, whether Jews or Gentiles. On that occasion he predicted that one of them would betray him, as Judas had betrayed Jesus; and, in consequence of it, would be reduced to great misery: all of which, as he asserts, actually took place ... (161)

After explaining how the Inquisition sentenced Cagliostro to life imprisonment, Barben strikes this work's anti-Masonic keynote: 'It will ... occur to every person of common sense, who happens to read and to weigh the facts contained in this history, that folly, superstition, and impiety are the distinguishing characteristics of those societies, at present known in Europe by the name of Free Masons' (267–8). Barben's conclusion also anticipates Robison's description of Freemasonry as a form of disease: 'We trust that it will please God, that all the rest of the world, convinced by the unspeakable miseries of the present times, may be enabled to deliver themselves from this dangerous contagion!' (269).

Publications like Barben's attest to the prevalence of the cabalistic semiotics attached to the Jew during the 1790s. The fact that such bastardization and demonization of the Jewish mystical tradition occurred during the very period when various projects were being undertaken throughout Europe to assimilate Jews along both religious and national lines were not sheer coincidence. The popular fictional representation of the secret society as an occult power-hungry cabal is inextricably bound up with the traditional stereotype of the dreaded demonic Jewish 'race' that threatened European society's spiritual values during this period. The resentment, fear, and hatred generated by the prospect of assimilation, of dismantling traditional exclusionary barriers, and of erasing ethnic and class differences, was channelled into Gothic fiction. Various works within that genre function as a testament to and furnish a barometer of this social anxiety.

'The British Inquisition': British nationalism, blood purity, and the threat of the Crypto-Jew

> From the early days of Christianity the Inquisition existed in the *spirit*, if not in the *form*. The wretched pack of controversial wolves, the so-called Fathers of the Church, when not flying at one another's throats, were ever busy in spewing forth their fanatical venom upon all not of their ilk.
>
> (Heckethorn: 172)

Nothing is more noteworthy with regard to British anxieties about the potential eradication of Jewish difference than the fact that so many Gothic novels are set against the backdrop of the Spanish Inquisition. This historic institution aimed to ferret out heretics and, more importantly for my examination, Christianized Jews, otherwise known as Marranos[33] or *conversos*. In the words of Henry Kamen, this body's 'entire concern was with judaizers' (*Spanish ... Historical*: 39): 'The figures indicate clearly who bore the brunt of the Inquisition: 99.3 per cent of those tried by the Barcelona tribunal between 1488 and 1505, and 91.6 per cent of those tried by that of Valencia between 1484 and 1530, were conversos of Jewish origin' (57). While its titular object was the salvation of souls (Roth, *Spanish*: 38) and the realization of the religious unity of Spain (57), the Spanish Inquisition was actually motivated by intense resentment, fears about progressive ideas, and growing nationalist sentiment. The establishment of this institution only a century after the forced conversion of thousands of Spanish Jews at the end of the fourteenth century was an anxious and jealous reaction, as Cecil Roth has persuasively illustrated, to the Marranos' social, political, and economic success (32). In these Marranos, Spaniards saw hypocritical Crypto-Jews 'who had lost none of their unpopular characteristics, pushing their way into the highest positions in the state' (30–1). As I will argue further, Jews were also blamed for the spread of dangerous progressive ideas. In order to rid their country permanently of the 'Jewish heresy', Spanish sovereigns signed a decree on 30 March 1492, to expel the remaining Jews from Spain (57–8). The Catholic Church continued its persecution of the Marranos by way of the Inquisition, and Catholic Spaniards supported this institution as indispensable for national preservation (71).

Spanish fanatical adherence during the Inquisition's operation to what became known as 'the cult of *limpieza de sangre'*, purity of blood (Kamen, *Spanish*: 123), signalled a momentous shift in European thought from religious/theological anti-Semitism to racial/secular anti-Semitism (Roth, *Spanish*: 58). Richard H. Popkin has explained how 'Until the Spanish Inquisition introduced biological criteria to answer "Who is a Jew?" or "Who is a New Christian?" the prevailing Christian view was that people were Jews by choice' (411). The Inquisition established the idea, however, that Jewishness was inherent and ineradicable and that Jews could not possibly convert to Christianity. In this new view, Jews were regarded as members of a race rather than followers of a religion. Considered in these terms, the possibility of religious conversion is eradicated. The persecution of *conversos* a century after their forced conversion in Spain, therefore, lends support to Jean-Paul Sartre's claim that 'the true opponent of assimilation is not the Jew but the anti-Semite' (143). Clearly, the annihilation of religious differences between Jews and Catholics – the assimilation of Jews into a Christian nation – disturbed many Spanish Catholics. The fact that Christianized Jews were labelled *conversos* suggests that assimilation had not actually occurred on the social level. Ironically and tragically, the Spanish Jew was damned if he did not convert (Jews were expelled from the country) and damned if he did (Christianized Jews were persecuted).

Léon Poliakov has further explained how the legend of the Wandering Jew was inextricably bound up with the inception of racial anti-Semitism. He notes how this legend spread after the Jews were expelled from Spain[34] and how its fascination increased in nineteenth-century Europe with the general emancipation of Western Jews. According to Poliakov, the legend of the Wandering Jew replaced the myth of Judas as the prevalent Jewish myth in the Christian imagination in order to reflect the changing Jewish situation in Europe. While the myth of Judas laid emphasis on the Jew's accursed, immoral action, the new myth of the Wandering Jew foregrounded the Jew's very essence and nature as accursed. The new myth of the Wandering Jew, therefore, signalled a significant transition from theological to racial anti-Semitism (352–3). Paul Lawrence Rose concurs, explaining that:

> ... Ahasverus represented now a collective guilt inherent in the wandering, homeless Jewish nation. Each individual Jew lay under a curse from which he had to redeem himself and his race, a curse symbolizing inherited ethnic guilt ... This shift is visible in the changed meaning of Ahasverus's epithet, the *Ewige Jude* or 'Eternal Jew'. (24)

Rose's argument that this racially based idea of the Eternal Jew became the dominant German conception of Judaism in the early part of the nineteenth century concurs with Poliakov's theory about the shift in the nature of anti-Semitism in early nineteenth-century Europe when Western Jews were emancipated. While Poliakov traces what he calls the 'innumerable off-spring' of Wandering Jew figures in French literature during this period (352), Rose does the same within the German tradition. He astutely describes the Wandering Jew legend as an 'allusive, plastic myth, comprehending themes of death, eternal Jewish character, and final redemption, ... [which] supplied the most potent vehicle for the secular mythology of the "destruction of Judaism" that came to dominate German revolutionary antisemitism in the nineteenth century' (23).

Although responses to the Jewish Question differed from nation to nation, racial anti-Semitism in Europe infused the Wandering Jew legend. Especially when emancipated Jews raised the prospect of national assimilation, the Wandering Jew legend was prevalent in popular culture. It is my contention that the often invoked scenario of the Spanish Inquisition and the appearance of this wanderer in the Gothic genre bespeak, among other things, anxieties in Britain about the nature of British national identity and the possibility of Jewish assimilation. These narrative elements are vital to the blood thematics of British Gothic literature which speak to the issues of ethnicity and national belonging. By reconfiguring the notorious Blood Libel which reflected cultural taboos, and transforming the Wandering Jew into an increasingly vampiric figure, Gothic writers articulated national fears and graphically defined the demonic nature of the non-belonging 'Other'. In the process, however, they also expressed fears about their own negative propensities.

Several critics have noted that the Spanish Inquisition is employed in such works as Matthew G. Lewis's *The Monk* in order to represent the more immediate and shocking events of the French Revolution, the most momentous phenomenon in eighteenth-century European history. Both the Spanish Inquisition and the French Revolution generated messianic hopes and eschatological concerns,[35] and both were regarded by Britons as crowning examples of Roman Catholic tyranny. It is often forgotten by twentieth-century readers, however, that the Spanish Inquisition was still in operation during the period when Gothic literature was being produced. In fact, the Spanish Inquisition was only finally abolished in 1834. Speaking about Ann Radcliffe's representation of that institution in her 1764 novel *The Italian*, Irene Bostrom explains that:

> The Inquisition was not regarded as merely an institution of an earlier age, since it still existed in Spain and Portugal. The result was that readers of Gothic novels did not always think of these scenes as part of a distant past but associated them with Catholicism. (159)

In its representation of the Spanish Inquisition during a period when that institution remained intact and the French Revolution and Terror were also occurring, British Gothic literature both reflected and fuelled national anti-Catholic prejudices.

Notably, the Spanish Inquisition's obsession with national racial purity and its fears regarding Jewish assimilation were also prevalent concerns during the French Revolution. Napoleon's pledge to grant Jews the rights of citizenship, resuscitated the threat to eradicate Jewish difference.[36] Since 28 September 1791 (Ausubel: 152), revolutionary France and most of the other countries under Napoleonic domination offered Jews complete emancipation in accordance with the Declaration of the Rights of Man (Poliakov: 213). The Jewish Question in both Spain and France was crucial to the process of defining national identity. As Gary Kates has astutely argued in the case of France, '[t]he debate over Jewish emancipation was … a debate over what it meant to be a French citizen' (109). As was also the case in Spain, the prospect of Jewish assimilation in France gave birth to racial anti-Semitism. Alain Finkielkraut has asserted that anti-Semitism in France 'turned racist only on the fateful day when, as a consequence of Emancipation, you could no longer pick Jews out of a crowd at first glance' (83). Confronted by the threat of Jewish assimilation, the spectre of the Crypto-Jew was born in the Christian imagination.

The semiotics surrounding the spectre of the Crypto-Jew and his putative acts of national subversion in Spain uncannily echo those evoked in the alarmist and imaginative works of Barben, Robison, and Barruel about the role of Jews and the Cabala in secret societies during the French Revolution. The fear of the Marrano parallels the fear of the French Revolutionaries and their covert Jewish leaders as depicted and disseminated in documents written primarily by Jesuits. Historical examinations chronicling the perception of the Jew by the Spanish Inquisition even read – as do the aforementioned Jesuit works – like Gothic novels. Indeed, the popular Gothic idea introduced by Horace Walpole in *The Castle of Otranto* that the sins of the fathers would be visited on subsequent generations was actually played out during the Spanish Inquisition. Henry Kamen relates how '[i]n theory the Inquisition visited the sins of fathers only up to the second generation, and this was supported by canon law' (128–9). Under this legislation, Marranos could be, and were, persecuted for their parents' conversions to Christianity.

As it is related in historic studies, the Spanish Inquisition's Gothic-sounding plot involved 'a vast conspiracy covering Spain in the interests of subverting Christianity' (Kamen: 65). The Jewish Marrano functioned as its featured multifaceted villain and 'Other' upon whom Catholic Spaniards projected their worst fears. As Kamen writes, '[i]n the constant struggle waged by the right-wing to preserve Catholic Spain, all that was hostile and sinister became personified in the Jew who was on the other side' (229). He was accused of having feigned Christian conversion in order to surreptitiously convert the members of his host nation. The Blood Libel assumed a central role in the Inquisition's Gothic plot as allegations of ritual murder were circulated (42). Further, the origins of the encroaching secret society 'heresies' of Illuminism (78–9) and Freemasonry (261) were attributed to Marranos (88). The terrifying spectre of speculative science was laid at the doorstep of the Jewish Marrano (106). As progressive scientific and political ideas were associated with secret societies, such organizations were purportedly extirpated (Roberts, *Mythology*: 6).

Two points should be made with regard to the popular and flawed British equation of the Spanish Inquisition and the French Revolution as examples of Roman Catholic tyranny. The first is that the supporters of the Spanish Inquisition were, like most Britons, extremely fearful of the French Revolution and its perceived anti-Christian tendencies. Kamen explains that very soon after the outbreak of the French Revolution, the Inquisition prohibited all French literature and pamphlets promoting democratic, anti-monarchist ideas (262). The Holy Office was openly hostile to Enlightenment ideas and subsequently censored French books. Included among them, rather ironically, was Edmund Burke's conservative, anti-Revolutionary tome *Reflections on the Revolution in France* which had been published in Spain in French (265). Perhaps because of the popular link between Jews and progressive ideas, seventeenth-century Spanish polemics against Judaism were reprinted during the period of the French Revolution (Manuel: 223).

The second and more crucial point to note with regard to the popular British equation of the Spanish Inquisition and the French Revolution is the lack of sympathy extended towards Jews in British Gothic novels featuring the Inquisition. Michael Ragussis has argued correctly that 'English discourse about the Inquisition, while consistently anti-Catholic, typically failed to be pro-Jewish' (135).[37] As is illustrated in the following chapter, Jewish and Catholic characters are depicted in novels like Godwin's *St. Leon* and Maturin's *Melmoth the Wanderer* as equally barbarous, tribal, and cannibalistic. Their authors assume a superior stance as enlightened, civilized, Protestant/Anglican onlookers.

Ironically, representations of the Jew in British Gothic literature reveal anxieties similar to those expressed by the Spanish Inquisition and by French citizens during the French Revolution. In their depiction of Jews and the Spanish Inquisition, Gothic novelists represent their own deep-seated concerns about the prospects of Jewish religious conversion and Jewish secular assimilation into the British nation. These anxieties were exacerbated by actual historical events in the eighteenth-century fin de siècle. The attempts of British missions to convert Jews had reached a fever pitch by the 1790s. Michael Ragussis explains that what 'had been throughout most of the eighteenth century a steady (if somewhat negligible) stream of literature on the conversion of the Jews and their restoration to Palestine became nothing short of a torrent in the 1790s' (4). This phenomenon generated intense social anxiety both because it was believed that Jewish conversion to Christianity would precipitate the Second Coming and, more importantly, because it heralded the Jews' assimilation into the British nation.

The spectre of Jewish assimilation had been raised earlier in the eighteenth-century in England in the form of the Jewish Naturalization Bill of 1753. Deemed by some historians to be 'one of the fiercest public issues of the eighteenth century ... [this Bill] had a very direct and serious effect on the Jews in England, for it kindled or rekindled latent anti-Semitism' (Rubin: 39). Ironically, the 'Jew Bill', as it was dubbed, did not promote radical change. As Abba Rubin explains, 'Its provisions would have permitted the future naturalization of professing Jews; [but] it would not have affected the Jews already in England, nor did it provide for any large scale naturalization' (37). The general population was nonetheless outraged and alarmed. In combination with the arrival of great numbers of Jews fleeing pogroms in Poland and Russia, and the growing wealth and influence of some English Jews, a virulent anti-Jewish campaign was begun (Ausubel: 182). Charges of Jewish conspiracies in the formation of new joint-stock trading companies were circulated (Levy, *Supposed*: 239)[38] and, before the end of 1754, 'roughly sixty pamphlets were published concerning the [naturalization] measure; most of them opposed it'. Attacked in part on economic grounds, the Bill generated a venomous campaign in London that foregrounded Jewish religious difference (Rubin: 41). Anti-Semitic caricature and violence became the order of the day (Ausubel: 182). The 'Jew Bill' controversy also made its way into light verse. In his comprehensive study of this Bill, Thomas Perry cites 'a widely reprinted occasional prologue, written by Garrick and spoken by the comedian Foote, [that reads] "The many various objects that amuse / These busy curious times, by way of news, / Are plays, elections, murders, lott'ries, Jews"' (104).

Popular response to the 'Jew Bill' sheds some light on the representation of the Jew in British Gothic literature. In particular, it exhibits the tenacity of medieval anti-Semitic stereotypes in mid-eighteenth century Britain. The anonymous author of a pamphlet entitled *Modest Apology for the Citizens and Merchants of London, who petitioned the House of Commons against Naturalizing the Jews*, argued that 'England was a Christian nation, "founded upon the doctrine of Jesus Christ", and could not admit these "crucifiers" without becoming involved in their inherited guilt' (Perry: 92–3). Nowhere is this idea more pronounced or more effectively relayed than in anti-Naturalization writings which comically manipulated the 'sanguinary' Jewish rite of circumcision (Wolper: 32). Also dubbed the 'Circumcision bill', the 'Jew Bill' elicited much black humour about circumcision which was predicated upon the dark stereotype of the barbarous, knife-wielding Jew who was ready, willing, and able to violently convert Christians to Judaism by way of circumcision (29). James Shapiro relates how the figure of Shylock was even incorporated into anti-Naturalization Bill writings:

> A good number of ... [their] allusions turned on a knife-wielding, circumcising, castrating Shylock. In 'The Prophesies of Shylock' that appeared in the *London Evening Post*, there is ... [mention that] an 'advertisement was found placed against the meeting house at Dartford in Kent' that reads: 'to all Jews ... pensioners and others whom it may concern: this is to give notice that this evening will be held at the Bull Inn a private circumcision feast, ... Benjamin Shylock, Scribe.' (219–20)

In one highly significant instance, the spectre of the circumcising Jew was united with the Blood Libel and the image of the venomous Christ-killer. A report from the *London Evening Post* stated that 'seven *Jews* were brought from Norwich, which had stolen a christen'd Child; had circumcised it, and minded to have crucified him at Easter' (Wolper: 35, n. 34). As Roy Wolper perceptively argues, the '[circumcision] fantasy threatened castration' (29). Deciphering this symbolism in terms of its more precise socio-political meaning, Wolper explains that the 'metonymy of circumcision' prevalent in discussions of the 'Jew Bill' in the popular press revealed English fear and anxiety about the distribution of power (33). That such fears were rendered in terms of a sexual threat is interesting. The perceived danger that Jewish naturalization posed to the British body politic is rendered more immediate and personal as a direct physical attack on the British man's body. This spectre of the converting, circumcising Jew is, as I illustrate in the following Chapter, used to convey religious anxieties in Maturin's *Melmoth the Wanderer*.

On 20 December 1753, on the heels of this popular uproar, the Jewish Naturalization Bill was repealed and the agitation subsided (Rubin: 42). A variety of economic, nationalistic, and religious factors clearly motivated this virulently anti-Semitic outrage (Wolper: 28). After a new wave of massacre in eastern Europe in 1768 forced more Jews to emigrate to England, increasingly violent anti-Semitic episodes occurred (Roth, *History*: 235), and legislation promoting Jewish rights and interests met with consistent opposition. Abba Rubin explains that these attitudes remained unaltered for the duration of the century:[39]

> ... in 1765 an attempt to revive the Jew Bill proved abortive. And when, in 1783, the Parliament passed the Irish Naturalization Act, the Jews were specifically excepted. As late as 1786, in *Isaac v. Gompertz* as in the earlier case of *Da Costa v. De Paz*, a Jewish behest for the support of a synagogue, this time in Magpie Alley, was disallowed. (45)

Especially at century's end during the period of the French Revolution and Terror, Jews were regarded as a nationally subversive force with Jacobin sympathies. According to Cecil Roth:

> The Aliens Act of 1793, which placed foreigners settled in England under strict control, resulted in sporadic raids on Jewish pedlars and petty traders throughout the country, and the deportation of a number of them. Thereafter there were recurrent alarms. When the French occupied Venice it was reported by the British representative there that the Jews of the city were in treasonable correspondence with their co-religionists in London. (*History*: 238)

The popular notion that Jews were Jacobin sympathizers was also upheld in Edmund Burke's *Reflections* which was written in response to a sermon by the famous Nonconformist minister Richard Price. Price's address praising the proceedings in France was delivered on the site of the old Jewish ghetto in London. In an analysis of Burke's rhetoric in *Reflections*, Michael Ragussis argues that Burke 'turns the simple designation of place – "the dissenting meeting house of the Old Jewry" – into the infectious sign of an as yet undefined (though nonetheless threatening) principle of Jewishness, so that the place-name eventually marks the speaker, the speech, the audience, the contents of the speech, and an entire species of discourse' (120). Ragussis's assessment of Burke's rhetorical strategy lends support to what I have described as the demonic semiotic yoking of the concepts of national Revolution, France, and Judaism. To this, Burke adds the notion of Jewish conspiracy with his repeated allusions to the act of 'caballing'. As Susan Manly astutely points out, in regard to Burke's employment of this term in *Reflections*, 'For Burke, caballing is an illicit and sinister political scheming contrary to the established government ideology of constitution, law, and nation. But with its Jewish associations of "cabbala", the rabbinical oral tradition of mystical interpretations from the scriptures, the word "cabballing" immediately calls up the fears of inhumanity, vengefulness, and subversive foreignness linked in the public mind to Jews' ('Burke': 157–8).[40] Ragussis also notes how Burke forges a significant historical connection between the English Puritan Revolution and the French Revolution:

> ... while Burke never directly discusses the French Revolution's emancipation of the Jews, he sneers at the French by speaking of their 'new Hebrew brethren'. Behind both the English 'Puritan Revolution' and the revolution in France, then, Burke discovers Judaizers, or at least Jewish sympathizers. In this light Price's sermon poses a genuine political threat to contemporary England; by capitalizing on the site of Price's sermon, Burke can designate Price as 'the preacher of the Old Jewry' who rearticulates, in 1789, the 'Old Jewry doctrine' of religious toleration, philo-Semitism, and revolution that rocked the English nation in the previous century. (121)

As I have discussed, the connection Burke draws between English Republicans and Jews was actually prevalent in the seventeenth century.

The fear articulated by Burke that Britons would be 'Judaized' was also not novel. James Shapiro has explained that since 'the word *Jew* had entered the English vocabulary in the thirteenth century as a catchall term of abuse, often directed at other Christians' the notion of the Jew 'as irredeemable alien and the Jew as bogeyman into whom the Englishman could be mysteriously "turned" coexisted at deep linguistic and psychological levels' (24). As James Picciotto notes in his *Sketches of Anglo-Jewish History*, '[t]he first mention made of the Jews in any document connected with English history, is found in the canons of Echbright, Archbishop of York, which contain an ordinance that no Christian shall presume to eat with a Jew or shall judaise, whatever that may have meant' (1). It is also noteworthy that one of the three accusations against the Jews which impeded their readmission into Britain in the mid-seventeenth century involved their 'unremitting efforts to convert their countrymen to Judaism' (Solomons: 22).[41]

At the level of British socio-historic reality, the greatly discussed conversion of Lord George Gordon to Judaism in 1787 exacerbated the fear of Judaization. Gordon, a rabidly anti-Catholic former MP and President of the United Protestant League, was behind the 'No Popery' Gordon Riots in June of 1780. These civil uprisings responded to a unanimously passed petition that allowed Catholics to serve in the Army and Navy in order to help fight in the American War. Notably, these riots coloured subsequent representations of the French Revolution,[42] which Gordon also later supported and for which he claimed the Riots as a precursor (Katz, *The Jews*: 309). In Birmingham in 1787, however, after championing Cagliostro in England (Solomons: 12–13), Gordon converted to Judaism. It was said that Gordon – the man Horace Walpole called 'The Lunatic Apostle' (9) whose imprisonment in Newgate after the Riots delighted Edmund Burke (Katz, *The Jews*: 310) – even underwent ritual circumcision (Solomons: 25). Predictable anti-Semitic rumours also circulated that Gordon had converted for reasons of financial self-interest and self-aggrandizement. His staunch friend Robert Watson, for example, speculated that 'Perhaps he hoped to give celebrity to his favourite scheme of finance by embracing Judaism … [or] perhaps he expected to have led back the Israelites to their fathers' land' (Solomons: 21). It would seem, however, in the light of Gordon's statements regarding Jews in the early 1780s, that he was genuinely in support of Jewish rights. He 'protested on 14 March 1782 to Emperor Joseph II against the poor treatment suffered by Jews in Germany, and on 10 August 1785 he sent a discourteous letter to the emperor, blaming his current political misfortunes on his tendency towards anti-Semitism' (Katz, *The Jews*: 305). Millenarianism was also a crucial aspect of Gordon's campaign. He aimed 'to advise the Jews of England to side with the Protestants and to oppose the Catholics irrevocably, not only in England, but in America as well' (306).

The popular rumour that Gordon was mentally unstable (Solomons: 45) illustrates how hard-pressed Britons were to explain an act they found inexplicable. Gordon clearly crystallized British fears about the prospect of Judaization. The *Public Advertiser* in January 1788 labelled him 'grotesque' (28), a quality suggested by his Ashkenazi pedlar 'makeover' in a satirical print published in Birmingham. Entitled *Moses Gorden [sic] or the Wandering Jew*, this print 'integrates pedlar and Wandering Jew by depicting the lank-haired and bearded figure of Lord George Gordon, a famous convert to Judaism, dressed in traditional Ashkenazi fashion, as a street-dealer with a bag of old clothes under his arm and some rabbit-skins in the other hand' (Felsenstein: 62–4). Although Gordon's conversion was an exceptional and rare event, it served to raise the spectre of Judaization among the public at large. If wealthy Lords could fall victim to the seductions of Judaism then no one was considered safe. The fact that Gordon was an ardent Protestant, rather than an ardent Catholic, prior to his conversion rendered the threat even greater.

Within this complex socio-historic landscape, a curious dynamic existed with regard to the eradication of Jewish difference: while British missionaries were avidly advocating the conversion of the Jews to Christianity, the popular view was that such a conversion was impossible. This was also the prevalent attitude regarding the Marranos in fifteenth-century Spain. As is discussed in the following chapter, Jewishness is regularly depicted in British Gothic literature as an essential characteristic that may not possibly be eradicated. Rather, it is frequently portrayed as a form of disease that may contaminate Christian Britain. This terrifying possibility was perhaps best captured in the figure of the Crypto-Jew which was popularized by the Spanish Inquisition. Indeed, in the figure of the nationless Wandering Jew, British Gothic writers have often presented what Ragussis refers to as the doppelgänger Crypto-Jew, 'an amoral double agent...or an amoral social climber...who keeps his race secret to invade and to subvert the Christian world' (149). A crucial component of this subversion threat involves the fear that Jews will convert Christians to their demonic religion and value system. Although British Gothic literature's Wandering Jew may be said to be a unique specimen of this body-snatching alien, he owes something to cultural cross-fertilization by way of his European literary counterparts. A brief examination will serve to illustrate that the German *Schauerroman*, a fictional form of terror popular in Britain throughout the 1790s, introduced several ingredients that became essential to British Gothic literature's cabalistic semiotics and its representation of the Wandering Jew.

4
The Rise of the Vampiric Wandering Jew: A Sinister German–English Co-Production

The German *Schauerroman*: Johann Christian Friedrich von Schiller's *The Ghost-Seer, or Apparitionist*

> In addition to particular turns of events and character types, German romantic narrative generally brought more explicit eroticism and violence to the realm of the English Gothic.
>
> (Kiely: 100)

British Gothic literature's cabalistic semiotics and its increasingly demonic Wandering Jew figure were not entirely home-grown products. The idea that secret societies and secret sciences were spectres haunting Europe was also disseminated by way of the German Terror-novel, otherwise known as the *Schauerroman*. Between 1794 and 1796, translations of several German *Schauerroman* treating the subject of secret societies became known in England. Four of the most important were Johann Christian Friedrich von Schiller's *The Ghost-Seer, or Apparitionist*, Cajetan Tschink's *Victim of Magical Delusions, or the Mystery of the Revolution in P——l, a magico-political tale*, Marquis Grosse's *Genius*, and Benedicte Naubert's *Herman of Unna*.[1] The genesis of this fictional genre in Germany was not surprising given Frederick the Great's tolerance towards secret societies during his reign as the King of Prussia (1740–86). His support stood in stark contrast to the tyranny of other governments. As a result, Germany 'seethed with societies, where prophets appeared who practised animal magnetism, professed to raise the dead, or to live a thousand years upon a tea' (Tompkins: 283). While J.M.S. Tompkins characterizes Germany as 'a fruitful bed for these fantastic ideas', she points out that 'even in England, where elemental spirits and natural magic were not taken very seriously, the disturbed atmosphere of the revolutionary period caused the idea of a grand political conspiracy to take root, though in shallow soil' (282–3).

The German *Schauerroman*'s popular secret society theme with its focus on politics and magic also appealed to Western Europe (281) where 'great changes were in progress, and men of liberal sympathies and men tenacious of ancient forms of life were alike prone to see something monstrous and abnormal in each other's activities' (282–3). Tompkins argues that the pattern this theme generally assumed was based on Schiller's *The Ghost-Seer* (1788) where a mysterious yet attractive man turns out to be an associate of a secret society (281). In the first English translation of Schiller's fragmentary prose romance published in 1795, the mysterious stranger is ultimately revealed to be an associate of the Holy Inquisition, an institution which is figured as a type of conspiratorial secret society engaged in the sinister activity of covertly converting influential people to Roman Catholicism.[2]

Schiller's *The Ghost-Seer* incorporates various narrative elements which later become critical to the construction of the vampiric Wandering Jew in British Gothic fiction: the metaphor of vampirism/parasitism, the themes of imposture, conspiracy, and conversion, a secret society, a religious Inquisition, and a mysterious, ageless, accursed wanderer. With an eye to the various configurations of these elements, I will trace the Wandering Jew's development into an increasingly demonic, mercenary, secular, and ethnically affiliated figure who attempts to convert or 'Judaize' upstanding Christians. It is noteworthy and rather ironic that authors who penned such Wandering Jew narratives have done so, in part, to capitalize on this portrait. While Schiller, for example, 'scorned the inferior *Schauerromane*, the profit motive nevertheless compelled the writer to solicit such popular material for his *Thalia*' (Stiffler: 36). Similarly, William Godwin's *St. Leon* 'was perhaps the first of Godwin's mature works to be inspired by commercial reasons' (Flanders: 534). It is also extremely significant that the Wandering Jew's make-up in both British Gothic literature and the German *Schauerroman* is progressively sinister and that this alteration is concurrent with the intensifying debates over the Jewish Question in both countries. Indeed, as Paul Lawrence Rose has expounded, the Wandering Jew had become an emblem for the Jewish Question in Germany by the early nineteenth century (27). This new emblematic role transformed the Wandering Jew from a predominantly religious figure into a secular one associated with liberation, revolution, and socio-political redemption. Generalizing about the Wandering Jew's significance in Europe, Rose states:

> Between 1770 and 1850, Ahasverus emerged as a powerful myth of Promethean revolutionism, and a major topos in non-Christian romantic literature and humanist philosophy alike. Ahasverus was transformed from theological legend into secular vision of human liberation and revolutionary redemption. He even lost for a time his Jewish significance. (25)

Although George K. Anderson in his magisterial study of the Wandering Jew, fails to recognize the secular shift in his representation of Germany or the connection between this transformation and socio-political events, he does note that, beginning especially in the 1820s, students of this legend – even those of a more Romantic persuasion – increasingly portrayed this character as 'another Cain or Satan'. For these writers, Anderson argues, the Wandering Jew's 'conversion...was an unconvincing business' (199). Rose relates that the debate over Jewish assimilation in Germany focused, similarly, on whether or not Jews could abandon their immoral character. The Jews, in Rose's view, 'lost by both sides':

> The offer of rights was poisoned by the condition that they effectively cease to be Jews and become 'real Germans', a notion that may have been clothed in practical political language but which was curiously mystical for all that. In the end, therefore, the very premise of the emancipation debate turned out to be profoundly anti-Jewish. (31)

Thus was the Wandering Jew in German literature – ever a doomed and accursed millenarian reminder – reconfigured for a new, secular era.

Rose rightly notes that British Romantic poets like Shelley also celebrated the Wandering Jew as 'a new Prometheus in messianic revolt against political and religious tyranny' (25). They generally rendered the legend of the Wandering Jew as an intensely personal myth that divested that figure of his Jewish significance and, instead, articulated the 'perpetual cycle of guilt and suffering' essential to the human condition (Bloom, *Visionary*: 207).[3] Although British Romantic poetry is not my generic focus, it is striking that such representations were devoid neither of anti-Semitic ideas nor of Gothic overtones. In Shelley's case, for example, Ahasuerus appears in 'The Wandering Jew's Soliloquy', *Queen Mab*, and *Hellas*, as a type of sage-like, living-dead being with 'cold pale limbs and pulseless arteries' (*Hellas*: 456, line 142) who is bitterly reproachful of, and in just revolt against, his curse by a tyrannical deity. Although Shelley breathes more passion and revolutionary zeal into his portrait than he possesses in established Gothic fiction, his Ahasuerus is nonetheless a *memento mori* figure. Notably, it is onto the Jew's deity, Jehovah, that Shelley projects the stereotypical characteristics of the vampiric Jew. Jehovah is a consummately vengeful and bloodthirsty tyrant in *Queen Mab*, an 'omnipotent Fiend, / Gorgeous and vast: [whose] costly altars smoked / With human blood' (VII: 97–9). This ghastly portrait is reiterated by Mary Shelley in her unfinished manuscript entitled 'History of the Jews' where she 'compares the cruel God of the biblical Jews to the bloodthirsty Mexitili' (Blumberg: 135). The explicit representation of Judaism as an irrational, primitive religion is also fundamental to both Deist dogma (Manuel: 186) and Enlightenment philosophy (Porter: 100).

The Wandering Jew's religious/moral conversion was also regarded as an increasingly unconvincing business in British Gothic literature, Britons' worst nightmares about Jewish conversion assuming flesh and blood in that genre where the Jew was represented as a spectral, seductive, and bloodthirsty proselytizer in league with the devil. While this immortal wanderer's Judaization threat always implies religious and/or racial conversion, it is variously rendered in each work under examination. Godwin depicts Judaization as a predominantly economic and moral threat, while Maturin represents it as a physical or sexual danger that may even generate castration anxiety. Croly hints at the phenomenon of Judaization as a predominantly economic threat that may lead to internal national division and erode religious certainties. Bram Stoker cleverly combines these components of the Judaization threat in *Dracula* as his alien Wandering Jew vampire simultaneously endangers both the health of individual British bodies and that of the British national body politic. Count Dracula is only made possible, however, thanks to these various literary forefathers.

I begin with a brief examination of Schiller's cryptic, incomplete novel *The Ghost-Seer*, which is vital to the genesis of the vampiric Wandering Jew who threatens Britain with Judaization. Set in Venice against the backdrop of the Holy Inquisition (which was, like the Spanish Inquisition, engaged in ferreting out heretics), and narrated in a fragmented format by way of excerpts from journals and letters written by one Count O – and his friend, Baron von F –, *The Ghost-Seer* chronicles the seductive conversion of their beloved associate, a wealthy, unnamed Protestant Prince, to Roman Catholicism. Enamoured of Venetian life, this young royal (who, we are expressly told, has never been a Freemason [6]) becomes the victim of a conspiracy masterminded by the Holy Inquisition. Undertaken with the hope that the Prince will 'subsequently disseminate Roman Catholicism among his subjects' (232–3), this conspiracy involves a charlatan Sicilian engaged with 'occult sciences' (118) and a Roman Catholic priest disguised as a wandering Armenian. After a long process during which the Prince becomes convinced of the authenticity of the Armenian's supernatural nature and abilities, and he falls in love with a beautiful young woman who forms part of the conspiracy, the young Prince converts to Roman Catholicism. After his failed attempts to murder the man who bars his ascent to the throne, the young Prince is poisoned by the conspiratorial Wandering Armenian and the charlatan Sicilian in order to avoid discovery of the plot. In this blatantly anti-Catholic novel, the young Protestant Prince dies 'in the bitterest agonies of contrition and remorse' (242).

The theme of secrecy shrouds *The Ghost-Seer*. Venice, the city in which the tale is set, subsequently became a popular locale in British Gothic literature. Associated with secrecy and gambling, this 'labyrinthine deathly city of alienated desire' (Coates: 1), is, as Tony Tanner suggests, the Gothic city *par excellence*. As Tanner describes it:

> ... in addition to being a powerful and enormously rich republic, Venice was effectively a police state with its notorious secret tribunals (the Council of Ten, the Council of Three); the fact of its famous masquerades

and carnivals (six months of the year were carnival time by the eighteenth century); the fact of its labyrinthine little streets and canals and endless bridges; the uncanny silence of its gliding traffic; the supposed 'super-subtlety' of its agents and citizens – all these attributes composed an easily available scenario or imaginary topography for writers from afar. Watery, dark, silent; a place of sensuality and secrecy; masks and masquerading; duplicity and desire; an always possible treacherous beauty; Othello and Shylock (and why *did* Shakespeare set his two plays with figures from marginalized groups – a black, a Jew – as protagonists, in Venice?); Volpone and greed; conspiracy and courtesans in Otway's *Venice Preserved* – all these associations made Venice an obvious setting for Gothic novels such as *The Mysteries of Udolpho* (Ann Radcliffe never visited Venice, but that is just the point – there is a 'Venice' compounded of just such reiterated association always to hand) and 'Monk' Lewis's *The Bravo of Venice*. (5)

Given these resonances of secrecy and seduction, the shady, marginal characters of Shylock and Gothic literature's Wandering Jew are comfortably at home in Venice. Paul Coates reinforces Tanner's portrait, arguing that Venice is associated with the key Gothic themes of conspiracy and identity politics. He maintains that 'one of the forms of the uncanny world of conspiracy is the Venetian Carnival … [during which] faces … [become] masks' (1). Ann Radcliffe's *The Mysteries of Udolpho* (1794) also capitalizes on Venice's association with secrecy and terror. Her protagonist Emily is removed to Venice where she becomes a prisoner of her Aunt's treacherous husband Montoni, and Emily's persistent suitor, Count Morano, is later imprisoned in 'one of those secret prisons, which were the terror of the Venetians' (423).

Schiller's prophetic Armenian in *The Ghost-Seer* makes his entry in the English translation of 1795 on the streets of Venice where he ominously informs the young Prince of the upcoming death of his cousin. This gloomy, masked figure is linked with the supernatural world and is present during two revelatory scenes involving the raising of the dead, acts he undertakes in order to establish his reputation as one who unmasks other occult-dabbling impostors. While in one instance he exposes a fratricide (130–85), in the other, he brings his Sicilian co-conspirator, who is engaged in cabalistic 'occult sciences', to justice (71–5). Disguised in both compelling sequences, the Armenian assumes the role of a truth-seeker with actual supernatural powers and a transfixing gaze who despises, and even revels in denouncing, fraudulent occult performances.

Believed to be modelled on the Wandering Jew-like Cagliostro (Birkhead: 51), Schiller's elusive wanderer is not explicitly identified as Jewish. According to George K. Anderson and Eino Railo, however, Schiller's Wandering Armenian seems to have been adapted from the Wandering Jew described in

Matthew Paris's thirteenth-century *Chronica majora* which was first published in English in the early seventeenth century (Anderson, *Legend*: 61).[4] Not only is Schiller's Wandering Armenian associated with the Wandering Jew through his peripatetic habit, he is of the same national background as the 'eyewitness' Armenian Bishop who relates the tale of the Wandering Jew in Paris's famous account. Another prominent and intriguing connection with Paris's Armenian *Bishop* lies in the fact that Schiller's Wandering Armenian is ultimately revealed to be a high-ranking Catholic official. As I will illustrate, Schiller's act of linking the supernatural pseudo-Wandering Jew with the conspiratorial Roman Catholic priest is important to Lewis's and Maturin's subsequent portraits of the Wandering Jew. Both groups – Catholics and Jews – are vital to the theme of religious inheritance in *The Monk* and *Melmoth the Wanderer* where they are depicted as the barbarian religious forefathers of enlightened Anglicans, and Protestants.

It is the Sicilian charlatan – a man repeatedly described as a 'Conjurer' (73) and a 'Juggler' (70) – who is instrumental in forging the connection between the mysterious wandering Armenian and his legendary counterpart, the Wandering Jew. He recounts various eyewitness reports that suggest that the Armenian possesses eternal youth (119) and other supernatural abilities. For example, several people claim to have seen the Armenian in various guises in different parts of the world at the same time (119–20). Curiously, Schiller's deceptive, gold-hungry Sicilian is also closely affiliated with the stereotype of the secret society Jew in *The Ghost-Seer*. It is suggested that he assumes the guise of a Jew when engaging in his deceptive secret society practices. When searched after his arrest, he is found to be in possession of a variety of alchemical materials along with 'a rosary, a Jew's beard, a dagger, and a brace of pocket pistols' (80). His love of cabalistic 'occult sciences' (131), a deceptive 'art' he exploits for material gain (he wins gold from sceptics), and the fact that his friends are 'zealous admirer[s] of the Cabala' (131) further establish the Sicilian's connection with the demonic religion of Judaism.

As the insidious, conspiratorial Holy Inquisition also leads the Prince away from Protestantism and into sinful crime, Schiller suggests that Roman Catholicism is yet another demonic secret society obsessed with power-mongering and engaged with the occult sciences. Schiller further implies that the Catholic conspirators are parasites who prey on innocent victims: while the Sicilian is a parasitic magician who exploits the spiritual needs and fears of innocent, gullible people, the Roman Catholic priest disguised as the Wandering Armenian preys, with the hope of material gain, on the naïve young Prince. This parasite motif is a cognate of the vampire theme which subsequently becomes central to the representation of the Wandering Jew in British Gothic literature. Indeed, vampirism is actually cryptically alluded to in Schiller's novel in relation to the Wandering Armenian. Addressing the curious Prince and his friends, the Sicilian provides a detailed description of the single limitation placed upon this mysterious man. This restriction suggests the presence of some vampiric force:

> 'Of the twenty-four hours in the day, there is only one which he cannot command; during which no person ever saw him, and during which he never was employed in any terrestrial occupation … When the clock strikes twelve, he at that moment ceases to belong to the living. In whatever place he is, he must immediately be gone; whatever business he is engaged in, he must instantly leave it. The terrible sound of the hour of midnight tears him from the arms of friendship, wrests him from the altar, and would drag him away even in the agonies of death. Whither he then goes, or what he is then engaged in, is a secret to every one. No person ventures to interrogate, still less to follow him. His features, at this dreadful hour, contract a degree of gravity so gloomy, and so terrifying, that no person has courage sufficient to look him in the face, or to speak a word to him. However lively the conversation may have been, a dead silence immediately succeeds it, and all around him wait for his return in an awful horror, without venturing to quit their seats, or to open the door through which he has passed.'

> 'Does nothing extraordinary appear in his person when he returns?' –

> 'Nothing, except that he seems pale and languid, nearly in the state of a man who has just suffered a painful operation, or received disastrous intelligence. Some pretend to have seen drops of blood on his linen, but with what degree of veracity I cannot affirm.'

> 'Did no person ever attempt to conceal the approach of this hour from him, or endeavour to engage him in such diversions, as might make him forget it?'

> 'Once only, it is said he passed his time. The company was numerous and remained together late in the night. All the clocks and watches were purposely set wrong, and the warmth of conversation hurried him away. When the fatal moment arrived, he suddenly became silent, and motionless; his limbs continued in the position in which this instant had arrested them; his eyes were fixed; his pulse ceased to beat. All the means employed to awake him proved fruitless, and this situation endured till the hour had elapsed. He then revived on a sudden without any assistance, cast up his eyes, and re-assumed his speech with the same syllable as he was pronouncing at the moment of interruption. The general consternation discovered to him what had happened, and he declared, with an awful solemnity, that they ought to think themselves happy in having escaped with no other injury than fear. The same night he quitted for ever the city where this circumstance had occurred.' (120–6)

In his paralysis, paleness, exhaustion, the impression of having 'suffered some painful operation', and the mysterious discovery of 'drops of blood on his linen', the Armenian is depicted as a type of vampire victim. In this state, he appears to be affiliated with the wealthy young Prince who is exploited by metaphoric parasites.

The Sicilian's explanation of the Armenian's unusual midnight hour paralysis further establishes the link between Schiller's Wandering Armenian and the Wandering Jew of legend. According to the Sicilian:

> The common opinion is that during this mysterious hour, he converses with his genius. Some even suppose him to be one of the departed, who is allowed to pass twenty-three hours of the day among the living, and that in the twenty-fourth his soul is obliged to return to the infernal regions, to suffer its punishment. Some believe him to be the famous *Apollonius of Tyana*; and others, the disciple of *John*, of whom it is said – *he shall remain until the last judgment.* (126–7)

This conjecture about the Wandering Armenian's true identity offers two opposite possibilities with different connotations. While Apollonius of Tyana is a wandering philosopher and a secret science adept who is believed to be the 'Master of the Rosicrucians' (Brewer: 55)[5] and later becomes 'known mainly as an antichrist' (Wilson: 197),[6] Christ's beloved disciple St John the Apostle is believed to be tarrying until Christ's return (John 21: 21–3). In the light of these widely divergent alternatives, the Wandering Armenian is an ambivalent, undead figure similar to the eternally accursed Wandering Jew of legend.

While *The Ghost-Seer* does not explicitly identify the Wandering Armenian as Apollonius of Tyana, their similarity is substantiated by the Wandering Armenian's abilities. Brewer's *Dictionary of Phrase and Fable* describes Apollonius as the 'Master of the Rosicrucians ... [who] is said to have had the power of raising the dead, of making himself invisible, and of being in two places at the same time' (55). Like Apollonius, the Wandering Armenian exhibits his ability to raise the dead in *The Ghost-Seer* and, as the Sicilian relates, 'There are several creditable persons, who remember having seen him, each at the same time, in different parts of the globe' (119–20). Given these uncanny resemblances, Schiller seems to have drawn fairly extensively on tales about Apollonius in the construction of his Wandering Armenian. One particularly famous anecdote about Apollonius, notably involving a vampire, is also incorporated into Schiller's portrait of the Wandering Armenian. Colin Wilson recounts it as follows:

> When his friend and disciple Menippus of Corinth introduced him to his (Menippus's) future bride, Apollonius instantly recognized her as a vampire ... Menippus refused to believe his warnings, but Apollonius came to the wedding, and with a few magical passes caused the guests and the feast to vanish – all were illusions conjured up by Lamia – and made the bride admit that she intended to eat Menippus. (197–8)

Apollonius assumes an ambivalent role in this tale: although he helps his friend avoid the fate of becoming a vampire's banquet, his dreaded supernatural association is not negated completely, as it is often demons who recognize their own. *The Ghost-Seer* features a similar revelatory wedding scene precipitated by the equally ambivalent Wandering Armenian in which a bride discovers on her wedding night that her husband, Lorenzo, has murdered Jeronymo, his brother and her former fiancé, in order to marry her. Raised vampire-like from the dead, 'covered with blood, and disfigured with horrible wounds' (183), Jeronymo exposes his brother as a bloodthirsty fratricide, a horrifying revelation which causes all of the wedding guests to lose consciousness. When they later reawaken, Lorenzo makes a private confession and dies (184). The truth of Jeronymo's revelation is subsequently borne out when his skeleton is discovered in a well in a neglected farmyard of his father's villa (185).

In their supernatural abilities to recognize and expose real and figurative vampires, Apollonius and Schiller's Wandering Armenian influence the Wandering Jew's earliest incarnation in British Gothic literature. As I will illustrate, a Faustian Wandering Jew figure and vampire-detector is featured in Matthew G. Lewis's *The Monk*. His engagement with the secret sciences is a noteworthy addition to the Wandering Jew of legend. In this preoccupation, Lewis's Wandering Jew may also be said to combine aspects of Schiller's shyster–magician Sicilian. Notably and ironically, the body parts necessary to the later incarnation of the *vampiric* Wandering Jew may also be exhumed from Schiller's novel. Indeed, in the complex portrait of his Janus-faced Wandering Armenian/conspiratorial Roman Catholic priest, Schiller forecasts the more treacherous Wandering Jew who will appear in works by Godwin, Maturin, and Stoker. This predatorial and conspiratorial Roman Catholic priest who assumes a disguise in order to achieve his victim's religious conversion is a particularly uncanny prototype of Bram Stoker's vampire proselytizer Count Dracula. Although Count Dracula is an unnatural figure who seems to resemble Schiller's vampire-detector Wandering Armenian who is never seen taking food, approaching a woman, or closing his eyes to sleep (120), Dracula also shares a great deal in common with Schiller's figuratively vampiric priest. In order to chart and assess the Wandering Jew's progressive 'fall' from supernatural vampire-detector to figurative vampire and, finally, to actual vampire in the pages of British Gothic literature, I now turn to an examination of the first stage in this legendary wandering immortal's metamorphosis in Matthew G. Lewis's explosive novel, *The Monk*.

Gothic Revelations and Religious Reformations: the case of *The Monk*

> Fenced round with spells, unhurt I venture
> Their sabbath strange where Witches keep;

Fearless the Sorcerer's circle enter,
And woundless tread on snakes asleep.

('The Gypsy's Song', Lewis: 35)

The Wandering Jew makes his memorable cameo début in British Gothic literature in Matthew G. Lewis's graphic porno-Gothic novel, *The Monk* (1795) where he, ironically, appears as a millenarian figure promoting a religious – and, more specifically, a Protestant – Reformation. This accursed but crucial exorcist of sexual excess, violence, and hypocrisy borne of Catholic repression, heralds nothing short of a religious revolution. Set largely in Madrid during the operation of the Spanish Inquisition and composed during the cataclysmic events of the French Revolution, *The Monk* is a deceptively disordered narrative that explores and denounces the devastating personal and socio-political effects of religious repression. In this strategically structured labyrinthine house of mirrors, the primary plot is not only mirrored by a subplot with various cognate tales focusing on temptation, transgression, and the question of redemption, it also functions on two connected levels as the personal experiences of a monk are paralleled to political events transpiring in Madrid. Both are enslaved by debilitating 'monkish fetters' (345) and, in what may be described as a combined sermon-striptease, the external theatre that is Madrid (7) is mirrored by the internal theatre of the monk's psyche, which becomes a 'Theatre of a thousand contending passions' (83). His unrestrained and excessive acts of rioting in carnal delights (224, 242, 329) are matched by the acts of the mob of 'Rioters [who heed] ... nothing but the gratification of their barbarous vengeance' (356). The outcomes are, predictably, violent.

The *Monk*'s primary plot anticipates Mary Shelley's *Frankenstein* in its consideration of the origin of monsters.[7] It charts the fall of a Faustian monk named Ambrosio who, after being abandoned in childhood, is raised by what is suggested as the dysfunctional family of the Roman Catholic Church. In adulthood, after a cloistered life devoid of temptation, he becomes the revered and proud abbot of the prestigious Capuchin monastery in Madrid. Targeted by Satan, Ambrosio is seduced by one of his demonic minions named Matilda, under whose tutelage he engages in secret sciences and commits murder in order to violate a beautiful young woman named Antonia. When he finally sells his soul to the devil in order to evade the Inquisition, Antonia is revealed to be his sister and her mother Elvira, his mother.

Lewis's accursed Wandering Jew forms part of a fairly lengthy subplot which was subsequently published as a separate and extremely popular chapbook. He functions as a storyteller who relates the tale of two enlightened young lovers named Raymond and Agnes whose escapades call modernity and rationalism into question. Intricate Gothic plotters in their own right, they wed their mockery of 'superstitious' beliefs with a defiance of parental authority. Bound against her will to enter a convent in Madrid due to her dying Mother's 'fatal vow' (133) during pregnancy to dedicate her child to the service of St Clare (130–1), the sixteen-year-old Agnes plots to defy her dead Mother's 'grossest superstition' (130) by manipulating another established superstition connected with her home, the Castle Lindenberg in Bavaria, where she lives with her aunt and uncle, the Baron and Baroness Lindenberg. The superstition involves a century-old ghost known as the Bleeding Nun who is said to inhabit a 'haunted Chamber' in the Castle from which she emerges 'on the fifth of May of every fifth year, as soon as the Clock strikes One' and thereafter terrifies her auditors for an hour (141). Raymond's first vision of the Bleeding Nun comes in the form of a sketch executed by Agnes who captures her in all of her sexual excess and subversively unreligious glory:

> [She was] a Female of more than human stature, clothed in the habit of some religious order. Her face was veiled; On her arm hung a chaplet of beads; Her dress was in several places stained with blood which trickled from a wound upon her bosom. In one hand She held a Lamp, in the other a large Knife, and She seemed advancing towards the Iron gates of the Hall. (138)

When the Baroness Lindenberg, who is also enamoured of the visiting Raymond, discovers that he is in love with her niece, she arranges for Agnes's immediate removal to Madrid. In desperation, the young lovers plot Agnes's escape. As it happens to be the fifth of May of the fifth year, Agnes cunningly decides to impersonate the Bleeding Nun and meet Raymond in a carriage near the Castle gate. At the appointed time the two meet but, after a dramatic escape and carriage accident during a ferocious tempest which leaves Raymond badly injured, 'Agnes' disappears and Raymond is taken to an Inn for recovery. Raymond discovers the following morning that he has actually eloped with the legendary Bleeding Nun, whom he describes as 'an animated Cor[p]se':

> Her countenance was long and haggard; Her cheeks and lips were bloodless; The paleness of death was spread over her features, and her eye-balls fixed stedfastly upon me were lustreless and hollow…The Apparition seated herself opposite to me at the foot of the Bed, and was silent. Her eyes were fixed earnestly upon mine: They seemed endowed with the property of the Rattle-snake's, for I strove in vain to look off her. My eyes were fascinated, and I had not the power of withdrawing them from the Spectre's. (160)

Raymond subsequently becomes 'the prey of habitual melancholy' and, after several months of these horrifying nocturnal visits, is 'so faint, spiritless, and emaciated, that … [he is unable to] cross the room without assistance' (163).

It is at this extremely desperate juncture that the Wandering Jew enters the novel in order to help the dejected and dying Raymond regain life by exorcizing his assailant. At least one critic has argued that the Bleeding Nun is a vampire (Anderson: 178),[8] and her expertise in draining her victim of all energy certainly supports the claim in figurative terms. Given this equation, Lewis's Wandering Jew might be described as a vampire hunter similar to Schiller's Apollonius-like Wandering Armenian. Raymond's first account of the Wandering Jew from his servant Theodore is also resonant of various passages from Schiller's *The Ghost-Seer*. Indeed, Lewis's Wanderer is a fascinating conflation of Schiller's Wandering Armenian and magician Sicilian:

> By his accent He is supposed to be a Foreigner, but of what Country nobody can tell. He seemed to have no acquaintance in the Town, spoke very seldom, and never was seen to smile. He had neither Servants or Baggage; But his Purse seemed well-furnished, and He did much good in the Town. Some supposed him to be an Arabian Astrologer, Others to be a Travelling Mountebank, and many declared that He was Doctor Faustus, whom the Devil had sent back to Germany. (167)

Raymond subsequently discovers the incredible extent of the mysterious stranger's life and experiences:

> He named People who had ceased to exist for many Centuries, and yet with whom He appeared to have been personally acquainted. I could not mention a Country however distant which He had not visited, nor could I sufficiently admire the extent, and variety of his information. (169)

In his overbearing gloom and the paradoxical feelings he inspires in Raymond, Lewis's Wandering Jew also anticipates Bram Stoker's 'malignant and saturnine' Count in his undead state (*Dracula*: 24):

> He was a Man of majestic presence: His countenance was strongly marked, and his eyes were large, black, and sparkling: Yet there was something in his look, which the moment I saw him, inspired me with a secret awe, not to say horror. He was drest plainly, his hair was unpowdered, and a band of black velvet which encircled his fore-head, spread over his features an additional gloom. His countenance wore the marks of profound melancholy; his step was slow, and his manner grave, stately, and solemn. (Lewis, *Monk*: 168)

Despite the fact that his good motives are made explicit to Raymond– 'the Stranger', as he is called, informs Raymond that 'amidst all the sorrows which oppress me, to think that I have been of use to you, is some consolation' (176) – a certain malice lurks in his face that leaves a powerful impression on Raymond. In the latter's words, 'There was in his eyes an expression of fury, despair, and malevolence, that struck horror to my very soul' (170). Indeed, as Edgar Rosenberg rightly comments, 'The Jew himself consciously emphasizes his gift for scaring people' (216) for, after perceiving Raymond's dread, he verbally alludes to his curse and the terror and charm it inspires (Lewis, *Monk*: 170). Like Schiller's dreaded, supernatural Wandering Armenian, therefore, Lewis's benevolent-malevolent Wandering Jew epitomizes ambivalence.

The Bleeding Nun experiences a similar ambivalent reaction to the Wandering Jew when confronted with his physiological abnormality. Apart from being afflicted with the singular curse of inspiring 'all who look[ed] on… [him] with terror and detestation' (170) and being an outcast, friendless Monster (169), this Wandering Jew is, true to tradition, physically inscribed. His extremely singular mark of Cain is 'a burning Cross impressed upon his brow' that undermines Raymond's courage with 'a mysterious dread' and garners a mixed reaction of 'reverence, and horror' from the Bleeding Nun (172).[9] Consistent with the established Medieval equation between the Jew and the Devil, Lewis's Lucifer possesses a similar emblem in the form of a 'bright Star sparkled upon his fore-head' (277). Also associated with sorcery and black magic like Lucifer, Lewis's Wandering Jew performs his role as the exorcist of the Bleeding Nun with the aid of his burning Cross, his mesmerizing eyes, and a small chest replete with instruments of sorcery ranging from a small wooden crucifix and a Bible, to a goblet actually containing Christ's blood. As Raymond discovers, this singular restless ghost derives from his own past and symbolizes a variety of taboos. Known in her lifetime as Beatrice, the Bleeding Nun is revealed to be the great-Aunt of Raymond's grandfather who was involved, a century earlier, with two of Agnes's ancestors (173). After being placed in a convent against her will, the Bleeding Nun escaped for the sake of her love for the Baron Lindenberg. As in the case of Madrid's idol monk Ambrosio, this 'fall' was the first on the slippery slope of depravity. She subsequently became a lover of the Baron's younger brother Otto, then murdered the Baron, and was thereafter killed by Otto. The Bleeding Nun's excesses were, Lewis suggests, the combined result of bad parental judgement and unnatural cloistering in a convent (173). As in the framing narrative involving Ambrosio, Lewis illustrates how repression breeds revolution: natural sexual desires, when unnaturally mortified, ultimately result in perversion and excess.

In a genre rife with what Maggie Kilgour calls 'incestuous narratives' (*Rise*: 155), the Bleeding Nun's tale functions as the 'incestuous narrative' *par excellence* as it involves both Raymond's and Agnes's ancestors and clearly mirrors their elopement tale. This mirroring is most explicitly suggested in the fact that Agnes and the Bleeding Nun become interchangeable figures in Raymond's mind during his illness (161). When recounting this extraordinary tale, he refers to the Bleeding Nun as 'the false Agnes' (164), which suggests she gives expression to Raymond's concerns regarding Agnes's faith-fulness. This tale also serves a monitory function, warning against trans-gression in general and sexual excess in particular, a warning that Raymond does not heed as he later 'sacrifices' Agnes's honour to his passion (186). She especially pays a heavy price for this transgression. Fortunately, however, they do not follow the bad examples of the Bleeding Nun and Ambrosio whose sins multiply. Raymond, in fact, helps to redress the sins of the past involving his and Agnes's ancestors, thus enacting one of Lewis's principal moral lessons, namely that while the sins of the fathers may be visited upon the sons and daughters, they are not necessarily doomed to repeat them. Moral revolutions may occur and cycles of violence may be broken.

The figure of the Wandering Jew is an exceptionally interesting player within this compelling subplot. The image of a repentant Jew exorcizing a lapsed Catholic Nun is nothing if not intriguing in the work of a British Anglican. In that his mesmerizing abilities are similar to the Bleeding Nun's, and that he repents his transgression against Christ (how else could he suc-cessfully employ the power of the Cross unless he has converted in his heart?), the Wandering Jew is the ideal exorcist. Who better to exorcize a woman guilty of the crimes of parricide and pseudo-incest than a repentant Christian convert and member of a group to whom these very taboos are tra-ditionally ascribed? In this significant allegorical scene where the Wandering Jew and the lapsed Catholic Nun are positioned as doppelgänger sinners, Lewis suggests a moral consanguinity between Jews and Roman Catholics. Both faiths are positioned as the tyrannical, parricidal religious forefathers of Anglicanism/Protestantism, an association also established in *The Ghost-Seer* in the mixed figure of the Wandering Armenian/Roman Catholic priest.

Lewis's novel is nonetheless particularly venomous in exposing the grotesque underbelly of an apparently righteous Roman Catholic Church – an institution whose doctrine of repression and violence is shown to create arrogant, hypocritical, sadistic monsters. The 'gothic obscurity' of the Church alluded to in the opening chapter (26) is an apt signpost of a domain Lewis describes as obscurantist, superstitious, and barbarian in its practices. This unenlightened institution is operated by what amounts to a dysfunc-tional, passion-consumed family comprised of a heartless father (Ambrosio) and a merciless mother (the Prioress). These spiritual siblings function as demonic doubles: while the former ends up repeatedly fornicating with his 'son' Rosario (43, 57) once he discovers 'he' is actually a woman, and later rapes and murders his 'daughter' Antonia (262, 381), the latter revives the old laws of her order (408) and subjects 'her beloved Daughter' Agnes (208), after discovering her pregnancy, to a torturous, inhumane imprisonment in a concealed, Bastille-like prison that lies beneath the convent burial vaults. There, the cruel Prioress advises Agnes to 'resign all hopes of liberty' (408).

The Spanish Inquisition, with its Grand Inquisitor and 'engines of torture' (422, 431), may not play an actual role in the narrative until Ambrosio is imprisoned for his heinous crimes near the novel's end (394), but it seems to be in full operation for the novel's duration in the form of both the Prioress's and Ambrosio's brutality. Ironically, the Inquisition's dreaded power especially haunts the 'voluptuous Monk' (225) as he becomes increasingly depraved (227, 425) and it is the only force that terrifies the sadistic Prioress (349). Indeed, the latter 'monastic Tyrant' (350) whom the Mother Superior, St Ursula, characterizes as 'a Tyrant, a Barbarian, and a Hypocrite' (355), acts like an exemplary Inquisitor when she visits Agnes and her deceased infant in the dungeon where she is enchained (409). As the astonishingly ever-merciful Agnes recounts:

> She then treated me with the most unrelenting cruelty: She loaded me with reproaches, taunted me with my frailty, and when I implored her mercy, told me to ask it of heaven, since I deserved none on earth. She even gazed upon my lifeless Infant without emotion; and when She left me, I heard her charge Camilla to increase the hardships of my Captivity. Unfeeling Woman! But let me check my resentment: She has expiated her errors by her sad and unexpected death. Peace be with her; and may her crimes be forgiven in heaven, as I forgive her my sufferings on earth! (414–5)

In her macabre role in the transformation of Agnes and her dead child into a grotesque Madonna and Child (369),[10] the Prioress certainly lives up to her billing as 'a dangerous Woman' who is 'haughty, inflexible, superstitious and revengeful' (219).

Lewis's indictment of the Roman Catholic Church as a type of Mammonistic pagan cult enacting literal sacrifices for its idol Ambrosio whose countenance, in Matilda's words, 'shone with the majesty of a God' (60–1) is further suggested by its engagement with both the illicit commerce of prostitution and the secret sciences. The Prioress's 'secret pride at displaying the pomp and opulence of her Convent' (348–9) seems a minor offence in comparison to the suggestion that the convent is a site of illicit commerce, a brothel where 'transactions' are made with prostitutes.

Ambrosio's comment that the Convent of St Clare threatens to become 'the retreat of Prostitutes' given the pregnant Agnes's presence there (46) assumes tremendous irony in the light of his subsequent 'illicit commerce' with Matilda (227, 236). Their recurrent sexual 'transactions' (226, 229) are rendered even more perverse when Matilda, like the prostitutes in Samuel Richardson's *Clarissa*, aids and abets Ambrosio's crime of drugging and raping an innocent virgin. Central to Matilda's power is her knowledge and manipulation of the secret sciences, taught her by an Uncle whom she refers to as 'a Man of uncommon knowledge' (267). These pursuits are, she claims, unjustly censured due to 'the blindness of superstition' and 'vulgar prejudice' (60). By way of this earnest guide, Matilda becomes versed in what is implied is a demonic enterprise that involves reading the future, commanding spirits, and reversing the order of nature (267). In her turn, Matilda initiates others into what appears to be a secret society. Indeed, with the aid of Matilda's Magic Mirror which provides unrestricted access to Antonia (270–1) and a powerful sleeping draught composed, among other things, of 'three human fingers, and an Agnus Dei' broken in pieces (276), Ambrosio is granted the tools with which to conduct his brutal transgressions. Ultimately, Ambrosio's instruments for black magic also serve to convict him on the charge of Sorcery as the constellated mirror[11] is later discovered in his room (423). Notably, the Prioress's control over access to the Laboratory that lies beneath the convent of St Clare (330) combined with her use of a similar opiate on Agnes, also implicates her in the secret sciences (407).

If an oppositional voice is raised in *The Monk* that indicts the Roman Catholic Church as a sinister cult that abuses authority, it belongs to Agnes who is ultimately, tragically in keeping with her name, literally converted into an *Agnus Dei*, a sacrificial and redemptive lamb of God. Hers is a heretical Protestant voice that denounces the Abbey and convent as 'abodes so falsely deemed religious' (372). In what seems, in part, to be a critique of the Roman Catholic idea of the Priest's position as a powerful mediator between men and God, Agnes reminds 'the Idol of Madrid' (48) that he is actually a man who, like all men, 'is weak and born to err' (49). Further to this, she extols a mixed doctrine of mercy and just retribution which is upheld at the narrative's end when, in keeping with the philosophy of both the British novel and Christianity, virtue and vice are justly rewarded.

In his marginal role, the Wandering Jew also serves as a *memento mori* signpost who provides evidence of God's mercy and justice. While the Bleeding Nun may be exorcized by the Wandering Jew, her spiritual peace is unavailable to her exorcist. The Wandering Jew may be a spiritually enlightened Christian convert whose transformation from the status of depraved sinner provides evidence of the merciful and righteous nature of Christianity (read Anglicanism), but his Jewish sins still cling to him. Indeed, the reader is reminded that the evils of Judaism are unequalled in history. In his representation of a Wandering Jew who mysteriously disappears with his sins unexorcized after a brief and cryptic cameo role, Lewis suggests that the Wandering Jew's crime of condemning Christ to Crucifixion is so formidable that it may only be pardoned by Christ at the Millennium.

In case the idea of Judaism's unequalled sins is lost on the reader, Lewis presents a Jewish character in *The Monk* who offers an especially significant reminder that Judaism is, much like Roman Catholicism as Lewis portrays it, demonic and, as its involvement with illicit commerce suggests, Mammon-obsessed. The only other Jewish character in this novel is the materialistic merchant who sells Ambrosio the Madonna portrait which precipitates his downfall. Although Matilda informs Ambrosio that she sat for the painting and then had her 'Emissary', the Jew, bring it to the monastery (81), the reader later discovers that Matilda is actually Lucifer's accomplice. While Lucifer, in his final revelatory statements to Ambrosio does not mention that he had the portrait purposely sent to Ambrosio – in fact, Lucifer only says that he 'observed … [Ambrosio's] idolatry of the Madon[n]a's picture … [and] bad a subordinate but crafty spirit assume a similar form in order to capture Ambrosio's attention' (440) – this does not discount the fact that the portrait functions as the crucial medium through which Lucifer commences his demonic handiwork. Despite the fact that the Jew might not actually have been Lucifer's Emissary, he is nonetheless instrumental in Ambrosio's fall as he is the middleman between the devil and his victims. This relationship maintains the established idea, represented in various illustrations dating from the medieval era to the Enlightenment, that the Jews and the devil were business partners who engaged equally in usury (Trachtenberg: 195).

Lewis's Wandering Jew functions primarily as a spiritual figure employed to address the related issues of Christian religious history and paternity. Although his connection with the supernatural is not novel, his magician-style paraphernalia is. In this aspect, he shares similarities with both the stereotypical Jewish charlatan magician[12] and *The Monk*'s Roman Catholic secret society adepts. The Wandering Jew is thus implicated in one of that novel's central concerns, namely the disjunction between righteous appearances and sinister covert realities. A decided ambivalence is at play, however, as a certain dread is associated with this figure despite the fact that, in contradistinction to the Prioress and Matilda, he is engaged in the secret sciences for benevolent reasons. This ambivalence carries over to his association with money. Lewis's wandering 'Fugitive' is distinct from his traditional legendary counterpart who is generally figured as anti-materialistic, abstemious, and penniless – when he is given groats, he says, he immediately gives them away to the poor (Anderson, *Legend*: 117).[13] Consistent with Lewis's representation of commercial enterprises as naturally and necessarily illicit, converted Jews may never entirely divest themselves of their morally tainted origins. His Wandering Jew may effect benevolent ends with his 'well-furnished' Purse – we are told that 'He did much good in the Town' with it – but the origin of this wealth is tainted by the references to Arabian Astrologers, Travelling Mountebanks, the Devil, and Doctor Faustus (167).

At this stage in his development, the Wandering Jew is not the nationally vampiric, conspiratorial, and depraved figure of sexual excess he will become in Bram Stoker's *Dracula*. In fact, Lewis's Wandering Jew seems, instead, to anticipate the vampire-hunting Van Helsing for he is an Apollonius-style exorcist of sexual excess who alone is capable of 'drying up' both Raymond's blood and that of the Bleeding Nun (167). The Wandering Jew has, however, taken his first decisive step on the slippery slope of degradation and demonization. In William Godwin's *St. Leon*, published only four years later, he falls significantly further.

Protestantism's Gothic House of Mirrors: The Gospel according to St Godwin[14]

> Look up! look up! O citizen of London, enlarge thy countenance! O Jew, leave counting gold! return to thy oil and wine. O African! black African! Go; winged thought, widen his forehead!
>
> (Blake: 71)

> The world knows no great deal of me: I do not deny but my monies may roll a little, but for myself, I do not roll at all. I live sparingly and labor hard, therefore, I am called a miser – I cannot help it – an uncharitable dog, I must endure it – a blood-sucker, an extortioner, a Shylock – hard names, ... but what can a poor Jew say in return, if a Christian chuses to abuse him?
>
> (Cumberland, *The Jew*: 6)

> Good Jew or bad, rich Jew or poor, tyrant or slave, money was almost bound to be at the root of his problem.
>
> (Rosenberg: 262)

In Lewis's *The Monk*, the Wandering Jew is a combined supernatural-scientific figure who furnishes a memorable reminder about the Millennium and is crucial to Protestantism's attempts to define the relationship with its own paternity. In Godwin's *St. Leon* (1799), however, the Wandering Jew heralds the advent of the modern era and thus anticipates pressing contemporary religious, political, and especially, economic matters. As Maggie Kilgour has insightfully noted about Godwin's experiments within the Gothic genre, it is there that he 'extends the Protestant tradition of self-scrutiny into a critique of Protestant bourgeois values' (*Rise*: 11). Kilgour specifically foregrounds Godwin's concern with unchecked individualism and notes his contribution to the tradition that extends to Stoker's *Dracula*:

> The location of authority within the individual, rather than in external systems, is suspected of leading to rampant and anti-social individualism, as is most clearly shown in satires of religious enthusiasm and non-conformity, such as Hogg's and Brockden Brown's. The gothic villain is frequently an example of the modern materialistic individual taken to an extreme, at which he becomes an egotistical and wilful threat to social unity and order: even Dracula, who is obviously a holdover from a foreign past, is, as Harker notes with admiration, a good modern businessman, who 'would have made a wonderful solicitor.' (*Rise*: 11–12)

Building on Kilgour's comments, I will suggest that Godwin's foremost cautionary warning in *St. Leon* involves what he perceives to be Britain's increasing Judaization at the eighteenth-century fin de siècle. Godwin implies that in its extreme aspect as hyper-capitalist, industrialist, and materialist, bourgeois Protestant Britain is being converted to values that are stereotypically associated with Jews. This transition in the domain of capitalist activity is intimated by William Reddy in his book *Money and Liberty*. Significant evidence exists, according to Reddy, that suggests that British élites were learning 'between about 1780 and 1820, to invest money in a thoroughly capitalist manner: "capitalist" in the strict sense of seeking to maximize return through the transformation of production methods' (12). The emphasis on returns in 'this developing capitalist and credit economy, a scheme based on market forces' (Henderson: 40) resembled the practice of usury that had long been associated with the Jews. Given this trend, Godwin suggests that the British nation has figuratively sold its soul and willingly embraced the demonic, anti-Christian, and anti-family values of the extortionist Jews mentioned in his 1817 novel *Mandeville: A Tale of the Seventeenth Century in England* (1:140–1).

In the figure of St Leon, his eponymous and ambiguous protagonist, Godwin portrays the unchecked individualist/scientist as a vampiric Wandering Jew who is 'suffered, with accursed and unnatural appetite, to feed on the vitals' of his loving family and countrymen (114).[15] Godwin's graphic representation of avarice as a type of poison that infects individual British bodies and the national body politic (130), and as a form of parasitism where 'a secret worm gnaw[s] at...[one's] vitals' (448), anticipates vampirism as a mode of Judaization in Bram Stoker's *Dracula*. St Leon is also a blood brother to Count Dracula in two other ways. First of all, both are Faustian figures. Stoker suggests that Count Dracula may have exchanged his soul for the knowledge he obtained from the devil at the Scholomance (302),[16] and St Leon exchanges his soul for knowledge of 'the great secret of nature, the *opus magnum*, in its two grand and inseparable branches, the art of multiplying gold, and of defying the inroads of infirmity and death' (1). Second, Count Dracula and St Leon are eth(n)ically affiliated as both are figured as vampiric Wandering Jews. While, as I will discuss, distinctions exist between them in terms of the degree of their immorality and the nature of their vampirism – St Leon is a *figurative* vampire while Dracula is an *actual* vampire – Godwin's creation of a parasitic, loveless, and materialist Wandering Jew helps, ultimately, to make Dracula possible.

Godwin was probably the most culturally, historically, and politically aware Gothic novelist of his age. He was well-versed in the Gothic tradition and acquainted with the Wandering Jew's various literary incarnations. He had read both Schiller's *The Ghost-Seer* and Lewis's *The Monk* prior to writing *St. Leon* (Clemit, Introduction: x, n.16), a variety of other *Schauerroman*, and Ann Radcliffe's *The Italian* (Kelly, *English*: 118). In terms of his political activities, Godwin was present at the famous lecture at the Old Jewry Chapel on 4 November 1789 given to the Revolutionary Society by the political radical

and Dissenter Richard Price (Godwin, *Enquiry*: 10). He had also read the conspiracy theories of Barruel and Robison while composing *St. Leon* (Clemit,
Introduction: xix) and, as I will illustrate, he appears to have been fairly
knowledgeable about the history of alchemical science and its cabalistic connections. Godwin channels all of this knowledge into *St. Leon*, a novel set
against the backdrop of the sixteenth-century religious wars but which condemns the prevalent British values of the 1790s. In Godwin's own unique
brand of demonic semiotics, the new modern age is, for all intents and purposes, 'Jewish' in its preoccupations. Indeed, St Leon's spiritual regression
mirrors the historical shift from an age of honour and chivalry to a new,
modern age characterized by the worship of 'craft, dissimulation, corruption, and commerce' (26). As it is the Wandering Jew who provides the tools
necessary for survival and success in this new era, it is suggested that his
co-religionists are naturally at home within it.

Set in the sixteenth century during the Protestant Reformation and while
the Spanish Inquisition is still in operation, *St. Leon* is a novel of ideas. It
chronicles the materialistic corruption of Count Reginald de St Leon, an
exiled French nobleman who exchanges the feudal, spiritual values of
chivalry and honour, as represented by his heroic actions with King Francis I
at the Field of the Cloth of Gold in 1520 (480, n. 4), for a materialist obsession with gold. The first stage in St Leon's fall involves his addiction to 'gam-
ing' (27), an activity long associated with the Jews and their endeavours in
financial speculation. St Leon's family suffers as a result of this all-consuming
vice. They starve while their father becomes a figurative vampire who 'is
suffered, with accursed and unnatural appetite, to feed on the vitals of all...
[he] love[s]' (114). St Leon preys upon his loving Christian family.

St Leon however reforms, and for six years he and his family live in a stable
'state of peace and tranquility' (124). This changes, however, after the arrival
of a mysterious stranger named Signor Francesco Zampieri who hails from
Venice (124). True to tradition, Godwin's accursed wanderer possesses a compelling mesmerizing ability coupled with a superhuman/inhuman nature:

> His eye-beam sat upon your countenance, and seemed to look through
> you. You wished to escape from its penetrating power, but you had not the
> strength to move. I began to feel as if it were some mysterious and superior
> being in human form, and not a mortal, with whom I was concerned. (136)

Like the traditional Wandering Jew of legend and Matthew Lewis's literary
version of that figure, Godwin's Zampieri has known people long since dead
and been an eye-witness at crucial historic events which transpired over a
century earlier (141).

St Leon subsequently exchanges his soul for the *elixir vitae* and the secret
science recipe for 'multiplying gold' (160). The traditional legend of the
Wandering Jew is thus abrogated in this exchange as 'Zampieri' actually dies

off after relating his secrets to St Leon. Godwin suggests that St Leon's act of exchanging his soul for the secrets of alchemical conversion and the ability to make endless amounts of gold involves his conversion along religious and ethical lines. A once moral Christian is effectively and unnaturally transformed into an immoral Jew. Moreover, St Leon assumes the mantle of the *Wandering* Jew in this instance and, as such, he epitomizes moral accursedness in the Christian worldview. His transformation into a Mammon-obsessed monster, however, is tragically forecast in the countenance of the Wandering Jew whose fate, by way of their secret compact, he essentially assumes. St Leon is confronted with his own fateful future in his initial reading of the Wandering Jew's physiognomy. St Leon observes, 'Ruined and squalid as he appeared, I thought I could perceive traces in his countenance of what had formerly been daring enterprise, profound meditation, and generous humanity' (124). St Leon perceives the Wandering Jew's radical and tragic transformation from mor(t)al to immor(t)al capitalist.

In the light of the Wandering Jew's assumed name – Zampieri – and a subsequent episode featuring a New Christian, Godwin implies that the Wandering Jew was once a Christian who was duped, like St Leon, into exchanging fates with the man who may perhaps have been the actual Wandering Jew of legend. Although the surname Zampieri signified an 'exoticism of a particularly Semitic kind' in eighteenth-century literature as it began with the letter 'z' (Michasiw: 270), it also carried with it strong Christian associations as it was the surname of the artist who came to be known as Domenichino (1581–1641). This famous painter of Christian subjects and chief Vatican architect was also a painter of landscapes that were often invoked in Gothic literature.[17] In further support of the speculation that Godwin's Zampieri is a Christian who converted to Judaism, St Leon recounts a significant encounter with a New Christian named Mordecai who helps St Leon escape the Inquisition. According to St Leon, Mordecai's countenance betrays the fact that he is a *New* Christian:

> I perceived, by certain indications in the countenance of my host, that he was by parentage a Jew. I presently concluded, that he was what in Spain they denominate a new Christian; for that otherwise he would not have been allowed to reside at large in a Spanish city. But, upon that supposition, I did not believe that Christianity was very deeply mingled up in him with the vital principle: the converts of the inquisition are not conspicuous for their sincerity. (342)

In this ironic and complex scene, St Leon articulates the traditional Christian view – and fear – that Jews may never actually convert to the Christian faith. Such signs are not found in Zampieri's countenance, thus supporting the idea that he was originally a Christian who later 'fell' into stereotypically Jewish pursuits.

True to his self-delusive nature, St Leon remains blind to his association with Mordecai in this episode. Anti-Semitic stereotypes abound as Godwin forges a decisive link between the Wandering Jew and his co-religionists. While 'Zampieri' describes himself as 'Hated by mankind, hunted from the face of the earth, pursued by every atrocious calumny, without a country, without a roof, without a friend' (127), Mordecai laments the general state of the Jewish community saying, 'We poor Jews ... [are] hunted on the face of the earth, the abhorrence and execration of mankind' (345). Notably, this systematic, longstanding persecution does not prevent St Leon from threatening to turn Mordecai over to the Inquisition and to kill Mordecai's daughter (344). Ever self-interested, St Leon reminds Mordecai that it is not in his interest to betray St Leon as the Inquisitors would not look well on a New Christian. He subsequently offers Mordecai six hundred pistoles as an added inducement. The threat and bribe achieve their desired effect as St Leon notes, 'While I talked to him, I easily perceived that the arguments I used, which produced the most sensible effect upon his features, were those of the dangers arising to him from betraying me, and the reward of six hundred pistoles which I promised him in the event of my success' (343). This episode reinforces the stereotype of the Jew as an avaricious usurer 'whose heart is in his bags' (Cumberland, *The Jew*: 11).

In his narrative treatment of the Spanish Inquisition, an institution which had its origins in Roman Catholic intolerance, Godwin combines a condemnation of the spiritual and economic Judaization of Britain with an indictment of what he suggests is that nation's increasingly intolerant political views. Through comments articulated by his immortal wanderer who has seen much of history due to his unnaturally long life, Godwin suggests that the British persecution of radicals in 1794 (Clemit, *Godwinian*: 88) and the passing of the Suspension of Habeas Corpus Act in 1798 (Clemit, Introduction: xiii) constitute a type of 'British Inquisition'. In the words of St Leon:

> ... human affairs, like the waves of the ocean, are merely in a state of ebb and flow: 'there is nothing new under the sun': *two centuries* perhaps *after* Philip the Second shall be gathered to his ancestors [he died in 1598], men shall learn over again to persecute each other for conscience sake; other anabaptists or levellers shall furnish pretexts for new persecutions; *other inquisitors shall arise in the most enlightened tracts of Europe.* (338; emphasis added)

This is a laudable and courageous critique of 1790s Britain as it daringly suggests that political persecution was not limited in Europe to France. Ironically, Godwin's unsympathetic portraits of the Jews and New Christians who were persecuted by the Spanish Inquisitors detracts from his critique and even aligns him with the Inquisitors he claims to despise. Godwin forges an equation between the vampiric, Mammon-obsessed Jews in *St. Leon* and the Spanish Inquisitors who are described as 'insatiable bloodsuckers' (330). To the latter anti-Catholic image, Godwin adds the portrait of a bloodthirsty Charles V (26, 439), the Holy Roman Emperor who was financed by Jewish capital and fought against Protestants during this era of religious wars.[18] As in Lewis's *The Monk*, Roman Catholics and Jews are portrayed by Godwin as doppelgänger sinners. In both works, these religious forefathers of Anglicanism/Protestantism are depicted as equally barbarian and tyrannical.

To enter the text of *St. Leon* is to enter an uncanny and labyrinthine Gothic house of mirrors populated by bloodthirsty monsters who function as doppelgängers to St Leon. The question of identity looms large and although St Leon sometimes recognizes his uncanny resemblance to his various doubles, he also suffers at times from a serious lack of self-knowledge and even delusion, so that he remains blind to their association with him. Subsequent to forging his secret compact, however, St Leon does recognize himself as a monster (176, 211) who is neither human nor moral and has succumbed to the poison of avarice. Lamenting his miserable and isolated fate, he states:

> How unhappy the wretch, the monster rather let me say, who is without an equal; who looks through the world, and in the world and cannot find a brother; who is endowed with attributes which no living being participates with him; and who is therefore cut off for ever from all cordiality and confidence, can never unbend himself, but lives the solitary, joyless tenant of a prison, the materials of which are emeralds and rubies! (211)

In another rare moment of self-awareness, St Leon says of himself, 'I still bore the figure and lineaments of a human creature; but I knew that I was not what I seemed' (356). In this monstrous, parasitic capacity, he is associated both with Bethlem Gabor, an illustrious Hungarian nobleman and soldier who is notorious for his anti-Christian, 'sanguinary' exploits (435), and the demonic Spanish Inquisitors who are described in this novel as 'insatiable bloodsuckers' (330).

One of Godwin's primary goals in this morality tale about money and the monsters it makes of those who worship it, is to condemn the impact of Jewish greed on Christian domestic ties. St Leon's devoted wife Marguerite, probably assuming the voice of Mary Wollstonecraft, Godwin's deceased former wife, articulates this key theme:

> The gift of unbounded wealth, if you possess it, and with wealth, apparently at least, distinction and greatness, is too powerful a temptation ... It destroys that communion of spirit which is the soul of the marriage-tie. A consort should be a human being and an equal. But to this equality and simple humanity it is no longer in your power to return. (209)

The mysterious stranger manages to corrupt St Leon by separating him from his beloved wife and exhorting him to make a decision without her advice (126). This loveless and egoistic Wandering Jew, therefore, assumes the position in *St. Leon* as one who threatens the British nation's Christian 'family values'.

The vow of silence that St Leon makes, once he is figuratively converted to the status of Jewish capitalist, further removes him from human society. After years of living in this anti-social manner, St Leon offers one of the novel's most tragic passages which makes the damnable nature of secrecy clear. After the death of his daughter Julia for which he is responsible, St Leon deems himself 'a monster that did not deserve to exist' (363) and denounces his own knowledge of the secret sciences:

> Fatal legacy! atrocious secrets of medicine and chemistry! every day opened to my astonished and terrified sight a wider prospect of their wasteful effects! A common degree of penetration might have shown me, that secrets of this character cut off their possessor from the dearest ties of human existence, and render him a solitary, cold, self-centered individual; his heart no longer able to pour itself into the bosom of a mistress or a friend; his bosom no longer qualified to receive upon equal terms the overflowing of a kindred heart. (362–3)

A victim of self-delusion, however, St Leon long hopes that this knowledge may be beneficial to mankind. Although the Wandering Jew's initial description of this knowledge is clearly geared to appeal to St Leon's nobler aspect (126), the Wandering Jew later highlights its ambivalent nature when he says that it is both 'God-given' and that it 'might render its possessor the universal plague or the universal tyrant of mankind' (135). St Leon, however, chooses to believe in its potential benefits. Despite the fact that the Neapolitan inquisitor who seeks the Wandering Jew prior to his death informs St Leon that 'the welfare of Christendom ... [demands] that the criminal, and the memory of his offences, should be buried together' (147), St Leon consistently refuses to acknowledge the dangers connected to the mysterious stranger.

St Leon's tendency to be bedazzled by mysterious, melancholic men is again played out in his fascination with another of his doubles, Bethlem Gabor. Critics have generally described Gabor as 'the novel's most Gothic creation' (Lévy, *Philosophical*: 59) beside whom 'the other characters pale into insignificance' (Birkhead: 114).[19] Although St Leon defends Gabor claiming he suffered a 'sanguinary catastrophe' when his entire family had been killed while he was away on a military excursion (400), St Leon's son Charles – the Christian voice of moderation and reason – sees only Gabor's figuratively vampiric, anti-Christian activities. He portrays Gabor as an 'intrepid, indefatigable and *sanguinary* partisan ... [who] had been the author of greater mischiefs to the Christian cause, than any of the immediate servants of the sultan of Constantinople' (435; emphasis added). St Leon's own anti-Christian activities are also observed by his estranged son who explains how the 'notorious Chatillon' (St Leon in disguise) is 'an infamous impostor, who, by his machinations...preserved the Turkish provinces of Hungary from being conquered by the Christian arms'. Neither delusive nor demonically possessed by avarice like his father, Charles regards the secret sciences as a Satanically associated and inspired domain of study. He says of the impostor Chatillon:

> The man is moreover a magician, the pretended or real possessor of the philosopher's stone. He is therefore doubly worthy of death, first as a traitor, the abettor and comforter of the common enemy of the Christian faith, and, secondly, as a dealer in the black art, and *a man notoriously sold and delivered over to the devil.* (472; emphasis added)

While the Wandering Jew claims that his knowledge of the secret sciences is God-given, Charles identifies it with a more sinister source. The figure St Leon perceives as a 'venerable sage' (136) who appeals to his generosity, is considered by Charles to be a diabolic parasite who knows the nature of human weakness and preys on his 'generous [Christian] host' (143).

In the introduction to the Oxford edition of *St. Leon*, Patricia Clemit explains that Godwin 'acknowledged as the inspiration for his tale a satirical work entitled *Hermippus Redivivus: Or, The Sage's Triumph Over Old Age and the Grave*' which was published in 1744. She hypothesizes, however, that 'another of these tales, which Godwin did not acknowledge, may have supplied the plot and title of *St. Leon*' (x). Clemit relates the tale as follows:

> ... [it is] the history of a fourteenth-century Rosicrucian, Nicholas Flamel, ... [which] gives two versions of how he gained his extraordinary wealth. According to some, he learned the secret of the philosopher's stone from a Jewish physician in the Spanish town of St. Leon; according to others, he defrauded Jewish refugees. The moral uncertainty surrounding Flamel's history may have provided the starting-point for Godwin's sceptical analysis of benevolent ideals. (x)

The Jewish connection in this tale and the ambivalence surrounding the knowledge of the philosopher's stone are noteworthy. They hint at the Jewish origins of the alchemical enterprise[20] and the moral ambivalence that was, even during the Enlightenment, attached to this knowledge. Indeed, Godwin's Wandering Jew articulates this ambivalence when he explains its origins as both God-given but potentially demonic depending on the uses to which it is put. I would like to suggest, however, on the basis of an allusion in the novel and the fact that Godwin's knowledge in this domain was far broader than critics to date have credited, that the life story of another significant alchemist lurks in the shadows of Godwin's novel. This theory might also help to explain the novel's title.

Cornelius Agrippa's name is mentioned in *St. Leon* by a Spaniard during a mini-inquisition of St Leon. After St Leon's mysterious wealth draws attention to him, he is pursued by a Spaniard who subjects him to an interrogation. The Spaniard asks if St Leon knew Cornelius Agrippa who died in Grenoble about twelve years earlier (307). As St Leon remarks at the beginning of that chapter that nineteen years had elapsed since his marriage to Marguerite de Damville (301) and as they had been married for seven years prior to 1544 when the 'Wandering Jew' arrived at their home in Constance (124), exactly 12 years had, in fact, elapsed between the time that St Leon encountered this mysterious stranger and his conversation with the Spaniard. Cornelius Agrippa, however, actually died in 1535 – and not 1544, as the events in *St. Leon* suggest, or 1534, as Godwin reports in his 1834 work *Lives of the Necromancers* (195) – in Grenoble. Perhaps Godwin's historical source was incorrect or he simply took poetic licence and manipulated the dates for his story's sake. Whatever the case, the dates do add up in the novel, lending some credibility to the theory that the Wandering Jew who tempts St Leon is Cornelius Agrippa. However, Agrippa actually died in Grenoble as the Spaniard states and not in Constance where the mysterious stranger visits St Leon and passes away. An explanation for this disjunction, however, is provided in the text. Before his death, the wanderer suggests that his place of burial may not be known for certain: 'My name shall be buried with me in the grave; nor shall any one who has hitherto known me, know how, at what time, or on what spot of earth, I shall terminate my existence' (125–6).

These dates and details aside, I am not suggesting that Godwin set out to use the Agrippa story in a historically realistic fashion. As Godwin's more factual account of Agrippa in his *Lives of the Necromancers* concedes, in fact, 'historic' details about Agrippa's life are extremely difficult to come by – instead, legends abound. In the light of this, Godwin seems to reference Agrippa's life more tenuously in *St. Leon*, while retaining the suggestion and indictment of his protagonist's Judaization. Notably, numerous points of contact exist between the Wandering Jew of legend and Agrippa, a figurative Wandering Jew. One of 'the two great occultists of the sixteenth century', Agrippa was a persecuted 'wandering scholar' (Wilson, *Occult*: 233) who travelled, according to Colin Wilson, 'like the Wandering Jew' (238). Perhaps most intriguingly, a famous legend involving the secret sciences recounts how Agrippa, like St Leon, actually encountered the Wandering Jew in the year 1525. That figure of legend is then reputed to have visited Agrippa in his alchemical laboratory in Florence where he

...begged Agrippa to show him his childhood sweetheart in a magic mirror.[21] Agrippa asked him to count off the decades since the girl died so that he could wave his wand for each decade; when the Jew reached 149, Agrippa began to feel dizzy; but the Jew went on numbering them until the mirror showed a scene 1,510 years earlier, in Palestine. The girl, Rebecca, appeared, and the Jew was so moved that he tried to speak to her – which Agrippa had strictly forbidden. The mirror immediately clouded over and the Jew fainted. On reviving, he identified himself as the Jew who struck Jesus when he was carrying the cross, and who has been condemned to walk the earth ever since. (238)

Agrippa's patron, for a time, was Charles V, the Holy Roman Emperor financed by Jewish capital who is negatively portrayed in *St. Leon*. Agrippa was also 'fascinated by the Kabbalah' (235), particularly the *Zohar* which was written around 1280 by a Spanish Jew, Moses *de Leon* (233), who, very significantly, shares the same surname as Godwin's eponymous protagonist. It was Agrippa's widely read treatise *On Occult Philosophy* (1531), in fact, that 'was largely responsible for the mistaken association of the Kabbalah in the Christian world with numerology and witchcraft' (Scholem, 'Kabbalah': 644). As de Leon's *Zohar* forms the groundwork for Agrippa's philosophy on magical-science, it is conceivable that Godwin adopted the name 'Leon' for his protagonist with this association in mind. It would be especially suitable given the strong Jewish–secret science bond forged in Godwin's novel. The combination of the Catholic 'St' with 'Leon', however, situates this protagonist at the crossroads between Catholicism and Judaism. These warring forces are key to St Leon's psychological torment and are also representative of the legendary Wandering Jew's position as a religious convert, the role St Leon assumes in this novel. In his presentation of an unrepentant, diabolical Wandering Jew, however, Godwin reverses the scenario: St Leon is a lapsed Christian who is converted to what is figured as a Jewish, Mammon-based religion. In this capacity, his use of magical science for monetary ends parallels Agrippa's. According to one story, Agrippa paid a bill 'in counterfeit money, which at the time of payment appeared of sterling value, but in a few days after became pieces of horn and worthless shells' (Godwin, *Lives*: 196). St Leon's shifting attitude towards secret science also followed Agrippa's. While St Leon becomes increasingly penitent, Agrippa abandons magic in favour of theology later in life. In 1530, the latter published a curious, nihilistic book in Antwerp entitled *On the Vanity of Sciences and Arts* whose central thesis is that knowledge only brings disillusionment and the recognition of man's fundamental ignorance (Wilson, *Occult*: 237–8). Despised by many monks in Europe, he died a lonely, tragic death.

Like Lewis's *The Monk*, *St. Leon* explores the issue of religious paternity and the sins of the fathers being visited upon the sons. Lewis also suggests that generational cycles may be broken. In a fascinating inversion at *St. Leon*'s conclusion, St Leon's son Charles, 'the gallant chevalier de Damville' (446), who is now older in appearance than his father thanks to the latter's use of

the *elixir vitae*, speaks as a father figure to St Leon. An honourable and honest Christian man, Charles laments the sixteenth-century religious wars
fought among Christians across Europe. Addressing St Leon, Charles states:

> Heaven knows how willingly I would have spent my blood for the over-
> throw of Mahomet and his blasphemous impieties. To me this is not per-
> mitted; to you it is. I shall be engaged in the painful scenes of civil
> contention between Christian and Christian, misguided and inflamed by
> the human inventions of Luther and of Calvin. (444)

Despite the fact that St Leon ends his narrative as a weary man who reviles
bloody wars and the demonic gold which perpetuates them (446), the suggestion is made that battles with non-Christians remain worth undertaking.
As a Wandering Jew figure plagued by the 'secret worm [of avarice] gnawing
at ... [his] vitals' (448), such a battle remains, for St Leon, tragically internal.
In his words, however, there are still things 'worth living for' (478).
Somewhat paradoxically, he is 'the [Christian] hero's father' (478), and this
suggests hope for the future in the form of the Christian bourgeois ideal of
marriage and family. In the union of Charles and Pandora at *St. Leon's*
conclusion, Godwin presents the restoration of an Edenic Christian past
dominated by 'family values', a similar state from which St Leon fell when
he underwent Jewish conversion. In St Leon's ostracism from society at
the novel's end, Godwin offers a tragic yet hopeful cautionary tale of social
re-conversion to Christian ideals.

Spanish 'Works of Blood': *Melmoth the Wanderer*

Charles Robert Maturin's *Melmoth the Wanderer* (1820) relates the tale of the
Faustian John Melmoth who sells his soul to the devil in exchange for pro-
longed life. As a result of dabbling in the secret sciences, he wanders for one
hundred and fifty years in search of someone with whom to exchange fates.
Melmoth has been accurately described by Mario Praz as 'a kind of
Wandering Jew crossed with Byronic vampire ('" ce pâle et ennuyé Melmoth"
Baudelaire called him)' (76). Rather curiously, another tale about the
Wandering Jew which was published in 1820, also establishes a connection
between that figure and the vampire. John Galt's *The Wandering Jew: Or the
Travels and Observations of Hareach the Prolonged*, pseudonymously published
in London under the name T. Clark, relates the cryptic, Gothic-style tale of
an unknown traveller – later revealed to be the Wandering Jew – who dies
mysteriously and then, vampire-like, abandons his coffin in the middle of
the night (Anderson, *Legend*: 149). While it is debatable whether Maturin
had read this work or not, Galt's tale illustrates how the figures of the vampire and the Wandering Jew were becoming increasingly identified in British
literature in the early nineteenth century.

Maturin's contribution to the development of the vampiric Wandering Jew in British Gothic literature is extremely intriguing. Although John Melmoth may be loosely classified as such a spectral figure, he is certainly not Jewish. Moreover, he is projected onto a series of doubles and subplots through which his story is indirectly developed. Maturin's contribution to this figure's evolution is perhaps best illustrated in his representation of several of Melmoth's Jewish doubles. In Volume Three of this 'dungeon of a book' (Baldick, 'Introduction', *Melmoth*: xix) set while the Spanish Inquisition is still in operation, the reader is introduced to two Jewish characters named Solomon and Adonijah. In combination, these figures might be described as Count Dracula's literary forefathers: Solomon threatens to enact a novel and bloody form of religious conversion and Adonijah is a Gothic immortal who resembles the Wandering Jew of legend. Like Lewis in *The Monk*, Maturin foregrounds the question of Christian religious paternity in his treatment of the Wandering Jew figure. As I will illustrate, however, Maturin is also indebted to Godwin for his treatment of the theme of religious conversion. In *Melmoth the Wanderer*, that fear is rendered through the figure of a demonic Jew who threatens Judaization by way of circumcision, which is portrayed as a pagan and barbaric ritual practice. Castration anxiety is clearly invoked, therefore, in Maturin's act of sexualizing the Gothic novel's popular spectre of Judaization.

Indeed, a vision of what Leslie Fiedler describes as the Ur-Gentile nightmare surfaces in the novel's preliminary Jewish portrait of a New Christian named Solomon. According to Fiedler,

> [w]hen the Gentile dreams the Jew in his midst … he dreams him as the vengeful and villainous Father: Shylock or Fagin, the Bearded Terror threatening some poor full-grown goy with a knife, or inducting some guileless Gentile kid into a life of crime. But Shylock and Fagin are shadows cast upon the Christian world by that First Jewish Father, Abraham, who is to them circumcizer and sacrificer rolled into one – castrator, in short. (*To*: 177)

With his 'red wolfish eyes' and terrifying 'sacrificial knife' (249), Solomon is introduced in the classic crypto-Abraham role as he prepares to circumcise his son to whom he has just confessed that he is actually a Jew and, therefore, a Catholic impostor. A castration fear clearly energizes this sexualized Blood Libel episode as Alonzo, the terrified unseen onlooker and narrator of the tale, describes Solomon as a type of fiery Old Testament deity enraged by the fact that his New Christian son does not bear the mark of his Jewish faith. The scene is richly described and symbolically loaded: the sorcerer-like Solomon stands beside his Hebrew Bible with a cock fastened to the leg of the table (presumably awaiting ritual slaughter) upon which the instruments necessary to his demonic sorcery lie arranged. Solomon's ethnicity is unmistakeable in his stereotyped features. He is described as a 'man of middle age, ... whose physiognomy had something peculiar in it, even to the eye of a Spaniard, from the clustering darkness of his eye-brows, his prominent nose, and a certain lustre in the balls of his eyes' (246). The mesmerizing gaze traditionally attributed to the Wandering Jew is adopted in Solomon's brief portrait.

Alonzo's expectation of 'some horrible sacrifice' (244) in this terrifying scene is not actually fulfilled. A more gruesome scene follows on its heels, however, for Alonzo witnesses the grotesque murder and dismemberment of a victim of the Inquisition later that evening on the streets of Madrid. As the juxtaposition of the two scenes suggests, Judaism is associated with both secret society sorcery and what Maturin describes as the Catholic Inquisition's 'work of blood' (255). In comparison with Catholicism's public blood baths, however, Judaism's bloody rituals are portrayed as private and limited in terms of their number of 'victims'. Although Alonzo is terrified by the potential bloody conversion ritual involving Solomon's son and he denounces Solomon as a type of infectious vampire, a 'Jew *innate*, an impostor, – a wretch, who, drawing sustenance from the bosom of our holy mother the church, had turned her nutriment to poison, and attempted to infuse that poison into the lips of his son' (249), Alonzo preserves his most gruesome denunciations for Roman Catholicism. Indeed, in his presentation of endless scenes 'alike horrible to humanity, and disgraceful to civilization' (255), Maturin spares no venom in his condemnation of Catholicism as a benighted, superstitious faith in *Melmoth the Wanderer*. In the face of such horrors, Alonzo yearns to escape to 'some Protestant country, beyond the reach of the Inquisition' (259). Alonzo's religious standpoint is not surprising given the fact that Maturin was an eccentric Dublin-born clergyman who always proudly reminded everyone of his Huguenot descent.

When the inquisitors arrive at Solomon's house to remove his son to a convent and away from what they refer to as Solomon's 'pestilential influence' (261), Alonzo makes his way through an underground passage to the secret home of another Jew named Adonijah. This learned man's tremendous antiquity and his role as a tragic and undying witness of death associate him with the Wandering Jew of legend. It is, in part, his role as a revered patriarch in Maturin's graphic narrative to assess and inveigh against the monstrous, bloodthirsty nature of the infernal Inquisition. Comparing his underground Jewish world with the realm of Catholic Madrid above ground, Adonijah tells Alonzo:

Within this apartment I have passed the term of sixty years, and dost thou shudder to visit it for a moment? These be the skeletons of bodies, but in the den thou hast escaped from were the skeletons of perished souls. Here are relics of the wrecks of the caprices of nature, but thou art come from where the cruelty of man, permanent and persevering, unrelenting and unmitigated, hath never failed to leave the proofs of its power in abortive intellects, crippled frames, distorted creeds, and ossified hearts. Moreover, there are around thee parchments and charts scrawled as it were with the blood of man, but, were it even so, could a thousand such volumes cause such terror to the human eye, as a page of the history of thy prison, written as it is in blood, drawn, not from the frozen veins of the dead, but from the bursting hearts of the living. (265–6)

Surrounded in his subterranean apartment by skulls and several parchment scrolls that appear to be inscribed with human blood, Adonijah essentially represents the old Jewish law, Catholicism's buried past. Although Alonzo initially believes he has encountered a 'grand wizard' (263) and an agent of Satan (264), and expects to be 'the involuntary witness of some infernal orgie' (263), he later provides another portrait of Adonijah: 'my eyes hung in reverence on the hoary majesty of his patriarchal figure, and I felt as if I beheld an embodied representation of the old law in all its stern simplicity – the unbending grandeur, and primeval antiquity' (267). Maturin's portrait of Judaism is undeniably ambivalent. Respectable in its stern, ancient, simplicity, it is also reprehensible in its primitive ritual practices. In comparison with the idolatrous and barbarian religiosity of Roman Catholicism, however, Judaism is represented as semi-civilized. Although a tremendous dread of forced and bloody religious conversion infuses this episode and Alonzo fears for his life at the hands of Adonijah, he remains unharmed. Instead, his energies ('blood') are employed by the patriarch to copy old manuscripts containing strange, fascinating tales.

Adonijah's domestic arrangement and location in a subterranean 'vault' has a sinister cast. Surrounded by the skeletons of four dead family members 'in a kind of upright coffin, that gave their bony emptiness a kind of ghastly and imperative prominence, as if they were the real and rightful tenants of that singular apartment' (263), Adonijah's macabre home anticipates the morbid domain of Castle Dracula which is inhabited by coffin-dwellers. The graphic description of 'human and brute abortions, in all their states of anomalous and deformed construction, not preserved in spirits, but standing in the ghastly nakedness of their white diminutive bones' (263) also invokes the Blood Libel. This scene echoes that featuring the menacing, circumcising Solomon and his son. The threat Jews pose to innocent children, however, is rendered more graphic in *Dracula*, where vampires actually consume children (39, 177).[22]

Given the prevalent anti-Catholic keynote of *Melmoth the Wanderer*, it is not surprising that Maturin establishes links between the theme of vampirism and the Catholics, rather than the Jews, in this novel. Chris Baldick has noted the vampire theme in *Melmoth* in the bloody tale of Guzman's family (Baldick, Introduction, *Melmoth*: xviii) which Marie Roberts has suggested is based on Polidori's *Vampyre*, published a year prior to *Melmoth the*

Wanderer (*Gothic*: 136). Another literary precursor for this scene might actually be Godwin's *St. Leon* where the avaricious eponymous protagonist figuratively vampirizes his family. A wealthy Catholic named Guzman initially refuses communication with his sister Ines and her 'heretic [Protestant] family', the Walbergs (401). Guzman later alters the terms of their relationship and sets the loving and loyal Walberg family up in luxury. Upon Guzman's death, however, the Catholic Church deceptively steals his fortune, thus rendering the expectant Walbergs penniless.[23] The ensuing events indict Roman Catholicism as a figuratively vampiric religion whose abuses are monstrous and barbarian. As they begin to starve, Walberg's faithful son Everhard repeatedly sells his blood to a surgeon in order to feed the family. This feast of metaphorical cannibalism is decisively brought home in Maturin's description of Everhard's arrival at the frugal family meal:

> 'Squabbling about your supper?' cried Everhard, bursting among them with a wild and feeble laugh, – 'Why, here's enough for to-morrow – and to-morrow.' And he flung indeed ample means for two day's subsistence on the table, but he looked *paler and paler*. The hungry family devoured the hoard, and forgot to ask the cause of his increasing paleness, and obviously diminished strength. (420)

The memorably grotesque description of the dying, bleeding Everhard could be that of a vampire victim:

> The snow-white limbs of Everhard were extended as if for the inspection of a sculptor, and moveless, as if they were indeed what they resembled, in hue and symmetry, those of a marble statue. His arms were tossed above his head, and the blood was trickling fast from the opened veins of both, – his bright and curled hair was clotted with the red stream that flowed from his arms, – his lips were blue, and a faint and fainter moan issued from them as his mother hung over him. (422)

As in the portrait of the Jewish knife-wielding Solomon who is introduced in a classic menacing stance as he prepares to circumcise his son, Walberg later becomes a monstrous, vampiric, crypto-Abraham who threatens to kill his children. This devastating episode may be described as the tale of Little Red Riding Hood gone nightmarishly bad. Hearing his family's groans of starvation, the wretched Walberg totters towards their beds like the Big Bad Wolf where he is supplicated by his children:

> 'Father! – father!' cried Julia, 'are these your hands? Oh let me live, and I will do any thing – any thing but' – 'Father! – dear father!' cried Ines, 'spare us! – to-morrow may bring another meal!' Maurice, the young child, sprung from his bed, and cried, clinging round his father, 'Oh, dear

father, forgive me! – but *I dreamed a wolf was in the room, and was tearing out our throats*; and, father, I cried so long, that I thought you never would come. And now – Oh God! oh God!' – as he felt the hands of the frantic wretch *grasping his throat*, – 'are *you the wolf?*' (430; emphasis added).

Walberg is reminiscent of St Leon in this instance when, due to the gambling addiction that results in his family's starvation, St Leon figuratively feeds on their vitals. In *Melmoth the Wanderer*'s haunting hunger scene, the faithful son adopts the traditional paternal role in his attempts to help his starving family.

While Maturin's specific target in *Melmoth the Wanderer* is the brutality, idolatry, and avarice of the Catholic Church (as in Lewis's *The Monk*, it is Catholics who engage in the most grotesque and violent crimes), his Jews are, paradoxically and true to legend, wolfish scapegoats who remain suspect for their original sin of betraying and killing Christ, the sacrificial lamb. Despite the benevolence of both of Alonzo's involuntary Jewish hosts – they heartily feed him in scenes that look forward to Jonathan Harker's meals in Dracula's castle – there exists a powerful underlying fear that they may also engage in diminutive but similar 'works of blood' that violate Christian scriptural law. The Blood Libel looms large. Just as the lupine-associated Dracula, a figurative wolf in sheep's clothing, proves to be a demonic host who literalizes the fundamental eucharistic notion that 'the blood is the life', Alonzo fears that his Jewish hosts will poison and/or cannibalize him (249, 265). Like Jonathan Harker, Alonzo worries, as he crosses himself after every mouthful and says an internal prayer over every sip of wine, that his body may become a banquet upon which his 'involuntary [Jewish] host', after some ritual fattening of the calf, will feed (Stoker, *Dracula*: 51, Maturin: 249).

As Edgar Rosenberg argues with regard to Shakespeare's cut-throat Jewish character Shylock in *The Merchant of Venice*, 'From cutting out the Christian's heart', an act committed in Chaucer's 'The Prioress's Tale', 'it was only a step to feeding on it [*The Merchant of Venice* II.v.: 14–15]; and occasionally the charge of mutilation carried with it obscure implications of cannibalism' (25). In Bram Stoker's *Dracula*, the feeding frenzy of the debauched and sexualized Wandering Jew, intent on infecting and converting Christians to his demonic religion, begins. Charles Robert Maturin's *Melmoth the Wanderer* helps to pave the way for Count Dracula by rendering the threat of Judaization more physically, and even sexually, violent.

5

Britain, Vampire Empire: Fin-de-Siècle Fears and Bram Stoker's *Dracula*

> ...the Jews presented a kind of grotesque mirror of the imperial powers; they were *secret colonizers*.
>
> (George Vacher de Lapouge, qtd. in Pick, 'Powers': 107)

One of the more important contributions to *Dracula* scholarship in recent years has been the examination of Bram Stoker's bloodthirsty Count as a stereotypical Jewish figure. Although this reading has helped to elucidate both the specific nature of the vampire's threat to fin-de-siècle England and the prevalent Christian thematics and iconography of Stoker's novel, literary critics have failed to consider Count Dracula's consanguineous connections with other characters within the Gothic literary tradition. Adapting Royce MacGillivray's claim that Stoker created in Dracula 'a myth comparable in vitality to that of the Wandering Jew, Faust, or Don Juan' (518), I would maintain that while the aristocratic figure of Count Dracula uniquely combines all three figures, he represents the apogee in the development of the vampiric Wandering Jew in British Gothic literature. As Henry Ludlam's 1962 biography of Stoker makes clear, the Wandering Jew had long haunted Stoker's imagination. As supportive evidence, Ludlam cites Stoker's lifelong friend, writer Hall Caine, the 'Hommy-Beg' to whom *Dracula* is dedicated. Thinking back over their attempts to fit Stoker's boss, acclaimed actor Henry Irving, with a suitable dramatic role, Caine wrote, 'I remember that most of our subjects dealt with the supernatural, and that the Wandering Jew, the Flying Dutchman and the Demon Lover were themes around which our imagination[s] constantly revolved' (97).

While all three themes may be said to be compellingly combined in the narrative whirlpool that is *Dracula* – the spectral ship central to the tale of the Flying Dutchman assumes the form of the Russian Demeter that transports the Count to England via Whitby – it is interesting to note that the subject of the Wandering Jew continued to fascinate Stoker subsequent to

Dracula's publication. In one of his final works entitled *Famous Impostors* (1910), a series of essays about various historical charlatans, Stoker proves his knowledge of both the legend of the Wandering Jew and its various literary treatments in the nineteenth century. What is perhaps most intriguing is the fact that Stoker's literary examination culminates with Eugène Sue's famous novel *Le Juif Errant* (1844–45), a book that Stoker adored and a dramatic version of which, given Irving's tremendous success with Shylock, Stoker tried to persuade him to perform (Malchow: 156). Notably, Stoker also lauds Sue's novel for tapping into a prevalent and deep-seated contemporary anxiety, namely, the spread of cholera.

Stoker was well aware of the cholera epidemic as his mother had survived it in Ireland in the early 1830s and had related chilling tales about it throughout Stoker's childhood. Emulating Sue's clever narrative strategy by adapting the Jew's curse as 'the fated carrier of that dreaded pestilence' (116) to his own time, Stoker's Dracula threatens to infect England – and, more specifically, English women who thereafter exhibit prostitute-like tendencies – with vampirism, an obvious metaphor for syphilis, the sexually transmitted disease prevalent in fin-de-siècle England that may have claimed Stoker's life.[1] Another significant connection between Dracula and Stoker's Wandering Jew in *Famous Impostors* lies in their ability to regenerate themselves. Stoker's description of this capacity is significant to his vampire's conception: 'the wanderer's life is miraculously prolonged. … Each hundredth year … [he] falls into a faint so that he lies for a time unconscious. When he recovers he finds that his age is restored to that which it was when the Lord suffered' (110). While the Wandering Jew is miraculously rejuvenated so that his punishment for his mockery of Christ may be prolonged, Dracula, in keeping with the tradition of the legendary vampire, is conceived as an anti-Christ figure who prolongs his life and regains youth by way of a literally bloody ceremony that produces degeneration and death in his victims. After centuries of demonically literalizing the Eucharist by imbibing sacrificial human blood, an act that violates communal Christian brotherhood, Dracula is fittingly punished in a pseudo-Crucifixion ritual.

That Stoker's Wandering Jew should have appeared in all of his bloodthirsty, proselytizing glory at the fin de siècle is understandable given the then changing nature of both British nationalism and capitalism. With these shifts, the Judaization threat also altered dramatically. As E.J. Hobsbawm explains, 'in the period from 1880 to 1914, nationalism took a dramatic leap forward, and its ideological and political content was transformed' (142). As a novel tendency developed 'to define a nation in terms of ethnicity and especially in terms of language' (144), nationalism became right-wing, anti-foreigner, anti-socialist, and anti-liberal (142). As was the case of Germany in the 1840s the Jewish Question became increasingly bound up with the issue of national identity. According to Judith Walkowitz, anti-Semitism was 'one articulation of a rising tide of nationalism and racism orchestrated by the popular media' (203). The fact that British Jews were able to assume public office since 1855 (Ausubel: 180) and had been granted full political emancipation by 1871 (Dinur: 701) did not, therefore, signify the unconditional acceptance of Anglo-Jews into British society. Anti-Semitic stereotypes persisted and other concerns emerged and were culturally registered, particularly regarding the economy and the issue of assimilation. Notably, the push to convert the Jews continued apace in British society throughout the 1870s– in fact, it picked up during that decade in the face of growing anti-Semitism (Ragussis, *Figures*: 299) – despite the fact that conversion ceased to be a useful option to English Jews (Endelman, *Radical*: 80).

Greater scrutiny was brought to bear during this period on the joint questions of the Jewish influence on British national character and Jewish patriotism. Economic factors played an especially central role in this regard given the popular public perception that a preponderance of Jews were not only engaged with, but at the forefront of, the nation's commercial institutions. In his characterization of Anglo-Jewish employment in the mid-nineteenth century, David Vital states:

> They were not engaged in moneylending to anything like the same extent as were the Jews of eastern France. The economic roles for which they were best known were stock-jobbing and wholesale and foreign commerce – spheres which were favoured by the government in London– and trades and crafts of the middle-lower rank: silversmithery, shopkeeping, diamond polishing, tailoring, watchmaking, and the like. Those who could not set up shop of their own account engaged in peddling and trading in old clothes as did many Jews in Germany, but among these the driving tendency to escape from the lower levels of the economy was evident and likely to be approved of. (41)

As Britain became 'less the "workshop of the world" than the world's banker' (Ward: 240) and those bankers and stockbrokers were popularly perceived to be Jews, that community was frequently scapegoated for the nation's economic volatility. And Britain certainly experienced economic volatility throughout the mid-nineteenth century. While it is true to say that she retained 'increasing industrial and imperial hegemony' throughout this era, a 'gradual erosion of British economic growth and imperial power ... [began] in 1873 which then marked the onset of a long depression' (Brantlinger, *Fictions*: 142). Market instability had earlier reared its treacherous head in the 1840s when shares collapsed during the Railway Mania speculation schemes. Another financial crisis occurred in 1857, on the heels of which came 'a money-market crash in 1866 and a massive panic in 1873 ... followed by a sustained depression' (Franklin, 'Victorian': 904). Financial woes were exacerbated in the early 1870s when an increase in foreign competition was combined with a transition in domestic manufacturing where 'the introduction of new machinery and techniques was throwing more and more men out of work' (Thornton: 20).

As a result of such economic developments and instability, the public attitude towards capitalist enterprises, in general, underwent a seismic shift. According to W.D. Rubinstein, since about 1870, Britain has been 'endemically anti-capitalist and in particular, anti-industrial and anti-manufacturing' (*Capitalism*: 45). Britain's commercial engagements both nationally and internationally were expanding and came under increasing scrutiny, especially by socialists and particularly on moral grounds. The once heralded creators of wealth were branded as inhumane exploiters, destroyers of established crafts, and despoilers of nature (Arnstein: 137; Rubinstein, *Capitalism*: 45).[2] In the process, Jewish 'sweaters' (the proprietors of deadly, back-breaking 'sweat shops') and stockbrokers were singled out for abuse.[3] In the eighteenth century, when the 'public association of Jews with the English financial markets ... [was a] truism generated throughout popular print and theatrical cultures' (Schoenfield: 39), pro-Semitic commentary crediting Jewish stockbrokers with ensuring national stability was produced alongside vicious anti-Semitic representations that suggested that market uncertainties were a Jewish-conceived fiction (39). In the mid- to late nineteenth century, however, the idea of stockbroking as nationally beneficial was virtually absent from public discussion. In fact, that enterprise became interchangeable in much of the period's literature with moneylending and gambling.[4] Stockbrokers were regularly portrayed as low, shady characters engaged in despicable dealings (Russell, *Novelist*: 34). Gothic imagery was, notably, frequently brought to bear on what was known as the 'jobbing' profession. As H.L. Malchow relates, 'in popular parlance generally, unscrupulous company promoters and (often Jewish) stock-jobbers were "vampires", "bloodsuckers", "wolves", and "vultures"' (160). These disturbing phenomena help to explain why, after the 1870s, the Jews were positioned as 'Other' to the British nation with greater urgency and frequency (Cheyette, *Constructions*: 53). Waves of anti-Semitism were also experienced throughout continental Europe beginning in the 1870s (Modder: 237), which resulted in the arrival in Britain of tens of thousands of desperate and unemployed Eastern European Jews fleeing pogroms and persecution (Zanger: 34).[5] Further to these events, openly anti-Semitic political parties like the Christian Socialists were formed (Finzi: 46–7) and in 1879, German agitator Wilhelm Marr coined the term 'anti-Semitism' and founded the Anti-Semitic League (43).

The wide-scale indictment of Jewish 'sweaters', 'jobbers', and immigrant workers in the mid-Victorian period was exacerbated by the widely unpopular foreign policy of imperialism – 'the view that Britain has the right and duty to annex new territories whenever it seems in her interest to do so' (Brantlinger, *Rule*: 6). This policy was promoted, and even said to have been invented by, Benjamin Disraeli, longtime Member of Parliament (1837–80) who held the office of Prime Minister briefly in 1868 and again between

1874 and 1880 (Thornton: 19). Despite his conversion from Judaism to Christianity at the age of 12, Disraeli was nonetheless regarded as a Crypto-Jew whose 'doctrine of empire and interest' (Feldman, *Englishmen*: 99) was subverting standard and stable British policy (104).[6] Although Disraeli argued that imperialism was an extension of Britain's Christian duty (Thornton: 26), Liberals were initially concerned about what they saw as an onerous commitment that could potentially upset the balance of power. In the words of one economic historian, Liberals viewed imperialism's promoters as nothing short of 'the sinister agents of the forces of wrong' (1). This attitude was prevalent until about 1880 when 'politicians at home were at most only "reluctant imperialists"' (Brantlinger, *Rule*: 7). Compounding early Liberal concern about this potentially financially burdensome enterprise was Disraeli's pro-Turkish and anti-Russian position on the Eastern Question. Although his was actually the traditional and long-standing English policy on that issue (Ragussis, *Figures*: 210), numerous caricatures of Disraeli during the 1870s present him as 'an actor, showman, or magician who is caught in the act, a variation on the theme of the secret Jew whose mask is finally penetrated by the Inquisition' (205).[7] At their most extreme and venomous, he was demonized as a 'figure of racial alchemy – possessing ambiguous powers to transmute or transform all that ... [he came] in touch with' (Freedman, 'Poetics': 477).

As a result of these political anxieties and the fact that he consistently celebrated Jewish contributions to European civilization by way of what he deemed 'the Semitic principle' (*Lord*: 496), Disraeli was popularly opposed between 1876 and 1880 (Feldman, *Englishmen*: 119). Various responses regarding Britain's ethnic/racial nature were generated to his pro-Jewish polemics. Matthew Arnold, for example, urged Britons to remedy the existing imbalance and embrace 'Hellenism' over 'Hebraism' and Anthony Trollope conceived the parasitic and imperialist Melmotte (I: 221–2; II: 44) in *The Way We Live Now* as a dark double of Benjamin Disraeli, his bête noire (Cheyette, *Constructions*: 26). While the push to convert the Jews continued apace in British society throughout the 1870s – in fact, it picked up during that decade in the face of growing anti-Semitism (Ragussis, *Figures*: 299) – authors portrayed the dark side of such campaigns. Trollope, for example, issued a scathing socio-political indictment of a nation he conceived as Judaized. Despite the promotion of Jewish assimilation and alongside a more racially grounded, coercive, and xenophobic nationalism (Feldman, 'Importance': 58; Hobsbawm: 142, 152) and aggressive imperialism, came a more physically demonic representation of the Judaizing 'Other' who endangered Britain.

Protestant Britain thus continued to displace its anxieties about its tendencies by projecting them onto a Jewish doppelgänger. That this 'dark double of empire' (Cheyette, *Constructions*: 92) had become a full-fledged vampire by century's end betrays a great deal about imperialist Britain's unconscious anxieties about itself. As Patrick Brantlinger has astutely argued, political and cultural concerns about the imperial enterprise often became gothicized in fin-de-siècle literature (227–9). In this regard, Stoker's *Dracula* cleverly taps two joint fears at the fin de siècle – the alien 'invasion' and domination of Britain by Eastern European Jews from without, and the threat of Anglo-Jewish takeover from within. The former scenario has been described by critics as enacting both the fear of 'reverse colonization' (Arata, 'Occidental': 623) perpetrated by an 'Occidental tourist' (621), and as reverse imperialism (Brantlinger, *Rule*: 233). Gothicized in Stoker's novel, these joint and dreaded scenarios involve a type of body-snatching, a covert conversion – or Judaization – of Britons that is terrifying for two reasons: it is propagated by a 'dark stranger' (177) who is not identifiable as a vampire and it is privately and willingly undertaken by its 'converts' without the notice of the public at large.

The complex nature of Count Dracula's Judaization threat may only be fully understood, however, when considered in the light of various prominent fin-de-siècle anxieties. Indeed, *Dracula* is a consummate 1890s cultural production which responded, albeit sometimes cryptically, to what Daniel Pick nicely describes as 'a distinct constellation of contemporary fears' ('Powers': 71) including syphilis, homosexuality, proto-feminism, the advent of monopoly capitalism, and 'the prospect of imperial and racial decline' (Arata, *Fictions*: 12).[8] To many Britons at the fin de siècle, like Bram Stoker, these fears were inextricably bound up with the idea of national degeneration that was then haunting Britain. Given a socio-political climate where 'fissures … [were] appearing in bourgeois hegemony, patriarchy and imperial power … [and] forces [were] gathering … against and within Victorian society' (Longhurst: 65–6), it is not surprising that the literature produced during Stoker's era was, consciously and unconsciously, 'saturated with the sense that the entire nation – as a race of people, as a political and imperial force, as a social and cultural power – was in irretrievable decline' (Arata, 'Occidental': 622).

What has remained unnoted is that 'Jewishness' functioned as the umbrella signifier, both in Stoker's *Dracula* and in his society, under which these diverse fears of national degeneration stood united. Even Max Nordau, the Jewish author of the famous anti-modernism polemic *Degeneration* (1895) which pathologized the fin de siècle (3), maintained that Jews were more susceptible than Christians to moral, mental, and physical degeneration (Chamberlin and Gilman: 292). These ideas were granted further support in new pseudo-scientific studies that traced the inception of syphilis, for example, to the Jewish community. In one such study by Henry Meige, a student of Dr Jean Martin Charcot, for example, the Wandering Jew is psychopathologized as a peripatetic neurotic whose co-religionists are deemed to be particularly prone to mental illness.

That several Jews were suspected of the Jack the Ripper murders in 1888, crimes which were considered to be the most degenerate of their era, was also unsurprising given the socio-cultural climate at the fin de siècle. Indeed, it was popularly claimed that the Ripper's bloodthirsty acts of butchery could not have been committed by an Englishman (Walkowitz: 203). The Whitechapel murders were one of several contemporary phenomena that were incorporated into *Dracula*'s dense narrative whirlpool. Notably, the popular media representations of the Ripper provide evidence that the Gothic Jew remained a vital bogey at the fin de siècle. Particularly in his fictionalized ethnic aspect and all that it signified culturally, Jack the Ripper may be said to be Count Dracula's semiotic blood brother.

Patrick Brantlinger relates further that imperialism 'grew particularly racist and aggressive from the 1870s on' (*Rule* 35). In the light of the changing face of nationalism, blood – *Dracula*'s most prevalent signifier – assumes rich symbolic meaning.[9] By way of this vital and resonant symbol, Stoker unifies his novel's most important themes. In Renfield's demonic parody of the Eucharistic phrase that 'the blood is the life', Stoker crystallizes the nature of the terror posed by his vampiric Wandering Jew. In keeping with established anti-Semitic stereotypes, Count Dracula is guilty of the Blood Libel, of desecrating the Host, and of endangering the national body politic, which was increasingly viewed as racialized. This desecration extends to the biological meaning of the term 'host' and gestures towards the Count's ultimate role in Stoker's novel: he is a parasite from a racially alien nation who vigorously feeds off Britain, his Christian host nation. In his figuration of vampirism as a type of blood disease, Stoker both draws upon longstanding anti-Semitic stereotypes associating Jews with plagues, and speaks to his era's syphilis epidemic and burgeoning racial nationalist ideology.

An iconography of filth is part and parcel of the infection motif central to Stoker's symbolic strategy. Building upon the perceptive anthropological work of Mary Douglas, Anne McClintock has shown that dirt exerted a compulsive fascination over the nineteenth-century imagination. More importantly, McClintock claims that, especially as that century wore on, 'the iconography of dirt became a poetics of surveillance, deployed increasingly to police the boundaries between "normal" sexuality and "dirty" sexuality, "normal" work and "dirty" work and "normal" money and "dirty" money' (154). While the trinity of dirty sex–work–money identified by McClintock was at play in anti-Semitic stereotypes since their inception, it became especially pronounced in racial anti-Semitism and in the degeneration debates at the Victorian fin de siècle. In its emphasis on excesses and the policing and transgression of boundaries, the Gothic genre proved to be a particularly suitable venue for the forging of such reactionary yet compelling critiques. Thus does *Dracula*, with Stoker in the role of principal surveillance officer, dramatically enact a multifaceted Judaization threat and ask the 'question appropriate to an age of imperial decline: ... to what extent can one be "infected" and still remain British?' (Punter, *Literature*: 239–40).

* * *

No reader could possibly suspect, based on the initial introduction to Count Dracula in Bram Stoker's classic novel, that a virile, bloodthirsty demon lurked within his person. As Jonathan Harker describes him during their first encounter:

> Within, stood a tall old man, clean-shaven save for a long white moustache, and clad in black from head to foot, without a single speck of colour about him anywhere. He held in his hand an antique silver lamp, in which the flame burned without chimney or globe of any kind, throwing long, quivering shadows as it flickered in the draught of the open door. The old man motioned me in with his right hand with a courtly gesture, saying in excellent English, but with a strange intonation: – 'Welcome to my house! Enter freely and of your own will!' (15)

As he further informs Harker shortly after his arrival, 'through weary years of mourning over the dead, [Dracula] is not attuned to mirth' (24). This is not the stuff, the reader might remark, of which seductive 'demon lover' vampires are traditionally made. As Lewis and Godwin's descriptions of their mysterious strangers clarify, however, this *is* the stuff of which the long-suffering, melancholic Wandering Jew – 'that sad and fabulous mythological oddity' (Rosenberg: 76) – is made. While Lewis's profoundly melancholic (Lewis: 168) Wandering Jew mournfully laments his lack of friends and his inability to die (169), Godwin's Zampieri is an incredibly afflicted man who is 'feeble, emaciated, and pale, [with] his forehead full of wrinkles, and his hair and beard as white as snow' (*St. Leon*: 124).

Dracula's description of historic Transylvanian battles 'as if he had been present at them all' (*Dracula*: 28) echoes earlier representations of the Wandering Jew in British Gothic literature. Both Raymond's servant Theodore in Lewis's *The Monk* and St Leon in Godwin's novel note how the mysterious wanderers they encounter are acquainted with people long dead (Godwin, *St. Leon*: 141; Lewis: 169). Stoker also adheres to earlier literary portraits of the Wandering Jew that present Faustian characters engaged with the secret sciences. Van Helsing, Dracula's foremost opponent and modern-day counterpart, provides the details relating to the Count's involvement with this field of knowledge. Dracula's engagement with these studies during his lifetime (prior to his 'undeath') is commendable according to Van Helsing:

> As I learned from the researches of my friend Arminius of Buda-Pesth, he was in life a most wonderful man. Soldier, statesman, and alchemist – which latter was the highest development of the science-knowledge of his time. He had a mighty brain, a learning beyond compare, and a heart that knew no fear and no remorse. He dared even to attend the Scholomance, and there was no branch of knowledge of his time that he did not essay. (302)

Dracula's participation in the Scholomance, effectively an exclusive educational secret society which admitted only ten scholars at a time and was located 'amongst the mountains over Lake Hermanstadt', may have resulted in his vampiric existence and the shift in his moral nature. As Stoker had learned from Madame E. de Laszowska Gerard's *Transylvanian Superstitions*, published in 1885, after the tenth scholar had been taught 'all the secrets of nature, the language of animals, and all magic spells and charms' by the devil himself (qtd. in Frayling, *Vampyres*: 322), he was exacted as the devil's payment due (Stoker, *Dracula*: 241). As the origins of Dracula's vampirism are not explained, it is possible that Dracula was the tenth scholar.[10] In the light of Dracula's association with the secret sciences, it is fitting that Van Helsing and his allies form a secret society of their own in order to combat him. In this 'Masonic narrative' (Glover: 4),[11] they undertake a modern Crusade, making 'a solemn compact' (Stoker, *Dracula*: 238) to 'go out as the old knights of the Cross to redeem more [souls]' (320).

Dracula's role as a Wandering Jew figure may be nowhere explicitly expressed in Stoker's novel but it is frequently and variously suggested. While his journey to England during the course of the narrative provides some evidence of his peripatetic inclination, the hoarded gold and jewels that Harker discovers in the Count's room in his Transylvanian castle attest to the extensive temporal and geographical nature of the Count's travels. As Harker describes this discovery:

> The only thing I found was a great heap of gold in one corner – gold of all kinds, Roman, and British, and Austrian, and Hungarian, and Greek and Turkish money, *covered with a film of dust*, as though it had lain long in the ground. None of it that I noticed was less than three hundred years old. There were also chains and ornaments, some jewelled, but all of them old and stained. (47; emphasis added)

This discovery of Dracula's literally filthy lucre and such acts as the Count's search for buried treasure in Transylvania on the dreaded eve of St. George's Day when, according to Eastern European folklore, the power of all evil things is said to be at its height (12–13), are significant for another reason. They suggest how, increasingly, secular anti-Semitic stereotypes were being grafted onto the Wandering Jew in British Gothic literature. I will hereafter turn to an examination of the economic implications of this development.

The ascetic, abstemious Wandering Jew of legend is certainly nowhere to be found in Stoker's Gothic thriller. Instead, 'a new, secularized, non-Christian myth of Ahasverus' such as emerged in Germany in the mid-nineteenth century (Rose: 54) is evident in *Dracula*. Numerous works of Stoker's era, both fictional and non-fictional, attest to the advent of a new racialized anti-Semitism in Britain that held the Jew to be nationally unassimilable and morally irredeemable. Among various other writers, Sir Richard Burton, the famous British adventurer, author of *King Vikram and the Vampire*, and one of Bram Stoker's acquaintances and heroes, was vital to the dissemination of anti-Semitic ideas in the 1890s. Burton's book, *The Jew, the Gypsy and El Islam*, published posthumously in 1898, shamelessly described the Jews as a 'parasitic race' (17) and upheld the longstanding Blood Libel.[12] Burton's work further sought an 'ample motive' for the 'tumultuous and wholesale massacres' of Jews throughout history (116). He found such justification in what he described as the eternally evil Jewish character. It is noteworthy that Dracula could have been the model for Burton's scathing, anti-Semitic portrait:

> His fierce passions and fiendish cunning, combined with abnormal powers of intellect, with intense vitality, and with a persistency of purpose which the world has rarely seen, and *whetted moreover by a keen thirst for blood engendered by defeat and subjection*, combined to make him the deadly enemy of all mankind, whilst his unsocial and iniquitous Oral Law contributed to inflame his wild lust of pelf, and to justify the crimes suggested by spite and superstition. (117; emphasis added)

Stoker's Count arguably incorporates aspects of such longstanding anti-Semitic stereotypes. He too lusts after blood and pelf and is portrayed as 'the deadly enemy of all mankind'.

Many of Burton's opinions had been expressed previously by Major E.C. Johnson whose book *On the Track of the Crescent: Erratic Notes From Piraeus to Pesth* was a primary source for Stoker's knowledge of the peoples inhabiting Transylvania. Johnson devotes an entire segment of his study on the Hungarian Jews and their pitiless commercial activities involving the peasantry (qtd. in Leatherdale, *Dracula*: 100). Drawing upon racialized portraits of the Jew by such writers as George Croly[13] and Samuel Roberts, and anticipating the Nazi stereotype of the unproductive, power-hungry and conspiratorial Jew, Johnson claims that the great talent of 'this strange people' is their

> … shrewdness in driving bargains, and … [their] marvellous aptitude for conducting financial operations, in consequence of which they have accumulated most of the wealth of the world, and control an immense proportion of the business transactions on the civilised globe. They have, however, never added one grain to the food supply of men, or done any physical work or handicraft labour. (100)

The exceptions to this rule, as Johnson points out, lie with 'the descendants of mixed marriages' (100).

Not everyone held Johnson's views at the fin de siècle, however, regarding the Jew's potential for assimilation into British society. Throughout the 1890s, Sir Arnold White, a regular Lyceum Theatre patron (Stoker, *Personal* I.: 326) and, like Stoker, a popular contributor to *The Nineteenth Century*, published articles on what he specifically referred to as 'The Jewish Question' (White: vii). White was an ardent supporter of the 1905 British Aliens Act (Feldman, 'Importance': 59) that, according to historian David Feldman was 'symptomatic of new formulations of the idea of the nation and of a more expansive and coercive state' (58). This Act effectively 'prevented the immigration of thousands of Russian Jews and was a source of trepidation for those already settled in Britain' (57–8). The necessary corollary of a fortified British nationalism was a stronger, clearer sense of who constituted the foreign 'Other' combined with the greater legal protection of British territory.

In his 1899 volume, *The Modern Jew*, White reiterated his stance on the subject of 'The Jewish Question'. Declaring 'the engine of international finance [to be] ... under Jewish control, and ... public opinion ... mediated by Jewish influence over the European press' (xv), White feared that the 'invasion of foreign paupers' (Feldman, 'Importance': 80, n. 10) would strengthen Jewish power in Britain and lead to a national crisis (x). According to him, the problem lay specifically with the Jewish resistance to assimilation. 'Except among the Jewish aristocracy', White wrote, 'they refuse to intermarry' (xiii), and remain an 'undigested mass' (192). Whether the resistance to intermarriage lay with the Jews or the Christians, the fact of the matter was that, at least among upper-class Jews, intermarriage and conversion were extremely rare occurrences (Endelman, *Radical*: 80). In the face of what he regarded as active resistance, White offered up disturbing yet prescient words. He presents two methods whereby the evil results of 'a Jewish imperium inside the English Empire can be obviated':

> It can be destroyed and its members expelled as was done in the thirteenth century in most countries in Europe, including England, and is likely to be done over again in France before many years have passed, or the Jewish community, frankly recognising the peril that besets them, must review their conduct and heartily work for instead of against the power of absorption which in two generations made French Protestants of the day of Louis XIV, an integral part of the English people. (xii–xiii)

The passing of the Aliens Act several years later attests to the fact that many in the legislature held White's opinions. One such individual was C. Russell who argued in conjunction with H.S. Lewis, that the 'invasion of the country by *hordes of hungry Israelites*, who seemed unfairly qualified for success in the industrial market by the combination of *a sleuth-hound instinct for gain*, with "an indefinitely low standard of life", naturally stirred up a certain amount of jealous hostility among the working-classes' (5; emphasis added). Russell's graphic description of parasitic Jewish aliens is notably Gothic and his sleuth-hound reference draws upon the popular stereotype of the fanging Jew. Russell claims further that incoming foreign Jews had a debilitating effect on the real estate market. While some were buying up property, rental fees were increasing due to overcrowding. As a result of these trends, he maintained, poor British Christians were being displaced from the increasingly Jewish East End neighbourhood of Whitechapel (17).

Although Russell describes Jews as a collective group who are 'isolated and peculiar...', self-centred in their organisation, and fundamentally alien in their ideas and aims' (8), he draws certain distinctions between the newly arrived foreign Jews and Anglo-Jews.[14] He essentially concurs with White that the distinction between these two groups lies in the area of their potential assimilation. While the latter is 'often an ardent patriot', the former pose a national threat (36). Unlike White, however, Russell locates the origins of this threat in Zionism, whose first Organization was formally established by Theodor Herzl in 1897, the year of *Dracula*'s publication (Shimoni: 97). Russell claims that this ideology undermines all attempts at assimilation and Anglicization. While resistance to assimiliation is laid at the doorstep of the newly arrived foreign Jews, White nonetheless casts doubt on the ability of any Jew to become English when he quotes a correspondent for the *Jewish World*, the organ of the English Zionists, who states, 'There is no such thing as an English Jew, just as there is no such thing as a "German Chinaman"' (111). That Jewish nationalism was also born in the 1880s and 1890s during the period of burgeoning British right-wing nationalism was cause for concern for some Britons. Although Zionism was conceived, according to Hannah Arendt, as an answer or 'counterideology' to antisemitism (xi), it also, unfortunately, helped to reinforce it by confirming what many long believed, namely that the Jews could never be assimilated into any nation. The popular prejudice, therefore, was that the Jew remained incontrovertibly alien or, as Count Dracula so aptly describes himself, 'a stranger in a strange land' (20).

In her chapter on 'The Jewish Community' in the 1889 publication *Life and Labour of the People in London*, noted Fabian Beatrice Webb also articulated the popular view regarding distinctions between suspect 'alien' immigrant Jews and good gentlemanly Anglo-Jews. Maintaining that the Polish or Russian Jew 'can in no sense be considered a fair sample of [Anglo-] Jews who have enjoyed the freedom, the culture, and the public spirit of English life' (185), she portrays immigrant Jews as notorious gamblers (185) who do not possess 'that highest and latest development of human sentiment – social morality' (191). Webb argues that in the domain of his commercial dealings

> [t]he small [Jewish] manufacturer injures the trade through which he rises to the rank of a capitalist by bad and dishonest production. The petty dealer or small money lender, imbued with the economic precept of buying in the cheapest and selling in the dearest market, suits his wares and his terms to the weakness, the ignorance, and the vice of his customers... (191)

She maintains that Jewish traders adhere to the political economy of 'an Always Enlightened Selfishness' as upheld by David Ricardo, 'the Hebrew economist' (192). Various claims were also made at the fin de siècle that Jews were displacing native Britons in certain trades (Malchow: 158).

Much historical evidence contradicts assertions that Jews were sheerly self-interested businessmen who undermined British national interests. As Hannah Arendt has articulately shown, the fact that the Jews were a wealthy and influential, supra-national European group was often crucial to the maintenance of national security throughout Europe (19). Associated initially with the aristocracy and later with the state, Jewish businessmen like the Rothschilds funded Britain during such national crises as the Napoleonic Wars and were crucial to negotiating peace treaties (20). This did not, however, stave off such accusations as that of war profiteering made against the great financier Nathan Mayer Rothschild after the Battle of Waterloo, which questioned the loyalty of all of England's Jews (Manly, 'Introduction': xxx). Thus did the popular conception of the Jews' role in Europe often run counter to historical fact. Although very few Jews held positions of political importance, their state connections and economic influence nonetheless gave rise to the popular misconception that they were conspiratorial puppet-masters intent on undermining national interests.

Such anxieties about Jewish economic practices and the degenerate Crypto Jew also spilled over into much fin-de-siècle literature. Although socio-political commentators like Arnold White proposed intermarriage as a resolution to the assimilation problem, great fears persisted with regard to this 'remedy'. The sense that Jews – especially male Jews – were sexually perverse and that religious conversion could not alter this make-up pervaded much of the era's literature. Trollope's unwritten message in *The Way We Live Now* with regard to relationships between Christian British women and Jewish men is, unarguably, 'put your good English daughters away!' Frank Danby's popular 1887 work *Dr. Phillips; A Maida Vale Idyll* carries on this crusade at the fin de siècle. Frank Danby was actually the pseudonym of Julia Frankau, a Dublin-born Jewess and converted Christian who was raised by Karl Marx's daughter, Mrs Paul Lafargue. As her brother, James Davis, was 'a journalist, dramatist, and composer of comic operas' (Zatlin: 97) and her sister was Eliza Aria, a 'journalist who became Irving's *chère amie* during the last seven or eight years of his life' (Gross: 160–1), Frankau had probably even met Bram Stoker. She published four novels dealing with Jews in her lifetime, all of which denigrated them and targetted what she felt was the wide-scale problem of Jewish materialism. *Dr. Phillips* relates the tale of an ambitious Jewish doctor who keeps a Christian mistress. Knowing that he is the beneficiary of his wife's will, he kills her, only to find that his mistress has left him for another man. As in Stoker's *Dracula*, one of the primary suggestions in Frankau's novel is that Jewish men are lascivious adulterers who may convert Christian women into prostitutes. Adhering to stereotype, Dr Phillips marries for money and in one telling passage Frankau relates how 'the luxurious prostitution of his marriage had developed in him an Eastern virility that brooked no denial' (77). Frankau carried her anti-Semitism into the domain of British patriotism and that nation's financial health in *Pigs in Clover* (1903), her next major novel dealing with a Jewish theme.[15]

Other anti-Semitic ideas were current in the literature of Stoker's day. H. Rider Haggard disseminates such ideas in *She*, for example, when he portrays the fin de siècle as 'Jewish' in nature. He makes allusion to 'the Jews whom everybody "wants" nowadays' (63), and foregrounds the fact that his primary female character Ayesha was driven into the wilderness by Jews (148). Although Ayesha shares some characteristics of the Wandering Jew as she 'tarries' until the man she once loved in ancient Egypt returns again (149), she functions as the vehicle through which Haggard condemns the Jews. She describes these people as Christ-killers (148), and mocks them for their lack of belief in the possibility of spiritual resurrection (149). Entries in Haggard's personal journals before and after the First World War reiterate this Christ killer idea (Katz, *Rider*: 150) and exhibit what one commentator describes as a 'frighteningly proto-fascist mentality' (149).[16]

Within the domain of Gothic literature, the villainous Jew also rears his head in works by Oscar Wilde, George Du Maurier, and Marie Corelli, three writers with whom Stoker was personally acquainted. It is striking that in all three works, this character poses a special threat to upstanding British womanhood. In Oscar Wilde's *The Picture of Dorian Gray* (1891), he appears as the 'hideous Jew' theatre manager (80, 48) to whom the 'sacred' Sibyl Vane (51) is effectively enslaved by debt. This immoral, urban monster (48) blasphemously reduces both art and women to their commercial exchange value. Borrowing from Wilde, Marie Corelli's own Lady Sibyl in *The Sorrows of Satan*, 'the biggest best-seller of the nineteenth century' (Wheeler, *English*: 163), is a vital commodity in her father's business transactions with Jews. Shortly before her suicide, Sibyl discovers that her father

> ...was crippled on all sides with debt – that he lived on advances made to him by Jew usurers, – and that these advances were trusted to him solely on the speculation that... [she], his only daughter, would make a sufficiently rich marriage to enable him to repay all loans with heavy interest. (403–4)

Corelli's feature character and personal mouthpiece is none other than Satan who, although an accursed immortal like the Wandering Jew (121), often spouts venomous anti-Semitic statements. In his worldview, the fin de siècle is dominated by Jewish Shylock-style merchants who are unfairly protected by God (121). Provoked by a sense of injustice, Corelli's Mephistophelean Satan articulates his theory to his next prospective victim, Geoffrey Tempest:

> By the way, have you noticed how the legended God still appears to protect the house of Israel? Particularly the 'base usurer' who is allowed to

get the unhappy Christian into his clutches nine times out of ten? And no remedy drops from heaven! The Jew always triumphs. Rather inconsistent isn't it, on the part of an equitable Deity! (121)

The Gothic Jew also makes an appearance in George Du Maurier's 1894 novel *Trilby* in the mesmerizing Svengali. This deceptive, theatre-associated man 'of Jewish aspect, well-featured but sinister' (11) threatens to reduce the upstanding British 'angel in the house' – in this case, Trilby – to the status of a figurative prostitute who generates his income. Described by Stoker's longstanding friend Du Maurier as 'a sticky, haunting, long, lean, uncanny, black spider-cat, if there is such an animal outside a bad dream' (84), Svengali is an undeniable relative of Stoker's animalistic Count. In fact, with his 'big yellow teeth baring themselves in a mongrel canine snarl' and his ability to 'oppress...and weigh...on... [Trilby] like an incubus' (104), Svengali's resemblance to Stoker's own literal and nightmarish incubus is particularly remarkable (Ormond: xxviii).[17] Both give powerful expression to what was clearly regarded by many at the fin de siècle as the extremely unsettling idea of the physical union of male Jew and female non-Jew.

The description of Immanuel Hildesheim, the only explicitly identified Jewish figure in Stoker's *Dracula*, provides some sense of Stoker's own anti-Semitism. While Hildesheim does not lust after blood, he is certainly money-hungry. A 'stereotypical Semitic middleman' (McBride: 117) who unwittingly aids Dracula in his return to Transylvania from England by receiving his coffin at Galatz, Hildesheim has a distinctly Jewish physiognomy and is, like Wilde's Jew in *The Picture of Dorian Gray* and Du Maurier's Svengali, also associated with the theatre. As Jonathan Harker describes him, he is 'a Hebrew of rather the Adelphi type, with a nose like a sheep, and a fez' (349). Almost predictably, when the men try to extract information from Hildesheim regarding the whereabouts of Dracula's 'box', he lives up to Harker's prejudicial billing for they discover that bribery is a successful approach: 'His arguments were pointed with specie – we doing all the punctuation – and with a little bargaining he told us what he knew' (349). Hildesheim has a similar cameo role in *Dracula* to that played by the Jewish merchant who sells Ambrosio the portrait of the Madonna in Lewis's *The Monk*. Like him, Hildesheim is also revealed to be in league with the devil. Dracula's avaricious associative blood brother, he aids in this demon vampire's escape.

Unlike the identifiably Jewish Hildesheim, Count Dracula is a fin-de-siècle Frankenstein monster borne of various established anti-Semitic stereotypes and contemporary anxieties relating to the Jewish Question in Britain. Stoker's 'occidental tourist' (Arata, 'Occidental': 621) hails from Eastern Europe, the region from which thousands of Jews, fleeing pogroms and persecution, were emigrating throughout the fin de siècle (Zanger: 34). A voracious scholar who is well-informed about England prior to his arrival in that country, Dracula adheres to the traditional stereotype of the Jews as 'the people of the Book'

(Blau: 5). His diversified knowledge in the legal, medical, political, and military professions is applauded by Van Helsing (*Dracula*: 302). Law, Harker's foremost domain of interest, is a profession which had been long associated with the Jews given their Talmudic scholarship. According to C. Russell:

> The Jews have always been 'a nation of students.' The Talmud sets the scholar above the king; and a thorough training in Hebrew is still held a matter of the highest importance. Five is recognised as the proper age at which a child should begin to study the Law ... (28–9)

Capping off Dracula's association with the law, Harker notes that a copy of the Law List is among the Count's many reference books (*Dracula*: 19). He also states that Dracula 'would have made a wonderful solicitor' (31). Notably, Jews were unable to practice law in England in the late nineteenth century (Adler, 'Jews': 145).

Like Hildesheim, Dracula is Mammon-obsessed and has a stereotypical Jewish physiognomy. Apart from his sinister 'pointed beard' (137) – a signature feature of the devil's traditional physiognomy – a figure with whom the Jews were traditionally associated (Russell, *Mephistopheles* 160, 164) – great care is taken to describe Dracula's nose which is strongly 'aquiline' (17), 'hooked' (137), and 'beaky' (172).[18] A passage from Stoker's *Personal Reminiscences of Henry Irving* illustrates that Stoker associated this type of nose with Jewishness. In his description of his employer, Henry Irving, as he applied his make-up for the part of Shylock, Stoker notes that he 'could never really understand ... how the bridge of the nose under painting [make-up] ... rose into *the Jewish aquiline*' (*Personal* I.: 140; emphasis added).

Dracula also has a distinct and pungent odour (19, 47) similar to the *foetor judaicus* long attributed to the Jews (Osborne: 129). One of the men who moves Dracula's requisite 50 cases of earth into his 'medieval' Carfax estate (23) comments that one 'might 'ave smelled *ole Jerusalem* in it' (228; emphasis added). Harker's description of the foul odour in Dracula's Carfax lair is especially noteworthy as it links Dracula's physical and moral decadence. In his entry dated 1 October, 5 a.m., Harker writes:

> There was an earthy smell, as of some dry miasma, which came through the fouler air. But as to the odour itself, how shall I describe it? It was not alone that it was composed of all the ills of mortality and with the pungent, acrid smell of blood, but it seemed as though corruption had become itself corrupt. Faugh! it sickens me to think of it. Every breath exhaled by that monster seemed to have clung to the place and intensified its loathsomeness.
>
> Under ordinary circumstances such a stench would have brought our enterprise to an end; but this was no ordinary case, and the high and terrible purpose in which we were involved gave us a strength which rose above merely physical considerations. (251)

Dracula is essentially a social *polluter* who threatens to infect the British nation. He is often accompanied by rats (252, 279), a longstanding symbol of the plague. Since at least the Middle Ages it was believed that Jews spread this and other infections while, as a result of demonic pacts made with the devil, they remained immune.[19] Van Helsing makes much of the fact that Dracula is one who 'can smile at death, as we know him; who can flourish in the midst of diseases that kill off whole peoples' (321).

While Dracula is a blood brother to the Wandering Jews in the works of Lewis and Godwin, therefore, he is far more dark, supernatural, and anti-Christian. Dracula's British alias, Count 'de Ville' (273), betrays his anti-Christ role as does Van Helsing's description of him as an 'arrow in the side of Him [Christ] who died for man' (237). Moreover, Stoker's Count is portrayed as simultaneously alien and alienated for his rejection of both love and Christ. Dracula's cryptic retort to the female vampire trinity that he too once loved (39) suggests that those days are long past. Although Count Dracula is careful not to violate British law, he repeatedly violates Christian law in his role as a demonic parasite.

Indeed, a thematics of the host may be said to be at work in *Dracula*. This theme incorporates several meanings of the word 'host' and taps into religious and economic anxieties emanating from Dracula's attempts at reverse imperialism. In religious terms, 'host' has two primary meanings. It refers to the unleavened bread representing the body of Christ used for the Eucharist and, in the sense of the phrase 'Heavenly Host', it refers to an armed company or multitude of men. In biological terms, the word 'host' denotes the living plant or animal in or upon which a parasite lives and obtains nourishment. Finally, it also refers to the 'man who lodges and entertains another in his home'. These various meanings are conjoined in *Dracula* which essentially plays out the economic fear of a new parasitic and consumer 'race' of alien Jews – as represented in the figure of Count Dracula – who will undermine their Christian British host nation. Dracula is, furthermore, a parasitic guest who is ultimately defeated by the Heavenly Christian Host composed of the Crew of Light. Given the Count's final 'look of peace' (377), this 'defeat' is figured as an act of saving grace where the protracted undeath he suffers is concluded and his soul returned to God. Thus are these British missionary imperialists successful in their enterprise of conversion.

Particularly through the character of Renfield, Dracula's English religious follower and servant who awaits his 'master's' arrival from Transylvania, Stoker cleverly manipulates the Eucharistic notion that 'the blood is the life'. In a rare moment of sanity, Renfield explains how he once interpreted this idea in a literal way:

> I used to fancy that life was a positive and perpetual entity, and that by consuming a multitude of live things, no matter how low in the scale of creation, one might indefinitely prolong life. At times I held the belief so

strongly that I actually tried to take human life. The doctor here will bear me out that on one occasion I tried to kill him for the purpose of strengthening my vital powers by the assimilation with my own body of his life through the medium of his blood – relying, of course, upon the Scriptural phrase, 'For the blood is the life'. (234)

Renfield's statements unarguably hearken back to the Blood Libel. Renfield's reductive, literal interpretation of this 'Scriptural phrase' is clearly anti-Christian in nature. His desecration of this sacred concept is, in fact, traditionally attributed to the Jews. This desecration is shown to be central to Dracula's vampire religion as his consumption of actual blood provides him with life. Indeed, in his particular love of the blood of children (39) – a taste that Lucy acquires after her transformation into the Bloofer Lady (178) – Count Dracula enacts the traditional Blood Libel crime ascribed to the Jews.

This violation is also carried over to the more secular meaning of the word 'host'. At the beginning of the novel, Dracula is frequently described as the host to Jonathan Harker (17, 24). After exploiting Harker's legal expertise in order to gain access to England, Dracula's new host nation, Dracula violates his role as Harker's host by leaving this young solicitor in the hands of his voracious harem. As Harker relates his last vision of his demonic host, 'The last I saw of Count Dracula he was kissing his hand to me, with a red light of triumph in his eyes, and with a smile that Judas in Hell might be proud of' (50). This allusion resuscitates the Jew as Christ-killer motif of which the Wandering Jew legend forms an essential part. It also foregrounds Dracula's parasitism. Judas, otherwise known as the arch-traitor, effectively received blood money – money obtained at the cost of another's life – when he betrayed Jesus with a kiss for 30 pieces of silver.

A blood-money theme is deftly manipulated throughout *Dracula* and underpins Stoker's critique of the changing face of British capitalism at the fin de siècle. Essentially, Stoker's novel distinguishes between two prevalent types of capitalism which had been respectively and repeatedly codified and classified in a variety of British historical documents as 'Christian' and 'Jewish'. According to Peter Stallybrass and Allon White, this distinction dates back as far as the early modern period when the Jew was regarded 'as a *calculating* enemy of carnival, a repressive bearer of cold rationality and profiteering individualism which ran counter to the communal spirit of free expenditure and careless exuberance characteristic of the festival' (55). It is also on exhibit in early sixteenth-century Britain in the anonymously published *The Death of Usury* which 'attempt[ed] to distinguish between acceptable and exorbitant interest rates ... [where] the Jews exemplif[ied] the latter' (Shapiro, *Shakespeare*: 99). Given that 'Catholics and Protestants repeatedly accused each other of Judaizing tendencies' in the decades following the Reformation when Protestant mercantile activity was rapidly expanding (Shapiro, *Shakespeare*: 8), it would seem that Protestant merchants felt increasing pressure to justify their commercial activities. Defining this involvement as beneficial to the Commonwealth necessitated defining what type of mercantile activity was detrimental. Designating Jewish usury as a pernicious, perverse, and parasitical form of capitalism, therefore, became a popular activity among Protestant writers of the day.

Perhaps the most recent description of these varying capitalist forms is provided in Max Weber's classic work, *The Protestant Ethic and the Spirit of Capitalism* where he outlines how:

> To the English Puritans, the Jews of their time were representatives of that type of capitalism which was involved in war, Government contracts, State monopolies, speculative promotions, and the construction and financial projects of princes, which they themselves condemned. In fact the difference may, in general, with the necessary qualifications, be formulated: that Jewish capitalism was speculative pariah-capitalism, while the Puritan was bourgeois organization of labour. (271)

Weber draws a further distinction between these two forms by designating Christian capitalism 'the rational capitalistic organization of (formally) free labour' (21), and Jewish capitalism as 'predominantly of an irrational and speculative character, or directed to acquisition of force, above all the acquisition of booty, whether directly in war or in the form of continuous fiscal booty by exploitation of subjects' (20). While Christian commerce is represented, therefore, as rational and productive, Jewish commerce is regarded as a form of gambling or a type of criminal activity as it is irrational, usurious, and unproductive. Weber adds a final distinction to his portrait by opposing the flashy Jewish merchant to the Christian-Puritan capitalist who 'avoids ostentation and unnecessary expenditure ... [and] is embarrassed by the outward signs of the social recognition which he receives' (71). According to Willa Z. Silverman, a similar attitude towards Jewish commerce existed in fin-de-siècle France where Jewish moneymaking was regarded as a type of magic or what she calls 'voodoo economics'. Jews were demonized by many in France as an 'evil empire' (157) composed of 'medieval alchemists ... [who] "create[d] something from nothing" through credit and speculation' (156).

An examination of Count Dracula in the light of contemporary anxieties about powerful, usurious Jews, and in connection to the distinction Weber draws between Jewish and Christian capitalism, locates him firmly in Weber's speculative Jewish capitalist camp. Dracula loves bloody war (29) and is distressed over what he refers to as the 'days of dishonourable peace' (30) in his native land. The nature of his investments are also typically 'Jewish' as he makes an international investment in London real estate. Notably, the Count's physically transformative abilities capture the immaterial, spectral nature of his capitalist activities. Further to this, he is also a class interloper in British terms as he purchases the signpost of a British gentleman's status – namely property. In this capacity, *Dracula* conflates two conjoined and preeminent fears about the British nation and the Jews at the fin de siècle – the 'invasion' of Britain by poor Eastern European Jews who were regarded as a financial drain on the nation, and the potential subversion of Britain by resident, wealthier Anglo-Jews. His act of initially purchasing real estate, however, is but the opening gambit by an invading Other in what amounts to an economic battle for the control of Britain. The Count's accumulation of a British harem is but a signpost of the commercial power he stands to gain as he kills off Britain's propertied gentlemen in a feeding frenzy. This strategy also falls under Weber's definition of Weber's definition of Jewish commerce as it involves war and the exploitation of subjects.

Stoker's clever blood-money equation particularly illuminates Dracula's fearsome aspect as an exploitative Jewish merchant. Like Shakespeare's *lupine* merchant Shylock (IV.i.: 73) in *The Merchant of Venice*[20] whose 'desires / Are wolvish, bloody, starv'd, and ravenous' (IV.i.: 137–8), Stoker's 'Shylock of the Carpathians' (Bouvier and Leutrat: 26) possesses claw-like hands with hairy palms (18) and an unusual ability to control wolves (13, 45, 49). As Harker learns shortly after his arrival in Transylvania, the laws of vampirism could in fact be rendered in Shylock's famous words: 'I will buy with you, sell with you, talk with you, walk with you and so following; but I will not eat with you, drink with you, nor pray with you' (I.3.: 33–5). Notably, Dracula only buys and sells with Christian Britons in order to gain access to, and safety within, their country. He neglects to inform Harker that he is unwilling to engage in further commercial transactions subsequent to Carfax's purchase. Further to this, this figurative big bad wolf in sheep's clothing cunningly neglects to inform Harker that he may attempt a 'black mass' by converting Harker's 'body [into] a banquet' (51). Given that victims of vampire attacks become vampires themselves, Dracula's menace carries with it the threat to convert Harker to the Count's demonic Jewish religion. In this regard, Jonathan Harker strikes the novel's most resonant note of terror when he articulates his fear that he is aiding and abetting Dracula in his aim of colonizing England in transferring this creature to London. In his horrified words, 'perhaps for centuries to come, he [Dracula] might, amongst its teeming millions, satiate his lust for blood, and create a new and ever widening circle of semi-demons to batten on the helpless' (51).

The threat of Judaization, or what the Germans referred to as 'Verjudung' (Rose: 44), was represented in 1840s Germany primarily in economic terms. Jewish economic practices were described as a form of parasitic usury that was rapidly *infecting* 'Christian' capitalism. This representation shares many points of contact with Stoker's *Dracula* and British anti-Semitism at the fin de siècle. According to Moses Hess in his 1843 work, *The Essence of Money*, vampiric capitalism, a Jewish specialty, was consuming the nation:

> We find ourselves at the apex of the social animal world; we are now social beasts of prey ... We are no longer herbivores like our gentle ancestors ... We are bloodsuckers. ... Man enjoys his life in the form of money

in a brutal, bestial, cannibalistic way. Money is social blood, but alienated spilled blood.

In the natural history of the social animal world the Jews had the world-historical mission of developing the beast of prey in mankind and they have now completed their task. The mystery of Judaism and Christianity has been revealed in the modern Jewish-Christian peddler-world. The mystery of the blood of Christ, like that of the ancient Jewish reverence for blood, appears now finally unveiled as the mystery of the beast of prey. (Rose 50)

Hess's words echo those of Karl Marx who states in chapter 10 of *Das Kapital* that 'Capital is dead labour which, vampire-like, lives only by sucking living labour, and lives the more, the more labour it sucks' (qtd. in Gelder: 20).[21] Like Hess, Marx characterizes what he regards as an age of extreme capitalism as Jewish in nature. In his unsettling work, 'On the Jewish Question', published in the same year as Hess's *The Essence of Money*, Marx makes the joint declarations that 'Money is the jealous god of Israel, beside which no other god may exist', and 'The god of the Jews has been secularized and has become the god of this world' (37). Marx's explanation of the nature of the problem and its solution runs as follows:

What is the profane basis of Judaism? *Practical* need, *self-interest*. What is the wordly cult of the Jew? *Huckstering*. What is his worldly god? *Money*.
Very well: then in emancipating itself from *huckstering* and *money*, and thus from real and practical Judaism, our age would emancipate itself. (34)

Discerning in Judaism 'a universal *antisocial* element of the *present time*' (34), Marx advocates the destruction of this Mammon-based religion. Only then, he argues, may society regain its health.[22]

While the writings of Hess and Marx are extremely resonant for Stoker's *Dracula* in which the vampire threatens to subvert the British nation, these thinkers regard all forms of capitalism as detrimental to Europe. Their proposed solution of purging society of its 'Jewishness' signified the destruction of capitalism *in all of its forms*. For Stoker, however, the Weberian distinction between 'good' Protestant and 'bad' Jewish capitalism remains fully operative. Delineating the exact nature of these moral and immoral capitalist forms is crucial to understanding *Dracula*'s economic critique. Most prevalent is the suggestion that Count Dracula's greatest threat is the eradication of all competition. As Franco Moretti has astutely commented, Dracula – despite his national origins – is the symbolic embodiment of monopoly capitalism: 'solitary and despotic, he will not brook competition' (*Signs*: 92). According to E.J. Hobsbawm, a new phase of capitalism had begun to emerge in fin-de-siècle Britain where 'combination [was] advanced at the expense of market competition, business corporations at the expense of private firms, big business and large enterprise at the expense of smaller' (44). Although Hobsbawm designates several labels for this new capitalist form – among them 'corporation capitalism' and 'organized capitalism' – perhaps the most longstanding and popular description of it is 'monopoly capitalism' (44). This new capitalist form went hand in glove with the growth of imperialism. According to Moretti, monopoly capitalism, a serious threat to free competition and individual liberty, was perceived in fin-de-siècle Britain as a 'foreign threat' because British 'monopolistic concentration was far less developed (for various economic and political reasons) than in the other advanced capitalist societies' like the United States (*Signs*: 93). Moretti claims further that, as the nineteenth-century British middle class could not imagine monopoly as the *future* face of capitalism, it was represented in the figure of Count Dracula as 'the tyranny of feudal monopoly' (93). Such a foreign threat is represented in Stoker's novel as endangering the future of British free enterprise.

Robert Smart likewise maintains that two narratives emerge in *Dracula*: the first is the domestic tale of the salvation of the Harkers and England, the other is 'a morality tale about money' (253). Smart, argues that the second story is 'embedded more deeply in the structure of the novel, [and] is about money and free enterprise, wherein the dangers of monopoly – symbolized by the greedy Count Dracula – are successfully thwarted by the combined enterprise of a young band of entrepreneurs' (253–4). Smart also notes that the blood transactions in *Dracula* are vitally connected to the monetary transactions:

> In the second story, blood is money, the 'life substance' of a free economy. A free flow of money is vital to an evolved capitalist economy, while the concentration of money and capital in the hands of a few monopolists staunches both free capital flow and movement up or down the socioeconomic ladder. (254)

The blood and monetary transactions in the novel support Moretti's and Smart's theoretical claims. The gold-hoarding Transylvanian Count only parts with his capital in England when he makes investments in London property. His Mammonism is further exhibited in a later episode where, when cornered by Van Helsing's crew in one of his haunts, he imperils himself attempting to recover some of his cash and figuratively 'bleeds' money when cut. After Harker cuts the cloth of Dracula's coat with his great Kukri knife (the very instrument which will later shear Dracula's throat on his final day of reckoning, 377), a wide gap produces 'a bundle of bank-notes and a stream of gold' (306). Thereafter, Dracula risks his life scrambling to retrieve some money before finally escaping (306). Such actions are contrasted to the healthy monetary circulation practised by the wealthy Christian Englishman, Lord Godalming, and the American adventurer, Quincey

Morris, who unreservedly finance the Dracula crusade. Just before setting off on their campaign, Mina states:

> Oh, it did me good to see the way that these brave men worked. How can women help loving men when they are so earnest, and so true, and so brave! And, too, it made me think of the wonderful power of money! What can it not do when it is properly applied; and what might it do when basely used! I felt so thankful that Lord Godalming is rich, and that both he and Mr. Morris, who also has plenty of money, are willing to spend it so freely. For if they did not, our little expedition could not start, either so promptly or so well equipped ... (356)

Mina's loaded words underline Stoker's economic critique about the polarized positive and negative ends to which money may be put. Count Dracula's self-interested, egoistic, monopolistic, and figuratively 'Jewish' capitalist practices battle against the selfless and charitable, 'Christian' capitalist practices of Van Helsing and his 'brotherhood'. Two different types of transactions compete for domination: the Crusaders undertake a 'transaction of life' (236) in order to defeat Dracula whose parasitic 'transactions' are usually fatal.

These morally divergent uses of money, 'the blood of civilization' (Osborne: 131), are also reflected in the novel's complex blood transactions. While Dracula parasitically and perversely drains blood from his female victims, the Christian Brotherhood who oppose him are portrayed as martyrs who selflessly donate their blood in a series of hazardous transfusions undertaken to revive the vampire's victims. This blood battle also serves to illustrate how Dracula's monopolizing tendencies extend into the human and, more specifically, the sexual domain. Count Dracula's words to the Van Helsing brotherhood illuminate his aspirations to become a harem-master in Britain. His taunt to the men is telling in this regard: 'Your girls that you all love are mine already; and through them you and others shall yet be mine – my creatures, to do my bidding and to be my jackals when I want to feed' (306). If nothing else, Dracula is a clever strategist who recognizes what his enemies consider to be valuable. Moreover, Dracula cunningly attacks England in the female population where Stoker intimates she is the most vulnerable.

As Moretti and Smart maintain, therefore, Count Dracula is a dreaded economic and sexual monopolist/imperialist. Subjecting *Dracula* to a Freudian psychoanalytic 'reading between the lines', however, Moretti further illustrates how Protestantism displaces anxieties about its own tendencies by projecting them onto an 'Other'. He argues that Dracula is actually a consummate *Protestant* whose practices herald the advent of monopoly capitalism in Europe.[23] In Moretti's words:

> Dracula (unlike Vlad the Impaler, the historical Dracula, and all other vampires before him) does not *like* spilling blood: he *needs* blood. He

sucks just as much as is necessary and never wastes a drop. His ultimate aim is not to destroy the lives of others according to whim, to waste them, but to *use* them. Dracula, in other words, is a saver, an ascetic, and upholder of the Protestant ethic. (91)

Stephen D. Arata offers a similar psychoanalytic reading when he argues that 'in Dracula the British characters see their own ideology reflected back as a form of bad faith, since the Count's Occidentalism both mimics and reverses the more familiar Orientalism underwriting Western imperial practices' ('Occidental': 634). While Moretti's disregard of the multi-layered anti-Semitic semiotics associated with *Dracula* neglects the more nuanced aspect of this novel's structural strategy, his projection theory is nonetheless insightful. In the cogent words of Stephen Arata:

> Dracula is the most 'Western' character in the novel. No one is more rational, more intelligent, more organized, or even more punctual than the Count. No one plans more carefully or researches more thoroughly. No one is more learned within his own spheres of expertise or more receptive to new knowledge. A reading that emphasizes only the archaic, anarchic, primitive forces embodied by Dracula misses half the point. (*Fictions*: 123).

The demonic, proselytizing Count does become a conduit for cultural guilt in whose being 'British culture sees its own imperial practices mirrored back in monstrous forms' (108).

In true Gothic fashion, Dracula's greatest threat thus lies in the elimination of the secure boundary between the novel's British gentlemen and the alien, Judaizing vampire they resemble and enable. Their resemblance, I would suggest, finds its historical origins in the controversial figure of Benjamin Disraeli who was, as I have explicated, popularly regarded as a hyper-imperialist national interloper. While Stoker's representation of Dracula as a Crypto-Jewish gentleman is suggested early on in the novel during Harker's trip to Transylvania thus extends the tradition of anti-Disraeli literary portraits inaugurated by Trollope, it proves ultimately uncontainable and casts dark shadows on British imperialism. The vampire–gentleman equation is suggested early on in the novel during Harker's trip to Transylvania when he does not perceive Dracula's reflection in the mirror despite the fact that Dracula is standing immediately behind him (25). Dracula's perpetration of brutal acts in Transylvania while wearing Harker's clothes further blurs the boundary of identity between vampires and imperialists (48). Albeit perhaps unconsciously, Stoker intimates an unsettling point of contact between these two groups. The Count's incredible assimilation skills further promote the uncanny vampire–imperialist affinity. This aristocrat is startlingly rapid in his acculturation to his newly adopted homeland. Before even visiting England, his English is, as Jonathan notes, 'excellent' and his voracious appetites extend, as his library clearly attests, to knowing all things English (19). After his arrival in England, when he is first spotted by Jonathan Harker on the streets of London, Dracula does not appear to be a foreigner (172). He proves extremely adept at passing for a British native. It is intriguing, however, that while Stoker erases Dracula's national difference in this scene, he does not extinguish his moral difference. This is, as Mina notes when she sees Dracula for the first time, inscribed on the Count's physiognomy. Rather appropriately given his lupine associations, Mina's description of Dracula is reminiscent of the Big Bad Wolf: his 'face was not a good face; it was hard, and cruel, and sensual, and his big white teeth, that looked all the whiter because his lips were so red, were pointed like an animal's' (172). What seems to be suggested by this scene, however, is that even good British Christians like Mina and her husband may have trouble recognizing the disguised Count Dracula as he lurks around London. Looking like one of them, Dracula and his 'big white teeth' are 'all the better to convert them with, my dear!' As Van Helsing relates, the threat of conversion, of becoming 'as him [Dracula]...without heart or conscience, preying on the bodies and the souls of those we love best' (237) is a foremost fear.

Drawing on the work of John Allen Stevenson and Stephen Arata who claim that if blood represents racial identity, Dracula deracinates his victims and renders them 'Other' (Stevenson: 144; Arata, *Fictions*: 116), I am arguing that Dracula threatens to Judaize Christian Britons by way of his very infectious bite. As the case of Lucy Westenra illustrates, Dracula's Christian victims who are repeatedly bitten become prey to a physical, mental, sexual, and moral decadence that is frequently signalled in the novel by way of an iconography of filth. In keeping with his 'Gothic Jew' forefather Fagin in Charles Dickens's *Oliver Twist*, who is portrayed as a conspiratorial (155, 188, 351), fanged (417), offal-eating (186) inhabitant of a filthy city district (102–3) and 'ugly ghost just rose from the grave' (187) who converts Britain's impoverished male children into heartless thieves and fathers prostitutes, Count Dracula combines the joint threat of immigrant alien Eastern European Jews and demonized, speculating capitalist Anglo-Jews. This literally 'monstrous' is also in keeping with the popular image of Disraeli as Crypto-Jew. Contact with Dracula, a hoarder of filthy lucre and 'filthy leech' (51), renders Lucy 'foul' (213) and Mina 'unclean' (284). Dracula's victims thus assume the characteristics associated with the Jews at the fin de siècle. Indeed, Britons do not even have to be bitten in order to be affected by Dracula. As the members of the Crew of Light discover, simply having contact with the Count emasculates them and induces hysteria (103, 174). This phenomenon, among others represented in the novel, is supported by a variety of contemporary pseudo-scientific treatises linking degeneration, mental illness, and syphilis specifically to the Jew.

The figure of the Wandering Jew played a significant role in fuelling the already established fires of anti-Semitism at the fin-de-siècle. It was at this stage that he wandered into the annals of European psychiatric literature. In a medical thesis published in 1893, Henry Meige had fostered a new image of the Wandering Jew as a psychopathologized type (Goldstein: 541). Notably, Meige was a student of Dr Jean Martin Charcot, the head of Paris's prestigious Salpêtrière School who had been a patron at the Lyceum Theatre's Beefsteak Room (*Personal* I.: 316), and a figure mentioned by Van Helsing in Stoker's novel in relation to hypnosis (191).[24] Deploying what came to be known as 'retrospective medicine', Meige argued that the bulk of the content of legends derived 'from straightforward "observations of material facts"'. In other words, 'what the folk authors had been observing' in the case of the Wandering Jew, was 'a medical reality' (542). As Meige outlined, the restless wanderings of the Jewish race had 'not been caused supernaturally, as punishment for their role as Christ-killers, but rather naturally, by their strong propensity to nervous illness' (543). Making 'a virtual career out of being patients' (542), these eternal wanderers were searching for a cure for their nervous afflictions. Sceptical about medicine and maligned as overly preoccupied with their psychological and physiological selves, they travelled extensively from one doctor to another, soliciting medical opinions about their neurotic ailments. Capping off this fictional portrait with a sleight of hand worthy of a Gothic novelist, Meige explicitly analogized 'the scepticism of such patients to the crime of the Wandering Jew: refusal to believe in medical power was tantamount to that fateful refusal to believe in the divinity of Christ' (542).

Bram Stoker's representation of the Count suggests this psychopathologized Wandering Jew as he 'unnerve[s]' the men who come into contact with him (248). Dracula's association with madness is emphasized by the fact that Renfield, the Count's foremost adherent in England, worships his 'master' from inside Dr Seward's insane asylum. Literalizing the Scriptural phrase 'the blood is the life' and engaging in demonic Black Masses with a variety of living creatures, Renfield is significantly described as suffering from something 'like *religious* mania' (100; emphasis added). The threat of insanity spreads, however, as the novel progresses. Dr John Seward initially fears that Van Helsing's 'mind can have become … unhinged' (204), and once he and the other Crusaders become engaged in the hunt for Dracula, Seward fears that 'we must be all mad and … we shall wake to sanity in strait-waistcoats' (274). As Lucy Westenra's nocturnal walks in Whitby illustrate, the vampire's bite also occasions somnambulistic wandering in his victims (who do manage, ironically, to garner several doctors' opinions as to the origin of their neuroses). The formulation of this psychopathologized type suggests pseudo-scientific embroidering on the traditional stereotype of the Jew as a neurotic wanderer. While the *Archives israélites* responded to Meige's claim arguing that Jewish wandering was a result of long-term, systematic persecution (545), many prominent European psychiatrists argued that due to generations of inbreeding, Jews were more prone to mental illness than other groups (Chamberlin and Gilman: 291).

Fin-de-siècle pseudo-scientific treatises on degeneration and criminality also fostered racially based anti-Semitic ideas that are current in *Dracula*. Mina deduces, for example, that 'The Count is a criminal and of criminal type, Nordau and Lombroso would so classify him, and *qua* criminal he is of imperfectly formed mind' (342). Despite the fact that Max Nordau was himself a Hungarian Jew – in fact he was 'one of Zionism's founding fathers' (Shimoni: 103) – in works like *Degeneration* where he outlined the proximity of genius and insanity, he argued that Jews were different from their Christian neighbours and more prone to insanity and moral and physical degeneration (Chamberlin and Gilman: 292). Although his claims were not racially based – he maintained that social pressures and persecutions rather than biology predisposed the Jew to insanity – he nonetheless produced material that was put to anti-Semitic use. The extent of its dissemination is extremely noteworthy, the first English edition of *Degeneration*, ostensibly a work of literary criticism, seeing seven printings in 1895 (Arata, *Fictions*: 27). This use of his evidence seems deeply ironic as Nordau consistently maintained that European anti-Semitism attested to 'European society's retreat from rational liberalism into irrational degeneracy' (Shimoni: 101). Lombroso, Nordau's 'Dear and Honoured Master' to whom he dedicated *Degeneration*, also furnished pseudo-scientific material that was readily referenced by anti-Semites. At the fin de siècle, Lombroso endeavoured to outline the physical characteristics of the criminal and, especially due to the shape of Dracula's *nose*, would have deduced that the Count was a criminal, a child-like throwback to an earlier stage of human development. According to Lombroso, the criminal's nose 'is often aquiline like the beak of a bird of prey' (Wolf, *Essential*: 403 n. 25). Such material fed into established anti-Semitic stereotypes.[25]

The serious, often fatal, and prevalent sexually transmitted disease of syphilis was also used to fuel anti-Semitism at the fin de siècle. Jews had been closely related to the spread and incidence of syphilis since the fifteenth century when the disease first appeared in Europe where it was 'commonly called the Peste of the Marranos' (Gilman, *Freud*: 61). As Sander Gilman relates, 'literature on syphilis in the nineteenth century contains a substantial discussion of the special relationship of Jews to the transmission and meaning of syphilis' (Gilman: 61). Joseph Banister's anti-Semitic work *England Under the Jews* (1901) charges Jews with the spread of various 'blood and skin diseases' (61). The fin de siècle was a period of intense moral panic when, in the face of shocking numbers of syphilitics, doctors predicted 'the unavoidable "syphilisation" of the Western world' (Showalter, *Sexual*: 188). The terror of contracting syphilis reached such epidemic proportions that the word 'syphilophobia' was coined to describe this pathological fear. In this regard, it is noteworthy that syphilis specifically symbolized *domestic* disease in the nineteenth century. As Elaine Showalter explains, 'Whereas in the Renaissance syphilis functioned as a religious symbol of the disease in the spirit, and during the Restoration became a political mètaphor for the disease in the state, fin-de-siècle English culture treats it as a symbol of the disease in the family' ('Syphilis': 89).

Stoker's representation of vampirism clearly taps contemporary syphilo-phobia. The Count imperils Christian British family values as he infects and transforms upright British women into sexually aggressive anti-mothers. Indeed, Stoker's Gothic narrative features an intriguing association between the Jew and the prostitute who were regarded, in the popular worldview of the period, as syphilis carriers.[26] Images of vampire women were ubiquitous in fin-de-siècle culture where they generally represented gold-digging, syphilitic prostitutes (Dijkstra: 351). Bram Dijkstra's description of the symbolic significance of female vampires illuminates the dynamic between Dracula and the sexually voracious, polyandrous women in Stoker's novel:

> By 1900 the vampire had come to represent woman as the personification of everything negative that linked sex, ownership, and money. She also came to represent the equally sterile lust for gold of woman as the eternal polyandrous prostitute. She was the absinth drinker, her fever for the gold of man's essence fed by her addiction, who was seen by Félicien Rops as lurking in the alleyways of Paris. She was the woman cloaked in darkness who beckoned man to his death … (351)

Like Dracula, whose 'sexualized' bite usually results in death, seductive fin-de-siècle prostitutes could transmit deadly syphilis through sexual intercourse.

The semiotic connection between Jews and prostitutes is actually a convention that dates back to at least the sixteenth century when 'Jewish usury was likened to the practice of female prostitution'. As one observer then reported, the 'beastly trade of courtesans and cruel trade of Jews is suffered for gain' in Italy; both 'suck from the meanest to be squeezed by the greatest' (Shapiro, Shakespeare: 99). Sander Gilman's chapter on Jack the Ripper in *The Jew's Body* examines the traditional 'deviant' coupling of the Jew and the prostitute on the margins of polite society. Posing '"dangers" to the economy, both fiscal and sexual, of the state' (120) as they 'represent[ed] a realm of exchange divorced from production' (Gallagher: 43), the prostitute and the Jew were united as heartless 'lovers of filthy lucre' (Shapiro, *Shakespeare*: 99). Indeed, they were yoked together by way of the stereotype of the Jewish pimp then prevalent in both Germany and England.[27] Their joint perversion lay in their 'sexualized relationship to capital'[28] which was ultimately sterile and unproductive as it entailed regarding money 'as a substitute for higher values, for love and beauty' (Gilman, *Jew's*: 124). L'Hermite made such a suggestion in 1899 with the rhetorical query, 'Are not all prostitutes "Jews", usurers in their way, since what they lend, they only lend for a large sum of money' (Geller: 31).

Stoker's loveless, Mammon-worshipping Count (47) is effectively an economically unproductive (parasitic) Jewish pimp who poses fiscal and sexual dangers to the British nation. While there are no prostitutes *per se* in *Dracula*, Lucy's New Woman-style, polyandrous inclination to marry three men (59) foreshadows her vampiric transformation into the 'Bloofer Lady', a supreme and terrifying anti-mother who preys on children in and around Hampstead Heath (178). As *The Westminster Gazette* report in *Dracula* makes clear, these children are like Jack the Ripper's murder victims: both sets of victims went missing at night and were discovered with their throats slightly torn or wounded (177).[29] Responding to the unconscious desires of British women – those creatures popularly referred to as lilies[30] and 'angels in the house' – Dracula assumes the role of a pimp who converts them into creatures/ladies of the night. It is noteworthy that Lucy's metamorphosis into the seductive, prostitute-like 'Bloofer Lady' is presaged by the series of blood transfusions undertaken by Dracula's opponents. Van Helsing explains that this act of blood-mixing is a form of sexual/marital transaction which transforms the 'sweet maid' Lucy into a 'polyandrist' (176).[31] Rather fittingly, therefore, Dracula's female victims become monopolists like him once they are infected by the vampire's bite. Robert Smart has noted that Lucy's tendency towards polyandry is not unlike Dracula's monopolizing tendency. While she yearns to monopolize all of the men, Dracula yearns to monopolize all of the women. It is perhaps this tendency which initially attracts the Count to her. According to Smart:

> ...Lucy at one point jests in a letter to Mina that she wishes she could marry them all [her three suitors] and that the law should be changed to allow it. This is an unusual remark for a proper Victorian maid and may account for the ease with which she falls into Dracula's power. She has the acquisitive instinct of the monopolist, something we do not see anywhere in Mina's character. (256)

Indeed, Mina does not exhibit the polyandrous, New Woman-associated tendencies we see in Lucy.

Although the proto-feminist New Woman is only actually mentioned twice in Stoker's novel (88, 89), she is a significant spectre haunting both that novel and the British fin de siècle. She was identified by her conservative critics, like Stoker, 'variously with feminism, mannishness, promiscuity and decadence' (Blain *et al.*: 792). In terms of the gender ideology of the British fin-de-siècle, the New Woman was often viewed as monstrous. This view was articulated in the February 1887 issue of *Lady's Realm* magazine where the New Woman is specifically described as 'this feminine Frankenstein' (Calder: 164). Marie Corelli's *The Sorrows of Satan* (1895) singles out this 'monster' for graphic and long-winded verbal attacks, and Stoker implies the inclusion of pen-wielding New Women in a scathing essay he published subsequent to *Dracula*. In 'The Censorship of Fiction' (1908), an article he wrote for *The Nineteenth Century and After*, Stoker denounces the 'class of works ... meant by both authors and publishers to bring to the winning of commercial success the forces of inherent evil in man' (485). He argues that the people involved in this venture '*prostitute* their talents' (487; emphasis added), and that women writers are 'the worst offenders in this form of breach of moral law' (485).[32]

Lucy Westenra represents this decadent, feminist, mannish, and promiscuous figure in *Dracula*. Given these attributes, she is appropriately matched with Stoker's decadent Transylvanian Count. This demonic union becomes understandable when read in the light of social preoccupations in fin-de-siècle Britain. As Anthony Julius notes in his recent, provocative work, *T.S. Eliot, Anti-Semitism, and Literary Form*, 'In late nineteenth-century Europe, misogyny and anti-Semitism were frequent partners. This alliance represented a reaction, in part, to a certain coincidence in demand by women and Jews for emancipation, especially in Germany and Austria' (19). Although British Jews had gained emancipation by the time of *Dracula*'s publication, other concerns existed regarding them, as I have outlined earlier in this chapter. Women and Jews were, however, 'becoming more visible in the civic culture of Western Europe' at the fin de siècle (Gilman, *Freud*: 83), and their dual threat was repeatedly represented in the cultural productions of that period. They stand united, for example, in the hugely popular work *Sex and Character* (1903) by Viennese theorist Otto Weininger. In that disturbing publication, Weininger connects women – significantly described along traditional anti-Semitic lines as 'human *parasites*' (Dijkstra: 219; emphasis added) – with various 'degenerate races', among them the Jews. According to Weininger, Judaism was 'saturated with femininity' (220), and both women and Jews were decadent creatures devoid of any moral sensibility. As Weininger expressed it:

> Greatness is absent from the nature of the woman and the Jew, the greatness of morality, or the greatness of evil. In the Aryan man, the good and bad principles of Kant's religious philosophy are ever present, ever in strife. In the Jew and the woman, good and evil are not distinct from one another. (221)

As Bram Dijkstra notes, 'Many of his [Weininger's] ideas had already been elevated to the status of commonplaces among the intellectuals of the 1890s' (218). Furthermore, many of these intellectuals were British. Ford Madox Ford observed that Weininger's book 'had spread through the serious male society of England as if it had been an epidemic' (218).

Stoker's polymorphously perverse Count and his seductive creatures of the night threaten to drain Britain of its vitality and infect its sacrosanct

Christian 'family values'. This national infection involves the violation of various taboos – particularly sexual ones – which terrify Stoker's xenophobic, 'gender-anxious culture' (Craft: 219). That Count Dracula should engender these transgressions is fitting given his role as an arch-transgressor. The suggestion is made, for example, that the Count is related to two of the 'weird sisters' (48) who attempt to attack Jonathan Harker in Dracula's Castle. Two are described as 'dark ... [with] high aquiline noses, like the Count's' (37). As Dracula may be said to be somewhat like Victor Frankenstein who single-handedly 'fathers' his own offspring, he threatens to blur familial and sexual boundaries, distinctions fundamental to Stoker's Christian Victorian society. As Clive Leatherdale cogently argues:

> There exists in the book an endogamous motif which, other than the Count, links nearly all the main characters as members of one large, figurative family. Most couplings can be slotted into parent–child or brother–sister relationships. Even Dracula's harem approach Mina with the words 'Come, sister'. (*Dracula*: 174)

Notably, as I have illustrated in Chapter 1, Jewish endogamy was often misrepresented as incest by anti-Semites. Dracula's figuratively Jewish 'sexual' practices, therefore, threaten Christian Britain. Given Dracula's Crypto-Jewishness and the figuration of his encounters with Christian British women as sexually perverse and even fatally infectious, the threat of 'racial'-religious miscegenation – specifically Jewish-Christian intercourse[33] – also hangs over Stoker's novel as it did many others of the era. Moreover, although Dracula limits his attacks in England to women, he does attack men on board the *Demeter*, the ship that brings him to England (81–6).[34] The suggestion of homosexuality was in keeping with longstanding anti-Semitic stereotypes. Among various other commentators, Voltaire regularly drew extravagant inferences from the Bible to illustrate that 'homosexuality and sodomy had been rife among the Hebrews' (Manuel: 235). The anti-Semitic charge aside, however, Dracula's illicit acts would have struck a special chord with Stoker's audience in the light of the 1895 trial of Oscar Wilde.

The threat of the Crypto-Jew in *Dracula* not only involves the blurring of racial/religious boundaries but the erasure of sexual difference. While the Count transforms feminine British lilies into mannish New Woman prostitutes, he feminizes British men. In psycho-sexual terms, virile British male Christians are threatened by the circumcised genitalia of the alien male Jew that, in the familiar racist folklore, are regarded as deviant and symbolically castrated.[35] This threat is especially foregrounded in the opening scenes in Transylvania. Imprisoned in Count Dracula's labyrinthine castle, and at the mercy of three sexually voracious, Lilith-like vampire women who consume infants, Jonathan Harker assumes the female role in Stoker's novel. Nowhere is this made more obvious than in the desperate final lines of Harker's opening travelogue of terror when he writes, 'At least God's mercy is better than that of these monsters, and the precipice is steep and high. At its foot man may sleep – *as a man*' (53; emphasis added). Upon his return to England, Harker reiterates that he '*felt impotent*, and in the dark, and distrustful' about whether his experiences in Transylvania were real or not (187–8; emphasis added).

This threat of emasculation is brought closer to home when Dracula immigrates to England. There, responding to deviant women like Lucy Westenra who possess voracious sexual and physical appetites which are generally attributed to the New Woman, Dracula begins to create his new race of phallic women who threaten castration. In a significant excerpt from Dr Seward's diary, Lucy is described as possessing wrinkled brows 'as though the folds of the flesh were the coils of Medusa's snakes' (212). The suggestion is later made that Mina's act of 'changing' into a vampire also involves becoming Medusa-like. When Harker watches her sleeping, he remarks how her 'forehead is puckered up into little wrinkles, as though she thinks even in her sleep' (267–8). According to Sigmund Freud in his essay 'Medusa's Head' (1922), the snake-haired Medusa threatens men with castration. Her serpentine locks of hair are trophies of penises in horrified reaction to which men gain erections (273). Her gaze literally petrifies them. Although Freud fails to acknowledge it, however, petrification also involves feelings of overwhelming desire. Such ambivalence marks Harker's initial confrontation with the female vampire trinity in Dracula's castle. As he relates this experience with these *vagina dentata*-style creatures:

> There was something about them that made me uneasy, some longing and at the same time some deadly fear. I felt in my heart a wicked, burning desire that they would kiss me with those red lips. (37)

Notably, the two most popular phallic women (pseudo New Women) represented in Stoker's culture were Jewesses. Salome and Judith were notorious symbolic castrators who robbed men of their power and vampirically drained them of their sexual potency by decapitating them.[36] As Bram Dijkstra notes, they signified the epitome of degeneracy in Stoker's day:

> Salome and Judith were both Jewish women, as the intellectuals of the turn of the century did not tire of pointing out. As such, they combined the crimes of women with those of a 'degenerate race'. If women's prosaic, everyday presence made it impossible for most men to maintain a constant sense of enmity toward them, the Jew was still there, guilty of the same crimes as women. (401)

As Salome had demanded the decapitation of St John the Baptist, she was regarded as particularly anti-Christian in her transgressive desires. Judith's Biblical role as 'a paragon of self-sacrificial martyrdom for a noble cause' was, however, radically altered to meet the demands of the age (377). In the images of many 'late nineteenth century painters, ... [Judith] is unmasked as a lustful predator, an anorexic tigress' (377). Further to this, this dangerous-yet-desirable, ambivalently submissive-dominant Jewess (Cohen-Steiner: 27) who 'invokes fantasies of desire, exoticism, and guilt' (Garb: 26) is frequently represented in the visual arts as prostitute-like at the fin de siècle. During this era, conversely yet significantly, 'the disease-disseminating prostitute was frequently represented as Jewish' (Geller: 29).[37] Moreover, Salome and Judith laid the groundwork for the cinematic vamp of the early twentieth century, a mesmerizing creature popularized, notably, by a Jewish actress named Theda Bara.[38] Lucy Westenra is sister to these symbolically castrating, power-hungry New Women. In the graphic staking and decapitation of Lucy, however, the tables are definitively turned on these diabolical female creatures in Stoker's *Dracula* (215–18).

In the light of the conjoined Jewish menace and the advent of the proto-feminist New Woman's movement, *Dracula* functions as a type of ritually purgative text whose task is 'to represent, externalize and kill off a distinct constellation of contemporary fears' (Pick, 'Terrors': 71). The fear of female prostitution and its multi-layered signification of sexual and monetary perversion is cunningly played out in Stoker's novel. These semiotic components were also at work in the literary and journalistic coverage of the Jack the Ripper murders which caused an incredible sensation in Stoker's day. Indeed, significant connections exist between *Dracula* and the Whitechapel murders which serve to illuminate the intensity of the semiotic coding and yoking of Jews and prostitutes in Britain at the fin de siècle. Like *Dracula*, the Ripper murders also had a 'capacity to play out an elaborate repertoire of contemporary anxieties – from heterosexual violence, to the "lavender menace", to the specters of imperial and domestic industrial decline' (Walkowitz: 4).

What must initially be noted is that Stoker consciously forged a connection between Dracula and Jack the Ripper. As Jean Goens has argued in *Loups-Garous, Vampires et Autres Monstres*, two greatly mythologized figures lurk in the shadows of the character of Count Dracula – Vlad the Impaler and Jack the Ripper. Concerning Stoker's inclusion of the 1888 Whitechapel murders, Goens writes:

> En effet, dans le roman de Bram Stoker, Dracula quitte la Transylvanie pour aller commettre une série de crimes sanglants à Londres, durant l'automne d'une année non précisée de la fin du XIXe siècle. Jack L'Éventreur avais commis ses crimes en automne 1888, et l'auteur a certainement subi leur impact inconscient, tout en percevant sans doute l'intérêt commercial de l'exploitation littéraire de cette série sanglante. (83)

The year after the initial publication of his compelling thriller, Stoker was asked to write an English introduction to the novel's first foreign-language translation.[39] Entitled *Makt Myrkranna* (*Powers of Darkness*), *Dracula* became available to Icelandic readers in 1901. The curious nature of this linguistic choice aside, Stoker's introduction to *Makt Myrkranna* forges a significant connection between *Dracula* and the 1888 Whitechapel murders. Despite Jonathan Harker's closing note to the novel which foregrounds the unbelievable nature of the *Dracula* 'manuscript' – he writes, 'We could hardly ask anyone even did we wish to, to accept these as proofs of so wild a story' (378) – Stoker effectively assumes his Count's role as a boundary-blurrer by extending his novel's crucial fiction–reality theme beyond its textual parameters in the introduction to the Icelandic edition. There, Stoker explains that 'for obvious reasons, ... [he] changed the names of the people and places concerned'. He makes the further claim that 'Both Jonathan Harker and his wife (who is a woman of character) and Dr. Seward are ... [his] friends and have been for so many years, and ... [he] never doubted that they were telling the truth' (*Makt*: 8). Finally, Stoker attempts to place his narrative within an actual historical context. Referring to Dracula's demonic London transactions, he writes:

> I state again that this mysterious tragedy which is here described is completely true in all its external respects, though naturally I have reached a different conclusion on certain points than those involved in the story. But the events are incontrovertible, and so many people know of them that they cannot be denied. This series of crimes has not yet passed from the memory – a series of crimes which appear to have originated from the same source, and which at the time created as much repugnance in people everywhere as the notorious murders of Jack the Ripper ... (7–8)[40]

That the Jack the Ripper serial prostitute slayings should be mentioned in connection with *Dracula* is not surprising. This reference directly contradicts Stoker's grand-nephew's claim that 'there is no hint in the novel [*Dracula*] or any of his writings of either the Ripper's violence or the subsequent panic' (Farson: 152). It serves, in fact, to support various critical claims by such writers as Grigore Nandris, Phyllis Roth, Clive Leatherdale, and Bernard Davies, that the Ripper was significant to Stoker's creation of *Dracula*. Curiously, fiction and reality actually did overlap to some degree for, as Belford relates, 1888 was not only 'the year Jack the Ripper terrorized Whitechapel, bringing evil into the drawing rooms of Mayfair and Kensington', it was also the year in which Stoker first conceptualized *Dracula*, 'a story that would intermingle Shakespeare's dark psychology with contemporary evils' (202).

In the light of their roles as bloodthirsty sexual predators, Dracula and Jack the Ripper may be described as blood brothers. Indeed, the depictions of the Ripper provided by contemporary commentators illustrate the semiotically consanguineous nature of London's degenerate serial killer and Dracula. In the words of Judith Walkowitz:

> Faced with a 'senseless crime', press commentary invoked the figure of the Gothic sex beast, a 'man monster' motivated by 'bloodthirsty lust' who 'goes forth stealthily and takes his victims when and where he already pleases', akin to the 'were wolf' of 'Gothic fiction'. Declared the *Daily Telegraph*, 'we are left...to form unpleasant visions of roving lunatics distraught by homicidal mania or bloodthirsty lust...or finally we may dream of monsters, or ogres'. (197)

The nature of the Ripper and his crimes also bears strong resemblances to Count Dracula's attacks on British women:

> ... [the Ripper's] 'lust murders' and sexual mutilations of prostitutes were... unnatural alternatives to heterosexual copulation...Often imagined as a seasoned urban traveler, the Ripper could move effortlessly and invisibly through the spaces of London, transgressing all boundaries, committing 'his' murderous acts in public, under the cover of darkness, exposing the private parts of 'public women' to open view. (3)

Similarly, Stoker's protean Count, another seasoned traveller, exports vampirism – an unnatural alternative to heterosexual copulation that involves mutilation – to England, and exposes women's private, repressed desires to public view. Notably, Jack the Ripper's notorious mutilations of women finds another reverberation in *Dracula*. A certain redemptive form of mutilation (165) is also performed by Van Helsing and his Crew of Light in order to save Lucy from her vampire state (215–17).

Dracula and Jack the Ripper may also be said to be blood brothers along ethnic lines as the Ripper was suspected of being Jewish. Notably, the impoverished district of Whitechapel where the Ripper conducted his bloody business became so densely populated with Jewish immigrants at the fin de siècle that it was called 'Jew-town' (Feldman, 'Importance' 56). Arthur Morrison's depiction of Whitechapel for the readership of the *People's Palace Journal* in April of 1889 – only several months after the murder of Jack the Ripper's last victim – betrays signs of the anti-Semitism current in Stoker's day:

> A horrible black labyrinth ... reeking from end to end with the vilest exhalations; its streets, mere *kennels of horrid putrefaction*; its every wall, its every object, slimy with the indigenous ooze of the place; swarming with *human vermin*, whose trade is robbery, and whose recreation is murder; the catacombs of London – darker, more tortuous, and more dangerous than those of Rome, and *supersaturated with foul life*. (Frayling, 'House': 203; emphasis added)

Physical and moral decadence pervade Morrison's disturbing verbal portrait, and the images of Whitechapel's filth, kennels, and vermin-like inhabitants anticipate Stoker's foul-smelling, fanging Count who conducts an army of rats (252).

Turning to a closer examination of the Ripper, a serial killer who occasionally cannibalized his victims (Showalter, *Literature*: 188), one discovers that many anti-Semitic stereotypes were at play in his 'story'. Not only was the Ripper suspected of being of a 'marked Hebrew type' (Walkowitz: 204) – 'Jacob the Ripper' (203) – he was specifically thought by many to be a Jewish *shochet* or ritual slaughterer. This figure was bastardized and demonized in the popular media as a 'kosher butcher,' one who was perhaps engaged in a type of ritual slaughter of harlots as decreed in the Talmud (Sharkey: 115). As Sander Gilman has written, 'The reality, at least that reality which terrified the London of 1888, was that the victims were *butchered*' (*Jew's*: 112; emphasis added). A result, in part, of the repeated assertion 'that no Englishman could have perpetrated such a horrible crime', the popular 'Jacob the Ripper' theory led, Walkowitz argues, to 'two local developments: denunciation of Jews at the inquests as ritual murderers and widespread intimidation of Jews throughout the East End' (203). As Christopher Frayling relates, 'Official visits were made to kosher abbatoirs, [and] two ritual slaughtermen were arrested' as Ripper suspects ('House': 200). This Ripper as *shochet* idea is explicitly suggested in *Dracula* in the heart-racing scene where the Count is cornered by Van Helsing's crew and figuratively bleeds money after being cut by Harker's Kukri knife. Before taunting them that the girls they love are his, Dracula says, 'You think to baffle me, you – with your pale faces all in a row, *like sheep in a butcher's*. You shall be sorry yet, each one of you!' (306; emphasis added). In keeping with the Count's role as a monstrous mirror to the Crew of Light, however, Lucy's purported 'saviours' are also revealed to be adept at Ripper-like mutilation when they stake and decapitate her.

The Blood Libel and the spectre of a Jewish conspiratorial secret society intent on world domination were resurrected during the Ripper investigations. Especially after 30 September, the night of the double murders of Lizzie Stride and Catherine Eddowes, Jewish 'revolutionaries' and socialists came under increasing suspicion. Stride's body had been discovered in front of a political club mostly frequented by Jewish socialists, and a portion of Eddowes's bloodstained apron was found in front of a building on Goulston Street which was inhabited by Jews (Walkowitz: 204). Although it is still debated, some argue that the Ripper's scrawled chalk message above the location of Eddowes's apron which read 'The Juwes are not the men that will be blamed for nothing' (Walkowitz: 204), attested, due to its poor English construction and orthography, to Jack's Eastern European, Jewish background (Gilman, *Jew's*: 122). The 'Jacob the Ripper' theory was further supported on the third of December when *The Times* reported that the Ripper was a Russian 'nihilist' and a member of a 'secret society'. While Clive Bloom argues that Jack became 'the focal point for an attack on foreigners (in particular Russians) and especially foreigners who ... [were] bent on under-mining society in secret *via covertly ritualised murder*' (120–1; emphasis added), the fact is that the 'Russians' entering England in the 1890s were pre-dominantly Jews, and it was the Jews who had long been associated with both ritual murder and conspiracy. As Arnold White complains in *The Modern Jew*, 'The immigration into this country of the poor of other lands is now almost entirely restricted to persons of the Jewish race' (xi).

In *Dracula*, with its central theme involving the alien invasion of the body and the body politic, Bram Stoker may be said to have evoked many of the sexual, political, and economic spectres haunting Britain during the period of the Jack the Ripper murders. Many of these spectres, specifically those involving the Jews, were long established. By way of Gothic narrative, Stoker compellingly enacted their ritual purgation. Indeed, the idea of purification in association with the syphilis menace was significant to both Stoker's *Dracula* and the media construction of Jack the Ripper. A popular rumour cir-culated that 'the Ripper was a mad doctor avenging himself on prostitutes for a case of syphilis' (Showalter, 'Syphilis': 94), and there is even one critic, Robert Tracy, who advances the highly controversial claim that Stoker, afflicted with syphilis, reenacted in *Dracula*, 'with a mixture of moral out-rage and prurience, the 1888 murders of Whitechapel prostitutes attributed to Jack the Ripper' ('Syphilis': 45).

Although the mirroring of the deviant woman with the deviant Jew was an established semiotic staple – in their earliest configuration they were con-sidered to be both dangerously seductive and easily seduced by fleshly and material pleasures – it would seem that Stoker adapts this connection in *Dracula* in order to lay to rest fin-de-siècle anxieties in general and anxieties awakened by the Ripper murders in particular. While, as Gilman argues, 'the carrier of disease can only be eliminated by one who is equally corrupt and diseased' (*Jew's*: 111) – thus only the deviant Jack the Ripper may kill the deviant prostitute – the tables are turned in *Dracula*. Dracula may respond to the call of the wild polyandrous woman lurking at the core of the sacred angel in the house who, as Mina explains, never entirely loses the taste of the original apple of sin (183), but Mina also functions as an intriguing 'dou-ble agent' who is used to defeat Dracula. Although the Count initiates her into vampirism so that he may gain a connection with his pursuers, she ends up supplying the crucial spiritual link that precipitates Dracula's demise.[41] As such, she taps into what Stoker describes as 'the mother' in herself in order to defeat evil (230).

The exorcism of Mina's 'inner prostitute' and the reinstatement of British Christian 'family values', therefore, are inextricably bound up with Dracula's bloody, violent, and ritualistic death. Only when the Count is killed does Mina's symbolic mark of Cain made by Van Helsing with the Host vanish (296). This mark stigmatizes Mina as one of Dracula's Wandering Jew-vampire brood, and its disappearance is figured as a Christian redemption. As Quincey Morris dies in his act of Christian 'service', Mina describes how:

> With one impulse the men sank on their knees, and a deep and earnest 'Amen' broke from all as their eyes followed the pointing of his finger as the dying man spoke:
> 'Now God be thanked that all has not been in vain! See! the snow is not more stainless than her forehead! The curse has passed away!' (378)

In this instance, Mina is also redeemed for the traditional and acceptable wifely motherly role. Mina's journal description of Dracula's final moments also foregrounds the idea of spiritual salvation: 'I shall be glad as long as I live that even in that moment of final dissolution there was in the face a look of peace, such as I never could have imagined might have rested there' (377). In the ritual, Crucifixion-like death scene where he is sheared through the throat by Harker's great Kukri knife (377), Bram Stoker's cut-throat, Shylock-like Count is finally released from his accursed, undead state which involves eternal, carnal bondage. In this dramatic 'fantasized genocide' (Arata, 'Occidental': 640), Stoker's demonic Wandering Jew is effectively converted to Christianity by monomaniacal imperialist missionaries who render Transylvania safe for tourism. Dracula is ultimately granted a violently inflicted peaceful rest while England makes her symbolic return to health in the form of good old-fashioned 'family values' monogamy and honest 'Christian' capitalism. Unsettling concerns about Britain's role as a vampire empire nonetheless remain and are symbolically signalled in the birth of Harker's son Quincey. While some of their 'brave [American] friend's spirit ... [may have] passed into him' as Harker claims (378), so too, by way of his adoring mother, did Dracula's infectious blood (288).

6

Afterword: Pathological Projection and the Nazi Nightmare

> He [the Jew] is and remains a parasite, a sponger who, like a pernicious bacillus, spreads over wider and wider areas according as some favourable area attracts him. The effect produced by his presence is also like that of the vampire; for wherever he establishes himself the people who grant him hospitality are bound to be bled to death sooner or later.
>
> (Hitler: 172)

> The portrait of the Jews that the [German] nationalists offer to the world is in fact their own self-portrait.
>
> (Horkheimer and Adorno: 168)

> They were drunk with blood.
> (Witness's statement at the trial of Adolf Eichmann describing the nature of the Nazis)

This study has attempted to illustrate how, in the pages of British Gothic literature, 'the English turned to Jewish questions to answer English ones' (Shapiro, *Shakespeare*: 1). To this end, it has traced the transformation of the largely benevolent Wandering Jew of legend into a dreaded-yet-desired and ultimately ethnically unidentified vampire figure in various British Gothic works published over the course of a century. It has delineated how anti-Semitic stereotypes involving the Blood Libel, secret societies, and the Cabala were progressively grafted onto that legendary figure in various reformulations of the Jewish Question in order to engage with shifting debates about British national identity. That these spectropoetics, as I have termed them, became manifest in the British Gothic novel, a literary form which emerged at the end of the eighteenth century, was significant: this genre betrayed conscious and unconscious desires and anxieties about national issues (Punter, *Literature*: 62) during 'one of the most formative periods in the making of the modern world and ... the forging of British identity' (Colley, *Britons*: 7).

Criticism of Gothic literature and religious/national questions has generally focused on the role of Roman Catholic France. This study has concentrated instead on the figure of the Jew, an Other who, while long demonized in Britain, became increasingly symbolically central to a variety of debates over modernity, particularly those involving the joint issues of ethics and economics. Indeed, the wandering signifier 'Jew' was so popularly and widely circulated in these debates to warrant the Jews' metaphoric classification, in the words of Derek Penslar, as 'Shylock's children'. According to Penslar, 'when capitalism's transfiguration of Europe was the guiding star of social thought, speculation about the position of the Jews in Europe – the Jewish question – could not be separated from anxiety about the new industrial order – the social question' (262). Max Horkheimer and Theodor Adorno have, similarly, astutely remarked in relation to this subject that the 'Jews remained objects, at the mercy of others…Commerce was not their vocation but their fate' (175). Questions concerning the ethics of economics seemed, in short, to have especially plagued the conscience of capitalist, missionary, imperialist Britain throughout the eighteenth and nineteenth centuries, and the nationally and morally transgressive figure of the vampiric Wandering Jew onto whom these anxieties were projected bespoke a deep-seated ambivalence regarding these engagements: while, on one hand, he was a religious throwback who reminded an expanding Christian British Empire of its 'superstitious' yet theologically secure past, he simultaneously attested to its enlightened yet possibly morally untethered future. This monitory projection, therefore, warned of Britain's 'Jewish' propensities and excesses in their various manifestations. Given the fin de siècle's preoccupations, it is not surprising that the culmination of the convergence of the Wandering Jew and the vampire occurred in Bram Stoker's *Dracula*. Perceived threats and actual socio-historic events were fictionalized in that novel that reflected the British Empire's then growing sense of vulnerability both at home and abroad.

To assume that Gothic literature's vampiric Wandering Jew entirely disappeared from the pages of twentieth-century British literature, however, is to make an extremely faulty assumption. In such works as Charles Williams's weird *All Hallow's Eve* (1948), the Gothic Wandering Jew is intact in all of his demonic glory. According to the Preface by Williams' longtime friend T.S. Eliot, *All Hallow's Eve* is a product 'of morbid psychology' (xv), and provides a singular anti-Semitic portrait of 'the single-minded lust for unlawful and unlimited power' (xvii). Williams's unnaturally aged, dark-skinned, alien Jew (52) is a satyr-like scientist who de-rationalizes and mesmerizes his victims and engages in chilling sexual/reproductive experiments – referred to as 'magical operation[s]' (110) – involving the use of homunculi physically modelled on himself (110–13). The fact that this novel appeared after the horrifying revelations of the Nazis' Final Solution, is not only extremely disturbing but indicative of the mesmeric power of what may be described as a dark 'archetype' in British consciousness. While various illuminating critical assessments of the Gothic tradition and anti-Semitism in British Modernist literature have been independently undertaken over the past decade, it is hoped that the present study may lay the groundwork for their future joint examination.[1]

By way of a conclusion and in order to establish a significant point of contact between the German and British treatments of the Gothic Wandering Jew, I will undertake a cursory examination of the vampiric Wandering Jew in another national setting and in another genre – namely, Nazi propaganda cinema. The genre of Gothic literature may be said to have been a product, in part, of reciprocal German–English dialogue at the end of the eighteenth century when the German Terror-novel, or *Schauerroman*, was popular in Britain, and British Gothic literature was garnering great attention in Germany. In the light of this literary cross-fertilization, German and British Gothic novels shared similar characters and themes. While the figures of the vampire and the Wandering Jew appeared separately in the *Schauerromanen*, however, their combined spectres haunted nineteenth-century German philosophical essays about the Jewish Question. As illustrated briefly in Chapter 5, a bloodthirsty, itinerant Jewish capitalist who threatened German national security was featured in essays by such writers as Karl Marx and Moses Hess.

Under the leadership of Adolf Hitler, the National Socialist Party resuscitated the figure of the vampiric Wandering Jew subsequent to Germany's defeat in the First World War when the humiliating 1919 Treaty of Versailles saddled that nation with a reparations bill amounting to 27 billion dollars. Subsequent to the ratification of this Treaty, various prominent Jewish politicians were scapegoated for their role in Germany's defeat. Although several perceptive writers have noted parallels between the concepts of racial purity and genocide in Stoker's *Dracula* and Nazi Germany,[2] a crucial distinction must be foregrounded regarding the uses to which the vampiric Wandering Jew was put in fin-de-siècle Britain and Nazi Germany. While this figure was central to the consolidation of national identity in both countries, his religious affiliation remained unidentified in Stoker's Gothic *fantasy* in stark contrast to his more *realistic* treatment in Germany. Through the medium of propaganda cinema, the Nazis thus fostered a new and terrifying stage in the development of the vampiric Wandering Jew: he blurred yet another boundary by purportedly wandering into 'reality' where he was deliberately manipulated to intend harm. As the immediate audience reactions to these films and the establishment of the death camps attest, these nightmarish projections were hugely successful in their aims.[3] That a deeply entrenched anti-Semitic tradition could be readily tapped – replete with a complex semiotics – to facilitate the Final Solution, illustrates the nefarious relationship and the complicity between anti-Semitic word and deed.

Notably, the vampiric Wandering Jew featured in Nazi propaganda cinema was drawn from the terrifying phantasmagoria of German Expressionist

cinema, an artistic movement which was itself influenced by Gothic literature. Such a figure was on exhibit in various German Expressionist classics,[4]
including Fritz Lang's famous *Metropolis* which featured the evil Jewish
alchemist-scientist Rotwang. This provenance was ironic given that the
Nazis considered German Expressionism to be fostered by decadent Jewish
'wheeler-dealer[s] and bloodthirsty Nosferatus' who had 'contaminated'
pure German cinema (Rentschler: 155).[5] Prior to 1940, the imagery of Jews
as peripatetic parasites had been disseminated in various Nazi publications.
Hitler described the Jews as vampires in *Mein Kampf* in 1925 (172), and a
horrifyingly illustrated issue of Julius Streicher's Nazi newspaper, *Der Stürmer*,
revived the Blood Libel in May of 1934. Its front cover depicted two rabbis
sacrificing a group of 'Aryan' children and collecting their blood (Ben-
Sasson: 1128). The Wandering Jew also played a prominent role in the largest
anti-Jewish exhibition of the prewar years organized by the Nazis. Displayed
in Munich's Deutsches Museum in November of 1937, the exhibition *Der
ewige Jude*, 'the Eternal Jew', was composed of anti-Semitic materials, caricatures, and slogans. Although a section was included on the Jews in film, the
Nazis only made major use of film in their propaganda effort at the beginning of the war (Friedländer: 383). In 1940, the vampiric Wandering Jew
assumed the starring role in two of these propaganda films. Specifically
produced to incite violence and prepare Germans for the Final Solution, Veit
Harlan's *Jud Süss* and Fritz Hippler's *The Eternal Jew* were both advertised as
realistic portraits of contemporary German Jews. While Joseph Goebbels, the
Nazi propaganda minister, insisted that Harlan's drama be billed as a realistic historic portrait (Rentschler: 151), Hippler's venomous cinematic work
was described as non-fiction. Following orders, one critic wrote that
The Eternal Jew is 'not a fiction film, but a documentary film about world
Jewry ... Its effect on the viewer lies precisely in this cool objectivity' (181).

Like Bram Stoker's *Dracula*, Nazi German propaganda cinema expressed
the theory that nationalism was inextricably bound up with the concept of
racial purity. As Anthony Synnott has argued, Nazism was, from its inception, 'an ideology based on blood' (31) according to which Jews were
national polluters who could never be assimilated into Germany. This idea
had been advanced in Arthur Dinter's *The Sin Against the Blood* (1918), one
of the top five German inter-war bestsellers (Geller: 33), which cautioned, 'If
the German people do not succeed in shaking off the Jewish vampire, which
they unwittingly feed with their very heart's blood, and do not render him
harmless – which could be done simply by legislative measures – the German
people will perish before long!' (qtd. in Bein: 17).[6] Hitler had articulated
these *völkisch* ideas as early as 24 February 1920 when, in a highly publicized
mass meeting at the Hofbrauhaus

> ... he delivered a venomous denunciation of the Jews, recited the Party's
> twenty-five point program, and concluded his presentation with another

attack on the Jews. Point Four of his announced program read: Only those who have German blood, regardless of creed, can be our countrymen. Hence no Jew can be a countryman. (Friedman, 'Edge': 55)

Drawing upon popular European fin-de-siècle, pseudo-scientific ideas about the Jews and degeneration, Hitler later publicly declared that the 'opinion that it is possible to co-exist or come to some sort of compromise with this ferment of decomposition among peoples, is like hoping that the human body might in the long run assimilate plague bacilli' (qtd. in Herzstein: 181). Further to this, as this chapter's epigraph illustrates, he blatantly labelled Jews 'vampires' (172). Goebbels's anti-Semitic descriptions also drew upon similar pseudo-scientific notions about disease and degeneration. Among other venomous statements, he called the Jew a 'bum parasite', 'the incarnation of evil, the ferment of decomposition, [and] the demon who brings about the degeneration of mankind' (Herzstein: 178). In response to this national plague, Goebbels assumed the role of hygienist (177). Propaganda films were a vital component in his program to 'purify' the nation.

Harlan's *Jud Süss* and Hippler's *The Eternal Jew* reflect Nazi Germany's *völkisch* ideology and its principal fear of Crypto-Judaism. As was the case with the *conversos* during the period of the Spanish Inquisition, the Nazis were particularly fearful of the Jews who had assimilated into their society. This group of non-ghettoized Jews was especially suspected, as Alain Finkielkraut articulates, of conspiring to undermine the nation:

Genocide [in W.W.II] was not imposed on the Jews *in spite of* their effort to assimilate, but *in response* to this very attempt. The more they hid their Jewishness, the more terrifying they became to others…It took a Jew without qualities to fit the part of spy or conspirator…Assimilated Jews thought they were being charged with excessively Jewish behavior, when it was their will to integration that was really the crime: the wary would only weaken their case in the very way they secured their defense. A kind of relentless mechanism had been set in place, turning every protestation of innocence into yet more evidence of guilt. (69–70)

The Eternal Jew illustrates, however, that ghettoized Jews also form a part of this terror – they are conspiring infiltrators in training. Hippler's film and *Jud Süss* were specifically produced in order to promote the punishment of both the dangerous Jewish infiltrators and their unassimilated co-religionists. Towards this end, both films revived the Blood Libel and portrayed the Jews as contaminated aliens who expertly feigned assimilation in order to pursue material gain through their 'Jewish' capitalist methods of usury, swindling, and fraud.

Described by one critic as a monster movie in the guise of a realistic portrait and a historical reconstruction (Rentschler: 158), Harlan's *Jud Süss* relates the story of Süss Oppenheimer, a Jewish moneylender who insinuates his way into the court of Karl Alexander, Duke of Württemberg, in the eighteenth century. Ironically, Harlan's film was based on Léon Feuchtwanger's lengthy philo-Semitic novel published in 1926 and followed on the heels of a British cinematic adaptation of that novel that rendered Süss with tremendous sympathy.[7] Feigning knowledge of the secret sciences in order to persuade Karl Alexander that his actions are divinely sanctioned, Süss gains control over him. In return for Süss's aid, the Duke grants him access to Stuttgart, a city closed to Jews, and appoints him finance minister. Public disfavour grows, however, as a result of Süss's burdensome taxation schemes and the coup d'état he engineers in order to expand the Duke's power. Süss's rape of the daughter of a prominent District Councillor and her subsequent suicide seal Süss's fate. Karl Alexander dies leaving his finance minister unprotected, and Süss's public execution follows. The film ends with a stern proclamation from the Chairman of the Council that ordered Süss's execution that all Jews have been banned from Württemberg. In statements directed at the 1940 German viewing audience, the Chairman invokes the Blood Libel. He cautions, 'May our descendants hold firmly to this law [of Jewish expulsion], so they can save themselves much suffering and save their goods and lives and the blood of their children and their children's children.'

A true product of anti-Semitic stereotypes that date back to the medieval period, Süss Oppenheimer is 'a personified Satan' (Hull: 169), and *Jud Süss* has been aptly described as 'dramatized *Stürmer*' (165). Particularly in his skill at assimilating into Stuttgart society, Süss Oppenheimer has also been characterized, more intriguingly, as 'a latterday Dracula, who ... infects the German corpus[,] dissembles and disseminates' (Rentschler: 156).[8] Süss's act of raping the young Dorothea Sturm is reminiscent of Count Dracula's symbolic acts of miscegenation in Britain, and the blood-money theme that is central to Stoker's novel is also prominent in Harlan's film. Indeed, in the first sequence shot in the Jewish ghetto where Süss lives, the shochet Itzak is shown cleaning his bloody knife while declaring that Süss should lend Karl Alexander money so that the Jews may 'take, take, take!' Jews, it is repeatedly suggested, bleed the nation dry. The power-hungry, well-travelled Süss who claims 'the world' as his home, is later denounced by Dorothea's fiancé Faber as a degenerate and unproductive gambler whose 'blood money' has been stolen from Stuttgart's productive families and their deserving children. Much like Stoker's Count Dracula, Süss is portrayed as a terrorizing anti-family-values force and his murder is figured as a redemption of German society.

Fritz Hippler's *The Eternal Jew* has been called the most vicious and repulsive anti-Semitic film produced by the Nazis. Indeed, some film critics have described it as 'the most evil film ever made' (Herzstein: 180). Intended to instill fear and anger in its viewing audience, this pseudo-documentary was presented as a realistic exposé of the Crypto-Jew in Germany. Having successfully 'infiltrated' European civilization for its own financial gain, this 'international power' is described as terrorizing 'world exchanges, world opinion, and world politics' with their capital. A particular warning is issued about the second and third generations of Jews who have left the ghetto. The commentator notes that their

> ... assimilation has reached its zenith. Outwardly, they try to act just like the host peoples. People without good instincts let themselves be deceived by this mimicry and consider Jews the same as they are. Therein lies the enormous danger. These assimilated Jews remain forever foreign bodies in the organisms of their host peoples regardless of appearances.

Extending this Draculaesque thematics of the host, the commentator informs the audience that this race of parasites never produces anything and always destroys its host nation:

> Wherever the body of a nation shows a wound, they anchor themselves and feed on the decaying organism. They make business out of the sickness of the nations and thereafter endeavour to deepen and prolong all conditions of sickness.

The film proceeds to show how the 'world-wide wanderings' of the Jews have paralleled the migrations of the rat: both have transmitted fatal plagues from one nation to another.

By far the most disturbing and controversial sequences in *The Eternal Jew*, however, occur at its conclusion. The ritual slaughter of a cow is screened on the heels of the claim that 'Judaism is not a religion [but] a conspiracy against all non-Jews by a sick, deceitful, poisoned race against the Aryan peoples and their moral laws.' This graphic and unsettling ten-minute episode features the stereotypical Shylock-style shochet and portrays Judaism as a bloodthirsty religion. The film concludes with the commentator's description of how implicitly 'humane' Nazis have banned such 'barbarian' practises. They enacted a law in 1933 forbidding Jewish ritual slaughter. The commentator concludes with the proclamation:

> ... National Socialist Germany has made a clean sweep of all Jewry. Jewish thinking and Jewish blood will never again pollute the German nation. Under the leadership of Adolf Hitler, Germany has raised the battle-flag against the eternal Jew.

Harlan's *Jud Süss* and Hippler's *The Eternal Jew* illustrate that Nazi anti-Semitism was borne of what Horkheimer and Adorno have called 'pathological projection'. Blaming the Jews for all things modern and the erosion of traditional values and institutions (Goodrick-Clarke: 5), the Nazis found a scapegoat upon whom they projected their own diseased self-image: 'in order to feel their own existence and confirm their own reality, the Nazis needed the Jews' (Rentschler: 154). Ironically, in its organization and belief system, Nazism resembled Judaism as it had been demonically portrayed in the European world-view: it was a conspiratorial, millenarian, cabalistically grounded secret society (Goodrick-Clarke 5)[9] whose leader regarded himself as the new German messiah (197).

As I hope this study has persuasively illustrated, anti-Semitism – in both word and deed – has been the real vampire throughout history. It has transgressed national borders engaging – in its most extreme forms – in a sinister form of cultural demonology. Despite the exact nature of the impact of anti-Semitism, however, this ideology of hatred has been crucial to the construction of national identity. Horkheimer and Adorno have perceptively highlighted the fact that anti-Semitism is, tragically, a 'ritual of civilization' and the pogroms the true ritual murders (171). *Night*, Elie Wiesel's haunting memoir about his experiences during the Holocaust, concludes with a graphic description of the fatal effects of anti-Semitism. After years of sadistic brutality at the hands of the Nazis and the tragic death of his father just months before his liberation from Buchenwald, the young Wiesel describes how he encountered his reflection in a mirror for the first time since his internment. All he saw, he says, was a corpse staring back at him whose look has since plagued his memory (127). Wiesel's account shares striking resonances with both the European stereotype of the spectral Jew and Gothic literature's variously represented Wandering Jews. It is, furthermore, the stuff of which that genre's nightmares and horror films are generally made. As Lester D. Friedman has perceptively written:

> Photographs and films taken in concentration camps grasp the strikingly sad resemblance between the tortured inmates and the walking dead of so many vampire movies. What demonic power could match Hitler's feat of turning members of the most humane professions into murderers and supporters of a totally immoral regime? Hitler and his followers transformed the world into a vast and terrifying horror movie in which good and evil battled to the death for mankind's soul. (56)

Among millions of 'Others', Elie Wiesel was the victim of the vampire called anti-Semitism. Tragically, and despite assertions to the contrary (Penslar: 262), the Jewish Question in the form of 'Shylock's ghost' does continue to haunt the Jews in a truly Gothic and illogical 'return of the repressed' manner. Although 'capitalism's transfiguration of Europe' may no longer be, as Derek Penslar has argued, 'the guiding star of social thought' (262), the idea of the Jew remains inextricably bound up with that transfiguration in the British unconscious where it continues, on an occasional but regular basis, to rear its spectral head. Likewise, anti-Semitism tragically continues to haunt nations – and notably even the cemeteries of those nations[10]– refusing to let Jews live or rest in peace.

Notes

Introduction: The Nation and the Spectral Wandering Jew

1. According to legend, Christ was driven from Ahasuerus's doorstep where he stopped to rest. In response to the Jew's action of striking him while shouting, 'Walk faster!', Christ replied, 'I go, but you will walk until I come again!' (Anderson, *Legend*: 11). By way of this curse, Christ figuratively transferred his burdensome cross to the Jew.
2. As Hyam Maccoby explains, 'One of the strongest beliefs of medieval Christians was that the Second Coming of Christ could not take place until the Jews were converted to Christianity. (Marvell's "till the conversion of the Jews" means simply "till the millennium".) The Jews, therefore, had to be preserved; otherwise the Second Coming could not take place' (239). According to Michael Ragussis, British conversionist societies justified their activities by claiming to 'aid in this divine plan, and with a kind of reverse logic their establishment was viewed as a sign of the proximity of the Second Coming' (*Figures*: 5).
3. Roger of Wendover's *Flores historiarum* and Matthew Paris's *Chronica majora* from the early thirteenth century provide all of the details of the legend, but the transgressor in their versions is Pilate's doorkeeper, a Roman named Cartaphilus, and not a Jew (Anderson, *Legend* 16–21). While in certain Italian versions of this tale the accursed wanderer is a Jew (19), he is not described as Jewish in the British legend until the early seventeenth century. The conjunction between the entry of this legend and Jews into England is in keeping with N.I. Matar's observation that 'anti-Jewish literature surfaced on the English scene when the Jews physically began entering England' ('The Idea ... Between the Reformation': 31, n. 53).
4. Cheyette traces this ambivalent 'semitic discourse' back to 'received Christological discourse' which positioned Jews as both Christ-killers and redemptive saviours. He cites a few examples of this discourse as follows: 'Jews are represented as *both* the embodiment of liberal progress *and* as the vestiges of an outdated medievalism; as a bastion of empire *and* one of the main threats to empire; as prefiguring a socialist world state *and* as a key force preventing its development; as the ideal economic man *and* the degenerate plutocrat *par excellence*; as the modern alienated artist *and* the incarnation of a corrupt worldliness' (*Constructions*: 9).
5. This shift in attitude toward usury actually commenced during the Renaissance. According to M. Lindsay Kaplan, 'as economic development made it an increasingly necessary transaction, public attitudes toward the charging of interest became more accepting. Hence, merchants and moneylenders, whose moneylending was regularly condemned in the Middle Ages, were viewed in an increasingly positive light. Public opinion changed, however, only through the process of vigorous debate; the older perspectives did not disappear overnight' ('Cultural': 188). Further to this, Benjamin Nelson relates how John Calvin's exegesis of the text of Deuteronomy that 'formed a cornerstone of the blood brotherhood morality of the Hebrew tribesmen' (xix), became 'a Gospel of the modern era' (74). While Jews interpreted that text as proscribing the taking of usury from one's brother and prescribing the taking of usury from foreigners (xix–xx), Calvin reinterpreted it more

liberally as permitting both the taking of usury from one's brother and foreigners (73–4). In Calvin's view, Scriptures only forbade 'biting usury (*neshek*), usury taken from the defenseless poor' (75).

6. E.J. Clery cites Montesquieu as explaining 'that bills of exchange, the first paper money, were the invention of the Jews, who were in constant danger of having their wealth confiscated by the ruling power. In the course of time this ghost money served to transgress national boundaries, shifting the balance of economic power from royal house and the aristocratic caste, with their immobile landed inheritances, to the cosmopolitan trading classes' (133). Susan Manly lends support to this theory in an editorial note about Maria Edgeworth's *Harrington* and Mr Montenero's claim that banknotes were a Jewish invention (Edgeworth, *Harrington* 120). According to Manly, 'Paper money was first issued in Europe by the Bank of Stockholm in the seventeenth century, and then by the Bank of Amsterdam. As a result of its stability and convertibility, the bills of the Bank of Amsterdam were exchanged and negotiated more frequently than coins, and often at rates above their face value. Amsterdam was home to a thriving Jewish commercial community at this time ... The antecedents of bank-notes were the receipts given in exchange for deposits of cash' ('Endnotes': 356, n. 104).

7. Linda Colley argues that the primary 'Other' against which Christian Britain defined itself was Catholic France. With the advent of British imperialist expansion, 'Others' later included a variety of colonized peoples. Colley explains her theory on national identity formation in general and British national identity formation in particular, as follows: 'Time and time again, war with France brought Britons, whether they hailed from Wales or Scotland or England, into confrontation with an obviously hostile Other and encouraged them to define themselves collectively against it. They defined themselves as Protestants struggling for survival against the world's foremost Catholic power. They defined themselves against the French as they imagined them to be, superstitious, militarist, decadent and unfree. And, increasingly as the wars went on, they defined themselves in contrast to he colonial peoples they conquered, peoples who were manifestly alien in terms of culture, religion and culture' (*Britons*: 5). While Colley does not mention the Jewish role in British national identity formation, her description of the process surrounding the forging of national identity would recognize the validity of their inclusion. Furthermore, in the light of the equation established between Jew and Jacobin in 1790s Britain that I chronicle in Chapter 2, the Jewish 'Other' found himself, to some degree, in the traditional 'French' enemy camp that Colley identifies.

8. According to Katharine M. Briggs, that legend was originally 'in almost all its forms, the story of the regeneration of a soul, of penitence and a hard long service rendered to humanity' (137). Hyam Maccoby identifies other variants, however, especially in Germany, 'which lacked the positive hope of reconciliation' with Christ at the Millennium. He characterizes them as follows: 'In those negative versions, the sufferings of the Wandering Jew are seen merely as just punishment for his depravity. He is not a convert to Christianity, but an unregenerate Jew, with evil magic powers derived from his long experience of life and his association with the Devil. It was this negative version that gave rise to the nineteenth-century anti-Semitic stereotype, taken up with enthusiasm by the Nazis, of the Jew as a "rootless cosmopolitan"' (252). In his impressive study of the medieval European conception of the Jews and its relation to modern anti-Semitism, Joshua Trachtenberg argues that this more negative strain of the Wandering Jew legend was formulated to suggest the intransigence of the actual Jewish community.

According to Trachtenberg, 'In most of the accounts the Wandering Jew had forsaken his false faith and adopted the true faith of Jesus, in contrast to the obduracy of his fellow Jews; several versions, however, have him remain a Jew, refusing to acknowledge through baptism the truth to which his own unique career testified, and thus typifying the attitude of all Jews' (17).

9. The Introduction to W.D. Rubinstein's *A History of the Jews in the English-Speaking World: Great Britain*, provides one such recent excoriating commentary. Like Eugen Weber who suggests that contemporary historians have a tendency to foist current preoccupations onto historical periods (8), Rubinstein accuses contemporary Anglo-Jewish historians of exaggerating British anti-Semitism. In his words, 'The younger school seem to be engaged in a kind of Dutch auction to determine who can discover the most insidious examples of British anti-semitism, reminiscent of the Four Yorkshiremen in the famous Monty Python skit who outdo one another to depict the exaggerated horrors of their youth' (32). Michael Ragussis provides a measured and intelligent response to Rubinstein when he cautions against 'self-congratulatory nationalism' amongst British historians (297) and suggests that we should not be 'inattentive to the subtle but nonetheless widespread powerful and deeply ingrained forms of anti-Semitism that are an important part of English history and culture' ('Secret': 296).

10. I do not mean to suggest by this list that philo-Semitic thinkers and activists were unheard of until the nineteenth century. John Toland's extremely articulate 1714 publication, *Reasons for Naturalizing the Jews in Great Britain and Ireland*, provides a wonderful case in point of a philo-Semitic work that predates the Victorian era. As to the endeavours of the cited nineteenth-century individuals, Owen submitted a petition in 1830 calling for the removal of disabilities from the Jews (Silberner: 30), which O'Connell supported, Hazlitt and Macaulay followed suit in 1831. For Hazlitt's and Macaulay's statements see Appendix VIII and IX in Rosenberg (331–7). Notably, in the course of his essay, Hazlitt deems anti-Semitic prejudice 'absurd and *Gothic*, because it is contrary to men's reason and feeling' (330; emphasis added). Hetherington, a staunch Chartist and Owenite, denounced the Archbishop of Canterbury in a newspaper article in 1834 for his declaration that the Jews were not fit to be trusted with the rights of citizenship (Silberner 31).

11. Linda Colley persuasively argues that a greater national consciousness was in evidence in England after 1750, due to a variety of factors – the development of communications and transportation infrastructure, the more widespread dissemination of print materials (especially newspapers and periodicals), a more mobile population, and the threats of invasion and war ('Whose': 100–3).

12. Curiously, Derrida does not use the term 'spectropoetics' in the course of his study. I borrow the term from the book's dust jacket. Derrida does refer, however, to Marx's deployment of 'something like a spectropolitics and a genealogy of ghosts' in *The Eighteenth Brumaire of Louis Bonaparte* (107). The most Gothic-inflected concept in that work is forged on its opening page and deals with the joint conceptions of history and inheritance. As Marx describes it, 'Men make their own history, but they do not make it just as they please; they do not make it under circumstances chosen by themselves, but under circumstances directly encountered, given and transmitted from the past. The tradition of all the dead generations weigh like a nightmare on the brain of the living. And just when they seem engaged in revolutionising themselves and things, in creating something that has never yet existed, precisely in such periods of revolutionary crisis they anxiously conjure up the spirits of the past to their service and borrow from them

names, battle cries and costumes in order to present the new scene of world history in this time-honoured disguise and this borrowed language' (97).
13. Although it has become commonplace to claim that Count Dracula possesses stereotypical Jewish features, Gothic specialists have failed to recognize his rich and extraordinary genealogy within the Gothic tradition. His gallery of ancestors yet remains in the shadows. My initial motivation to undertake this project involved answering the question, 'Did the "Jewish" Count Dracula have forefathers within the Gothic tradition?' While more specific details of the Count's immediate fin-de-siècle family are provided in Chapter 5, this entire study works towards unearthing his genealogy.
14. While Amanda Anderson describes the literary figure of the Jew in general in this manner, I am limiting my claim to the figure of the Wandering Jew given his explicitly transnational make-up.
15. See my forthcoming entry on 'Victorian Gothic Literature' in *The Grolier Encyclopedia of the Victorian Era*.
16. Lynn Pykett advances a similar claim when she delineates how ' "Gothic traces" ... [are] embedded in a range of popular fictional genres' – crime novels, the ghost story, the detective story, degenerationist fantasies, imperial romances, and scientific romance (192–3).

1   The Contested Enlightenment, the Contested Castle

1. The question of the origin and development of European nationalism is a very complex and contentious subject that has engendered a growing body of scholarship. While such a detailed examination is beyond the scope of this study, I am obviously making certain presuppositions about the topic that should be concisely laid out. I concur with Eli Sagan's assertion that nationalism is a '*sine qua non* of any society existing in the Modern world' (9). I am also essentially in agreement with Conor Cruise O'Brien that '[n]ationalism, as a collective emotion (as distinct from a body of doctrine, or ideology), is far older than the Enlightenment' (19). Adrian Hastings agrees. In *The Construction of Nationalism* (1997), he cogently considers the complex issue of the development of English national identity. In his Introduction he sets forth several of the most prominent claims relating to the subject. O'Brien draws a useful distinction between an older, spiritual and a newer, secular form of nationalism that I am also working on. In his words, 'With the Enlightenment what emerges is a distilled form of the old nationalism. Purified of supernatural religious and monarchist ideology, the new nationalism becomes self-sufficient, acknowledging and needing nothing superior to the nation' (19). While I am not convinced that such a comprehensive purification occurred in Britain, its sense of itself as a nation seems to have become more widely embraced during the Enlightenment, a process that intensified throughout the nineteenth century.
2. Such fears would be explicitly articulated half a century later in such works as Bruno Bauer's *The Jewish Question* (1843) that deemed Jewish emancipation a hopeless and socially dangerous experiment (Vital: 190).
3. As Norman Cohn noted in 1961, 'even today the Jew – the man who clings to the Old Testament and rejects the New, the member of the people into which Christ was born – is imagined by many Christians as typically an "old Jew", a decrepit figure in old wornout clothes' (*Pursuit*: 86).

4. Moses Mendelssohn, the foremost voice from the *Haskalah* (Jewish Enlightenment) who is celebrated as 'the Jewish Socrates' in Maria Edgeworth's *Harrington* (38), campaigned for Jewish rights and advocated the retention of Jewish particularities within a larger nation. He also responded to thinkers like Voltaire who portrayed Judaism as hopelessly superstitious by redefining Judaism as a rational faith, 'compatible with the rational deism favoured by the Enlightenment' (Robertson, *German-Jewish*: x). Ultimately, he unwittingly assumed an 'ambiguous position between preserving the traditions of Judaism and contributing to its dissolution' (Robertson, *'Jewish'*: 20).

5. Anti-Enlightenment thinkers in Germany, like the young Romantic writers Clemens Brentano and Achim von Arnim, positioned the Jews in a disparaging manner with 'humanity and enlightenment' (Robertson, *German-Jewish*: xv). Such views serve to support Bryan Cheyette's argument that Jews 'were constructed *at one and the same time* both as embodying the aspirations of an enlightened State and as undermining the essential characteristics of a particularist nation. Such was the disturbing ambivalence of "the Jew" who, in the end, embodied simultaneously both "culture" *and* "anarchy"' (*Constructions*: 269).

6. In explaining why the French decided not to have a type of English House of Peers in their country, Paine states, 'Because aristocracy has a tendency to degenerate the human species. By the universal economy of nature it is known, and by the instance of the Jews it is proved, that the human species has a tendency to degenerate, in any small number of persons, when separated from the general stock of society, and intermarrying constantly with each other. It defeats even its pretended end, and becomes in time the opposite of what is noble in man' (43). Paine's equation of Jews and aristocrats as morally degenerate is in keeping with their representation in published French Republican documents. Ronald Schechter notes an intriguing shift with regard to such representations where the image of the aristocrat 'comprised the vices most anathema to citizenship' during the Revolution while the Jew 'embodied what the ideal citizen was not' prior to the Revolution (87). It would seem that this shift occurred, in large part, because such disparaging images were not conducive to the Republican agenda to convert the Jews into full-fledged citizens.

7. Ronald Paulson first noted Burke's tendency to read the events of the French Revolution in terms of the Gothic (60–1). Frans De Bruyn has since commented on 'Burke's reliance on a gothic "paradigm" to structure and order the chaos of revolutionary events to which he ... [was] witness' (418). De Bruyn foregrounds how this allowed Burke to promote anti-Catholicism based on the 'established convention that locates the unsavory events of gothic romances in some dark corner of Catholic Europe – France, for example' (417). Maggie Kilgour has provided further evidence of this rhetorical strategy in her observation of Burke's concern with generational violence, a Gothic preoccupation. She insightfully notes 'Burke represents the Revolution in terms of the gothic imagery of grave robbing, parents dismembering their children and children dismembering their parents' (*Rise*: 29).

8. This phenomenon is in evidence in other European nations and at other historic moments. Speaking of the 1870s, for example, when Jews were generally associated with the primitive past, Ritchie Robertson notes, 'public discussion of the "Jewish Question" in Germany became sharply more hostile, as Jews were made the scapegoats for the drawbacks of modernity' (*Jewish*: 1). This equation remained in force in Germany into the twentieth century, especially during the Weimar Republic and Nazi eras.

9. The heated debate continues with regard to the Gothic's exact relationship to the past. Robert Mighall counters Maggie Kilgour's viewpoint about the Gothic's backward-looking glance and its role as 'a nightmare vision of a modern world made up of detached individuals, which has dissolved into predatory and demonic relations which cannot be reconciled into a healthy social order' (*Rise*: 12). In his opinion, 'These novels do not reject the advantages of enlightenment, modernity, and civilization in an irrational gesture of historical reversal; rather, they cling to these totems more insistently through their troubled recognition of the alternative' (xviii). Chris Baldick concurs with Mighall in his argument that the Gothic 'is a middle-class tradition, and its anxiety may be characterized briefly as a fear of historical reversion; i.e:, of the nagging possibility that the despotisms buried by the modern age may prove to be yet undead' (*Oxford*: xxi). Further to this, the principal distinction he draws between ghost stories and Gothic literature involves their attitude to the past. In his view, while ghost stories promote belief in an older superstitious worldview, 'Gothic fiction … usually shows no such respect for the wisdom of the past, and indeed tends to portray former ages as prisons of delusion' (xv). Intriguingly, Toni Wein arrives at the opposite conclusion when she focuses on attitudes towards the past to draw a generic distinction between the Gothic and the historical novel. Arguing that 'Gothic novels do more than rehearse the past; they figure that past as a lost Golden Age that can be recovered', Wein maintains that '[t]he yearning expressed in that backward glance helps us distinguish the Gothic novel from the historical novel with which it has frequently been compared, and with which it shares an episodic, retrogressive structure' (4). Based on these statements and my own observations while reading numerous Gothic works, I would caution against generalizations about the Gothic's attitude towards the past. Indeed, its position on this subject seems to be profoundly ambivalent, a standpoint suggested in its very label. As Maggie Kilgour has perceptively noted, '[t]he very name "gothic novel" which was ultimately given to the form he [Walpole] created is an oxymoron that reflects its desire to identify conflicting impulses: both towards newness, novelty, originality, and towards a return to nature and revival of the past' (*Rise*: 17–18).

10. In this regard, the Wandering Jew is associated with the Jews who were long known as the people of the book and the keepers of secret knowledge. The Wandering Jew's access to forbidden knowledge in Gothic literature is in keeping with the phrase Immanuel Kant coined as the *Wahlspruch* of the Enlightenment– *Aude sapere*, or 'dare to know' (qtd. in Foucault, 'What': 35) – and positions him, in general terms, as emblematic of a rapidly expanding educated public. As Patrick Brantlinger has perceptively argued about the representation of reading in the eighteenth and nineteenth centuries, 'All of the monsters bred by and in the shadow of the French Revolution are, to greater or lesser extent, enlightened; they are all the Gothic spawn of the Enlightenment Terror, the phantasmal domain of monsters, proves to be the domain also of literacy and "learning"' (Brantlinger, *Reading*: 68). Given that so much Gothic fiction plays on the idea of transgressing boundaries of knowledge and gaining access to that which is regarded as secret and forbidden, it seems curious to me that so little has been said to date about how Gothic fiction dialogues with the Enlightenment mantra of 'daring to know'. Brantlinger's *The Reading Lesson: The Threat of Mass Literacy in Nineteenth-Century British Fiction* – particularly Chapters 2 and 3, which deal with various Gothic novels – provides a noteworthy step in this direction.

11. Various scholars have commented upon this phenomenon. Bryan Cheyette mentions the irony that 'in recent years, much of the "semitic" indeterminacy that we have situated historically has been evoked by cultural theorists in a more generalized post-Holocaust and postmodern context. The impossibility of permanently situating "the Jew" within any given textual order has been universalized in numerous theoretical works to characterize the absence of any absolute meaning' (*Constructions*: 274). The Jew, he notes further, has been 'embraced and rehumanized as a paradigmatic representation of an exuberant post-modernity' (274). Further to this, Susan Shapiro observes that the trope of the Jewish Uncanny has 'perhaps been most prevalent and influential in its appearance in contemporary French critical theory, from the writings of Maurice Blanchot and Jean-François Lyotard to those of Jacques Derrida, Edmond Jabès, and Emmanuel Levinas' (74). Michael Weingrad is notably disturbed by the fact that postmodern theory is 'entangled ... in the darker legacies of Western attitudes toward Jews' (257). He traces the origins of this offensive tradition back to Jean-Paul Sartre's 1948 work *Anti-Semite and Jew*, which, problematically, deems Jewishness to be 'at bottom an existential condition created by antisemitism'. Weingrad notes further that this perspective 'was echoed in a more offensive register forty years later by Jean-François Lyotard, who said: "What is most real about real Jews is that Europe, in any case, does not know what to do with them: Christians demand their conversion; monarchs expel them; republics assimilate them; Nazis exterminate them." Derrida and his followers tend to see Jews as texts and ciphers, as metaphors, tropes, and traces; stripped of both historical and corporeal reality, these theoretical Jews hover about like pale shades, ironically fulfilling Toynbee's conviction that the Jews are a *Geistesvolk*, a phantom people' (257). Julia Kristeva's characterization of the Jew in *Powers of Horror* provides a single case in point. The Jew is 'phantasmatic' and the epitome of ambivalence (180) and abjection as s/he does not 'respect borders, positions, rules' and 'disturbs identity, system, [and] order' (4).

12. Susan Shapiro has provocatively suggested that the figure of Jew is repressed in all of Freud's writings (70), especially 'The Uncanny'. There, however, Freud revises the idea of the Uncanny Jew by displacing it onto the figure of the mother. In Shapiro's view, therefore, the maternal haunts 'The Uncanny' (70) as Freud 'turns the trope of the Uncanny from the Jew to everyman, returning the specter to its familial origin in the mother's body, her "womb", the first home' (71). As regards Hoffmann's tale, Ritchie Robertson concludes, on the basis of Coppelius's outfit, that he 'resembles a figure from the *ancien régime* which was then re-establishing itself after the fall of Napoleon' ('Introduction', *Golden*: xx). Unfortunately, Robertson fails to extrapolate on why such a spectre would generate such terror in Nathanael.

13. With specific reference to *The Interpretation of Dreams*, Robert J.C. Young suggests that Freud 'pulled off ... a fictional coup, unparalleled in literary history' (208) for he produced 'a [Gothic] novel that pretended to be a real work of scientific psychology' (206–7). Tipping his hat to 'his greatest literary precursor, the Romantic Gothic writer Thomas De Quincey' (213), Freud created a work whose real project was 'to make the reader undergo an experience – typically, a frisson of horror or of sexual excitement' (217).

14. Notably, Nicholas Royle's recent formidable study of the uncanny makes no mention of Judaism or the figure of the Jew.

15. I borrow this term from Kate Ferguson Ellis's wonderful 1989 study, *The Contested Castle: Gothic Novels and the Subversion of Domestic Ideology*.

16. Although my project concentrates on what Antony Easthope deems the *ideal* aspect of national culture as 'reproduced through narratives and discourses' as opposed to the *material* aspect, which is 'produced through institutions, practices and traditions which historians and sociologists can describe' (12), I never lose sight of the fact that these ideal and material aspects are connected as narratives and discourses help to determine and support such things as institutional policy.

17. While one of Goddu's foundational claims is that the Gothic is frequently repressed in American literary criticism (6), she is guilty of a great deal of suppression throughout her study. The significant contributions of both canonical American Gothic authors and pioneering literary critics are grossly ignored and/or distorted in order to uphold her principal claim that studies of American Gothic, to date, have been problematically ahistorical. It is slavery, she says, that especially 'haunts the American gothic' (3), which is 'most recognizable as a regional form' (3). In Goddu's view, '[b]y so closely associating the gothic with the South, the American literary tradition neutralizes the gothic's threat to national identity' (76). This claim denies the works of some of the most powerful Gothic writers such as Charles Brockden Brown, Nathaniel Hawthorne, and Herman Melville whose works, although set primarily in the North or at sea, nonetheless repeatedly engage with the question of national identity. As such, they underline Goddu's theory that the 'benighted South is able to support the irrational impulses of the gothic that the nation as a whole, born of Enlightenment ideals, cannot' (4). In terms of her critical transgressions, Goddu is especially guilty of grossly minimizing Leslie Fiedler's inestimable contributions to the field and even distorting his principal insights. In contradistinction to the phenomenon of repressing the Gothic to which Goddu alludes, it was Fiedler who, in 1960, brazenly claimed of American literature that 'of all the fictions of the West, our own is most deeply influenced by the gothic, is almost essentially a gothic one' (*Love*: 129). The boldness of this statement at a time when the Gothic was yet regarded as a culturally illegitimate form cannot be overemphasized. Contrary to Goddu's claims that Fiedler's reading of the American Gothic is limited to 'a Calvinist exposé of natural human corruption' (9), Fiedler consistently and firmly tethers his insights to the specificities of American history, particularly as regards race relations. In the brief list of particular issues in American history that he claims 'awaited projection in the gothic form', he includes 'the slaughter of the Indians ... and the abominations of the slave trade' (130). Although Goddu rightly observes that race relations issues in American Gothic fiction required further exploration, the distortion of her creative and critical predecessors was unwarranted to make the case.

18. Piggybacking on Andrea Henderson's claim that the Gothic model of subjectivity is the 'eerie *doppelgänger*' of 'the canonical Romantic model' in that 'other people "lose psychological depth" ' (38), I would reinforce Salisbury's statements with the claim that the Gothic also haunts the Enlightenment's *ontological* certainties.

19. Salisbury is by no means unique in this tendency. In fact, such a tradition may be traced among both non-Jewish and Jewish writers from the Romantic era through to the Victorian era and the Modernist and postmodernist movements. Bryan Cheyette notes and criticizes Matthew Arnold's ultimately anti-Semitic conceptualization of Hebraism (*Constructions*: 4–5) and Susan Shapiro comments upon Sigmund Freud's 'attempts to embed the Jew (and Jewishness) within a universalized male subject' during the First World War (70). Notably, not everyone is critical of this tendency. Writing in 1949, Leslie Fiedler, for example, looks

forward to the day 'when the Jew will come to seem the central symbol, the essential myth of the whole Western world' ('What': 418).

20. See Royce MacGillivray's essay for the earliest reference associating Dracula with Judaism (518). Other critics have, to varying degrees, undertaken the Dracula as Jew theme. See page 96 in Phyllis Roth, pages 342–3 in Bram Dijkstra, and Daniel Pick's and William Thomas McBride's articles on *Dracula*. For the three most detailed examinations of Dracula's 'Jewishness', however, see Jules Zanger, Judith Halberstam, and H.L. Malchow.

21. See Terry Castle's brief overview of two histories, W.E.H. Lecky's *History of the Rise and Influence of the Spirit of Rationalism in Europe* and Keith Thomas's *Religion and the Decline of Magic* (1971), that chronicle the profound effect that the shift from magic to science/reason had on human consciousness (14–15).

2   The Primal Scene: The Skeleton in Britain's Closet

1. Edgeworth wrote *Harrington* in response to a critical letter she received in the summer of 1816 from a young Jewish American woman. According to Susan Manly, this letter writer 'questioned how an author "who on all other subjects shows such justice and liberality, should on one alone appear biased by prejudice: should even instill that prejudice into the minds of youth?"' ('Introductory': xxvii). For a more detailed account of Edgeworth's anti-Semitic representations see Rosenberg: 49–60.

2. Edgeworth's brief but weighty description of Mr Mordicai, through the eyes of Lord Colambre, squares uncannily with the image of the spectral, alien, corpse-like Jew whose tradition is delineated in Chapter 1. As Colambre relates, 'Mr Mordicai stood without moving a muscle of his dark wooden face – indeed, in his face there appeared to be no muscles, or none which could move; so that, though he had what are generally called handsome features, there was, altogether, something unnatural and shocking in his countenance. When, at last, his eyes turned and his lips opened, this seemed to be done by machinery, and not by the will of a living creature, or from the impulse of a rational soul' (7). The unnaturalness of this Jewish character is later echoed in *Harrington* where the young Harrington declares with regard to the 1753 Jew Bill, to the delight of his Member of Parliament father, that the Jews cannot be naturalized as they are unnatural (22).

3. This name is repeatedly used to taunt Jacob, the son of Simon, the Jewish Old Clothes Man who so terrifies Harrington in childhood (24–5; 95). It would seem that the name 'Wandering Jew' was as popular a taunt as 'Shylock' in the early nineteenth century. These labels are used in combination throughout *Harrington*.

4. Imprisoned by Falkland, Caleb describes himself as 'govern[ed] ... by terror' (145). Caleb says that he 'envied the victim of the inquisition in the midst of his torture' (145), and when Thomas, Falkland's footman, visits Caleb in jail, he is shocked and disgusted by Caleb's state. Thomas's remarks in the face of Caleb's situation suggest that it is not such a fine thing to be an Englishman as liberty is not truly upheld and protected. In this regard, England is like France where unlawful imprisonment is an everyday event (202). That novel's greatest critique of England echoes Thomas's reaction. In an extreme moment of despair, Caleb enjoins his readers to go and visit British prisons and see their tyrannical governors and the misery of their inmates firsthand. 'After that', he states, 'show me the man shameless enough to triumph, and say, England has no Bastille!' (181). In *St. Leon*, Godwin suggests that the British persecution of radicals in 1794

(Clemit, *Godwinian*: 88) and the passing of the Suspension of Habeas Corpus Act in 1798 (Clemit, 'Introduction': xiii) constitute a type of British Inquisition. St. Leon prophesies that 'two centuries perhaps after Philip the Second shall be gathered to his ancestors [1798] ... other inquisitors shall arise in the most enlightened tracts of Europe' (338).

5. This dating is suggested in Harrington's allusion to his father's act of 'five-and-twenty years ago ... [voting] against their [Jews'] naturalization in England' (45). That vote occurred in 1753.

6. Whether Edgeworth had read Hoffmann's story or knew of it is entirely a matter of conjecture. In 1827, five years after Hoffmann's death and a decade after *Harrington's* publication, her great friend, Sir Walter Scott, did review several of Hoffmann's fictional collections, including *Nachtstucke* in which 'The Sandman' first appeared. In that famous review, Scott deems Hoffmann a 'Genius' (348) with an extremely fertile fancy, an ill-regulated imagination (335), and a diseased mind (332–3). The driving idea of Scott's commentary, however, is the inscrutability of Hoffmann's work and criticism's deficiencies in the face of it. Scott notes the impossibility of subjecting tales like 'The Sandman' to criticism. Indeed, in his view, 'the inspirations of Hoffmann so often resemble the ideas produced by the immoderate use of opium, that we cannot help considering his case as one requiring the assistance of medicine rather than of criticism' (352). The exact date of Scott's introduction to Hoffmann's work is also unknown. Ioan Williams notes the first mention of Hoffmann in Scott's letters in March of 1823 when he asks his son Walter to purchase some of Hoffmann's works in Leipzig (Scott, 'On the Supernatural': 312). With regard to the general awareness of Hoffmann in nineteenth-century England, E.F. Bleiler writes, 'Although certain major authors like Scott, Carlyle, Poe, and Hawthorne have known his work, translations into English have been few, poor, and difficult to obtain' (xv).

Despite the fact that Edgeworth probably did not read 'The Sandman' prior to composing *Harrington*, there are numerous uncanny resemblances between them, especially in their opening primal scenes. 'The Sandman' also features a threatening nursery maid frustrated by her sleepless charge. In Hoffmann's tale, Little Nathaniel is told that the Sandman is a bad man who flings sand into the eyes of little children who refuse to go to bed. This idea long haunts him as do the players in that primal scene who, in keeping with the narrative's 'Return of the Repressed' dynamic and the narrator's overwhelming conspiracy fears, never seem to go away. A similar situation applies with both the characters and the plot in *Harrington*.

7. An alternate meaning of the image of the Jew with a bag is commercial – namely, the Jew with the money-bags. According to U.R.Q. Henriques, a popular early Victorian parlour game, now held in the Mocatta library, consisted 'of a board upon which is represented a villainous-looking bearded Jew. The players have to get their counters onto his money bags' (134).

8. In *The Origins of Satan*, Elaine Pagels also notes that 'because Christians as they read the gospels have characteristically identified themselves with the disciples, for some two thousand years they have also identified their opponents, whether Jews, pagans, or heretics, with forces of evil, and so with Satan' (xxiii). Pagels illustrates how the very construction of Satan in the Gospels was grounded in anti-Semitism. 'Satan', Pagels writes, 'along with diabolical colleagues like Belial and Mastema (whose Hebrew name means "hatred"), did not materialize out of the air. Instead, ... such figures emerged from the turmoil of first-century Palestine, the setting in which the Christian movement began to grow' (xviii).

9. According to the *Encyclopaedia Judaica*, allegations of Jews desecrating the Host began after the Fourth Lateran Council of 1215 when the doctrine of Transubstantiation, which holds that the consecrated wafer becomes 'the actual body of Jesus', was officially recognised: 'After that period therefore it was widely held that in certain circumstances – for instance disbelief or desecration – the Host might show supernatural powers. At the same time, it was imagined in some Christian circles that the Jews, believing paradoxically (which they could not if they remained Jews) that the consecrated wafer was in fact the very body of Jesus, desired to renew upon it and him the agonies of the Passion, by stabbing, tormenting, or burning it. Such was the intensity of their paradoxical hatred that they would not abandon their Jewish perfidy even if the sacred wafer manifested its indignation and its miraculous essence by shedding blood, emitting voices, or even taking to flight. There is no need to regard as a wholly spiteful invention the statement that the consecrated wafer shed drops of blood, the most common manner in which the outrage became known, for a scarlet fungoid organism (called for this reason the *Micrococcus prodigiosus*) may sometimes form on stale food kept in a dry place, having an appearance not unlike blood. The charge of desecrating the Host was leveled against Jews all over the Roman Catholic world, frequently bringing in its train persecution and massacre' (Gaster: 1040–3). As to other purposes to which Christian blood was apparently put, the *Encyclopedia Judaica* notes that '[t]he strange medley of ideas about the use of blood by the Jews is summed up by the end of the Middle Ages, in 1494, by the citizens of Tyrnau (Trnava). The Jews need blood because firstly, they were convinced by the judgment of their ancestors, that the blood of a Christian was a good remedy for the alleviation of the wound of circumcision. Secondly, they were of opinion that this blood, put into food, is very efficacious for the awakening of mutual love. Thirdly, they had discovered, as men and women among them suffered equally from menstruation, that the blood of a Christian is a specific medicine for it, when drunk. Fourthly, they had an ancient but secret ordinance by which they are under obligation to shed Christian blood in honor of God, in daily sacrifices, in some spot or other ... the lot for the present year had fallen on the Tyrnau Jews' (Ben-Sasson: 1123).

10. It would appear, however, based on Martin Luther's claims in 1543, that the Jewish predilection for human blood was not limited to that of children or Christians. While Luther does allude to the established Blood Libel in his reference to 'Jews kidnap[ping] children and pierc[ing] them through' (58), he also conveys details of another story about bloodthirsty Jews: 'I have heard that one Jew sent another Jew, and this by means of a Christian, a pot of blood, together with a barrel of wine, in which when drunk empty, a dead Jew was found' (63). The great irony regarding Luther's obsessive anti-Semitism is that his radical new theological beliefs were regarded as a heresy by his enemies and branded as a Jewish conspiracy (Manuel: 47).

11. There were many other claims of such mutilations and murders. As illustrated by an excerpt from the 1715 publication, *A Confutation of the Reasons for Naturalizing the Jews Containing the Crimes, Frauds and Insolencies, For which they were Convicted and Punished in former Reigns*, in some instances, the alleged crimes were compounded in order to incite greater outrage. In 1204, for example, Jews were said to have circumcised and then crucified a child on Good Friday (13).

12. Joshua Trachtenberg implies that Edward I's reasons for expelling the Jews played upon popular prejudices and fears. These served to veil the primary reason behind

the expulsion in 1290, which was an economic one. He outlines how 'when non-Jewish commercial activity increased to such an extent that the Jew no longer counted for much in the field, his importance as a source of governmental revenue vanished. The state's investment in the protection of the Jew no longer paid and was therefore hastily withdrawn. He was mulcted of what little he still possessed and unceremoniously shown the gate. During the thirteenth and fourteenth centuries a number of major expulsions took place in England and on the Continent (the first, in England, in 1290) wholly for reasons affecting the royal exchequer' (189).

13. Jewish circumcision involves the ritual of *metsitsah*, the sucking of the infant's newly circumcized penis by the *mohel* in order to staunch the bleeding. Sander Gilman has argued that this practice was considered to be a possible route of syphilis transmission in the late nineteenth century (*Jew's*: 93). As I discuss in Chapter 6, Jews were popularly regarded as syphilis carriers.

14. There would appear to be some dispute over the frequency and duration of the Jewish male's menstrual cycle. While Lawrence Osborne cites Franco de Piacenza, a Jewish convert to Christianity, as claiming that this phenomenon occurred 'a mere four times a year!' (129), Sander Gilman cites the same source as stating four days a year (*Jewish*: 74).

15. Hemorrhoids were regarded as an occupational hazard of scholars. As Susan Kassouf explains, 'Often referred to as the golden vein because they made blood-letting costs irrelevant, hemorrhoids were considered a classic Jewish disease, stemming from male Jews' scholarly lifestyle and the requisite hard benches, but it quickly became a disease they shared with all those bookishly inclined' (102).

16. W.D. Rubinstein has explained that the 'presence of the Jewish community in medieval England had one purpose only, to permit them to act as money-lenders to the king and as … "treasury agents", advancing large sums of money to the Crown to defray its expenses' (36–7). It has been estimated 'that at the end of the twelfth century Jews, who constituted no more than 1 per cent of the English population (and probably less), owned up to one-third of the mobile weath of England – an incredible sum' (37).

17. This metaphor of the biting Jew is rendered almost literal in the notorious coin-clipping affair of 1278 when Jews were accused of filing the edges of England's silver pennies. This accusation resulted in the largest ever massacre of English Jews. In retaliation for this alleged filing, Edward I arrested and imprisoned the head of every Jewish household in the Tower of London. While 269 were hanged, over £16 000 was collected from the sale of their forfeited property (Richmond: 46).

18. The act of dentition is graphically described in both the 1715 *Confutation* (13) and in Sir Walter Scott's *Ivanhoe* (1817): 'The kings of the Norman race, and the independent nobles, who followed their example in all acts of tyranny, maintained against this devoted people a persecution of a more regular, calculated, and self-interested kind. It is a well-known story of King John, that he confined a wealthy Jew in one of the royal castles, and daily caused one of his teeth to be torn out, until, when the jaw of the unhappy Israelite was half disfurnished, he consented to pay a large sum, which it was the tyrant's object to extort from him. The little ready money which was in the country was chiefly in possession of this persecuted people, and the nobility hesitated not to follow the example of their sovereign, in wringing it from them by every species of oppression, and even personal torture' (68–9).

As will be more fully discussed in this chapter, a painting entitled the 'Dentition of the Jew' is also featured in Maria Edgeworth's *Harrington* (1817). This piece is purchased and then burned by Mr Montenero, a rich, benevolent Jew and refugee from the Inquisition. This act is deemed an 'auto da fè' by the narrator (133), and Montenero regards it as a symbolic purgation ritual signifying his destruction of 'every record of cruelty and intolerance ... [and] all that can keep alive feelings of hatred and vengeance between Jews and Christians!' (133).

The Nazis also practised their own form of lucrative dentition by extracting the gold from the teeth of their Jewish victims in the concentration camps. The 1976 film, *Marathon Man*, features a former Nazi dentist named the White Angel who once performed such extractions. In what is perhaps that film's most unforgettable scene, the sadistic White Angel attempts, in later years, to extract information from an unwitting Jewish graduate student by torturing him with various dental instruments. Notably, as the film *Blade* attests, dentition also functions as a form of torture equally suitable for literal and figurative vampires.

19. This image of the Jew as a canine/lupine usurer is maintained in much nineteenth-century literature. In Scott's *Ivanhoe*, for example, the moneylender Isaac is described, among other things, as the 'whelp of a she-wolf' and the 'dog of an unbeliever' (79). This figuration is also at work in Dickens' novel *Oliver Twist*, which borrows much from the Gothic genre. The notorious fence, Fagin, who corrupts and preys upon young British boys, is described by Bill Sykes as a type of undead figure, an 'ugly ghost just rose from the grave' (187). A truly Gothic Jew, the avaricious Fagin is also depicted as 'a blackhearted wolf' (400) who possesses 'withered old claw[s]' for hands (398) and 'fangs as should have been a dog's or rat's' (417). Stephen Gill renders Fagin's latent vampirism explicit when he describes him as feeding on his own kind (xxii). Fagin is also portrayed as a sinister conspiratorial figure and master-plotter who uses a lot of directing signals with his minions, Barney (55) and Dodger and Charley (351), in order to manipulate Bill Sikes and Nancy. Bill actually calls attention to and denounces Fagin's wily ways when, at one point in the narrative, he tells Fagin not to wink and communicate with his eyes (188).

20. Thomas Babington Macaulay notably subverted this Jew = wolf, Christian = lamb equation in his speech of January 1831 on the 'Civil Disabilities of the Jews'. In his words, 'If the Jews have not felt towards England like children, it is because she has treated them like a step-mother. There is no feeling which more certainly develops itself in the minds of men living under tolerably good government than the feeling of patriotism ... To make it therefore ground of accusation against a class of men, that they are not patriotic, is the most vulgar legerdemain of sophistry. It is the logic which the wolf employs against the lamb' (122).

21. Adalbert von Chamisso's protagonist Peter Shlemihl (the Yiddish word 'Schlemihl' means an unlucky, ridiculous person) is an unemployed Jewish man who first sells his shadow and later his soul to the devil in exchange for Fortunatus's purse which produces endless gold ducats. The Blood Libel motif is retained here as Schlemihl signs over his soul in blood. The Wandering Jew motif is even incorporated as he ends up wandering through the world with seven-league boots at story's end. Leopold von Loewenstein-Wertheim notes in his brief introduction to *Peter Schlemihl* that von Chamisso could empathize with this wanderer. In a letter to Madame de Staël, von Chamisso once wrote, 'I am nowhere at home. I am a Frenchman in Germany and a German in France. A Catholic among Protestants, a Protestant among Catholics, a Jacobin among aristocrats, an aristocrat among democrats' (11).

22. Adolf Hitler rearticulates the equations between the Jew and Satan and the Jew and Mephistopheles in his notorious 1925 work *Mein Kampf*. Comparing the

Jew to Satan, Hitler writes, 'His utterly low-down conduct is so appalling that one really cannot be surprised if in the imagination of our people the Jew is pictured as the incarnation of Satan and the symbol of evil' (184). After describing the Jew as lacking 'the creative abilities ... necessary to the founding of civilization', Hitler claims that 'the Jewish intellect will never be constructive but always destructive. At best it may serve as a stimulus in rare cases but only within the meaning of the poet's lines: "The Power which always wills the Bad, and always works the Good"' (171). As Hitler explains in a footnote, the poet is Goethe and the work is *Faust*: 'When Mephistopheles first appears to Faust ... Faust inquires: "What is thy name?" To which Mephistopheles replies: "A part of the Power which always wills the Bad and always works the Good." And when Faust asks him what is meant by this riddle and why he should call himself "a part," the gist of Mephistopheles' reply is that he is the Spirit of Negation and exists through opposition to the positive Truth and Order and Beauty which proceed from the never-ending creative energy of the Deity. In the Prologue to *Faust* the Lord declares that man's active nature would grow sluggish in working the good and that therefore he has to be aroused by the Spirit of Opposition. This Spirit wills the Bad, but of itself it can do nothing positive, and by its opposition always works the opposite of what it wills' (172).

23. Although Shell examines Goethe's *Faust* (1808), Christopher Marlowe's *The Tragical History of Doctor Faustus* (1588) includes the same stipulation (I.v.: 53–8).

24. It would seem that the connection between Judaism and the Faust myth was quite firmly established in European folk culture. This association is later channelled into Gothic literature, a combination Eino Railo calls the 'Faust-group' (201). Railo isolates Lewis's *The Monk*, Godwin's *St. Leon*, and Maturin's *Melmoth the Wanderer* as novels that fall into this category. In his comprehensive study of the Wandering Jew, George Anderson comments on the 'unattractive' combination of the Wandering Jew and Faust in *Melmoth the Wanderer* (189–90), and Phyllis Roth is the first critic to claim that the character of Dracula represents a combination of the Wandering Jew and Faust (96). She explains how in *Dracula* the Count is a descendant of the Wandering Jew: 'like the Wandering Jew, Dracula cannot die and "speaks of nations long extinct as though personally acquainted with them". Like his biblical prototype, his immortality is, in one sense, a punishment and a torment. However, like Faust, Dracula not only could not die, he would not die. Thus, the fusion of the Faust myth with the legend of the Wandering Jew "give[s] rise to the legend of the exchange of eternal bliss for everlasting life and happiness on earth"' (96–97). Anderson may feel that these 'two legends should be kept separate' (42) but various authors have clearly felt compelled to combine them.

25. See note 17 in this chapter for the details of this notorious event.

26. Michael Ragussis maintains that *Harrington* self-consciously reworks *The Merchant of Venice* (69). In response to Ragussis, Neville Hoad notes that 'Montenero is different from Shylock in the sense that he does not resent the cost of the comic ending. He is happily assimilated, even if it means giving up his money and his daughter. This ... renders him highly suspect as a sympathetic portrayal of a Jew' (137, n. 10). Hoad's comparative reading entirely overlooks Edgeworth's revised conversion plot where Harrington's family exchanges their anti-Semitism for philo-Semitism and the fact that Montenero does not undergo forced conversion.

27. With regard to this conclusion, Neville Hoad astutely argues that anti-Semitism, 'which is shown to be rife throughout English society, [is displaced] onto the

socially marginal figure of the maidservant. Fowler, as the disease of the national body, can be excluded and is sent to America on the very boat that was to take Berenice and her father away' (123). Further to the case of Fowler, however, Hoad notes that 'the class and gender markers of the protagonists in ... [the novel's primal] scene suggest a much wider and fraught national narrative' (134). Hoad's claims about what he identifies as a 'female economy of prejudice' in *Harrington* (123) is undermined by the fact that it is a working-class Irishwoman, a vendor of oranges, who saves the generous Mr Montenero and his family during the Gordon Riots. After commenting on their common humanity and religious ties – 'we were all brothers and sisters once ... in the time of Adam, sure, and we should help one another in all times' – she removes their name from their front door so that the mobs won't attack their house (187). The national narrative in *Harrington* is clearly more fraught than Hoad's argument allows.

3   Cabalistic Conspiracies and the Crypto-Jew

1. Intriguingly, much of the rhetoric in what J.M.S. Tompkins has referred to as the second phase in British Gothic fiction (243) is found in at least one British history of the French Revolution, namely Thomas Carlyle's *The French Revolution*. It is difficult to say in Carlyle's case, however, where the influence of Edmund Burke ends and that of the British Gothic novel begins. Carlyle's ostensible history illustrates and further consolidates a link between the French Revolution and the Gothic. Mary Desaulniers notes the 'paradox involved in Carlyle's use of Gothicism' (9): despite explicitly and repeatedly rejecting popular fiction, he adopted it for this magisterial work. Carlyle draws on Burke's framing of the Revolution 'as a Faustian sale, the "brave people" having sacrificed all for an equivocal liberty' (32), to construct his own Gothic vision of the French Revolution as partaking of 'a brotherhood of Death' (80). See Desaulniers for a more detailed examination of 'the economics of terror' (33) in Carlyle's *The French Revolution*.

2. The fear of a French invasion of Great Britain was not new. On the heels of fears of a Jacobite invasion, came the fear of a Jacobin invasion. See pages 3–4 in Colley that explain why these fears were not unfounded.

3. For example, Robert Clifford, the translator of Barruel's *Memoirs* and author of *Application of Barruel's Memoirs of Jacobinism, to the Secret Societies of Ireland and Great Britain*, mentions 'associations of a similar tendency [to French secret societies] appear[ing in Great Britain] under a great diversity of names indeed, but all actuated by a similar spirit' (29). In the light of this, he asks, 'Are the *sans culottes* then to lord it in London streets, bearing on pikes in sanguinary triumph the heads of the best men of England, with the hideous yells of *Equality* and *Liberty*? Vainly shall such sycophants, in the hope of partaking of the general pillage and of despoiling their fellow-countrymen (for, from the *king to the peasant*, ALL are declared *monopolizers*) spread the terror of French arms and the impossibility of resisting them' (41). Although he concludes that they need not fear as 'ENGLISHMEN are *loyal, manly*, and *brave*' and they need never doubt of victory – they will unmask this foe (41), this alarmist rhetoric is later taken up by Thomas Carlyle in 'Chartism'.

4. Maggie Kilgour provides the best synopsis, to date, of the debate about the political nature of the Gothic. In her view, the Gothic is a decidedly ambivalent form: 'Like the carnivalesque, the gothic appears to be a transgressive rebellion against

norms which yet ends up reinstating them, an eruption of unlicensed desire that is fully controlled by governing systems of limitation. It delights in rebellion, while finally punishing it, often with death or damnation, and the reaffirmation of a system of moral and social order' (*Rise*: 8).

5. One notable exception to this claim is Margaret Jacob who has argued 'that freemasonry provided at least a "social nexus" for the discussion and publication of the "radical Enlightenment," even if no deliberate conspiracies were set going' (Simpson: 87–8). According to Jacob, speculative Freemasonry possessed 'decidedly political overtones' (*Radical*: 114) and an 'important and radical underside' (111). Amongst Whigs, it helped engender 'a radical faction given to heresy and republicanism' (119).

6. According to the *OED*, theurgy is 'A system of magic, originally practised by the Egyptian Platonists, to procure communication with beneficent spirits, and by their aid produce miraculous effects; in later times, [it is] distinguished as "white magic" from GOETY or "black magic" ' (II.: 3288).

7. These may be traced back to the original Sanhedrin and the figure of Judas. They are prevalent in various European documents such as *A Confutation* (1715) where the author maintains that the Jews 'undermine our Merchans, Betray our Secrets, and correspond with our Enemies' (35).

8. See my commentary on this in Chapter 1 and J.G.A. Pocock's Introduction to his 1987 edition of *Reflections* where he states, in relation to Burke's foregrounding of an association between speculators and members of the radical, anti-religious intelligentsia, 'He was not far from that identification of Freemasons and Jews as the revolutionary underground which was to haunt the imagination of the Catholic Right for at least a century and a half, but he did not articulate it' (xxx–xxxi). Ironically, Burke was himself the subject of a religious conspiracy theory, which involved 'England, protectress of European Protestantism, ... being secretly infiltrated by clandestine Papists'. According to Conor Cruise O'Brien, 'Burke may not actually have been a crypto-Catholic, but in the eyes of a strong Protestants in eighteenth-century Britain and Ireland, he was as near to being a crypto-Catholic as made no difference' (qtd. in Robinson: 41).

9. Not everyone agreed with Barruel's assessment of who was responsible for the socio-political disorder. One of Barruel's most vocal detractors was the Savoyard, Joseph de Maistre who, at the end of 1811, published his views on secret societies. He criticized Barruel's book saying that the French freemasons were, like the English freemasons, innocent. De Maistre did, however, claim that the Illuminés were the true enemies of Roman Catholicism and the monarchy. Rather notably, their association with the Jews – they had advanced pleas for relief for the Jews in Russia – was regarded as especially problematic (Roberts, *Mythology*: 294).

10. Specific reference to Judaism as an anti-Christian religion comes in *A Confutation* (1715) where the author cites I John 4.3 which reads, 'For every Spirit that confesseth not that Jesus Christ is come in the Flesh, is not of God, and this is the Spirit of Anti-Christ' (36).

11. According to Ronald Paulson, Barruel was an adept Gothic fictionalizer in his own right. In reference to Barruel's interpretation of French Revolutionary events in his *Mémoires*, Paulson argues that Barruel 'offered an extremely symbolic explanation (down to the detection of the masonic triangle in the guillotine blade, invented by Dr Guillotine, a freemason), one that could be called gothic in its emphasis on historical explanations and extreme causality, on devious and secret plotting, and on pseudoscience and occult philosophy' (241). Barruel's impact on

the popular understanding of freemasonry has been tremendous. One astute French scholar has justifiably claimed that 'nous sommes tous plus ou moins victimes – bien souvent plus que moins – de la légende barruellienne' (Roberts, *Mythology*: 202). Barruel's impact on the Gothic novel, however, has yet to be assessed. Lee Sterrenburg has begun the process by suggesting that Barruel had a tremendous impact on both Mary and Percy Shelley. The Abbé's *Memoirs* was a favorite work of Percy's during his days at Oxford, and he and Mary studied Barruel during their continental tour of 1814 (155–6).

12. Bernard McGinn relates an intriguing tale about Napoleon's role as the Anti-Christ. Writing about Hester Thrale Piozzi, Samuel Johnson's friend, who 'collected contemporary English witnesses to popular apocalyptic expectations in a diary she kept between 1776 and 1809 called the *Thralliana*,' McGinn explains that, 'Always opposed to the French Revolution, she was happy to cite increasing evidence of its Antichrist-like character, culminating in Napoleon whose name she believed meant "the Destroyer" in Corsican, and who she asserted "does come forward followed by a Cloud of Locusts from ye bottomless Pit" (see Revelation 9: 1–11). She even noted that some women in Wales told her that Napoleon's titles added up to 666' (244).

13. Sometimes referred to as the 'British Israel Theory', Brothers's philosophy was a controversial idea popular in Britain into the twentieth century. It is important to note, however, that advocates of this theory are very careful to discount the British = Jewish equation that the 'British Israel Theory' might seem to suggest. In his fascinating 1871 treatise, *The English Nation Identified with the Lost House of Israel by Twenty-Seven Identifications* 'dedicated to the (so-called) British people by their Kinsman', Edward Hine cautiously draws a distinction between the Jews and Israel. He maintains that while the Jews are 'of Israel', they are *not* Israel (24). Hines then provides 27 pieces of evidence in support of his main argument that the British people constitute the Ten Lost Tribes of Israel. The 'blessings' they have inherited stem from the fact that the British are the 'Heirs to Israel, ... the very descendants of this lost people, in whom, so many valuable promises are vested' (iii). Hines's aim in suggesting that the Jews are imposters is clearly to establish Britain's claim to the role of God's elect, the 'chosen people', without simultaneously assuming the negative mantle associated with the traditional 'chosen people', namely the Jews. While some critics of the British Israel theory have found it absurd, others have been uncomfortable with the proximity they perceive it creates between the Jews and the British. In his 1933 publication *The British Israel Theory*, H.L. Goudge counters the theory whose recent popularity, he says, is attested to by the appearance of the fourteenth edition of a work called *British Israel Truth* (1932) produced by the Covenant Publishing Company.

14. As David Simpson astutely and concisely points out, Burke looked back 'to the 1640s and to an English radicalism that "bore no sort of resemblance to your present reforming doctors in Paris" at the same time as he focuses on 1688 as an essentially English and positive "revolution"' (57).

15. This phenomenon was occurring in Britain even in the late sixteenth century when there were very few Jews in England. Cambridge-educated minister, Ralph Durden, was 'imprisoned in 1586 for "predicting the downfall of the Tudor monarchy" and for prophesying that "he would lead the Jews and all the saints to rebuild Jerusalem"' (Shapiro, *Shakespeare*: 142).

16. As in the case of the claims that Napoleon was the Antichrist, numerological theories were advanced about Cromwell's name. Although the mathematical

calculations are not provided, Christopher Hill claims that, in his 1654 book *A Trumpet Sounded*, 'John More, a London apprentice or journeyman, added Cromwell's names and titles up to make 666' (122).

17. In his 1714 publication, John Toland anticipates that he will be accused of 'Judaizing' for supporting Jewish naturalization in Britain (56). It would seem that this accusation was made about any individual who supported the Jews in any way over any issue.

18. While alchemy was an extremely minor component of the Cabala, other speculative areas of study such as numerology (known as *gematria*), and acrostic and anagrammatic word-play (respectively known as *notarikon* and *themurah*) were of major importance. On the nature of *gematria*, *notarikon*, and *themura*, see pages 8–9 in Blau.

19. It is particularly curious that the anonymous English translator of the 1795 version of Schiller's *The Ghost-Seer* makes reference to the Christian *abuse* of the term Cabala:

> *Cabbala* is properly a mysterious kind of science delivered by revelation to the ancient Jews, and transmitted by oral tradition to those of our times, serving for the interpretation of difficult passages in Scripture, and to discover future events by the combination of poetic words, letters and numbers. It is likewise termed the oral law. But *Cabbala* among the Christians is also applied to the use, or rather abuse, which visionaries and enthusiasts make of Scripture for discovering futurity, by the study and consideration of the combination of certain words, letters, and numbers in the sacred writings. All the words, terms, magic characters or figures with stones and talismans, numbers, letters, charms, &c. employed in magic operations, are comprised under this species of *Cabbala*, and the word is used for any kind of magic, on account of the resemblance this art bears to the Jewish *Cabbala*. The Jews, however, never use the word in any such sense, but always with the utmost respect and veneration. (131–2)

This translator's awareness of the nature of the distinction between Jewish and Christian uses of the term is rare for the period.

20. It is additionally noteworthy that the *OED* connects the word 'cabal' with an important event in seventeenth-century history. It explains how the first initials of the last names of the five ministers of Charles II who signed the Treaty of Alliance with France for war against Holland in 1672 actually spelled the word 'cabal'. These ministers were Clifford, Arlington, Buckingham, Ashley (Earl of Shaftesbury), and Lauderdale. While the *OED* points out that this was 'merely a witticism ... [as] these five men did not constitute the whole "Cabal", or Committee for Foreign Affairs', it also cites Thomas Babington Macaulay's explanation about this word's negative connotations. In Macaulay's words, 'It happened by a whimsical coincidence that, in 1671, the Cabinet consisted of five persons the initial letters of whose names made up the word Cabal. These ministers were therefore emphatically called the Cabal; and they soon made the appellation so infamous that it has never since their time been used except as a term of reproach' (1. 311). The alliance forged in the seventeenth century between the concept of a cabal – whether associated with Judaism and/or a secret group or society – and Catholic France, Protestant Britain's arch-enemy, was retained in classic British Gothic literature of the 1790s.

21. It would seem that schemes like Harrington's to 'solve' the 'Jewish Problem' were not exclusive to England. Furthermore, such schemes often linked the fate of the

Jews to other marginalized groups who assumed the role as 'Other' to the British. In 1819, for example, one German pamphleteer 'suggested a solution linking Germany's Jews and the British empire's blacks by calling for a system of eugenics: "Let the children of Israel be sold to the English, who could employ them in their Indian plantations instead of the blacks. That they may not increase, the men should be emasculated, and their wives and daughters be lodged in houses of shame"' (Ragussis, *Figures*: 22).

22. Jacob Katz explains that 'King Solomon was designated as the founder of the Order in Masonic legends, and his Temple was the structure symbolizing the perfection which Masons were striving to attain' (*Jews*: 200).

23. The association between the Jews and a secret cabalistic language was also a well-established idea. John Wilkins, a member of the 'Invisible College' and Royal Society, 'revealed that the real master of secret communication were the Jews' and 'showed that Kabbalistic number – letter manipulations could be used to develop secret diplomatic codes' (Schuchard: 120). This myth about Jews and a secret language persisted into Nazi Germany. As George L. Mosse relates about that period, 'Some racists, once again making a connection with illicit sexuality, asserted that contemporary pimps communicated through a "Jewish secret language"' (147). I examine the popular anti-Semitic association between the Jew and the prostitute in Chapter 5.

24. For more on this fascinating figure see Gershom Scholem's *Sabbatai Sevi: The Mystical Messiah, 1626–1676*.

25. At least one critic has suggested a connection between Mary Shelley's creature in *Frankenstein* and the Golem of cabalistic tradition. In his essay 'Rava's Golem', David M. Honigsberg writes, 'Nowhere are the dangers of creation more poignantly elaborated on than in Mary Shelley's *Frankenstein*. The parallels between Victor's creation and the golem are apparent in such things as their size, strength, and lack of the power of speech, although Victor's creation does have the ability to learn language and speaks eloquently to Victor upon meeting him on the Mer de Glace. Grimm's *Journal for Hermits* was written only eight years before *Frankenstein* was published. It is well known that Shelley was inspired to write her tale after trading German ghost stories at the home of Byron. It is certainly possible that the stories included tales of golems, which were popular at that time' (143).

26. As regards this connection, see Gustav Meyrink's *The Golem* (1915), which was originally titled *The Eternal Jew* (Irwin: 5). Like the Wandering Jew, the Golem is a type of anti-Christ figure who emerges in a room every thirty-three years. Meyrink had, notably, studied the Cabala (5), had 'made textual and practical researches into alchemy', and was a founding member of the Theosophical Order of the Blue Star (4).

27. Lester D. Friedman describes Wegener's 1920 cinematic rendition of the Golem tale as a form of horror story. As the Jews are represented as wizards who inhabit cave-like dwellings in a sinister ghetto, Wegener's celluloid Golem represents a threat to the film's Gentiles posed by the Jews (53). In his 1941 publication *Golem … Geissel der Tschechen* (*Golem … Scourge of the Czech*), Walter Jacobi represents the Golem as a type of anti-Christ and connects the Jews with the Freemasons whom he accuses of an international conspiracy to gain control of Czech society. Jacobi distorts the Golem story by citing the Golem as an instrument used by the Jews to enslave and destroy non-Jews. The cover of Jacobi's book depicts Prague's New Town Hall statue of Rabbi Loew and a variation of the Freemasonry symbol which resembles a Star of David (Bilski: 72).

28. The date of 1717 provided by Katz as marking the origins in England of the Freemasonry movement is based on his claim that 'the first [Masonic lodge], the London Grand Lodge, was founded in 1717' (2). This claim has been disputed by Frances Yates. She cites 1646 as marking 'the earliest known record of speculative masonry in an English lodge' (210). She notes this, however, after remarking also how 'The origin of Freemasonry is one of the most debated, and debatable, subjects in the whole realm of historical enquiry. One has to distinguish between the legendary history of Freemasonry and the problem of when it actually began as an organized institution. According to masonic legend, Freemasonry is as old as architecture itself, going back to Solomon's building at the Temple, and to the guilds of medieval masons who built the cathedrals' (209). Yates's date of 1646 does not undermine Katz's contention that the simultaneous advent of Freemasonry and the entry of Jews into European society forever yoked them together in the minds of their various adversaries. Rather, the readmission of the Jews into England shortly after 1646 lends support to the popular conception of a Jewish–Freemasonry relationship. The fact that the legend of the Wandering Jew also made its début in England around this time also explains, in part, why this figure was so often connected to secret societies and secret sciences in the British popular world-view.

29. As Jacob Katz notes, in Freemasonry the Jew met with both neutral symbols such as the angle-bar and the compass and symbols which derived from his own cultural and religious heritage. King Solomon, for example, was said to be the founder of the Masonic Order, and his Temple symbolized the structural perfection Masons set out to attain (200–1). Cecil Roth has also explained how the English Freemasons' coat of arms was said to have been designed by a rabbi. In 1765, Rabbi Judah Leão (called Templo) apparently exhibited a model of Solomon's Temple at Court (*History*: 226).

30. A fascinating and rare secret society that practised non-exclusion was the Order of the Asiatic Brethren. An offshoot of the Freemasons, it originated in Vienna in 1780 at a time when Jews were systematically banned from Masonic membership throughout Germany (Katz: 26). Based, as Gershom Scholem relates, on a conglomeration of Cabalistic, Sabbatian, and Christian theosophic doctrines (35), the philosophy of the Order of the Asiatic Brethren began as one of the most liberal secret societies to emerge during the Enlightenment. Its two founders – Hans Heinrich von Ecker, a Christian, and Ephraim Josef Hirschfeld, a Jew – reflected its syncretistic make-up. Strong anti-Semitic public opinion, however, tragically undermined this Order. Allegations that it was composed of 'money grubbers' and possessed 'a false and confused ideology' led to its fall from prominence (42). In the final analysis, social discrimination undermined the relations between Ecker and Hirschfeld. As a result, Jewish members left the Order throughout the 1790s and it subsequently went into decline (53).

31. Specific reference is made, for example, to the 'cabalistical words and symbols' used by various secret societies in Robert Clifford's *Application of Barruel's Memoirs of Jacobinism, to the secret societies of Ireland and Great Britain*. The Martinists were also associated with the Jews. According to Robert Clifford, they were 'the same sect as the Swedenborgian Illuminées' who pretended 'to the powers of ghost raising, evoking spirits, and raising and interrogating the dead' (xvii). In reference to the founder of Martinism, J.M. Roberts notes, 'He was often said to be a Jew, but he seems to have been a Roman Catholic and certainly numbered an Archbishop of Bordeaux among his admirers and patrons his admirers and patrons' (104).

32. The nature and duration of this episode is extremely significant to the Christian tradition where the number 40 is associated with forbearance and spiritual transformation. In the Old Testament, Moses was 40 years of age when he struck the first blow for Israel's freedom (Exodus 2: 11–12), he was on the Mount with God for 40 days and nights (Exodus 24: 18), and he wandered for 40 years. Christ's temptation by Satan in the New Testament occurs after 40 days and nights of fasting (Matthew 4: 2). While Barben's portrait of Cagliostro's conspiratorial pro-Jewish sensibility stops short of labelling Cagliostro a Jew, it obviously adheres to the traditional pattern where the demonic Jew parodies sacred Christian practices.

33. About the exact meaning of the term 'Marrano', Norman Roth has explained that, despite the lack of supportive evidence, it is popularly understood to mean 'pig' (3). Given that pork was taboo meat for both Jews and Moslems, and the term 'Marrano' was applied to both Christianized Jews and Christianized Moslems, it was clearly intended as an insult. Medieval European illustrations of Jews engaged in various grotesque acts with pigs served as a similar type of religious affront. In the revised version of his study on the *Spanish Inquisition*, Henry Kamen provides an interesting speculation regarding the term 'Marrano'. He says 'the association between "Marrano" and "pig" is etymologically undocumented'; however, he notes, 'there are several examples of the word being used to refer to one who "mars", i.e. spoils, the Christian faith' (323–4, n. 11).

34. Poliakov's theory about the correlation between the spread of the legend of the Wandering Jew in Europe and the movement of actual Jews in that region is supported by R. Edelmann. He provides evidence illustrating that, during the sixteenth century, the Wandering Jew legend was known in the towns of Hamburg and Danzig, the only towns in northern Germany numbering Marranos among their population (7–8).

35. I have already examined these issues in revolutionary France. With regard to the second half of the fifteenth and first decades of the sixteenth century when the Spanish Inquisition was first established, Andrew Colin Gow explains that both 'Christians and Jews paid anguished attention to possible signs that the Last Days were at hand. The expulsion of the Jews from Spain and Messianic hopes among the Jews left in the Iberian peninsula and among those in Italy and Germany contributed to renewed Jewish hopes for the imminent arrival of the Messiah – regarded by many Christians as the Antichrist' (16–17).

36. As excerpts from Napoleon's letters quoted by Poliakov reveal, Napoleon intended to destroy a 'race' he regarded as accursed: 'I do not intend to rescue that [Jewish] race, which seems to have been the only one excluded from redemption, from the curse with which it is smitten, but I would like to put it in a position where it is unable to propagate the evil ... When one in every three marriages will be between a Jew and a Frenchman, the Jew's blood will cease to have a specific character' (226). Other anti-Semitic revolutionaries proposed a radically different solution to the pressing 'Jewish Question'. For example, Baudot, 'a member of the National Convention and commissary for the armies of the Rhine and Moselle [suggested] that the Jews should be regenerated by guillotine' (221). Likeminded individuals recommended, in terms recalling the Spanish Inquisition, that 'an *auto da fé* be made to Truth and all Hebrew books be burned' (222).

37. This was the case, in part, because British representations of the Inquisition until the nineteenth century foregrounded its role as an anti-Protestant tribunal and rarely mentioned that its principal victims were people of Jewish and Muslim origin (Kamen, *Spanish ... Historical*: 296, 299). Gothic novels set during the

operation of the Holy Roman Inquisition also adhered to this pattern. In Ann Radcliffe's *The Italian*, for example, the demonic Catholic inquisition is even associated with Judaism by way of the Hebrew language. When Vivaldi is delivered into the prisons of the Inquisition, the narrator relates how he passes 'through a gallery to an anti-chamber, where, being delivered into the custody of some persons in waiting, his conductor disappeared beyond a folding door, that led to an inner apartment. Over that door was an inscription in Hebrew characters, traced in blood-colour. Dante's inscription on the entrance of the infernal regions, would have been suitable to a place, where every circumstance and feature seemed to say, *"Hope, that comes to all, comes not here!"'* (200). Further, the Marquese and Schedoni are repeatedly described as having engaged in a 'cabal' against Ellena di Rosalba (102, 390).

38. For a specific instance of these Jewish conspiracy charges in 1753, the year of the Naturalization Bill, see S. Levy.

39. Rubin should have added that these attitudes persisted in the British Parliament in the nineteenth century. For example, the fight to remove the Parliamentary disabilities of the Jews which began just before the Reform Bill of 1832 faced tremendous opposition. Opponents maintained that Jews were a separate nation who looked forward to their restoration to Palestine and had greater ties to their fellow Jews around the world than they did to other Britons (Rubinstein, *History*: 75). This view of the Jews as representing a separate nation was popular since the Jews' re-entry into Britain. The idea was rarely put forward that the Jews could be more readily assimilated into Britain because they did not have a country of their own. This rare argument was made, however, by Toland in the 1714 publication *Reasons for Naturalizing the Jews in Great Britain and Ireland, On the same foot with all other Nations. Containing also, A Defence of the Jews Against All vulgar Prejudices in all Countries*. Toland supported the very unpopular argument that British Jews should be naturalized. Among other points, he maintained that Jews would not enter into political engagements counter to British interests because Jews had no other national allegiance (12–13).

40. Steven Blakemore disagrees with Manly's interpretation of Burke's use of the term 'caballer' and deems her argument tenuous. In his words, 'one would think that the centrality of "Cabal" – in the sense of a conspiratorial association – in the eighteenth-century vocabulary – would be another semantic candidate for something other than anti-Semitism'. As evidence, he cites Dr Johnson's 1755 *Dictionary* which defines 'Caballer' as 'He that engages in close designs; an intriguer.' In response to Blakemore, it should be noted that while the term 'cabal' may have gained broader meaning by the eighteenth century, the manner in which Burke deploys the term throughout *Reflections* in relation to an England that he suggests has been Judaized (11, 85, 111, 154, 218) is consistent with his anti-Semitic rhetoric.

41. The other two accusations involved their employment of 'the blood of a Christian child in the performance of their Passover ceremonies' and the impoverishment 'by their usury [of] the country in which they lived' (Solomons: 22). In keeping with the theory that Christians have often projected their worst tendencies onto the Jew, Frank Felsenstein argues that 'the reiterated anti-Semitic charge that the Jews would stop at nothing to convert or "Judaize" the English may be interpreted as a distorted mirror image of the message of Christian hope offered by evangelists to the survivors of God's biblical chosen people' (112). It is interesting to note that Judaism, although 'no proselytising faith, and [one that] admits freely that

"the righteous of all creeds have a part in life eternal"' (Roth, *Great*: 90), was widely libelled in Britain as hyper-proselytizing. The resettlement of the Jews during Cromwell's time was conditional upon the prohibition of Judaizing (89). In the face of several subsequent claims regarding its continuation, however, a communal ban on proselytization was passed by the Great Synagogue in London in 1751 (90). For more on these events, see pages 89–93 in Roth's *Great Synagogue*.

42. Ronald Paulson notes that '[a]fter 1780 the crowd was inextricably linked, in the minds of the English, with the burnings and devastations of the Gordon Riots – an event which provided the terms that would be used in the first accounts of the French Revolution in 1789' (134).

4   The Rise of the Vampiric Wandering Jew: A Sinister German–English Co-Production

1. As J.M.S. Tompkins explains, 'The order of translation was: – *Herman of Unna* (1794), ascribed to Professor Cramer; *The Ghost-Seer* (1795); *The Victim of Magical Delusions* (1795), by P. Will and *The Genius*, which was twice translated in 1796, as *The Genius: or the Mysterious Adventures of Don Carlos de Grandez*, by Joseph Trapp, and as *Horrid Mysteries* by P. Will' (281).

2. Tompkins's description of *The Ghost-Seer*'s plot is curious for two reasons: there is no reference to a secret society in the first English translation of Schiller's novel in 1795, and in the subsequent 1853 English translation the mysterious stranger is nowhere even implicitly connected to the secret society which is known as the Bucentauro. I am unfortunately unable to read Schiller's novel in the original German in order to discover which version actually constitutes the authentic translation. This is further complicated by other problems. Henry G. Bohn, the English translator for the 1853 version, relates that 'The *Ghost-Seer*...was first published between 1785 and 1789, in the periodical work called the *Thalia*, and soon after (1789) in a separate volume. Schiller could never be prevailed on to finish it, but the *denouement* is to be gathered from a series of letters, published in the same periodical. Various Grub Street authors (for Germany, too, has its Grub Street), invented sequels, none of which has outlived its hour. The first English translation appeared in 1795, abridged, and without the letters, but well executed' (xi). Curiously, while Bohn notes that the first English translation of *The Ghost-Seer* was abridged, he does not remark upon a substantial difference between the representation of the Armenian in the 1795 translation and his own.

3. A similar treatment of the Wandering Jew is also found in German poetry by such writers as Christian Friedrich Daniel Schubart (Anderson: 172–3) and Heinrich Heine. For a detailed examination of Heine's treatment of this character see Rose: 158–70.

4. Matthew Paris's wanderer in the *Chronica majora* is also not a Jew, but many of the elements of Paris's tale are subsequently integrated into the legend of the Wandering Jew that enters British folklore in the seventeenth century. As to Schiller's use of Paris's tale, George K. Anderson argues that 'Very likely he [Schiller] got the idea of using an Armenian from the pages of Matthew Paris' (177). Eino Railo further argues that 'No mention is made of the name Ahasuerus, and, as the reader can see, the picture contains features developed beyond those of the traditional Ahasuerus. Nevertheless, the Armenian is obviously founded upon the legend' (197).

5. Brewer's *Dictionary of Phrase and Fable* describes Apollonius as the 'Master of the Rosicrucians' (55). This is further supported by Edward Bulwer-Lytton's romance novel *Zanoni* where it 'is darkly hinted … that Apollonius's teachings were the inspiration behind the true Rosicrucian order' (Roberts, *Gothic*: 159). Although Colin Wilson claims that Christian Rosencreutz – and not Apollonius – was the legendary founder of Rosicrucianism, both figures were adepts in the Cabala and other occult sciences (3). Whatever the case, both are associated with a branch of Jewish religious culture that became increasingly demonized in modern Europe.

6. According to Colin Wilson, Apollonius of Tyana was a wandering philosopher who was the most famous disciple of Pythagoras. Not only was Apollonius often figured as diametrically opposed to Christ's disciple, St John the Apostle (197), a note in the 1795 translation of *The Ghost-Seer* relates that he was described frequently as the antithesis of the miracle worker, Jesus Christ (126–7). As the anonymous translator notes, 'The heathens opposed the pretended miracles of this man to those of our Saviour, and gave the preference to this philosopher … Mr du Pin has published a confutation of Apollonius's life, in which he proves that the miracles of this pretended philosopher carry strong marks of falsehood, and that there is not one which may not be imputed to chance or artifice' (128).

7. Lewis is explicit in his suggestion that Ambrosio is made into, rather than born, a monster. See Volume 2, Chapter 3, especially pages 236–9 on this issue.

8. Peter Grudin makes a similar suggestion when he describes the Bleeding Nun as a revenant (22).

9. Percy Bysshe Shelley retains this feature in his 1810 poem *The Wandering Jew*, which draws a great deal from Lewis's novel. When Paolo (Shelley gives his Wanderer a name) loosens the grey band encircling his head, this unique mark of Cain is graphically described: 'A burning Cross was there; / Its colour was like to recent blood, / Deep marked upon his brow it stood, / And spread a lambent glare./ Dimmer grew the taper's blaze, / Dazzled by the brighter rays' (39, ll: 817–22). Further to this, Shelley's Wanderer is also a magician-scientist who draws 'magic circle[s]', and is capable of summoning Satan (41), with whom he shares certain physical characteristics. For example, the dreaded, spectral Paolo with 'his skeleton hand' and 'gorgon eye' (21) is strikingly similar to Satan who possesses a 'basiliskine eye' (61).

10. This association is prevalent when Lorenzo finally discovers Agnes. She is then described as 'a Creature stretched upon a bed of straw, so wretched, so emaciated, so pale, that He doubted to think her Woman. She was half-naked: Her long dishevelled hair fell in disorder over her face, and almost entirely concealed it. One wasted Arm hung listlessly upon a tattered rug, which covered her convulsed and shivering limbs: The Other was wrapped round a small bundle, and held it closely to her bosom. A large Rosary lay near her: Opposite to her was a Crucifix, on which She bent her sunk eyes fixedly, and by her side stood a Basket and a small Earthen Pitcher' (369).

11. Although their nature is not explicitly identified, it is highly possible that the 'various strange and unknown characters' on the borders of the constelled Magic Mirror (270) are Hebrew characters given that language's longstanding association in Europe with magic and sorcery (Rochelson: 400). Hebrew functioned as another signpost of the Jew's Otherness (400). Ambrosio also notes 'a variety of unknown characters' on the 'long sable Robe' Matilda wears before calling upon Lucifer (274), she converses with that fallen angel 'in a language unintelligible to the Monk' (277), and the Book that Matilda leaves with the Monk when he is

imprisoned in the dungeons of the Inquisition is described as being written 'in a language, whose import was totally unknown to him' (432).

12. The best examination of this stereotype is provided, in my opinion, by R. Po-chia Hsia who argues that the 'magical reputation of Jews was already firmly established before the Christianization of the Roman Empire. But in medieval Christianity Jewish magic came to be seen as essentially demonic. In its fight to establish orthodoxy and control, the mediaeval church gradually eroded away any conceptual distinctions between heretics, magicians, and Jews, lumping all under the realm of darkness, attacking all as the enemy of true religion' (116).

13. Another literary work contemporary with Lewis's *The Monk* also portrays the Wandering Jew as a wealthy man. Andrew Franklin's *The Wandering Jew or, Love's Masquerade* was first produced at the Drury Lane Theater in 1797 and features a young adventurer in the guise of the Wandering Jew. In order to dupe the money-obsessed father of the woman he loves, the adventurer places an article in the newspaper saying that the Wandering Jew is in London and predicts that 'the hour of his dissolution will be within a twelvemonth'. The 'subject of his journey to London is, to wed some British beauty, by whom he may leave an heir to his wealth and his longevity' (30). Franklin clearly discarded the notion of the Wandering Jew's accursed state and the popular millenarian tradition for the basis of his plot.

14. I borrow the idea for 'St. Godwin' from a satire which appeared a year after *St. Leon* was published entitled *St. Godwin: A Tale of the 16th, 17th, and 18th Century* (Rosenberg: 371, n. 18).

15. In its skeletal plot framework, *St. Leon* may be deemed a father-text to Mary Shelley's *Frankenstein*. In Shelley's own Gothic tale, the unchecked individualist/scientist is Victor Frankenstein whose destructive monster-double is significantly described by his creator as 'my own vampire, my own spirit let loose from the grave, and forced to destroy all that was dear to me' (57). Among other narrative elements, this image of avarice and the quest for power as parasitic/vampiric is retained in both novels. According to Marilyn Butler in her Introduction to the 1994 Oxford edition of *Frankenstein*, 'Mary's greatest debt intellectually and emotionally is probably to *St. Leon* (1799), which anticipates *Frankenstein*'s themes of science and gender, its plot and its central figure: in both novels, a selfish intellectual trades domestic happiness and marital love for the chimaeras of scientific knowledge, success, and power' (xiv–xv). For a more detailed examination of the intertextual relationship between Godwin's *St. Leon* and Mary Shelley's *Frankenstein* see Gregory Maertz.

16. I discuss this idea at greater length in Chapter 5.

17. As Bonamy Dobrée explains in the notes to the Oxford edition of *The Mysteries of Udolpho*, Ann Radcliffe refers to Domenichino (Domenico Zampieri) in that novel as he influenced the development of seventeenth-century Italian landscape painting. These works are peopled with shepherds and *banditti*, and are characterized by wildly craggy landscapes which 'create an atmosphere in which awe serves only to heighten the sense of imminent danger and permanent terror which goes into an experience of the sublime' (674).

18. Although Godwin may not have been aware of it, an actual Roman Catholic–Jewish association existed during the era of the religious wars as 'Jewish money was enabling the Emperor Charles V to proceed against those German princes who had embraced evangelical truth' (Rose: 4).

19. For an exception to the usually positive responses to Bethlem Gabor as an impressive character, see Gary Kelly's article. In Kelly's opinion, *St. Leon* is a novel 'grand

in conception ... but a failure in execution' (118) and Bethlem Gabor provides the 'best example of this failure' (119). Onto the real historical figure of Gabor, 'a leader of the Transylvanian Calvinists in their struggle for independence from both Moslem Turk and Catholic Austrian' (119), Godwin grafts the fictional character of Wolfe, the hero–villain of Flammenberg's Gothic work, *The Necromancer* (1795). As a result, Kelly says, Godwin 'succeeded only in creating a monster' who 'has neither the weight of moral example of "philosophical history" nor the weight of authenticity lent by the historical characters who are scattered through the first three volumes of the novel' (120).

20. Raphael Patai's research supports the aspect of Flamel's story relating his act of gaining alchemical knowledge from a Jewish scholar. As there was a widely held view that such Jewish Biblical figures as Adam, Tubal-Cain, Moses, and Solomon were alchemists, 'This belief gave rise to the fashion, widespread among medieval and later European Christian alchemists, to seek out a Jewish master – usually in the lands of the south and the east, where ancient traditions were supposed to have survived more fully than in the west – and become his disciple in acquiring the secrets of the Royal Art' (11). Patai further explains how 'Another factor in the high estimation of Jewish alchemical expertise by Christian alchemists was the attribution of alchemical–mystical efficacy to Hebrew divine, angelic, and demonic names, to Hebrew words, and even to the letters of the Hebrew alphabet. The Jew who knew Hebrew was believed, due to that very fact, to possess an advantage over the Christian when it came to acquiring mastery of the Great Art. Thus the Hebrew language had for the alchemist a greater importance than Latin has had down to the present time for the physician' (11). Patai also relates, however, that these ideas in the popular culture were manipulated for anti-Semitic ends: 'The widely held belief that Jews were experts in alchemy was grist for the mills of anti-Semitic authors ... Indeed, the overvaluation by gentiles of the Jewish role in the origin and development of alchemy survived the European Enlightenment and continued unabated into the eighteenth and nineteenth centuries' (12).

21. Godwin relates a similar story in *Lives of the Necromancers* involving different players – namely, Lord Surrey and his mistress Geraldine. Godwin cites his source as Thomas Nash's *Adventures of Jack Wilton* (1593).

22. The Count's 'terrible bag' (44) with which he goes out baby-snatching is, in fact, reminiscent of the Jewish old clothes man Simon's bag in Maria Edgeworth's *Harrington* that terrifies the young Harrington. As explicated in Chapter 2, this novel, published three years before *Melmoth the Wanderer*, also plays on the Blood Libel charge.

23. Eugène Sue's *Le Juif Errant* (1844–45) deals with a similar situation with regard to money. In his book, the Jesuit 'secret society' is the avaricious, parasitic force. Guided by their ruthless leader Rodin, the Jesuits attempt to gain a fortune of millions of francs that rightfully belongs to the several heirs of the Huguenot family of Rennepont.

5 Britain, Vampire Empire: Fin-de-Siècle Fears and Bram Stoker's *Dracula*

1. In the Postscript to his 1975 biography about the life and literary production of his grand-uncle, Daniel Farson speculated that Bram Stoker died of syphilis (233). Describing him as 'chained to a beautiful but frigid wife' (214), Farson postulated

that Stoker sought his sexual pleasure from prostitutes and could have contracted the illness 'as early as the year of *Dracula*, 1897'. Farson further argued that the effects of this devastating disease became manifest in Stoker's literary works. As he described it, 'When his wife's frigidity drove him to other women, probably prostitutes among them, Bram's writing showed signs of guilt and sexual frustration' (234). This theory remains highly controversial and has most recently been disputed by Leslie Shepard in his essay, 'A Note on the Death Certificate of Bram Stoker'. Whether Stoker died of syphilis or not, the spectre of syphilophobia which menaced his society certainly haunts *Dracula*.

2. Further to this characterization of the shifting public attitude, Walter Arnstein says 'Successful industrialists preferred their sons to become gentlemen instead, and gentlemen preferred their sons to become lawyers or civil servants or colonial administrators rather than captains of industry' (133).

3. The popular anti-Jew-jobber propaganda was in evidence as early as the 1820s and 1830s. The Chartists were particularly guilty of promoting this in their various publications. Alongside expressions of sympathy for the oppressed Jews of Russia (Silberner: 32), they advocated that England had essentially been delivered into the 'thraldom of the Jews and jobbers' (33). See Silberner 32–4 for more details on this topic. In his fictional work on Chartists, Charles Kingsley also has his protagonist Alton indict his young employer as a Jew-like 'sweater' in *Alton Locke, Tailor and Poet: An Autobiography* as early as 1850. In Chapter X, 'How Folks Turn Chartists', Alton relates how, subsequent to the death of his old employer, the son succeeded to the business and 'resolved to make haste to be rich' (101). To this end, Alton says, he became 'emulous of Messrs. Aaron, Levi, and the rest of that class' (102) and set up a sweat-shop. In a despicably anti-Semitic contemporary review of that novel, W.E. Aytoun launches a polemic against what he variously describes as 'human leeches' and 'such inhuman vampires' (599). Clearly, Kingsley was striking a chord with some readers.

4. According to J. Jeffrey Franklin, 'The obvious similarities between stockbroking and gambling increased general anxiety about market stability, and those in the commercial world concerned with respectability strove to maintain a precarious distinction between the two' (904). Goldwin Smith also draws a direct equation between stockbroking and gambling in his essay on 'The Jewish Question' in 1881.

5. Jules Zanger claims that between '1881 and 1900, the number of foreign Jews in England increased by 600 per cent' (34). More specific statistics that do not support Zanger's 600 per cent claim are provided by Linda Gertner Zatlin. She writes, 'The 100 000 new [Jewish] arrivals between 1881 and 1905 created a major problem, one which threatened to split the Anglo-Jewish community. By 1900 approximately 150 000 Jews lived in London alone, almost two-thirds were émigrés clustered in the East End. Of the approximately 60 000 Jews in England in the 1880s, more than one half were born in England. The more accultur[at]ed of this group were repelled by the lower-class immigrants' (106). Nathan Ausubel's statistics on London's Jewish population concur with Zatlin's. He maintains that in '1883 there were 47,000 Jews living in the city [of London], many of them the descendants of late eighteenth-century Polish immigrants. By 1902 the number had more than tripled, to a total of 150,000' (185–6).

6. This view was maintained as late as 1890 in J.A. Froude's biography of the Earl of Beaconsfield where he concludes that Disraeli 'was only English by adoption, and he never completely identified himself with the country which he ruled. At heart

he was a Hebrew to the end, and of all his triumphs perhaps the most satifying was the sense that a member of that despised race had made himself the master of the fleets and armies of the proudest of Christian nations' (261–2).

7. As late as 1985, A.P. Thornton promoted the association between Disraeli and a mysterious imperialism. In fact, Thornton suggests that Disraeli purposely wielded imperialism in order to mystify people and maintain power. In Thornton's words, 'In Disraeli's hands it [imperialism] was a mantle – spuriously attractive, perhaps, to weaker minds – thrown over policies whose essence and purpose were mysterious, and whose consequences were generally hidden from the watchful eye of Parliament until it was too late to prevent the presentation of a *fait accompli*' (30–1).

8. In her consideration of the significance of the vampire figure in Stoker's novel, Maud Ellmann expands Pick's 'constellation of contemporary fears' ('Terrors': 71) to include 'perversion, menstruation, venereal disease, female sexuality, male homosexuality, feudal aristocracy, monopoly capitalism, the proletariat, the Jew, the primal father, the Antichrist, and the typewriter' (xxviii). Like other critics of *Dracula*, however, she fails to recognize how the figure of the Jew (notably included in her list) subsumes these various apparently disparate threats.

9. The literary representation of the vampire reflected this racially obsessed environment. In her essay, 'Vampires and the Empire: Fears and Fictions of the 1890s', Alexandra Warwick elucidates how the racial aspect of the vampire was foregrounded in British literature in the nineteenth-century fin de siècle (208, 216).

10. Stoker adopted these details about the Scholomance from Emily de Laszowska Gerard's two-volume work *The Land Beyond the Forest*. As Clive Leatherdale has noted, 'Stoker's debt to Emily Gerard is immense' (*Origins*: 108).

11. David Glover argues that 'secrecy is textualized in Stoker's writing in several ways, and his books are full of mystery, deception, and concealment, often bringing into play *a kind of Masonic narrative* in which – as in *Dracula* – a group of men and women privately pledge themselves to fight against some terrible and overwhelming force' (4; emphasis added). Although it remains disputed, Stoker may have been a member of the famous secret society known as Golden Dawn in the Outer (Leatherdale, *Dracula*: 81–2).

12. Sir Richard Burton resuscitated the Blood Libel charge in his argument in *The Jew, the Gypsy and El Islam* 'that Sephardic Jews still practiced ritual murder and cites specific instances that he knew about in Damascus, Rhodes, and Corfu. Suppressed from publication in this volume … was an "Appendix on the Alleged Rite of Human Sacrifice among the Sephardim"' (101). Many of the anti-Semitic ideas promoted by Burton also inform a curious pamphlet entitled *The Hebrew Talisman*. Originally published in 1840 and subsequently updated and reprinted by the Theosophical Publishing Society in 1888, several years after the death of Benjamin Disraeli, *The Hebrew Talisman* is subtended by the fear of the usurious Crypto-Jew who aims to undermine British national interests. It features a Wandering Jew who possesses a magic talisman that he bestows on prominent Jews dedicated to advancing Jewish interests and exposes a purported Jewish conspiracy to regain Palestine by exerting power in Britain. Notably, *The Hebrew Talisman* also lends credibility to the notorious Blood Libel as the Wandering Jew, an accomplished magician, tells of an invaluable root called Baara which Jews use 'to cast out evil demons from people possessed' (10). As it may 'only be drawn from its parent earth, on being sprinkled with human blood', the suggestion is made that Jews engage in ritual murder in order to secure it.

13. George Croly actively engaged with the Jewish Question in the form of two polemics published in the 1840s – 'Judaism in the Legislature'. (1847) and *The Claims of the Jews Incompatible with the National Profession of Christianity* (1848). In these works Croly raises the spectre of national dechristianization should Jews be allowed entry into the legislature and reconceptualizes Judaism as *Rabbinism* ('Judaism': 735), a 'faith' characterized by 'coldness, craft, and avarice' ('Judaism': 731). Notably, Croly made his own contribution to the development of the Faustian Wandering Jew in his popular 1828 novel *Salathiel: A Story of the Past, the Present, and the Future*. Due to length restrictions, I am unable to examine that work here.

14. A more class-based version of this popular prejudice is articulated by Mrs Davilow in George Eliot's *Daniel Deronda*. In her view, 'the great Jewish families who were in society were quite what they ought to be both in London and Paris, but [she] admitted that the commoner unconverted Jews were objectionable' (775).

15. For more on this novel and other anti-Semitic novels at the fin de siècle, see Bryan Cheyette's essay in David Cesarani's 1990 edited collection, *The Making of Modern Anglo-Jewry*.

16. For more comprehensive detail regarding Haggard's anti-Semitic letters and diary entries, see pages 149–52 in Wendy R. Katz's critical study of his experiments with imperial fiction.

17. George Du Maurier was at Whitby in the summer of 1890 while he was completing *Trilby* and 'had featured the Stokers in a *Punch* cartoon' (Belford: 227). Describing the mesmerist Svengali as 'an enduring mythic character to rival Dracula', Stoker's recent biographer Barbara Belford wonders, 'Was Dracula born from Svengali, as critic Nina Auerbach suggests, with his powers still further extended over time and space? Both deal with the fear of female sexuality and the loss of innocence, and with brave men who rescue the mother figure from a foreigner's embrace' (228). Leonee Ormond has also perceptively noted the Dracula–Svengali connection: 'There are parallels here with Bram Stoker's Dracula, another man of sinister and Central European origins, practising diabolic arts on British womanhood' (xxviii). On the question of Svengali's Jewishness see Daniel Pick's *Svengali's Web: The Alien Enchanter in Modern Culture* (2000).

18. For more on the nose as a representative Jewish signifier, see Chapter 7 in Sander Gilman's *The Jew's Body*.

19. F.W. Murnau's *Nosferatu* (1922), the first adaptation of *Dracula* to the screen, retains this plague connection. Rats accompany Graf Orlok to England, and Orlok himself resembles a rat with his pointed ears, rat-like fangs, bald cranium, and inordinately long, claw-like fingers.

20. Shakespeare's *The Merchant of Venice* was a play Stoker knew exceptionally well as his employer, acclaimed English actor Henry Irving, 'played Shylock over a thousand times' (Gross: 147). Shylock 'was the part ... [Irving] chose for his last appearance at the Lyceum in 1902, and the part he had been due to play the night after he collapsed and died in Bradford in 1905' (Gross: 147). Notably, while Irving revolutionized the role of Shylock on the nineteenth-century stage by rendering the merchant in a sympathetic way, Stoker's Count Dracula shares much in common with Shylock.

21. See page 20 in Gelder regarding Marx's obsessive vampirism = capitalism equation.

22. Although Immanuel Kant neither refers to Jewish capitalist practices nor calls for such an extreme measure, he conceives of Judaism somewhat similarly a half century earlier. In recently published reports of private conversations, Kant discussed

what he perceived as the Jewish resistance to assimilation with his friend Johann Friedrich Abegg where he purportedly said, 'As long as the Jews are Jews and allow themselves to be circumcised, they never will become more useful than harmful to civil society. They are now vampires of society' (Manuel: 286).

23. Various religious affiliations have been attributed, to date, to Count Dracula. Kathleen Spencer, for example, interprets the Count as being a Roman Catholic. Ignoring Dracula's aristocratic background and the fact that the peasants use Catholic iconography *against* him, Spencer writes, 'his roots are in Eastern Europe – Slavic, Catholic, peasant, and superstitious where England is Anglo-Saxon, Protestant, industrial, and rationalist' (213).

24. According to a list of patrons compiled by Bram Stoker, Dr Charcot had actually been a guest at the Lyceum's famous Beefsteak Room (*Personal* I.: 316).

25. Lombroso and Nordau were actually severely critical of anti-Semitism. In his 1894 work, *Antisemitism and Modern Science*, Lombroso – who did not reveal in that study that he was Jewish – argued that anti-Semites were diseased with an 'epidemic bacillus'. As Sander Gilman explains in *Freud, Race, and Gender*:

> For Lombroso the 'epidemic' of anti-Semitism was caused by syphilis, for 'the most fanatic anti-Semites have syphilis or they show the signs of having had the disease'. They demonstrate signs of the 'delirium ... incited everywhere by the same virus'. It is a disease, indeed, caused by the presence of the intact penis and the anxiety of castration. (82)

Lombroso's Freudian assessment of anti-Semitism is particularly noteworthy as it incorporates the spectre of syphilis which was often associated with the Jewish community and used to generate anti-Semitism at the fin de siècle. Unfortunately, Lombroso also promotes certain anti-Semitic ideas in *Antisemitism and Modern Science* and is guilty of blaming the victims for their persecution. He maintains that the character of the Jewish community – its segregation and distinctiveness in particular – contributed to their persecution. Assimilation, in his view, was the solution.

26. This Jew-prostitute-disease connection is retained in the infamous *Protocols of the Elders of Zion* which was published in its earliest form in Russia in 1901. Presented as a series of 24 lectures in which a subversive group known as the Elders of Zion expound their plot to achieve world domination, these Protocols outline how 'drunkenness and prostitution must be vigorously fostered' in order to undermine Gentile morality. They explain how any surviving remnants of opposition 'can always be inoculated with frightful diseases' (Cohn: 3). Twenty years later in Germany, Adolf Hitler articulated what he perceived to be the combined sexual-economic threat posed by the Jew. In *My Struggle* (1925), he writes, 'In the case of syphilis especially the attitude of the State and public bodies was one of absolute capitulation. ... The discovery of a remedy which is of a questionable nature and the excellent way in which it was placed on the market were only of little assistance in fighting such a scourge. Here again the only course is to adopt is to attack the disease in its causes rather than in its symptoms. But in this case the primary cause is to be found in the manner in which love has been prostituted. ... This Judaizing of our spiritual life and mammonizing of our natural instinct for pro-creation will sooner or later work havoc with our whole posterity' (141–2). As Gilman notes, 'Hitler also linked Jews with prostitutes and the spread of infection. Jews were the "arch-pimps"; Jews ran the brothels; Jews infected their prostitutes and caused the weakening of the German national fiber' (*Freud*: 62). In recent

years, Nation of Islam leader Louis Farrakhan, a notorious anti-Semite, has suggested 'that Jewish doctors invented the AIDS virus to infect black children'.
Farrakhan's claim is, as Goran Larsson has commented, but 'a modern version of
the medieval Black Death-accusation and the superstition that Jews poisoned the
wells and even killed Christian children!' (Larsson: 52–3).

27. Among various other prints see illustration 62 of the Jewish 'flesh-merchant' in
Eduard Fuchs' fascinating study of stereotyped anti-Semitic caricatures, which
portrays a lascivious Jewish merchant exhibiting his wares in the form of a naked
Christian woman (42).

28. Although George Simmel does not mention Jews in his essay on prostitution, he
does state that 'the nature of money resembles the nature of prostitution. The
indifference with which it lends itself to any use, the infidelity with which it
leaves everyone, its lack of ties to anyone, its complete objectification that
excludes any attachment and makes it suitable as a pure means – all this suggests
a portentous analogy between it and prostitution' (122).

29. In the introduction to *Makt Myrkranna*, the Icelandic translation of *Dracula*, Stoker
seems to suggest that Lucy's attacks constitute a fictionalization of the Ripper
murders in *Dracula*. He states, somewhat cryptically, that 'the notorious murders
of Jack the Ripper, ... came into the story [*Dracula*] a little later' (8). My argument,
however, is that the Jack the Ripper murders are not only extensively integrated
into *Dracula*, along both technical and thematic lines, but that both Dracula and
Jack the Ripper share, rather significantly, a certain semiotic 'costume'.

30. This description of women as lilies was especially popularized by John Ruskin in
his book *Sesame and Lilies* which contains 'Of Queens' Gardens', his famous essay
about women's roles in the Victorian family and society. Stoker does use this
imagery in *Dracula*. In one scene, for example, Van Helsing refers to the vampi-
rized Lucy as 'that poor lily girl' (182).

31. Rather significantly, the term 'polyandrous' was also used in journalism about the
Jack the Ripper murders as a euphemism for the word prostitute. In one article
about these 1888 Whitechapel murders, for example, a *Star* reporter was said to
have 'made inquiries among a number of "polyandrous" women in the East End'
(Walkowitz: 203).

32. Stoker actually published two articles on this subject in the early 1900s for *The
Nineteenth Century and After* – 'The Censorship of Fiction' (1908) and 'The
Censorship of Stage Plays' (1909). Ironically, *Dracula* cannot be defended totally
against the charge of sexual titillation and graphic violence. Stoker would maintain, however, that his novel portrays the truly seductive nature of evil and the
terrible price to be paid for succumbing to it. Several literary critics have reiterated this reading, describing *Dracula* as a Christian allegory (Frayling, *Vampyres*:
79) that unapologetically promotes conservative 'family values'.

33. The theme of miscegenation is central to other Gothic works where it functions
as a transgression or type of original sin for which subsequent atonement is necessary. In keeping with the Gothic's dynamic of the return of the repressed, a sin
like miscegenation is later visited upon the sons and/or daughters of the sinner.
In *The Monk*, this taboo is class-related as opposed to race-related. Ambrosio's
mother Elvira, the daughter of a shoemaker, violated the social code when she
secretly married a nobleman (13). This sin is paid for by her children.

34. Christopher Craft argues that 'all erotic contacts between males [in *Dracula*],
whether directly libidinal or thoroughly sublimated, are fulfilled through a mediating female, through the surrogation of the other, "correct", gender' (224). While

this is the case when Dracula is in England, it is certainly not the case prior to his arrival.

35. James Shapiro explains that 'Paradoxically, even as descriptions of Jews focused almost exclusively on men (except for some notable exceptions in plays), the Jews as a people were often thought of collectively as feminine, especially when juxtaposed to the masculine English (hence the ease with which analogies could be drawn between Jews and female prostitutes)' (38–9).

36. For more on these two significant fin-de-siècle female figures, see Dijkstra's *Idols of Perversity*, 376–401.

37. Further to this, Geller adds, 'The vast migrations of East European Jewry in the wake of poverty and pogroms contributed to the perception that Jewish women were leaving private homes and entering public houses. In fact, the horrendous conditions in Eastern Europe did lead to a large increase in Jewish prostitution' (29).

38. Until the opening of the film *A Fool There Was* starring Theda Bara in 1915, the word 'vamp' referred either to 'a piece of stage business or music done over and over between acts (to "vamp until ready"), or the upper part of a shoe' (Golden: 55). By the end of 1915, however, this word had entered the American vocabulary in reference to 'a woman who uses her charms and wiles to seduce and exploit men' (55). Notably, Theda Bara was a mesmerizing dark-featured Jewish actress from Cincinnati whose real name was Theodosia Goodman. Her character in *A Fool There Was* that of an illegitimate gypsy who seduces a WASP diplomat from his family. Bara played a variety of similar roles in numerous subsequent films, among them *Salome* in 1918. The vamp figure develops out of a common convention in the nineteenth-century novel, which was identified by Northrop Frye, of using two heroines, one dark and one light. Citing *Ivanhoe* and *The Woman in White* as examples, he writes, 'The dark one is as a rule passionate, haughty, plain, foreign or Jewish, and in some way associated with the undesirable or with some kind of forbidden fruit like incest' (101).

39. Although this translation did not appear until 1901, Stoker's introductory comments were written in August of 1898.

40. In *The Vampire Omnibus*, Peter Haining refers to a curious 'suggestion … [that] floated in America that *Dracula* … [was] actually a cryptic novelization of the Jack the Ripper mystery based on certain secret information that was only known to Bram Stoker and a close circle of his friends!' (3). Given his tantalizing introduction to the Icelandic edition, Stoker would no doubt have been delighted by this rumour.

41. Mina's role as a spiritual link to Dracula is similar to that of female spiritualists, like the famous Georgina Weldon, who tried their hand at armchair detection during the Ripper affair by attempting to commune with the spirits of the murdered women (Walkowitz: 189).

6   Afterword: Pathological Projection and the Nazi Nightmare

1. See in particular, works by Neil R. Davison, Anthony Julius, and Jean Paul Riquelme. Both classic Modernist works alongside some lesser-known fictions might be rewardingly examined, I think, in the light of the Gothic Wandering Jew's trajectory. In the latter category, I would include such works as George Sylvester Viereck and Paul Eldridge's curious productions, *My First Two Thousand Years: The Autobiography of the Wandering Jew* (1928) and *Salome, The Wandering Jewess: My First Two Thousand Years of Love* (1930).

2. It is interesting to note how frequently critics have drawn parallels between Stoker's novel and the Holocaust. Curiously, Count Dracula has been mentioned in association with both the persecuted Jews and the barbaric Nazis. In terms of the former perspective, Stephen Arata has argued that if Dracula stands for an entire race, his death becomes a fantasized genocide (*Fictions*: 460). H.L. Malchow has made a similar point about the Count's 'ritual murder' stating that it anticipates, among other things, 'the mass destruction of both European Jews and sexual deviants at the hands of Nazi racial hygienists' (166). In terms of the association forged between Dracula and the Nazis, see the studies by Richard Wasson and Paul Oppenheimer. David Pirie mentions, further to this, Hans W. Geissendorfer's 1970 film *Jonathan, Vampire Sterben Nicht*, which portrays Dracula as a demonic Hitler-style figure who oppresses the population around his remote castle (173), and Rick Worland alludes to William Nigh's 1942 film *Black Dragons* where Bela Lugosi plays a crazed, scalpel-wielding Nazi spy. According to Worland, 'Within its limited means, *Black Dragons* thus associates the supernatural threat of Dracula with a popularized caricature of fascist ideology. In one of the most florid lines of the time, Dracula-as-Nazi-fanatic coolly avers, "Anything I can do to hasten the establishment of our New Order and to destroy the archaic democracies is an honor and a privilege" ' (49). Clive Leatherdale has noted how Stoker's novel actually played a part in the Second World War. The Allies exploited the equation of Dracula and the Nazis: American propaganda posters featured a German soldier with canine teeth dripping with blood ... [and] free copies of *Dracula* were issued to US forces serving overseas (*Dracula*: 235–6).

3. The German film version of *Jew Suss*, for example, was shown to the non-Jewish population when the Jews were about to be deported. In fact, by 1943, 20.3 million viewers had seen it (Rentschler: 154). At the Auschwitz trial in Frankfurt one SS officer admitted that the effects of screening this film was to instigate the maltreatment of prisoners (Rentschler: 165).

4. Film critics like Siegfried Kracauer, Lotte Eisner, and Lester D. Friedman have argued that German Expressionist cinema was an extension of the Gothic style in literature and anticipated the rise of fascism. Kracauer describes the transformation of cinematic monsters from German Expressionist fantasy to Nazi reality as follows:

> [C]onspicuous screen characters now came true in life itself. Personified daydreams ofminds to whom freedom meant a fatal shock, and adolescence a permanent temptation, these figures filled the arena of Nazi Germany. Homunculus walked about in the flesh. Self-appointed Caligaris hypnotized innumerable Cesares into murder. Raving Mabuses committed fantastic crimes with impunity, and mad Ivans devised unheard-of tortures. Along with this unholy procession, many motifs known from the screen turned into actual events. (272)

Film critics like Lester D. Friedman and Baxter Phillips have similarly illustrated how Paul Wegener's *The Golem* (1920) plays out, in more subtle terms, the anti-Semitic ideas later upheld by the Nazis in their promotion of the Final Solution.

5. The notorious anti-Semite Lucien Rebatet who ran the art section of the Institut d'Études des Question Juives in France during the Occupation years, wrote a book in 1941 entitled *Les Tribus du cinéma* in which he accused Jews of monopolizing cinema to the detriment of French filmmakers (Cone: 180). Rebatet circulated a conspiracy theory in his claim that Jewish artists had infiltrated the Paris art world

and were popular thanks to an organized network of partisan dealers and critics (Cone: 181).

6. Notably, in 1946, 'many thought that he [Dinter] should be tried at Nuremberg for the same charges that were used to indict Julius Streicher' (Schmidt: 132). Given the case I am making in this Afterword that anti-Semitic words and actions go hand-in-glove, I would have supported Dinter's indictment.

7. In contradistinction to Harlan's portrayal of Süss as an unrepentant rapist, the British film directed by Lothar Mendes portrays Karl Alexander as a rapist whose victims are furnished by his pimp, Süss. In Mendes's version, Süss grows repentant and is rendered with extreme sympathy. Notably, Nazi Propaganda Minister Joseph Goebbels saw Mendes's film and thought a Nazi version could be produced that would benefit National Socialism.

8. For a more detailed comparative analysis of Harlan's *Jew Süss* and Bram Stoker's *Dracula* see Linda Schulte-Sasse.

9. Ariosophy, the official name of the Nazis' occult-based philosophy, ironically incorporated 'ideas and symbols of ancient theocracies, secret societies, and the mystic gnosis of Rosicrucianism, *Cabbalism*, and Freemasonry' (Goodrick-Clarke: 5; emphasis added).

10. In reference to the Nazis, Horkheimer and Adorno have astutely described what I have argued is the undying, vampiric aspect of anti-Semitism: 'Anyone who seeks refuge must be prevented from finding it; those who express ideas which all long for, peace, a home, freedom – the nomads and players – have always been refused a homeland. ... Even the last resting place is emptied of peace. The destruction of cemeteries is not a mere excess of anti-Semitism – it is anti-Semitism in its essence' (183).

Works Cited

Adler, Hermann. 'Can Jews Be Patriots?' *The Nineteenth Century* 3 (May 1878): 637–46.
——. 'Jews and Judaism: A Rejoinder'. *The Nineteenth Century* 4 (July 1878): 133–50.
Anderson, Amanda. 'George Eliot and the Jewish Question'. *The Yale Journal of Criticism* 10 (1997): 39–61.
Anderson, George K. *The Legend of the Wandering Jew*. Hanover: Brown UP, 1965.
Anderson, Ken. *Hitler and the Occult*. Amherst, NY: Prometheus Books, 1995.
Arata, Stephen D. *Fictions of Loss in the Victorian Fin de Siècle*. Cambridge: Cambridge UP, 1996.
——. 'The Occidental Tourist: *Dracula* and the Anxiety of Reverse Colonization'. *Victorian Studies* 33 (1990): 621–45.
Arendt, Hannah. *Antisemitism*. New York: Harcourt, Brace & World, 1951.
Arnold, Matthew. *Culture and Anarchy: An Essay in Political and Social Criticism*, 1869. Indianapolis and New York: Bobbs-Merrill, 1971.
Arnstein, Walter L. *Britain Yesterday and Today: 1830 to the Present*. 1966, 5th edn. Lexington, MA: D.C. Heath & Company, 1988.
Atkinson, Thomas. *An Oblique View of the Grand Conspiracy, against Social Order; or A Candid Inquiry, tending to shew what part The Analytical, the Monthly, the Critical Reviews, and the New Annual Register, have taken in that Conspiracy*. London: J. Wright, 1798.
Auerbach, Nina. *Our Vampires, Ourselves*. Chicago and London: Chicago UP, 1995.
Ausubel, Nathan. *Pictorial History of the Jewish People: From Bible Times to Our Own Day Throughout the World*. New York: Crown Publishers, 1953.
Aytoun, W.E. Rev. of *Alton Locke, Talilor and Poet: An Autobiography*, by Charles Kingsley. *Blackwood's Edinburgh Magazine* 68 (1850): 592–610.
Bacon, Francis. *New Atlantis. Advancement of Learning and New Atlantis* 1627, London: Oxford UP, 1960, 257–98.
Baczko, Bronislaw. 'Enlightenment'. *A Critical Dictionary of the French Revolution*, eds François Furet and Mona Ozouf. 1988. Trans. Arthur Goldhammer. Cambridge, MA: Belknap Press, 1989, 659–67.
Baldick, Chris, ed. Introduction. *Melmoth the Wanderer*. By Charles Robert Maturin. 1820. Oxford: Oxford UP, 1989, vii–xix.
——, ed. Introduction. *The Oxford Book of Gothic Tales*. Oxford: Oxford UP, 1992. xi–xxiii.
Banister, Joseph. *England Under the Jews*. London: Joseph Banister, 1907.
Barben, Monsignor. *The Life of Joseph Balsamo, commonly called Count Cagliostro*. Dublin: Printed for Messrs: P. Byrne, W. M'Kenzie, A. Greuber, W. Jones, J. Jones, R. White and R. M'Allister, 1792.
Barfoot, C.C. 'The Gist of the Gothic in English Fiction; Or, Gothic and the Invasion of Boundaries'. *Exhibited by Candlelight: Sources and Developments in the Gothic Tradition*, eds Valeria Tinkler-Villani, Peter Davidson, with Jane Stevenson. Amsterdam and Atlanta, GA: Rodopi, 1995, 159–72.
Baring-Gould, Sabine. *Curious Myths of the Middle Ages* 1866, ed. Edward Hardy. London: Jupiter Books, 1977.
Barruel, Abbé Augustin. *Memoirs Illustrating the Antichristian Conspiracy*. 1797–98. Trans. Robert Clifford. Dublin: William Watson & Son, 1798.

Barzilay, Isaac Eisenstein. 'The Jew in the Literature of the Enlightenment'. *Jewish Social Studies* 18 (1956): 243–61.

Bauer, Bruno. *The Jewish Question*. Braunschweig, 1843.

Bauman, Zygmunt. 'Allosemitism: Premodern, Modern, Postmodern'. *Modernity, Culture and 'the Jew'*, eds Bryan Cheyette and Laura Marcus. Cambridge: Polity Press, 1998, 143–56.

Beaconsfield: A Mock-Heroic Poem, and Political Satire. London: Abel Heywood & Son, 1878.

Bein, Alex. 'The Jewish Parasite: Notes on the Semantics of the Jewish Problem with Special Reference to Germany'. *Leo Baeck Institute Yearbook* 9 (1964): 3–40.

Belford, Barbara. *Bram Stoker: A Biography of the Author of Dracula*. New York: Knopf, 1996.

Ben-Sasson, Haim Hillel. 'Blood Libel'. *Encyclopaedia Judaica*. Vol. 2. Jerusalem: The Macmillan Company, 1971, 16 vols, 1120–28.

Bilski, Emily D., ed. *Golem! Danger, Deliverance and Art*. New York: The Jewish Museum, 1988.

Birkhead, Edith. *The Tale of Terror: A Study of the Gothic Romance*. 1921. New York: Russell & Russell, 1963.

Black, Henry Campbell. *Black's Law Dictionary*, 6th edn St. Paul, MN: West Publishing Co., 1990.

Blade. Dir. Steve Norrington. Perf. Wesley Snipes, Stephen Dorff and Kris Kristofferson. Newline: 1998.

Blain, Virginia, Patricia Clements and Isobel Grundy, eds 'New Woman'. *The Feminist Companion to Literature in English: Women Writers from the Middle Ages to the Present*. New Haven and London: Yale UP, 1990, 792.

Blake, William. 'A Song of Liberty'. 1792. *The Norton Anthology of English Literature*. Vol. 2, 5th edn Gen. Ed. M.H. Abrams. New York: Norton, 1986, 2 vols, 71.

Blakemore, Steven. Rev. of *Edmund Burke's Reflections on the Revolution in France: New Interdisciplinary Essays*, ed. John Whale. Manchester: Manchester UP, 2000. *Romantic Circles Reviews* 4 (2001): 10 pars. 4 July 2001. <http://www.rc.umd.edu/reviews/whale.html>

Blanning, T.C.W. 'The Commercialization and Sacralization of European Culture in the Nineteenth Century'. *The Oxford History of Modern Europe*, 1996. Oxford: Oxford UP, 2000, 126–52.

Blau, Joseph Leon. *The Christian Interpretation of the Cabala in the Renaissance*. New York: Columbia UP, 1944.

Bleiler, E.F. Introduction. *The Best Tales of Hoffmann*. 1814–1821. New York: Dover Publications, 1967, v–xxxiii.

Bloom, Clive. 'The House that Jack Built: Jack the Ripper, Legend and the Power of the Unknown'. *Nineteenth-Century Suspense From Poe to Conan Doyle*, eds Clive Bloom *et al*. London: Macmillan, 1988, 120–37.

Bloom, Harold. *The Visionary Company: A Reading of English Romantic Poetry*, 1961. Ithaca and London: Cornell UP, 1971.

Blumberg, Jane. 'A Question of Radicalism: Mary Shelley's Manuscript "History of the Jews"'. *Revolution and English Romanticism: Politics and Rhetoric*, eds Keith Hanley and Raman Selden. New York: St. Martin's Press, 1990, 131–46.

Bohn, Henry G. Preface. *The Works of Frederick Schiller: Early Dramas and Romances*. Trans. Henry G. Bohn. London: Bell & Daldy, 1873, v–xii.

Bostrom, Irene. 'The Novel and Catholic Emancipation'. *Studies in Romanticism* 2 (1962): 155–76.

Botting, Fred. *Gothic*. London and New York: Routledge, 1996.

——. *Making Monstrous: Frankenstein, Criticism, Theory*. Manchester: Manchester UP, 1991.

Bouvier, M. and J.-L Leutrat. *Nosferatu*. Paris: Gallimard, 1981.

Brantlinger, Patrick. 'Disraeli and Orientalism'. *The Self-Fashioning of Disraeli 1818–1851*, eds Charles Richmond and Paul Smith. Cambridge: Cambridge UP, 1998. 90–105.

——. *Fictions of State: Culture and Credit in Britain, 1694–1994*. Ithaca and London: Cornell UP, 1996.

——. 'Nations and Novels: Disraeli, George Eliot, and Orientalism'. *Victorian Studies* 56 (1992): 255–75.

——. *The Reading Lesson: The Threat of Mass Literacy in Nineteenth-Century British Fiction*. Bloomington and Indianapolis: Indiana UP, 1998.

——. *Rule of Darkness: British Literature and Imperialism, 1830–1914*. Ithaca and London: Cornell UP, 1988.

Brennan, Timothy. 'The National Longing for Form'. *Nation and Narration*, ed. Homi K. Bhabha. New York: Routledge, 1990, 44–70.

Brewer, E. Cobham. *The Dictionary of Phrase and Fable*, 1894. New York: Avenel Books, 1978.

Briggs, Katharine M. 'The Legends of Lilith and of the Wandering Jew in Nineteenth-Century Literature'. *Folklore* 92 (1981): 132–40.

Brinton, Crane. *A Decade of Revolution 1789–1799*. New York and London: Harper & Brothers, 1934.

Burke, Edmund. *Reflections on the Revolution in France*, 1790. London: J.M. Dent & Sons, 1955.

Burton, Richard F. *The Jew, The Gypsy and El Islam*, 1898. Hollywood, CA: Angriff Press, 1970.

Butler, Marilyn. Introduction. *Frankenstein*. By Mary Shelley, 1818. Oxford and New York: Oxford UP, 1994, ix–li.

Calder, Jenni. 'New Women'. *Women and Marriage in Victorian Fiction*. London: Thames and Hudson, 1976, 159–70.

Castle, Terry. *The Female Thermometer: Eighteenth-Century Culture and the Invention of the Uncanny*. Oxford: Oxford UP, 1995.

Chamberlin, J. Edward and Sander L. Gilman, eds *Degeneration: The Dark Side of Progress*. New York: Columbia UP, 1985.

Chamisso, Adalbert von. *Peter Schlemihl*. 1813. Trans. Leopold von Loewenstein-Wertheim. London: Calder and Boyars, 1957.

Cheyette, Bryan. *Constructions of 'The Jew' in English Literature and Society: Racial Representations, 1875–1945*. Cambridge: Cambridge UP, 1993.

——. 'The Other Self: Anglo-Jewish Fiction and the Representation of Jews in England, 1875–1905', ed. David Cesarani, *The Making of Modern Anglo-Jewry*. Oxford: Basil Blackwell, 1990, 97–111.

——. Introduction. *Between 'Race' and Culture: Representations of 'the Jew' in English and American Literature*, ed. Bryan Cheyette. Stanford: Stanford UP, 1996, 1–15.

Clemit, Pamela. Introduction. *St. Leon*. By William Godwin, 1799. Oxford: Oxford UP, 1994, vii–xxiii.

——. *The Godwinian Novel: The Rational Fictions of Godwin, Brockden Brown, Mary Shelley*. Oxford: Clarendon Press, 1993.

Clery, E.J. *The Rise of Supernatural Fiction 1762–1800*. Cambridge: Cambridge UP, 1995.

Clery, E.J. and Robert Miles, eds *Gothic Documents: A Sourcebook 1700–1800*. Manchester and New York: Manchester UP, 2000.

Clifford, Robert. *Application of Barruel's Memoirs of Jacobinism, to the Secret Societies of Ireland and Great Britain*. London: E. Booker, 1798.

Coates, Paul. *The Gorgon's Gaze: German Cinema, Expressionism, and the Image of Horror*. Cambridge: Cambridge UP, 1991.

Cohen, Derek. 'Constructing the Contradiction: Anthony Trollope's The Way We Live Now'. *Jewish Presences in English Literature*, eds Derek Cohen and Deborah Heller. Montreal and Kingston: McGill-Queen's UP, 1990, 61–75.

Cohen-Steiner, Olivier. 'Jews and Jewesses in Victorian Fiction: From Religious Stereotype to Ethnic Hazard'. *Patterns of Prejudice* 21 (1987): 25–34.

Cohn, Norman. *The Protocols of the Elders of Zion*. Montreal: Concordia University, 1982.

——. *The Pursuit of the Millennium: Revolutionary Messianism in Medieval and Reformation Europe and Its Bearing on Modern Totalitarian Movements*. New York: Harper & Row, 1961.

Cohn-Sherbok, Dan. *The Crucified Jew: Twenty Centuries of Christian Anti-Semitism*. New York: Harper Collins, 1992.

Colley, Linda. *Britons: Forging the Nation 1707–1837*. New Haven and London: Yale UP, 1992.

——. 'Whose Nation? Class and National Consciousness in Britain, 1750–1830'. *Past and Present* 113 (1986): 97–117.

The Compact Edition of the Oxford English Dictionary, 1971. Oxford: Oxford UP, 1989. 2 vols.

Cone, Michèle C. 'Vampires, Viruses, and Lucien Rebatet: Anti-Semitic Art Criticism During Vichy'. *The Jew in the Text: Modernity and the Construction of Identity*, eds Linda Nochlin and Tamar Garb. New York: Thames and Hudson, 1995, 174–86.

A Confutation of the Reasons for Naturalizing the Jews Containing the Crimes, Frauds and Insolencies, For which they were Convicted and Punished in former Reigns. London: Edm. Powell, 1715.

Corelli, Marie. *The Sorrows of Satan*. London: Methuen, 1895.

Craft, Christopher. ' "Kiss Me with Those Red Lips": Gender and Inversion in Bram Stoker's *Dracula*'. 1984. *Speaking of Gender*, ed. Elaine Showalter. New York and London: Routledge, 1989, 216–42.

Croly, George. *The Claims of the Jews Incompatible with the National Profession of Christianity*. London: Seeleys, 1848.

——. 'Judaism in the Legislature'. *Blackwood's Magazine* 62 (December 1847): 724–35.

——. *Salathiel: A Story of the Past, the Present, and the Future*, 3 vols. London: Henry Colburn, 1828.

Cumberland, Richard. *The Observer. The British Essayists*, ed. A. Chalmers. Vol. 32. Boston: Little, Brown, 1866.

——. *The Jew: A Comedy*. London: C. Dilly, 1794.

Danby, Frank. *Dr. Phillips: A Maida Vale Idyll*. London: The Keynes Press, 1989.

Davis, David Brion. *The Slave Power Conspiracy and the Paranoid Style: Images of Conspiracy in the Slavery Controversy*. Baton Rouge, LA: Louisiana State UP, 1969.

Davison, Carol Margaret. 'Victorian Gothic Novel'. *The Grolier Encyclopedia of the Victorian Era*, eds Tom Pendergast and Sara Pendergast, 4 vols. Danbury, CT: Grolier Academic Press, 2004.

Davison, Neil R. *James Joyce, Ulysses, and the Construction of Jewish Identity*. Cambridge: Cambridge UP, 1996.

De Bruyn, Frans. 'Edmund Burke's Gothic Romance: The Portrayal of Warren Hastings in Burke's Writings and Speeches on India'. *Criticism* 29 (1987): 415–38.

Der Golem: Wie er in die Welt kam. Dir. Paul Wegener. Perf. Paul Wegener, Lyda Salmonova, and Hans Sturm. UFA, 1920.

Derrida, Jacques. *Specters of Marx: The State of the Debt, the Work of Mourning, and the New International.* Trans. Peggy Kamuf. New York and London: Routledge, 1994.

Desaulniers, Mary. *Carlyle and the Economics of Terror: A Study of Revisionary Gothicism in the French Revolution.* Montreal and Kingston: McGill-Queen's UP, 1995.

Dickens, Charles. *Oliver Twist,* 1837–38. Harmondsworth: Penguin, 1980.

——. *Our Mutual Friend.* 1864–1865. Oxford: Oxford UP, 1991.

Dijkstra, Bram. *Idols of Perversity: Fantasies of Feminine Evil in Fin-de-Siècle Culture.* New York and Oxford: Oxford UP, 1986.

Dinur, Benzion, ed. 'Emancipation'. *Encyclopaedia Judaica,* Vol. 6. Jerusalem: The Macmillan Company, 1971, 16 vols, 696–718.

Disraeli, Benjamin. *Coningsby, or The New Generation.* 1844. New York: Signet, 1962.

——. *Lord George Bentinck: A Political Biography.* London: Colburn and Co., Publishers, 1852.

——. *Tancred; or The New Crusade.* 1847. London: Peter Davies, 1927.

Dobrée, Bonamy. 'Explanatory Notes'. *The Mysteries of Udolpho.* By Ann Radcliffe. 1794, ed. Bonamy Dobrée. Oxford: Oxford UP, 1980, 673–6.

Du Maurier, George. *Trilby,* 1894. London: Everyman, 1994.

During, Simon. 'Literature – Nationalism's Other? The Case for Revision'. *Nation and Narration,* ed. Homi K. Bhabha. London and New York: Routledge, 1990, 138–53.

Easthope, Antony. *Englishness and National Culture.* London and New York: Routledge, 1999.

Edelmann, R. 'Ahasuerus, the Wandering Jew: Origin and Background'. *The Wandering Jew: Essays in the Interpretation of a Christian Legend,* eds Galit Hasan-Rokem and Alan Dundes. Bloomington, IN: Indiana UP, 1986, 1–10.

Edgeworth, Maria. *The Absentee,* 1811. *Tales and Novels, The Longford Edition (1893).* Vol. 6, 10 vols. Hildesheim: Georg Olms Verlagsbuchhandlung, 1969, 1–264.

——. *Castle Rackrent.* 1800. Oxford: Oxford UP, 1980.

——. *Harrington.* 1817. London: J.M. Dent & Co., 1893.

——. *Moral Tales for Young People,* 1801, 3 vols. New York: Garland, 1974.

Efron, John M. *Defenders of the Race: Jewish Doctors and Race Science in Fin-de-Siècle Europe.* New Haven and London: Yale UP, 1994.

Eisner, Lotte H. *The Haunted Screen: Expressionism in the German Cinema and the Influence of Max Reinhardt,* 1952. Trans. Roger Greaves. Berkeley and Los Angeles: University of California Press, 1973.

Eliot, George. *Daniel Deronda.* 1876. Harmondsworth: Penguin, 1987.

Eliot, T.S. Preface. *All Hallow's Eve.* By Charles Williams. New York: Pellegrini & Cudahy, 1948, ix–xviii.

Ellinger, M. 'The Wandering Jew'. *The Menorah* 16 (February 1894): 99–102.

Ellis, Kate. *The Contested Castle: Gothic Novels and the Subversion of Domestic Ideology.* Urbana, IL: University of Illinois Press, 1989.

Ellmann, Maud. Introduction. *Dracula.* By Bram Stoker. Oxford: Oxford UP, 1996, vii–xxviii.

The Eternal Jew. Dir. Fritz Hippler. UFA, 1940.

Endelman, Todd M. *Radical Assimilation in English Jewish History 1656–1945.* Bloomington and Indianapolis: Indiana UP, 1990.

Evans, Jessica. Introduction. *Representing the Nation: A Reader,* eds David Boswell and Jessica Evans. London and New York: Routledge, 1999, 1–8.

Farson, Daniel. *The Man Who Wrote Dracula: A Biography of Bram Stoker.* London: Michael Joseph, 1975.

Feldman, David. *Englishmen and Jews: Social Relations and Political Culture 1840–1914.* New Haven and London: Yale UP, 1994.

——. 'The Importance of Being English: Jewish Immigration and the Decay of Liberal England'. *Metropolis London: Histories and Representations Since 1800*. London and New York: Routledge, 1989, 56–84.

——. 'Was Modernity Good for the Jews?' *Modernity, Culture and 'the Jew'*, eds Bryan Cheyette and Laura Marcus. Cambridge: Polity Press, 1998, 171–87.

Felsenstein, Frank. *Anti-Semitic Stereotypes: A Paradigm of Otherness in English Popular Culture, 1660–1830*. Baltimore: Johns Hopkins UP, 1995.

Ferguson, Niall. *The House of Rothschild: The World's Banker 1849–1998*, 1998. London: Penguin, 2000.

Fiedler, Leslie A. *Love and Death in the American Novel*, 1960. New York: Dell, 1966.

——. *To the Gentiles*. New York: Stein and Day, 1972.

——.'What Can We Do About Fagin? The Jew-Villain in Western Tradition' *Commentary* 7 (1949): 411–18.

Finkielkraut, Alain. *The Imaginary Jew*, 1980. Trans. Kevin O'Neill and David Suchoff. Lincoln, Nebraska & London: University of Nebraska Press, 1994.

Finzi, Roberto. *Anti-Semitism: From its European Roots to the Holocaust*. Trans. Maud Jackson. New York: Interlink Books, 1999.

Fisch, Harold. *The Dual Image*. New York: Ktav Publishing House, 1971.

Fitzgerald, F. Scott. *The Great Gatsby*, 1926. Harmondsworth: Penguin, 1950.

Flanders, Wallace Austin. 'Godwin and Gothicism: *St. Leon*'. *Texas Studies in Language and Literature* 8 (1966–67): 533–45.

Foucault, Michel. *Madness and Civilization: A History of Insanity in the Age of Reason*. 1965. Trans. Richard Howard. New York: Vintage, 1973.

——. 'What is Enlightenment?' *The Foucault Reader*, ed. Paul Rabinow. New York: Pantheon Books, 1984, 32–50.

Frank, Frederick S. *The First Gothics: A Critical Guide to the English Gothic Novel*. New York and London: Garland Publishing, 1987.

Franklin, J. Jeffrey. 'The Victorian Discourse of Gambling: Speculations on *Middlemarch* and *The Duke's Children*'. *ELH* 61 (1994): 899–921.

Frayling, Christopher. 'The House that Jack Built: Some Stereotypes of the Rapist in the History of Popular Culture'. *Rape: An Historical and Social Enquiry*, eds Sylvana Tomaselli and Roy Porter, 1986. Oxford: Basil Blackwell, 1989, 174–215.

——. *Vampyres: Lord Byron to Count Dracula*. London: Faber and Faber, 1991.

Freedman, Jonathan. *The Temple of Culture: Assimilation and Anti-Semitism in Literary Anglo-America*. Oxford: Oxford UP, 2000.

——. 'The Poetics of Cultural Decline: Degeneracy, Assimilation, and the Jews in James's *The Golden Bowl*'. *American Literary History* 7 (1995): 477–99.

Freud, Sigmund. 'Medusa's Head'. 1922. *The Standard Edition of the Complete Psychological Works of Sigmund Freud*, Vol. 18, ed. James Strachey. London: The Hogarth Press, 1962, 272–4. 24 vols.

——. 'The Uncanny', 1919. *An Infantile Neurosis and Other Works. The Standard Edition of the Complete Psychological Works of Sigmund Freud*. Vol. 17, ed. James Strachey. London: The Hogarth Press, 1962, 217–56. 24 vols.

Friedländer, Saul. *Nazi Germany and the Jews: The Years of Persecution, 1933–1939*. Vol. 1. New York: HarperCollins, 1997.

Friedman, Lester D. 'Canyons of Nightmare': The Jewish Horror Film'. *Planks of Reason: Essays on the Horror Film*, ed. Barry Keith Grant. Metuchen, New Jersey and London: The Scarecrow Press, Inc., 1984, 126–52.

——. 'The Edge of Knowledge: Jews as Monsters/Jews as Victims'. *Melus* 11 (1984): 49–62.

Froude, J.A. *Lord Beaconsfield*. 2nd edn London: Sampson Low, Marston, Searle and Rivington, 1890.

Gallagher, Catherine. 'George Eliot and Daniel Deronda: The Prostitute and the Jewish Question'. *Sex, Politics, and Science in the Nineteenth-Century Novel*, ed. Ruth Bernard Yeazell. Baltimore and London: Johns Hopkins UP, 1986, 39–62.

Gamer, Michael. *Romanticism and the Gothic: Genre, Reception, and Canon Formation.* Cambridge: Cambridge UP, 2000.

Garb, Tamar. 'Modernity, Identity, Textuality'. Introduction. *The Jew in the Text: Modernity and the Construction of Identity*, eds Linda Nochlin and Tamar Garb. London: Thames and Hudson, 1995, 20–30.

Garrett, Clarke. *Respectable Folly: Millenarians and the French Revolution in France and England.* Baltimore, MD: John Hopkins UP, 1975.

Gaster, Theodor H. 'Host, Desecration of'. *Encyclopaedia Judaica*, Vol. 8. Jerusalem: The Macmillan Company, 1971, 16 vols, 1040–4.

Gelder, Ken. *Reading the Vampire.* London and New York: Routledge, 1994.

Geller, Jay. 'Blood Sin: Syphilis and the Construction of Jewish Identity'. *Faultline: Interdisciplinary Approaches to German Studies* 1 (1992): 21–48.

Gill, Stephen. Introduction. *Oliver Twist.* By Charles Dickens, 1837–38, ed. Stephen Gill. Oxford: Oxford UP, 1999, vii–xxv.

Gilman, Sander. *Freud, Race, and Gender.* Princeton: Princeton UP, 1993.

——. ' "I'm Down on Whores": Race and Gender in Victorian London'. *Anatomy of Racism*, ed. David Theo Goldberg. Minneapolis, MN: University of Minnesota Press, 1990. 146–70.

——. *The Jew's Body.* New York and London: Routledge, 1991.

Glassman, Bernard. *Anti-Semitic Stereotypes Without Jews.* Detroit, IL: Wayne State UP, 1975.

Glover, David. *Vampires, Mummies, and Liberals: Bram Stoker and the Politics of Popular Fiction.* Durham, NC: Duke UP, 1996.

Goddu, Teresa A. *Gothic America: Narrative, History, and Nation.* New York: Columbia UP, 1997.

Godwin, William. *Enquiry Concerning Political Justice*, 1793, ed. F.E.L. Priestley. Vol. 1. Toronto: University of Toronto Press, 1946. 3 vols.

——. *Lives of the Necromancers; or, An Account of the Most Eminent Persons in Successive Ages Who Have Claimed for Themselves, or to Whom Has Been Imputed by Others, the Exercise of Magical Power*, 1834. New York: Gordon Press, 1976.

——. *Mandeville: A Tale of the Seventeenth Century in England*, Vol. 1. Edinburgh: A. Constable and Company, 1817. 3 vols.

——. *St. Leon.* 1799. Oxford: Oxford UP, 1994.

——. *Caleb Williams.* 1794. Oxford: Oxford UP, 1988.

Goens, Jean. *Loups-Garous, Vampires et Autres Monstres.* Paris: CNRS Éditions, 1993.

Goethe, Johann Wolfgang von. *Faust: A Tragedy, Part One*, 1808. Trans. Alice Raphael. New York: Rinehart, 1960.

Golden, Eve. *Vamp: The Rise and Fall of Theda Bara.* Vestal, NY: Emprise Publishing, 1996.

Goldhagen, Daniel Jonah. *Hitler's Willing Executioners: Ordinary Germans and the Holocaust*, 1996. New York: Vintage, 1997.

Goldsmith, Arnold. 'Elie Weisel, Rabbi Judah Lowe, and the Golem of Prague'. *Studies in American Jewish Literature*, ed. Daniel Walden. Albany, NY: State University of New York Press, 1986, 15–28.

Goldstein, Jan. 'The Wandering Jew and the Problem of Psychiatric Anti-Semitism in Fin-de-Siècle France'. *Journal of Contemporary History* 20 (1985): 521–2.

Goodrick-Clarke, Nicholas. *The Occult Roots of Nazism: Secret Aryan Cults and Their Influence on Nazi Ideology.* New York: New York UP, 1992.

Goudge, H.L. *The British Israel Theory*. London: A.R. Mowbray & Co., 1933.

Gow, Andrew Colin. *The Red Jews: Apocalypticism and Antisemitism in Medieval and Early Modern Germany*. Ann Arbor, MI: UMI, 1993.

Gregg, Joan Young. *Devils, Women, and Jews: Reflections of the Other in Medieval Sermon Stories*. Albany, NY: State University of New York Press, 1997.

Gross, John. *Shylock: A Legend and Its Legacy*. 1992. New York: Touchstone, 1994.

Grudin, Peter. *The Demon-Lover: The Theme of Demoniality in English and Continental Fiction of the Late Eighteenth and Early Nineteenth Centuries*. New York: Garland, 1987.

Haggard, H. Rider. *She*, 1887. New York: Signet, 1994.

Haining, Peter, ed. *The Vampire Omnibus*. London: Orion, 1995.

Halberstam, Judith. *Skin Shows: Gothic Horror and the Technology of Monsters*. Durham and London: Duke UP, 1995.

Hallman, Diana R. *The French Grand Opera La Juive (1835): A Socio-Historical Study*. Ann Arbor, MI: UMI, 1995.

Hampson, Norman. *The Enlightenment*. 1968. Harmondsworth: Penguin, 1990.

Hansard's Parliamentary Debates, 3rd series. 356 vols. London: T.C. Hansard, 1829–91.

Hardy, Barbara. Introduction. *Daniel Deronda*. By George Eliot, 1876. Harmondsworth: Penguin, 1967, 7–30.

Harrington, James. *The Art of Lawgiving*. 1659. *The Oceana and Other Works of James Harrington*. Ann Arbor, MI and London: UMI Press, 1978, 359–438.

——. *The Commonwealth of Oceana*, 1656. *The Oceana and Other Works of James Harrington*. Ann Arbor, MI and London: UMI Press, 1978, 31–210.

Hastings, Adrian. *Construction of Nationalism*. Cambridge and New York: Cambridge UP, 1997.

The Hebrew Talisman, 1840. London: The Theosophical Publishing Society, 1888.

Heckethorn, Charles William. *The Secret Societies of All Ages and Countries*, Vol. 1. New York: University Books, 1965. 2 vols.

Henderson, Andrea K. *Romantic Identities: Varieties of Subjectivity, 1774–1830*. Cambridge: Cambridge UP, 1996.

Henriques, U.R.Q. 'The Jewish Emancipation Controversy in Nineteenth-Century Britain'. *Past and Present* 40 (1968): 126–46.

Hertzberg, Arthur. *The French Enlightenment and the Jews*. New York: Columbia UP, 1968.

Herzstein, Robert Edwin. 'The Jew in Wartime Nazi Film: An Interpretation of Goebbels' Role in the Holocaust'. *Literature, the Arts, and the Holocaust*, eds Sanford Pinsker and Jack Fischel. Greenwood, FL: The Penkevill Publishing Company, 1985, 177–88.

Hess, Jonathan M. 'Forum: Jewish Questions'. Introduction. *Eighteenth-Century Studies* 32 (1998): 83–110.

Hill, Christopher. *Antichrist in Seventeenth-Century England*. London: Oxford UP, 1971.

Hine, Edward. *The English Nation Identified with the Lost House of Israel by Twenty-Seven Identifications*. Manchester: Country Publishers, 1871.

Hitler, Adolf. *Mein Kampf*. 1925. Trans. James Murphy. London: Hurst and Blackett Ltd., 1942.

Hoad, Neville. 'Maria Edgeworth's *Harrington*: The Price of Sympathetic Representation'. *British Romanticism and the Jews: History, Culture, Literature*, ed. Sheila A. Spector. Palgrave Macmillan, 120–37.

Hobsbawm, E.J. *The Age of Empire 1875–1914*. London: Weidenfeld and Nicolson, 1987.

Hoffmann, E.T.A. 'The Sandman', 1816. *The Golden Pot and Other Tales*. Trans. Ritchie Robertson. Oxford: Oxford UP, 1992, 85–118.

Honigsberg, David M. 'Rava's Golem'. *Journal of the Fantastic in the Arts* 7 (1995): 137–45.

Horkheimer, Max and Theodor W. Adorno. *The Dialectic of Enlightenment*, 1944. Trans. John Cumming. New York: Seabury, 1972.

Hsia, R. Po-Chia. *The Myth of Ritual Murder: Jews and Magic in Reformation Germany*. New Haven and London: Yale UP, 1988.

Hull, David Stewart. *Film in the Third Reich: A Study of the German Cinema 1933–1945*. Berkeley and Los Angeles: University of California Press, 1969.

Hutson, Lorna. *The Usurer's Daughter: Male Friendship and Fictions of Women in Sixteenth-Century England*, 1994. London and New York: Routledge, 1997.

Invasion of the Body Snatchers. Dir. Don Siegel. Perf. Kevin McCarthy, and Dana Wynter. Allied Artists, 1956.

Irwin, Robert. 'Gustav Meyrink and His Golem'. Introduction. *The Golem*. By Gustav Meyrink, 1915. Trans. M.Pemberton. Sawtry, Cambridgeshire: Dedalus, 1991, 1–6.

Jacob, Margaret C. *Living the Enlightenment: Freemasonry and Politics in Eighteenth-Century Europe*. New York and Oxford: Oxford UP, 1991.

——. *The Radical Enlightenment: Pantheists, Freemasons and Republicans*. London: George Allen & Unwin, 1981.

Jameson, Frederic. *The Political Unconscious: Narratives as a Socially Symbolic Act*. Ithaca, NY: Cornell UP, 1981.

Jud Süss. Dir. Veit Harlan. UFA, 1940.

Jew Süss. Dir. Lothar Mendes. Gaumat Studies, 1934.

Julius, Anthony. *T.S. Eliot, Anti-Semitism, and Literary Form*. Cambridge: Cambridge UP, 1995.

Kamen, Henry. *The Spanish Inquisition*, 1965. New York: NAL, 1975.

——. *The Spanish Inquisition: A Historical Revision*, 1997. New Haven and London: Yale UP, 1998.

Kaplan, M. Lindsay. 'Cultural Contexts'. *The Merchant of Venice*. By William Shakespeare. Boston and New York: Bedford/St. Martin's Press, 2002, 123–351.

Kassouf, Susan. 'The Shared Pain of the Golden Vein: The Discursive Proximity of Jewish and Scholarly Diseases in the Late Eighteenth Century'. *Eighteenth-Century Studies* 32 (1998): 101–9.

Kates, Gary. 'Jews into Frenchmen: Nationality and Representation in Revolutionary France'. *The French Revolution and the Birth of Modernity*, ed. Ferenc Fehér. Berkeley, CA: University of California Press, 1990, 103–16.

Katz, David S. *Philo-Semitism and the Readmission of the Jews to England, 1603–1655*. Oxford: Oxford UP, 1982.

——. 'The Marginalization of Early Modern Anglo-Jewish History'. *Immigrants and Minorities* 10 (1991): 60–77.

——. *The Jews in the History of England 1485–1850*. Oxford: Oxford UP, 1994.

Katz, Jacob. *From Prejudice to Destruction: Anti-Semitism, 1700–1933*. Cambridge, MA: Harvard UP, 1980.

——. *Jews and Freemasons in Europe 1723–1939*. Trans. Leonard Oschry. Cambridge, MA: Harvard UP, 1970.

Katz, Wendy R. *Rider Haggard and the Fiction of Empire: A Critical Study of British Imperial Fiction*. Cambridge: Cambridge UP, 1987.

Kelly, Gary. *The English Jacobin Novel*. Oxford: Oxford UP, 1976.

——. 'History and Fiction: Bethlem Gabor in Godwin's *St. Leon*'. *English Language Notes* 14 (1976): 117–20.

Kiely, Robert. *The Romantic Novel in England*. Cambridge, MA: Harvard UP, 1972.

Kilgour, Maggie. *From Communion to Cannibalism: An Anatomy of Metaphors of Incorporation*. Princeton, NJ: Princeton UP, 1990.
——. *The Rise of the Gothic Novel*. London: Routledge, 1995.
Kingsley, Charles. *Alton Locke, Tailor and Poet: An Autobiography*. 1850. Oxford: Oxford UP, 1983.
Kracauer, Siegfried. *From Caligari to Hitler*. Princeton: Princeton UP, 1947.
Kristeva, Julia. *Powers of Horror: An Essay on Abjection*. Trans. Leon S. Roudiez. New York: Columbia UP, 1982.
LaCapra, Dominick. *Representing the Holocaust: History, Theory, Trauma*. Ithaca and London: Cornell UP, 1994.
Larsson, Goran. *Fact or Fraud? The Protocols of the Elders of Zion*. Jerusalem: AMI-Jerusalem Center for Biblical Studies and Research, 1994.
Leatherdale, Clive. *Dracula: The Novel and The Legend*. East Sussex: Desert Island Books, 1985.
Levine, Robert S. *Conspiracy and Romance: Studies in Brockden Brown, Cooper, Hawthorne, and Melville*. Cambridge: Cambridge UP, 1989.
Lévy, Ellen. 'The Philosophical Gothic of *St. Leon*'. *Caliban* 32 (1996): 51–62.
Levy, S. 'A Supposed Jewish Conspiracy in 1753'. *TJHSE* 6 (1908): 234–9.
Lewis, Matthew G. *The Monk*, 1795. Oxford: Oxford UP, 1980.
Loewenstein-Wertheim, Leopold von. Introduction. *Peter Schlemihl*. By Adalbert von Chamisso, 1813. Trans. Leopold von Loewenstein-Wertheim. London: Calder and Boyars, 1957, 9–12.
Longhurst, Derek. 'Sherlock Holmes: Adventures of an English Gentleman 1887–1894'. *Gender, Genre, and Narrative Pleasure*. London: Unwin Hyman, 1989, 51–66.
Ludlam, Harry. *A Biography of Dracula: The Life Story of Bram Stoker*. London: W. Foulsham & Co., 1962.
Luther, Martin. *On the Jews and Their Lies*, 1543. Trans. Martin H. Bertram. 14 May, 2002 <http://www.humanitas-international.org/showcase/chronography/documents/luther-jews.htm>.
Macaulay, Thomas Babington. 'Civil Disabilities of the Jews', January 1831. *Critical and Historical Essays*. New York: McGraw-Hill, 1965, 116–29.
McBride, William Thomas. 'Dracula and Mephistopheles: Shyster Vampires'. *Literature Film Quarterly* 18 (1990): 116–21.
McClintock, Anne. *Imperial Leather: Race, Gender and Sexuality in the Colonial Context*. New York and London: Routledge, 1995.
Maccoby, Hyam. 'The Wandering Jew as Sacred Executioner'. *The Wandering Jew: Essays in the Interpretation of a Christian Legend*, eds Galit Hasan-Rokem and Alan Dundes. Bloomington, IN: Indiana UP, 1986, 236–60.
MacGillivray, Royce. '*Dracula*: Bram Stoker's Spoiled Masterpiece'. *Queen's Quarterly* 79 (1972): 518–27.
McGinn, Bernard. *Anti-Christ: Two Thousand Years of the Human Fascination with Evil*. San Francisco, CA: Harper, 1994.
Malchow, H.L. *Gothic Images of Race in Nineteenth-Century Britain*. Stanford: Stanford UP, 1996.
Manly, Susan. 'Burke, Toland, Toleration: the Politics of Prejudice, Speculation, and Naturalization'. *Edmund Burke's 'Reflections on the Revolution in France': New Interdisciplinary Essays*, ed. John Whale. Manchester and New York: Manchester UP, 2000, 145–67.

Manly, Susan. 'Endnotes'. *Harrington*, 1817. *The Pickering Masters The Novels and Selected Works of Maria Edgeworth*, Vol. 3, eds Marilyn Butler and Susan Manly. London: Pickering & Chatto, 1999, 346–61.

——. Introductory Note. *Harrington*, 1817. *The Pickering Masters The Novels and Selected Works of Maria Edgeworth*, Vol. 3, eds Marilyn Butler and Susan Manly. London: Pickering & Chatto, 1999, xxvi–xxxiii.

Manuel, Frank E. *The Broken Staff: Judaism through Christian Eyes*. Cambridge, MA: Harvard UP, 1992.

Marathon Man. Dir. John Schlesinger. Perf. Dustin Hoffman, Laurence Olivier, and Marthe Keller. Paramount, 1976.

Marigny, Jean. *Vampires: Restless Creatures of the Night*, 1993. Trans. Lory Frankel. New York: Thames and Hudson, 1994.

Marlowe, Christopher. 'The Tragical History of Doctor Faustus. 1588'. *Christopher Marlowe: The Complete Plays*, ed. J.B. Steane. Harmondsworth: Penguin, 1988, 259–344.

Marx, Karl. *The Eighteenth Brumaire of Louis Bonaparte*, 1852. *Karl Marx and Frederick Engels: Selected Works in One Volume*. New York: International Publisheres, 1977, 95–180.

——. 'On The Jewish Question', 1843. *Karl Marx: Early Writings*. Trans. T.B. Bottomore. New York: McGraw-Hill, 1964, 3–40.

Matar, N.I. 'The Idea of the Restoration of the Jews in English Protestant Thought: Between the Reformation and 1660'. *The Durham University Journal* 78 (1985): 23–35.

——. 'The Idea of the Restoration of the Jews in English Protestant Thought, 1661–1701'. *Harvard Theological Review* 78 (1985): 115–48.

Maturin, Charles Robert. *Melmoth the Wanderer*, 1820. Oxford: Oxford UP, 1992.

Mergenthal, Silvia. 'The Shadow of Shylock: Scott's *Ivanhoe* and Edgeworth's *Harrington*'. *Scott in Carnival*, eds J.H. Alexander and David Hewitt. Aberdeen: The Association for Scottish Literary Studies, 1993, 320–31.

Meyrink, Gustav. *The Golem*, 1915. Trans. M. Pemberton. Sawtry, Cambridgeshire: Dedalus, 1991.

Michasiw, Kim Ian. Appendix. *Zofloya, or The Moor*. By Charlotte Dacre. 1806. Oxford: Oxford UP, 1997, 269–71.

Mighall, Robert. *A Geography of Victorian Gothic Fiction: Mapping History's Nightmares*. Oxford: Oxford UP, 1999.

Miles, Robert. *Gothic Writing 1750–1820: A Genealogy*, 1993. Manchester: Manchester UP, 2002.

——. Rev. of *Gothic*. By Fred Botting. *Gothic Studies* 1 (1999): 119–20.

Modder, Montagu Frank. *The Jew in the Literature of England*, 1939. New York and Philadelphia: Meridian Books, 1960.

Moncure, Daniel Conway. *The Wandering Jew*. New York: Henry Holt and Company, 1881.

Moretti, Franco. *Signs Taken for Wonders: Essays in the Sociology of Literary Forms*. London: Verso Editions & NLB, 1983.

——. *The Way of the World: The Bildungsroman in European Culture*. London: Verso, 1987.

Morrison, Toni. *The Nobel Lecture in Literature, 1993*. New York: Knopf, 1994.

——. *Playing in the Dark: Whiteness and the Literary Imagination*. Cambridge, MA: Harvard UP, 1992.

Mosse, George L. *Nationalism and Sexuality: Middle-Class Morality and Sexual Norms in Modern Europe*. Madison, WI: University of Wisconsin Press, 1985.

Mundill, Robin R. *England's Jewish Solution: Experiment and Expulsion, 1262–1290.* Cambridge: Cambridge UP, 1998.

Nelson, Benjamin. *The Idea of Usury: From Tribal Brotherhood to Universal Otherhood,* 1949. Chicago and London: The University of Chicago Press, 1969.

Newman, Gerald. *The Rise of English Nationalism: A Cultural History, 1740–1830.* New York: St. Martin's Press, 1987.

Nordau, Max. *Degeneration.* New York: D. Appleton and Co., 1895.

Nosferatu: Eine Symphonie des Grauens (A Symphony of Terror). Dir. F.W. Murnau. Perf. Max Schreck, Greta Schroeder, and Gustav von Wagenheim. Prana Film, 1922.

Nurbhai, Saleel. 'Metafiction and Metaphor: *Daniel Deronda* as Golem'. *George Eliot Review* 25 (1994): 39–44.

O'Brien, Conor Cruise. 'Nationalism and the French Revolution'. *The Permanent Revolution: The French Revolution and its Legacy 1789–1989,* ed. Geoffrey Best. London: Fontana Press, 1988, 17–48.

Oliver, W.H. *Prophets and Millennialists: The Uses of Biblical Prophecy in England from the 1790s to the 1840s.* New Zealand: Auckland UP, 1978.

Oppenheimer, Paul. *Evil and the Demonic: A New Theory of Monstrous Behaviour.* London: Duckworth, 1996.

Ormond, Leonee. Introduction. *Trilby.* By George Du Maurier, 1894. London: Everyman, 1994, xxiii–xxx.

Ormsby-Lennon, Hugh J. 'Nature's Mystick Book: Renaissance *Arcanum* into Restoration Cant'. *Secret Texts: The Literature of Secret Societies,* eds. Marie Mulvey-Roberts and Hugh Ormsby-Lennon. New York: AMS Press, 1995, 24–96.

Osborne, Lawrence. *The Poisoned Embrace: A Brief History of Sexual Pessimism.* New York: Pantheon, 1993.

Pagels, Elaine. *The Origins of Satan.* New York: Random House, 1995.

Paine, Thomas. *Rights of Man,* 1791–92. Mineola, NY: Dover, 1999.

Patai, Raphael. *The Jewish Alchemists: A History and Source Book.* Princeton, NJ: Princeton UP, 1994.

Paulson, Ronald. *Representations of Revolution (1789–1820).* New Haven and London: Yale UP, 1983.

Penslar, Derek J. *Shylock's Children: Economics and Jewish Identity in Modern Europe.* Berkeley, Los Angeles, and London: U of California P, 2001.

Perry, Thomas W. *Public Opinion, Propaganda, and Politics in Eighteenth-Century England: A Study of the Jew Bill of 1753.* Cambridge, MA: Harvard UP, 1962.

Phillips, Baxter. *Swastika: Cinema of Oppression.* New York: Warner Books, 1976.

Pick, Daniel. 'Powers of Suggestion: Svengali and the Fin-de-Siècle'. *Modernity, Culture and 'the Jew',* eds Bryan Cheyette and Laura Marcus. Cambridge: Polity Press, 1998, 105–25.

——. ' "Terrors of the Night": *Dracula* and Degeneration in the Late Nineteenth Century'. *Critical Inquiry* 30 (1988): 71–87.

Picciotto, James. *Sketches of Anglo-Jewish History.* London: Trübner &Co., 1875.

Pinsker, Leo. 'Auto-Emancipation: An Appeal to His People by a Russian Jew'. 1882. *Modern Jewish History: A Source Reader,* eds Robert Chazan and Marc Lee Raphael. New York: Schocken Books, 1974, 160–74.

Pirie, David. *The Vampire Cinema.* New York: Crescent Books, 1977.

Pocock, J.G.A. Introduction. *Reflections on the Revolution in France.* By Edmund Burke, 1791. Indianapolis, IN: Hackett Publishing Company, 1987, vii–lvi.

Pocock, J.G.A. *Virtue, Commerce, and History: Essays on Political Thought and History, Cheifly in the Eighteenth Century.* Cambridge: Cambridge UP, 1985.

Poliakov, Léon. *The History of Anti-Semitism: From Voltaire to Wagner*, 1968. Trans. Miriam Kochan. London: Routledge & Kegan Paul, 1975, Vol. 3 of *The History of Anti-Semitism*, 1955–77, 4 vols.

Popkin, Richard H. 'Medicine, Racism, Anti-Semitism: A Dimension of Enlightenment Culture'. *The Languages of Psyche: Mind and Body in Enlightenment Thought*. ed. G.S. Rousseau. Berkeley, CA: University of California Press, 1990, 405–42.

Porte, Joel. 'In the Hands of an Angry God: Religious Terror in Gothic Fiction'. *The Gothic Imagination: Essays in Dark Romanticism*, ed. G.R. Thompson. Washington: Washington State UP, 1974, 42–64.

Porter, Roy. *Enlightenment: Britain and the Creation of the Modern World*. London: Penguin, 2000.

Probatum Est. 'Terrorist Novel Writing'. *Spirit of the Journals for 1792*. London: James Ridgway, 1802, 227–9.

Punter, David. *Gothic Pathologies: The Text, the Body and the Law*. Houndmills, Basingstoke: Macmillan, 1998.

——. *The Literature of Terror: A History of Gothic Fictions From 1765 to the Present Day*. London and New York: Longman, 1980.

——. 'Of apparitions'. Introduction. *Spectral Readings: Towards a Gothic Geography*. eds Glennis Byron and David Punter. Houndmills, Basingstoke: Macmillan, 1999, 1–8.

Pykett, Lynn. 'Sensation and the Fantastic in the Victorian Novel'. *The Companion to the Victorian Novel*, ed. Deirdre David. Cambridge: Cambridge UP, 2001, 192–211.

Radcliffe, Ann. *The Italian*, 1797. Oxford: Oxford UP, 1981.

——. *The Mysteries of Udolpho*, 1794. Oxford: Oxford UP, 1980.

Ragussis, Michael. *Figures of Conversion: 'The Jewish Question' and English National Identity*. Durham and London: Duke UP, 1995.

——. 'The "Secret" of English Anti-Semitism: Anglo-Jewish Studies and Victorian Studies'. Rev. of *The Origin of the Modern Jewish Woman Writer: Romance and Reform in Victorian England*, by Michael Galchinsky, *Jerusalem Recovered: Victorian Intellectuals and the Birth of Modern Zionism*, by Michael Polowetzky, and *Antisemitism, Misogyny, and the Logic of Cultural Difference: Cesare Lombroso and Matilde Serao*, by Nancy A. Harrowitz. *Victorian Studies* 40 (1997): 295–307.

Railo, Eino. *The Haunted Castle: A Study of the Elements of English Romanticism*. London: George Routledge & Sons, Ltd, 1927.

Ray, Rhonda Johnson. 'The Last Things: Apocalypse and Eschatology in British Dark Romanticism'. Diss. Emory University, 1990. *DAI* 50 (1990): 2068A.

Reddy, William H. *Money and Liberty in Modern Europe: A Critique of Historical Universtanding*. Cambridge: Cambridge UP, 1987.

Reid, William Hamilton. *The Rise and Dissolution of the Infidel Societies in this Metropolis: Including the Origin of Modern Deism and Atheism; the Genius and Conduct of Those Associations; Their Lecture-Rooms, Field-Meetings, and Deputations; From the Publication of Paine's Age of Reason till the Present Period*. London: J. Hatchard, 1800.

Rentschler, Eric. *The Ministry of Illusion: Nazi Cinema and Its Afterlife*. Cambridge, MA: Harvard UP, 1996.

Riquelme, Jean Paul. 'Introduction: Toward a History of Gothic and Modernism from Bram Stoker to Samuel Beckett'. *Modern Fiction Studies* 46 (2000): 585–605.

Richmond, Colin. 'Englishness and Medieval Anglo-Jewry'. *The Jewish Heritage in British History*, ed. Tony Kushner. London: Frank Cass, 1992, 42–59.

Roberts, J.M. *The Mythology of the Secret Societies*. London: Secker & Warburg, 1972.

Roberts, Marie. *British Poets and Secret Societies*. Totowa, NJ: Barnes & Noble Books, 1986.

——. *Gothic Immortals: The Fiction of the Brotherhood of the Rosy Cross*. London and New York: Routledge, 1990.

Robertson, Ritchie. Introduction. *The German-Jewish Dialogue*. Oxford: Oxford UP, 1999, vii–xxviii.

——. Introduction. *The Golden Pot and Other Tales*. By E.T.A. Hoffmann. Oxford: Oxford UP, 1992, vii–xxxii.

——. *The 'Jewish Question' in German Literature 1749–1939: Emancipation and its Discontents*. Oxford: Oxford UP, 1999.

Robison, John. *Proofs of a Conspiracy against all the Religions and Governments of Europe, carried on in the Secret Meetings of Free Masons, Illuminati and Reading Societies, 1797*. London: T. Cadell, jun. and W. Davies [etc.], 1798.

Robinson, Nicholas K. *Edmund Burke: A Life in Caricature*. New Haven and London: Yale UP, 1996.

Rochelson, Meri Jane. 'Language, Gender, and Ethnic Anxiety in Zangwill's *Children of the Ghetto*'. *English Literature in Transition (1880–1920)* 31 (1988): 399–412.

Rose, Paul Lawrence. *Revolutionary Antisemitism in Germany From Kant to Wagner*. Princeton, NJ: Princeton UP, 1990.

Rosenberg, Edgar. *From Shylock to Svengali: Jewish Stereotypes in English Fiction*. Stanford: Stanford UP, 1960.

Ross, Alexander. *A View of the Jewish Religion Containing the Manner of Life, Rites, Ceremonies and Customes of the Jewish Nation throughout the World at this Present Time; Together with the Articles of their Faith, as now received*. London, 1656.

Roth, Cecil. *The Great Synagogue London 1690–1940*. London: Edward Goldston & Son Ltd, 1950.

——. *A History of the Jews in England*, 1940. Oxford: Clarendon Press, 1964.

——. *The Spanish Inquisition*, 1937. New York and London: Norton, 1964.

Roth, Norman. *Conversos, Inquisition, and the Expulsion of the Jews from Spain*. Madison, WI: The University of Wisconsin Press, 1995.

Roth, Phyllis A. *Bram Stoker*. Boston: Twayne, 1982.

Royle, Nicholas. *The Uncanny*. Manchester: Manchester UP, 2003.

Rubin, Abba. *The English Jew in English Literature 1660–1830*. Westport, CT: Greenwood Press, 1984.

Rubinstein, W.D. *A History of the Jews in the English-Speaking World: Great Britain*. London: Macmillan, 1996.

——. *Capitalism, Culture, & Decline in Britain, 1750–1990*. London: Routledge, 1993.

Ruderman, David B. *Jewish Thought and Scientific Discovery in Early Modern Europe*. New Haven and London: Yale University Press, 1995.

Russell, Jeffrey Burton. *Mephistopheles: The Devil in the Modern World*. Ithaca and London: Cornell UP, 1986.

Russell, Norman. *The Novelist and Mammon: Literary Responses to the World of Commerce in the Nineteenth Century*. Oxford: Clarendon Press, 1986.

Russell, C. and H.S. Lewis. *The Jew in London: A Study of Racial Character and Present-Day Conditions*. London: T Fisher Unwin, 1900.

Sacks, Chief Rabbi Jonathan. 'The Modern Jewish Dilem[m]a', 1997. <www.chiefrabbi.org/speeches/dilema.html>.

Sade, Marquis de. 'Reflections on the Novel', 1800. *One Hundred and Twenty Days of Sodom*. Trans. Austryn Wainhouse and Richard Seaver. London: Arrow Books, 1989, 91–116.

Sagan, Eli. *Citizens & Cannibals: The French Revolution, the Struggle for Modernity, and the Origins of Ideological Terror*. New York: Rowman and Littlefield Publishers, Inc., 2001.

Sage, Victor. *Horror Fiction in the Protestant Tradition*. London: Macmillan, 1988.

Salisbury, Jay D. 'Gothic and Romantic Wandering: The Epistemology of Oscillation'. *Gothic Studies* 3 (2001): 45–60.

Sartre, Jean-Paul. *Anti-Semite and Jew*, 1948. Trans. George J. Becker. New York: Schocken Books, 1965.

Schechter, Ronald. 'The Jewish Question in Eighteenth-Century France'. *Eighteenth-Century Studies* 32 (1998): 84–91.

Schiller, Johann Christoph Friedrich von. *The Ghost-Seer*, 1785–89. *The Works of Frederick Schiller*, Vol. 4. Trans. Henry G. Bohn. London: Henry G. Bohn, 1853, 377–482, 4 vols.

——. *The Ghost-Seer; or Apparitionist*, 1788. London: Vernor, 1795.

Schmidt, Josef. 'Artur Dinter's "Racial Novel" *The Sin Against the Blood* (1917): Trivial Stereotypes and Apocalyptic Prelude'. *Hinter dem schwarzen Vorhang: Die Katastrophe und die epische Tradition*, eds Friedrich Gaede, Patrick O'Neill, and Ulrich Scheck. Tübingen: Francke Verlag, 1994, 129–38.

Schmitt, Cannon. *Alien Nation: Nineteenth-Century Gothic Fictions and English Nationality*. Philadelphia, PA: University of Pennsylvania Press, 1997.

Schoenfield, Mark L. 'Abraham Goldsmid: Money Magician in the Popular Press'. *British Romanticism and the Jews: History, Culture, Literature*, ed. Sheila A. Spector. Palgrave Macmillan, 37–60.

Scholem, Gershom G. 'Kabbalah'. *Encyclopaedia Judaica*, Vol. 10. Jerusalem: The Macmillan Company, 1971, 489–655, 16 vols.

——. *On the Kabbalah and Its Symbolism*, 1960. Trans. Ralph Manheim. New York: Schocken Books, 1969.

——. *Sabbatai Sevi: The Mystical Messiah, 1626–1676*, 1957. Princeton: Princeton UP, 1973.

Schuchard, Marsha Keith. 'Yeats and the "Unknown Superiors"': Swedenborg, Falk, and Cagliostro'. *Secret Texts: The Literature of Secret Societies*, eds. Marie Mulvey-Roberts and Hugh Ormsby-Lennon. New York: AMS Press, 1995, 114–68.

Schulte-Sasse, Linda. 'Courtier, Vampire, or Vermin? *Jew Süss*'s Contradictory Effort to Render the "Jew" Other'. *Perspectives on German Cinema*, eds Terri Ginsberg and Kirsten Moana Thompson. New York: G.K. Hall & Co., 1996, 184–220.

Schweizer, Karl W. and John W. Osborne. *Cobbett in his Times*. Leicester and London: Leicester UP, 1990.

Scott, Sir Walter. *Ivanhoe*, London: Thomas Nelson & Sons Ltd, n.d.

——. 'On the Supernatural in Fictitious Composition; and particularly on the Works of Ernest Theodore William Hoffmann'. *Sir Walter Scott On Novelists and Fiction*, ed. Ioan Williams. London: Routledge & Kegan Paul, 1968, 312–53.

Shakespeare, William. *Hamlet, Prince of Denmark*, 1602. *The Riverside Shakespeare*. Boston: Houghton Mifflin, 1974, 1135–97.

——. *The Merchant of Venice*, 1596–97. *The Riverside Shakespeare*. Boston: Houghton Mifflin, 1974, 254–83.

Shapiro, James. *Shakespeare and the Jews*. New York: Columbia UP, 1996.

Shapiro, Susan E. 'The Uncanny Jew: A Brief History of an Image'. *Judaism* 46 (1997): 63–78.

Sharkey, Terence. *Jack the Ripper: 100 Years of Investigation*. London: Ward Lock Limited, 1987.

Shell, Marc. *Money, Language, and Thought: Literary and Philosophic Economies from the Medieval to the Modern Era*. Baltimore and London: The Johns Hopkins UP, 1982.

Shelley, Percy Bysshe. *Hellas*. 1821. *The Complete Poetical Works of Percy Bysshe Shelley*, ed. Thomas Hutchinson, 1905. London: Oxford UP, 1965. 446–82.

——. *Queen Mab*, 1813. *The Complete Poetical Works of Percy Bysshe Shelley*, ed. Thomas Hutchinson, 1905. London: Oxford UP, 1965, 762–800.

——. *The Wandering Jew*, 1810, ed. Bertram Dobbell. New York: AMS Press, 1975.

——. 'The Wandering Jew's Soliloquy' n.d. *The Complete Poetical Works of Percy Bysshe Shelley*. ed. Thomas Hutchinson, 1905. London: Oxford UP, 1965, 881–2.

Shepard, Leslie. 'A Note on the Death Certificate of Bram Stoker'. 1992. *Bram Stoker's Dracula: Sucking Through the Century, 1897–1997*, ed. Carol Margaret Davison. Toronto and Oxford: Dundurn Press, 1997, 414–5.

Shimoni, Gideon. *The Zionist Ideology*. Hanover, New Hampshire and London: Brandeis UP, 1995.

Showalter, Elaine. *A Literature of Their Own: British Women Novelists From Brontë to Lessing*. Princeton: Princeton UP, 1977.

——. *Sexual Anarchy: Gender and Culture at the Fin de Siècle*. Harmondsworth: Penguin, 1990.

——. 'Syphilis, Sexuality, and the Fiction of the Fin de Siècle'. *Sex, Politics, and Science in the Nineteenth-Century Novel*, ed. Ruth Bernard Yeazell. Baltimore and London: Johns Hopkins UP, 1986, 88–115.

Silberner, Edmund. 'British Socialism and the Jews'. *Historia Judaica* 14 (1952): 27–52.

Silverman, Willa Z. 'Anti-Semitism and Occultism in Fin-de-siècle France: Three "Initiates"'. *Modernity and Revolution in Late Nineteenth-Century France*, eds Barbara T. Cooper and Mary Donaldson-Evans. Newark, DE: University of Delaware Press, 1992. 155–63.

Simmel, Georg. 'Prostitution'. 1907. *On Individuality and Social Forms: Selected Writings*, ed. Donald N. Levine. Chicago: The University of Chicago Press, 1971. 121–6.

Simpson, David. *Romanticism, Nationalism, and the Revolt Against Theory*. Chicago and London: The University of Chicago Press, 1993.

Singer, Brian. 'Violence in the French Revolution: Forms of Ingestion/Forms of Expulsion'. *The French Revolution and the Birth of Modernity*, ed. Ferenc Fehér. Berkeley, CA: University of California Press, 1990. 150–73.

Smart, Robert A. 'Blood and Money in Bram Stoker's *Dracula*: The Struggle Against Monopoly'. *Money: Lure, Lore, and Literature*, ed. John Louis DiGaetani. Westport, CT: Greenwood, 1994, 253–60.

Smith, Goldwin. 'Can Jews Be Patriots?' *The Nineteenth Century* 3 (May 1878): 875–87.

——. 'The Jewish Question'. *The Nineteenth Century* 10 (October 1881): 494–515.

——. 'The Jews. A Deferred Referrnder (*sic*)'. *The Nineteenth Century* (November 1882): 687–709.

Smith, Paul. Introduction. *The Self-Fashioning of Disraeli 1818–1851*. eds Charles Richmond and Paul Smith. Cambridge: Cambridge UP, 1998, 1–15.

Solomons, Israel. *Lord George Gordon's Conversion to Judaism*. London: Luzac & Co., 1914.

Spencer, Kathleen L. 'Purity and Danger: *Dracula*, the Urban Gothic, and the Late Victorian Degeneracy Crisis'. *ELH* 59 (1992): 197–225.

Stallybrass, Peter and Allon White. *The Politics and Poetics of Transgression*. Ithaca, New York: Cornell UP, 1986.

Sterrenburg, Lee. 'Mary Shelley's Monster: Politics and Psyche in *Frankenstein*'. *The Endurance of Frankenstein: Essays on Mary Shelley's Novel*, eds George Levine and U.C. Knoepflmacher. Berkeley, CA: University of California Press, 1979. 143–71.

Stevenson, John Allen. 'A Vampire in the Mirror: The Sexuality of *Dracula*'. *PMLA* 103 (1988): 139–49.

Stiffler, Muriel W. *The German Ghost Story as Genre*. New York: Peter Lang, 1993.

Stoker, Bram. 'The Censorship of Fiction'. *The Nineteenth Century and After* 64 (September 1908): 479–87.

Stoker, Bram. 'The Censorship of Stage Plays'. *The Nineteenth Century and After* 66 (December 1909): 974–89.

——. *Dracula*, 1897. Oxford: Oxford UP, 1992.

——. *Famous Impostors*. New York: Sturgis & Walton Company, 1910.

——. Introduction, 1898. *Makt Myrkranna*. Trans. Valdimar Asmundsson. *Bram Stoker Society Journal* 5 (1993): 7–8.

——. *Personal Reminiscences of Henry Irving*. 2 vols. 1906. Westport, CT: Greenwood Press, 1970.

Sue, Eugène. *The Wandering Jew*, 1844–45. Sawtry, Cambridgeshire: Dedalus, 1990.

Summers, Montague. *The Gothic Quest: A History of the Gothic Novel*. London: The Fortune Press, 1938.

Synnott, Anthony. *The Body Social: Symbolism, Self and Society*. London and New York: Routledge, 1993.

Tanner, Tony. *Venice Desired*. Cambridge, MA: Harvard UP, 1992.

Tarr, Mary Muriel. *Catholicism in Gothic Fiction in England: A Study of the Nature and Function of Catholic Materials in Gothic Fiction in England (1762–1820)*. Washington, DC: The Catholic University of America Press, 1946.

Thompson, E.P. *The Making of the English Working Class*. Harmondshire: Penguin, 1963.

Thornton, A.P. *The Imperial Idea and Its Enemies: A Study in British Power*, 1959, 2nd edn. Houndmills, Basingstoke: Macmillan, 1985.

Toland, John. *Reasons for Naturalizing the Jews in Great Britain and Ireland, On the same foot with all other Nations. Containing also, A Defence of the Jews Against All Vulgar Prejudices in all Countries*. London: J. Roberts, 1714.

Tompkins, J.M.S. *The Popular Novel in England 1770–1800*. London: Methuen, 1932.

Trachtenberg, Joshua. *The Devil and the Jews: The Medieval Conception of the Jew and Its Relation to Modern Antisemitism*. New Haven: Yale UP, 1943.

Tracy, Robert. 'Loving You All Ways: Vamps, Vampires, Necrophiles and Necrofilles in Nineteenth-Century Fiction'. *Sex and Death in Victorian Literature*, ed. Regina Barreca. Bloomington and Indianapolis: Indiana UP, 1990, 32–59.

Trollope, Anthony. *An Autobiography*, 1883, eds Michael Sadleir and Frederick Page. Oxford: Oxford UP, 1989.

——. *The Way We Live Now*, 1875. Oxford: Oxford UP, 1991.

Varma, Devendra P. *The Gothic Flame*. London: Arthur Barker, 1957.

Viereck, George Sylvester and Paul Eldridge. *My First Two Thousand Years: The Autobiography of the Wandering Jew*. New York: The MacAulay Company, 1928.

——. *Salome, The Wandering Jewess: My First Two Thousand Years of Love*, 1930. New York: Gold Label Books, 1945.

Vital, David. *A People Apart: The Jews in Europe 1789–1939*. Oxford: Oxford UP, 1999.

Walker, Barbara G. *Woman's Encyclopedia of Myths and Secrets*. New York: HarperCollins, 1983.

Walkowitz, Judith R. *City of Dreadful Delight: Narratives of Sexual Danger in Late-Victorian London*. Chicago: The University of Chicago Press, 1992.

Walpole, Horace. *The Castle of Otranto*, 1764. Oxford: Oxford UP, 1982.

The Wandering-Jew, Telling Fortunes to English-men. London, 1640.

Ward, Geoff, ed. *A Guide to Romantic Literature: 1790–1830*. London: Bloombsbury, 1993.

Wasson, Richard. 'The Politics of *Dracula*'. *English Literature in Transition* 9 (1966): 24–7.

Webb, Beatrice. 'Chapter IV: The Jewish Community'. *Life and Labour of the People in London*. By Charles Booth, 1889. New York: Augustus M. Kelley, 1969, 166–92.

Weber, Eugen. 'Reflections on the Jews in France'. *The Jews in Modern France*, eds Frances, Malino and Bernard Wasserstein. Hanover and London: UP of New England, 1985.

Weber, Max. *The Protestant Ethic and the Spirit of Capitalism*, 1930. London: George Allen & Unwin, 1985.

Wein, Toni. *British Identities, Heroic Nationalisms, and the Gothic Novel, 1764–1824.* Houndmills, Basingstoke: Palgrave Macmillan, 2002.

Weinbrot, Howard D. *Britannia's Issue: The Rise of British Literature From Dryden to Ossian*. Cambridge: Cambridge UP, 1993.

Weingrad, Michael. Rev. of *Marrano as Metaphor: The Jewish Presence in French Writing*, by Elaine Marks, and *Albert Cohen, une quête solaire*, by Carole Auroy. *Prooftexts* 21 (2001): 255–75.

Wheeler, Michael. *Heaven, Hell, and the Victorians*. Cambridge: Cambridge, 1994.

——. *English Fiction of the Victorian Period 1830–1890*. London and New York: Longman, 1985.

White, Arnold. *The Modern Jew*. London: William Heinemann, 1899.

Wiesel, Elie. *Night*, 1958. New York: Avon, 1969.

Wilde, Oscar. *The Picture of Dorian Gray*, 1891. Oxford: Oxford UP, 1994.

Williams, Charles. *All Hallow's Eve*. New York: Pellegrini & Cudahy, 1948.

Wilson, Colin. *The Occult: A History*. New York: Vintage, 1971.

Wolf, Leonard. *The Essential Dracula: The Definitive Annotated Edition of Bram Stoker's Classic Novel*. 1975. New York: Plume, 1993.

Wolper, Roy S. 'Circumcision as Polemic in the Jew Bill of 1753: The Cutter Cut?' *Eighteenth-Century Life* 7 (1982): 28–36.

Wordsworth, William. 'Preface to *Lyrical Ballads*', 1802. *Romanticism: An Anthology*. ed. Duncan Wu. Oxford: Blackwell, 1996, 250–69.

Worland, Rick. 'OWI Meet the Monsters: Hollywood Horror Films and War Propaganda, 1942 to 1945'. *Cinema Journal* 37 (1997): 47–65.

Yates, Frances. *The Rosicrucian Enlightenment*. London and Boston: Routledge & Kegan Paul, 1972.

Young, Robert J.C. 'Freud's Secret: *The Interpretation of Dreams* was a Gothic novel'. *Sigmund Freud's The Interpretation of Dreams: New Interdisciplinary Essays*. Manchester and New York: Manchester UP, 1999, 206–31.

Zanger, Jules. 'A Sympathetic Vibration: Dracula and the Jews'. *English Literature in Transition 1880–1920* 34 (1991): 33–44.

Zatlin, Linda Gertner. *The Nineteenth-Century Anglo-Jewish Novel*. Boston: Twayne Publishers, 1981.

Žižek, Slavoj. *The Sublime Object of Ideology*. London: Verso, 1989.

Index

Adler, Rabbi Herman, 13
Adorno, Theodor, 158, 159, 165, 199n10
adversus judaeos literature, 40
Agrippa, Heinrich Cornelius, 112
  On Occult Philosophy (1531), 113
  On the Vanity of Sciences and Arts
    (1530), 113
Akenside, Mark, 48
alchemy, ix, 72, 92, 107, 111, 112, 138,
    183n18
  see also Jew and alchemy
Aliens Act
  of 1793, 84
  of 1905, 130
American Gothic, 27, 173n17
Anderson, Amanda, 169n14
Anderson, George K., 88, 91, 179n24,
    188n4
anti-capitalism, 123
anti-Catholicism, 80, 90, 100–3, 109,
    116, 170n7
anti-Enlightenment, 81, 170n5
anti-Semitism
  in Britain, 5, 121–6, 168n9
  continental, 123
  and misogyny, 149, 156
  and projection, 14
  as psychopathology, 53
  political parties, 123
  racial/secular, 18, 78, 79
  religious/theological, 78
  as vampiric, 14, 165, 199n10
Apollonius of Tyana, 94–5, 103, 189n5,
    189n6
Arata, Stephen D., 143, 144, 198n2
Arendt, Hannah, 131
Ariosophy, 199n9
Arnim, Achim von, 170n5
Arnold, Matthew, 12, 124, 173n19
Arnstein, Walter, 192n2
Atkinson, Thomas, 58
Auerbach, Nina, 56, 194n17
Austen, Jane
  Northanger Abbey (1818), 35
Ausubel, Nathan, 67, 192n5

Bacon, Francis
  New Atlantis (1627), 69
Baldick, Chris, 171n9
Banister, Joseph, 146
Bara, Theda, 152, 197n38
  see also vamp
Barben, Monsignor, 10, 75, 186n32
Barfoot, C.C., 11
Baring-Gould, Reverend Sabine, 42
Barruel, Abbé Augustin, 10, 59, 60, 61,
    62, 66, 180n3
  as Gothic novelist, 181–2n11
Bauer, Bruno, 169n2
Bauman, Zygmunt, 18
Blade, 178n18
Blake, William, 104
Blakemore, Steven, 187n40
Blanchot, Maurice, 172n11
Bleeding Nun, 97–100, 103, 189n8
  see also Lewis, Matthew, *The Monk*
Bleiler, E.F., 175n6
blood and money, 137, 139, 141–2,
    163
Blood Libel, 9, 10, 35, 39–46, 66, 75, 79,
    80–1, 83, 115, 117, 119, 126, 129,
    137, 155, 158, 162, 163, 164,
    176n9, 176n10, 178n21, 187n41,
    191n20, 193n12
Blount, Henry, 65
Bostrom, Irene, 29, 79
Botting, Fred, 57
Brantlinger, Patrick, 26, 58, 124, 126,
    171n10
Brennan, Timothy, 26
Brentano, Clemens, 170n5
Briggs, Katharine M., 167n8
British imperialism, 13, 30–1, 122, 123,
    125, 136, 141, 142, 143, 157, 159,
    193n9
British Israel Theory, 182n13
Brontë, Charlotte
  Jane Eyre (1847), 38
Brothers, Richard, 63
Brown, Charles Brockden,
    173n17

Bulwer-Lytton, Edward
  Zanoni: A Rosicrucian Tale (1842),
    189n5
Burke, Edmund, 10, 60, 63, 81, 170n7,
    180n1, 181n8, 182n14
  on France's Judaization, 20
  Letters on a Regicide Peace (1795–7), 20
  Reflections on the Revolution in France
    (1790), 20, 36, 84
Burton, Sir Richard
  The Jew, the Gypsy and El Islam
    (1898), 128–9, 193n12

Cabala, 32, 45, 66–77, 92, 113, 158, 165,
    183n18, 183n19, 184n25, 184n26,
    199n9
  bastardization of, 66, 68, 76
  and cabals, 68, 69, 84, 183n20, 187n40
  demonization of, 70, 71, 76
  and Gothic literature, 35, 68
  and the Occult, 68
  and secret societies, 70
Cagliostro, 75–7, 85, 91, 186n32
Cain, 41, 42, 72, 89, 99, 156
Calvin, John, 114, 166–7n5
Calvinism, 44, 173n17
cannibalism, 55, 81, 118
Cantimpré, Thomas de, 42
capitalism,
  and Protestantism, 3, 138, 141–4
  and vampirism, 139
  see also Jew and capitalism
Carlyle, Thomas, 180n1, 180n3
Castle, Terry, 21, 22, 174n21
Chamisso, Adalbert von
  Peter Schlemihl (1813), 45, 178n21
Charcot, Dr. Jean Martin, 125, 145,
    195n24
Charles V (Holy Roman Emperor), 109,
    113, 190n18
Chartists, 168n10, 192n3
Chaucer, Geoffrey
  'The Prioress's Tale,' 119
Cheyette, Bryan, 2, 5–6, 13, 23, 30,
    166n4, 170n5, 172n11, 173n19,
    194n15
circumcision, 40, 41, 45, 83, 85, 115,
    117, 177n13, 195n22
Clemit, Patricia, 111
Clery, E.J., 10, 26, 58, 59, 167n6

Clifford, Robert, 180n3, 185n31
Coates, Paul, 91
Cobbett, William, 6
Cohn, Norman, 169n3
coin-clipping affair (1278), 177n17
Colley, Linda, 4, 29, 167n7, 168n11
A Confutation of the Reasons for
    Naturalizing the Jews Containing
    the Crimes, Frauds and Insolencies,
    For which they were Convicted and
    Punished in former Reigns (1715),
    44, 176n11, 177n18, 181n7, 181n10
conversion, 51
  see also Count Dracula and Christian
    conversion
  see also Jew and Christian conversion
Corelli, Marie
  The Sorrows of Satan (1895), 133–4,
    148
Count Dracula, 95, 98, 115, 119, 127,
    129, 134–57, 191n22
  as anti-Christ, 136
  see also Jew and anti-Christ
  and Christian conversion, 136, 157
  as Crypto Jew, 143, 150
  as Faust figure, 45
  see also Faust
  and filth, 144
  see also filth, iconography of
  see also filthy lucre
  and genocide, 157
  and homosexuality, 150, 196–7n34
  see also homosexuality
  see also Jew and homosexuality
  as imperialist, 13, 142–3
  see also British imperialism
  see also Disraeli, Benjamin, and Count
    Dracula
  and Jack the Ripper, 152–7
  as Jew, 134–9, 146, 155, 169n13,
    198n2
  as Judaizer, 144
  see also Judaization
  and miscegenation, 163
  see also Jew and miscegenation
  as Nazi, 198n2
  see also Nazism
  as pimp, 148
  as Roman Catholic, 195n23
  as Shylock figure, 139

countersubversion, imagery of, 58
Craft, Christopher, 196n34
Croly, George, 90, 129
*The Claims of the Jews Incompatible with
    the National Profession of Christianity*
    (1848), 194n13
  'Judaism in the Legislature' (1847),
    194n13
  *Salathiel: A Story of the Past, the Present,
    and the Future* (1828), 194n13
Cromwell, Oliver, 5, 63, 64, 65
Crypto-Jews, 12, 31, 61, 74, 77, 80, 86,
    124, 132, 162, 163, 193n12
  see also Count Dracula as Crypto-Jew
  see also Disraeli, Benjamin as
    Crypto-Jew
Cumberland, Richard, 47, 104

Danby, Frank [Julia Frankau]
  Dr. Phillips; A Maida Vale Idyll (1887),
    132
  Pigs in Clover (1903), 133
Davies, Bernard, 153
Davis, David Brion, 58
Davison, Carol Margaret, 169n15
Davison, Neil R., 197n1
De Bruyn, Frans, 170n7
Declaration of the Rights of Man, 80
degeneration, 125, 144, 146, 151, 152,
    169n16
Deists, 20, 89
dentition, 44, 177n18
Dentition of the Jews, 48, 177n18
Derrida, Jacques, 7, 168n12, 172n11
Desaulniers, Mary, 180n1
Dickens, Charles
  Great Expectations (1860–1), 38
  Oliver Twist (1837–8), 178n19
  see also Fagin
Dijkstra, Bram, 149, 151, 174n20, 197n36
Dinter, Arthur
  The Sin Against the Blood (1918),
    161, 199n6
Disraeli, Benjamin, 34, 65, 193n12
  Coningsby; or The New Generation
    (1844), 12, 65
  and Count Dracula, 13, 143
  as Crypto-Jew, 144, 192n6
  see also Crypto-Jews
  and imperialism, 13, 123, 193n7

  *Lord George Bentinck: A Political
    Biography* (1852), 12
  as magician, 124
Domenichino (Domenico Zampieri),
    107, 190n17
double, 10, 24, 30, 32, 71, 86, 100, 109,
    110, 115, 123, 124, 173n18
Douglas, William Fettes
  The Spell (1864), ix
Drumont, Edouard, 65, 66
Du Maurier, George
  Trilby (1894), 5, 8, 133, 134, 194n17
Durden, Ralph, 182n15

Easthope, Antony, 173n16
Edelmann, R., 186n34
Edgeworth, Maria
  The Absentee (1811), 34
  Castle Rackrent (1800), 34, 35
  Harrington (1817), 9–10, 34–9, 46–54,
    167n6, 170n4, 191n22
  Moral Tales for Young People (1801), 46
Edward I, 176n12, 177n17
Ehrmann, Dr., 66
Eichmann, Adolf, 158
Eisner, Lotte, 198n4
Eldridge, Paul, 197n1
Eliot, George, 53
  Daniel Deronda (1876), 12, 194n14
Eliot, T.S., 159
elixir vitae, 33, 106, 114
  see also opus magnum
Ellis, Kate Ferguson, 172n15
Ellmann, Maud, 193n8
Enlightenment, 15, 19, 111, 169n1,
    171n10
  demonization of, 15
  and the Jews, 9, 16, 17–18, 20
  and national identity, 16
eschatology, 62, 65, 79
'Eternal Jew' (art exhibition, Munich
    1937), 161

Fagin, 23, 46, 115, 144, 178n19
Farrakhan, Louis, 196n26
Farson, Daniel, 191n1
Faust, 45, 95, 103, 105, 114, 120, 127,
    179n22, 179n23, 180n1, 194n13
Feldman, David, 3, 6
Felsenstein, Frank, 19, 41, 63, 187n41

Female Gothic, 27, 38, 51
Feuchtwanger, Léon, 163
Fiedler, Leslie, 23, 46, 53, 115, 173n17, 173n19
Fifth Monarchy Men, 63, 65
filth, iconography of, 144
filthy lucre, 128, 144, 147
  see also Jew and capitalism
Final Solution, 14, 159, 160, 198n4
Finkelkraut, Alain, 19, 80, 162
Flying Dutchman, 120
foetor judaicus, 135
Foucault, Michel, 15, 56
forbidden knowledge, 171n10
Franklin, Andrew
  The Wandering Jew, or, Love's Masquerade (1797), 190n13
Franklin, J. Jeffrey, 192n4
Frayling, Christopher, 155
Frederick the Great, 87
Freedman, Jonathan, 16, 32
Freemasonry, 62, 72, 73, 76, 81, 128, 181n5, 182n11, 184n22, 185n28, 185n30, 193n11, 199n9
  British, 59, 181n9
  and guillotine, 181n11
  see also Jew and Freemasonry
French Revolution, 10, 12, 20, 25, 55, 56, 57, 62, 76, 79, 81, 83, 84, 96, 170n7, 171n10, 188n42
  see also Jew and the French Revolution
Freud, Sigmund, 38, 41, 142, 173n19
  as Gothic novelist, 24, 172n13
  'The Medusa's Head' (1922), 151
  'The Uncanny' (1919), 21, 22
  see also Jew as uncanny figure
  see also Uncanny
Friedländer, Saul, 41
Friedman, Lester D., 165, 184n27, 198n4
Froude, J.A., 192n6
Frye, Northrop, 197n38
Fuchs, Eduard, 196n26

Gabor, Bethlem, 109–11, 190–1n19
  see also Godwin, William, St. Leon
Gagging Acts (1795), 57
Galt, John
  The Wandering Jew (1820), 114
gambling, 45, 90, 131, 138, 163, 192n4

Garb, Tamar, 23
Geissendorfer, Hans W., 198n2
Gelder, Ken, 194n21
Geller, Jay, 31, 197n37
genocide, 198n2
German Expressionist Cinema, 14, 25, 160–1, 198n4
Gill, Stephen, 178n19
Gilman, Sander, 41, 146, 155, 156, 177n13, 177n14, 194n18, 195n25
Glassman, Bernard, 19
Glover, David, 193n11
Goddu, Teresa, 8, 27, 173n17
Godwin, William
  Caleb Williams (1794), 37, 174n4
  Lives of the Necromancers (1834), 112, 191n21
  Mandeville: A Tale of the Seventeenth Century in England, 105
  St. Leon (1799), 11, 37, 81, 88, 90, 103, 104–14, 115, 118, 127, 135, 174–5n4, 179n24, 190–1n19
Goebbels, Joseph, 162, 199n7
Goens, Jean, 152
Goldhagen, Daniel Jonah, 46
Golem, 72, 184n25, 184n27
Gordon, Lord George, 85–6
Gordon Riots (1780), 50, 85, 180n27, 188n42
Gothic novel
  and Enlightenment, 6–7, 26, 173n18
  and the French Revolution, 25
  and modernity, 9, 26
  and national identity, 7, 8, 27–33, 158
  as parasite, 32
  political nature of, 180n4
  and religion, 28–33
Goudge, H.L., 182n13
Green, Sarah
  Romance Readers and Romance Writers (1810), 35
Grosse, Marquis, 87
Grudin, Peter, 189n8

Haggard, H. Rider, 133, 194n16
Haining, Peter, 197n40
Halberstam, Judith, 174n20
Harlan, Veit
  Jud Süss (1940), 14, 161, 162, 164, 198n3, 199n7, 199n8

Harrington, James
  The Art of Lawgiving (1659), 52, 68
  The Commonwealth of Oceana
    (1656), 52, 68, 183n21
Haskalah (Jewish Enlightenment),
    170n4
Hastings, Adrian, 169n1
Hawthorne, Nathaniel, 173n12
Hazlitt, William, 6, 168n10
The Hebrew Talisman (1840), 193n12
Heine, Heinrich, 188n3
Henderson, Andrea, 173n18
Henriques, U.R.Q., 175n7
Hermippus Redivivus (1744), 111
Herzl, Theodor, 131
D'Hesmivy, Abbé d'Auribeau, 71
Hess, Moses, 160
  The Essence of Money (1843), 139
Hetherington, Henry, 6, 168n10
Hill, Christopher, 183n16
Hines, Edward, 182n13
Hippler, Fritz
  Der Ewige Jude (*The Eternal Jew*), 14,
    161, 162, 164
Hitler, Adolph, 158, 160, 161, 178n22,
    195n26
  see also Nazism
Hoad, Neville, 36, 179n26, 179n27
Hobsbawm, E.J., 121, 140–1
Hoffmann, E.T.A.
  The Sandman (1816), 24, 38, 175n6
Holocaust, 14, 17, 165, 198n2
Holy Roman Inquisition, 76, 90, 187n37
homosexuality, 13, 152, 193n8
  see also Jew and homosexuality
  see also Count Dracula and
    homosexuality
Horkheimer, Max, 158, 159, 165, 199n10
Host, thematics of, 111, 126, 136–7, 164
Hsia, R. Po-Chia, 44
Hugh of Lincoln, 40

Illuminati, 59, 62, 70, 81, 181n9,
    185n31
Industrial Revolution, 26
Invasion of the Body Snatchers (1956), 31

Jabès, Edmond, 172n11
Jack the Ripper, 125–6, 148, 153–6,
    196n29, 196n31, 197n40, 197n41

and Count Dracula, 152–7
  as Jew, 126
Jacob, Margaret, 181n5
Jacobi, Walter, 184n27
Jacobinism, 180n2
  English, 56
  see also Abbé Augustin Barruel
  see also Jew and Jacobinism
Jacobites, 180n2
James, Henry, 8
Jew
  and alchemy, 191n20
  see also alchemy
  and ambivalence, 166n4, 170n5
  and anti-Christ, 62, 193n8
  as anti-citizen, 20, 21, 170n6
  and assimilation, 13, 31, 52, 69, 76–7,
    78, 82, 89, 122, 128, 132, 162,
    163–4, 195n25
  see also Jew and miscegenation
  as body snatcher, 125
  and British Emancipation debates, 20
  and British 'invasion,' 125, 139, 156
  see also Jew and immigration to Britain
  and cannibalism, 31, 40, 43, 44, 119
  and capitalism, 3, 32–3, 41, 43, 44,
    102, 103, 105, 107, 108, 109, 110,
    114, 122, 125, 130, 132, 137–43,
    159, 162, 167n6, 190n18,
    194n22, 197n38
  as castrator, 115
  and Christian conversion, 4, 18, 31,
    78, 81, 86, 107, 122, 166n2
  as conspirator, 60, 61, 65, 82, 144,
    164, 165, 178n19, 187n38,
    193n12, 198n5
  and degeneration, 151, 162
  and the devil, 39, 41, 45, 102–3, 163
  and disease, 61, 126
  as dog, 44, 178n19
  as effeminate, 149, 197n35
  expulsion from England, 40
  as fanged, 44, 130, 144, 178n19
  as father figure, 30
  and filth, 42
  see also filth, iconography of
  see also filthy lucre
  and Freemasonry, 72–7, 181n8,
    184n27, 185n29
  see also Freemasonry

Jew – *continued*
  and the French Revolution, 65
  and hemorrhoids, 42, 177n15
  and homosexuality, 150
  and immigration to Britain, 13, 82,
    83, 125, 130, 138, 156
  see also Jew and British 'invasion'
  as imperialist, 65, 130, 138, 159
  see also British imperialism
  see also Disraeli, Benjamin, and
    imperialism
  as incestuous, 40, 41
  see also Cain
  and Jacobinism, 21, 83–4
  and the law, 13, 145
  and magic, 45, 190n12
  see also magic
  and menstruation, 40, 42
  and miscegenation, 46, 130, 150, 163
  and modernity, 17–18
  and nervous illness, 145
  as old clothes man, 86, 122, 169n3,
    174n3, 191n20
  and parasitism, 49, 164
  as pimp, 147
  and postmodernity, 172n11, 173–4n19
  and projection, 23, 158, 159, 164–5
  readmission to England, 63–4
  and revolution, 61, 66, 75
  as ritual murderer, 40, 193n12
  see also shochet
  and secret language, 184n23
  and secret societies, ix, 10, 45, 61, 65,
    92, 159
  and sodomy, 150
  as spectre, 1, 172n11, 172n12
  as stockbroker, 122, 123, 192n3
  and syphilis, 144, 146
  as uncanny figure, 9, 25, 172n12
  see also Freud, Sigmund, 'The
    Uncanny'
  see also Uncanny
  and vampirism, 6, 11, 13, 44–5, 46,
    158, 161, 195n22
  and war, 61
  as word in the English language, 85
  as wolf, 44, 115, 119, 139, 178n19,
    178n20
Jew badge, 41
Jewish disabilities, 187n39

Jewish Emancipation, 34, 36
Jewish messianism, 71–3
  see also Zevi, Sabbatai
Jewish Naturalization Bill (1753), 20, 39,
    82–3, 174n2, 175n5, 187n38
  repeal of, 83
Johnson, Major E.C., 129
Judaization, 31, 65, 75, 84, 85, 88, 90,
    105, 112, 115, 121, 124, 125, 126,
    137, 139, 155, 183n17
  fears in Britain, 7, 108, 187n41
  fears in Germany, 139, 195n26
Judas, 43, 78, 181n7
Judeophobia, 1
Judith, 151–2
Julius, Anthony, 149, 197n1

Kamen, Henry, 77, 80, 186n33
Kant, Immanuel, 16, 171n10, 194n22
Kaplan, M. Lindsay, 166n5
Kassouf, Susan, 177n15
Kates, Gary, 80
Katz, David S., 9
Katz, Jacob, 73, 184n22, 185n29
Kelly, Gary, 190–1n19
Kilgour, Maggie, 26, 31, 32, 99, 104,
    170n7, 171n9, 180n4
Kingsley, Charles
  *Alton Locke, Tailor and Poet: An
    Autobiography* (1850), 192n3
Kracauer, Siegfried, 198n4
Kristeva, Julia, 172n11

Leatherdale, Clive, 150, 153, 193n10
Lecky, W.E.H., 174n21
Levinas, Emmanuel, 172n11
Levine, Robert S., 58
Lewis, Matthew
  The Monk (1795), 5, 11, 28, 42, 79,
    92, 95–103, 104, 105, 113, 127,
    134, 179n24, 189n7, 189n10,
    189n11, 190n13, 196n33
Loew, Rabbi Judah, 72, 184n27
Loewenstein-Wertheim, Leopold von,
    178n21
Lombroso, Cesare, 146, 195n25
Ludlam, Henry, 120
Luther, Martin, 17, 44, 66, 67, 114,
    176n10
Lyotard, Jean-François, 172n11

Macaulay, Thomas Babington, 6, 51, 168n10
'Civil Disabilities of the Jews' (1831), 178n20
Maccoby, Hyam, 42, 166n2, 167n8
MacGillivray, Royce, 174n20
magic, 48, 99, 102, 103, 174n21, 181n6
see also Jew and magic
Maistre, Joseph de, 181n9
Malchow, H.L., 9, 11, 44, 123, 174n20, 198n2
Manly, Susan, 34, 36, 52, 84, 167n6, 174n1
Marathon Man (1976), 178n18
Marlowe, Christopher
The Tragical History of Doctor Faustus (1588), 179n23
The Jew of Malta (1590), 19
Marranos, 77, 80, 81, 86, 107, 108, 115, 162, 186n33
Martinism, 185n31
Marx, Karl, 7, 132, 160
The Eighteenth Brumaire of Louis Bonaparte (1852), 168–9n12
Das Kapital (1867, 1885, 1895), 140
Manifesto of the Communist Party (1848), 2
'On The Jewish Question' (1843), 140
Matar, N.I., 63
Maturin, Charles Robert
Melmoth the Wanderer (1820), 11, 28, 81, 83, 92, 95, 114–19, 179n24, 191n20
McBride, William Thomas, 174n20
McClintock, Anne, 126
McGinn, Bernard, 62, 182n12
Medusa, 151
Meige, Henry, 145
Melville, Herman, 173n17
Mendelssohn, Moses, 17, 170n4
menstruation, 193n8
see also Jew and menstruation
Mephistopheles, 45, 179n22
mesmerism, 71
Metropolis (1927), 161
Meyrink, Gustav, 184n26
Mighall, Robert, 22, 171n9
Miles, Robert, 26, 59
millenarianism, 62, 63, 71, 81, 85, 96, 165, 186n35

miscegenation, 196n33
see also Jew and miscegenation
monstrosity, 57, 96, 100, 109, 110, 134
Montesquieu, 167n6
Moretti, Franco, 26, 56, 140, 142
Morrison, Toni, 14
Mousseaux, Chevalier Gougenot des, 66
Murnau, F.W.
Nosferatu (1922), 194n19

Nandris, Grigore, 153
Napoleon, Bonaparte, 55, 61, 80, 186n36
as anti-Christ, 62, 182n12, 182n16
as Jewish Messiah, 62
national identity, 121, 158, 169n1
Naubert, Benedicte, 87
Nazism, 19, 158–65, 167n8, 178n18, 198n4, 199n7, 199n10
as secret society, 199n9
New Woman, 13, 148, 151–2
Nigh, William, 198n2
Nordau, Max, 195n25
Degeneration (1895), 125, 146
novel
and national identity, 26–7, 36, 173n16
see also national identity
historical, 171n9

Oberammergau Passion Play, 42
O'Brien, Conor Cruise, 16, 169n1, 181n8
O'Connell, Daniel, 6, 168n10
Oppenheimer, Joseph Süss, 19
see also Harlan, Veit
opus magnum, 105
Order of the Asiatic Brethren, 185n30
originality, 32
Osborne, Lawrence, 42, 177n14
Owen, Richard, 6

Pagels, Elaine, 175n8
Paine, Thomas, 170n6
The Rights of Man (1791–2), 20
Paris, Matthew, 92, 166n3, 188n4
Patai, Raphael, 67, 191n20
Paulson, Ronald, 170n7, 181n11, 188n42
Peacock, Thomas Love
Nightmare Abbey (1818), 35
Penslar, Derek, 165
Perry, Thomas, 82
Phillips, Baxter, 198n4

philosopher's stone, 33, 111
Picciotto, James, 85
Pick, Daniel, 125, 174n20
Pico della Mirandola, Giovanni, 67
Pinsker, Leo, 1, 23
Pocock, J.G.A., 181n8
Poliakov, Léon, 60, 78–9, 186n34
Polidori, John
    The Vampyre (1819), 117–18
Popkin, Richard H., 78
Porte, Joel, 29, 30
Porter, Roy, 15–16, 29, 30
Praz, Mario, 114
Price, Richard, 20, 84, 106
prostitution, 101, 121, 132, 144, 147,
    152, 156, 184n23, 192n1, 195n26,
    196n28, 196n31, 197n37
Protestantism, 29, 92, 104, 118, 124, 137
    see also capitalism and Protestantism
Protocols of the Elders of Zion, 61, 66,
    195n26
Prynne, William, 43
Punter, David, 26, 32
Pykett, Lynn, 169n16

Radcliffe, Ann
    The Italian (1764), 79, 105, 187n37
    The Mysteries of Udolpho (1794), 50,
    91, 190n17
Ragussis, Michael, 1, 5, 7, 8, 36, 38, 46,
    51, 81, 84, 168n9, 179n26
Railo, Eino, 91, 179n24, 188n4
Ray, Rhonda Johnson, 65
Rebatet, Lucien, 198n5
Reddy, William, 105
Reid, William Hamilton, 58, 63
Reik, Theodor, 41
repression, 173n17
    return of the repressed, 36, 37, 165,
    196n33
Restoration to Palestine, 64, 81
Reuchlin, Johann, 67
Ricardo, David, 131
Richardson, Samuel
    Clarissa, 101
Riquelme, Jean Paul, 197n1
Roberts, J.M., 185n31
Roberts, Marie [Mulvey], 57, 69–70, 117
Roberts, Samuel, 129
Robertson, Ritchie, 170n8, 172n12

Robison, John, 10, 59, 62
Roger of Wendover, 166n1
Roman Catholic Church, 4, 29, 77, 79,
    88, 90, 95, 96, 100–3, 113, 116, 117,
    119, 137, 159, 167n7
    and conspiracy, 92
    as secret society, 92, 102–3, 191n23
Rose, Paul Lawrence, 18, 78, 88
Rosenberg, Edgar, 8, 11, 99, 104, 119
Rosicrucianism, 59, 69, 70, 94, 111,
    189n5, 199n9
Ross, Alexander, 64
Roth, Cecil, 77, 84
Roth, Norman, 186n33
Roth, Phyllis, 153, 174n20, 179n24
Rothschild, Nathan Mayer, 132
Royle, Nicholas, 172n14
Rubin, Abba, 64, 65, 82, 84
Rubinstein, W.D., 168n9, 177n16
Ruskin, John, 196n30
Russell, C., 130–1, 135

Sacks, Chief Rabbi Jonathan, 18
Sade, Marquis de, 55
    'Reflections on the Novel' (1800), 26
Sagan, Eli, 169n1
Sage, Victor, 29
*St. Godwin: A Tale of the 16th, 17th, and
    18th Century*, 190n14
Salisbury, Jay, 28, 173n18, 173–4n19
Salome, 151–2
Sanhedrin, 61, 62, 181n7
Sartre, Jean-Paul, 78, 172n11
Schauerroman (shudder novel), 55, 86,
    87–8, 105, 160
Schechter, Ronald, 170n6
Schiller, Johann Christoph Friedrich von
    The Ghost-Seer (1788), 87, 88, 90–5, 98,
    105, 183n19, 188n1, 188n2, 189n6
Schmitt, Cannon, 27
Scholem, Gershom, 184n24, 185n30
Scholomance, 105, 128, 193n10
Schubart, Christian Friedrich Daniel,
    188n3
Schulte-Sasse, Linda, 199n8
Scott, Sir Walter, 175n6
    Ivanhoe (1817), 4, 177n18, 178n19
secret sciences, 70, 92, 96, 101, 103,
    106, 110, 111, 112, 114, 125, 189n9
    and the French Revolution, 59

secret societies, 57–62, 74, 103, 116,
158, 165, 185n28, 185n31, 193n11
and repression, 70
see also Jew and secret societies
see also Nazism as secret society
see also Roman Catholic Church as
secret society
Secret Societies Act (1799), 57
September Massacres, 55, 79, 83
Shakespeare, William, 27
Hamlet (1602), 25
The Merchant of Venice (1596–7), 19,
52, 179n26, 194n20
see also Shylock
Shapiro, James, 3, 4, 5, 82, 197n35
Shapiro, Susan, 43, 172n11, 172n12,
173n19
Shell, Marc, 45
Shelley, Mary, 182n11
Frankenstein (1818), 72, 96, 134, 148,
150, 184n25, 190n15
'History of the Jews' (n.d.), 89
Shelley, Percy Bysshe, 182n11
Hellas (1821), 89
Queen Mab (1813), 89
The Wandering Jew (1810), 5, 189n9
'The Wandering Jew's Soliloquy'
(n.d.), 89
Shepard, Leslie, 192n1
shochet (ritual slaughterer), 155, 163, 164
Showalter, Elaine, 17
Shylock, 19, 44, 46, 82–3, 91, 115, 119,
133, 157, 159, 165, 174n3, 179n26,
194n20
see also Count Dracula as Shylock
figure
see also Shakespeare, William, *The
Merchant of Venice*
Silberner, Edmund, 5, 192n3
Silverman, Willa Z., 138
Simmel, George, 196n28
Simpson, David, 16, 57, 182n14
slavery, 173n17
Smart, Robert, 141–2
Smith, Goldwin, 13, 192n4
Spanish Inquisition, 36–7, 47, 48, 77–86,
96, 100–1, 106–9, 115–16, 162
European cultural representations of,
4, 18, 186n37
Spencer, Kathleen, 195n23

Spinoza, Baruch, 16
Spiritualism, 197n41
Stäel, Madame de, 178n21
Sterrenburg, Lee, 182n11
Stoker, Bram
'The Censorship of Fiction' (1908),
149, 196n32
'The Censorship of Stage Plays'
(1909), 196n32
Dracula (1897), 8, 11, 13, 29, 72, 95,
104, 105, 117, 120–57, 161,
179n24, 199n8
Dracula (*Icelandic edition*, 1901), 153,
196n29, 197n39, 197n40
Famous Impostors (1910), 121
Personal Reminiscences of Henry Irving
(1906), 135
and secret societies, 193n11
Stolz, Alban, 66
Der Stürmer, 161
Streicher, Julius, 161, 199n6
Sue, Eugene
Le Juif Errant (1844–5), 121, 191n23
Summers, Montague, 11, 29
Svengali, 134, 194n17
Sweeney Todd, 38
syphilis, 13, 121, 125, 126, 144, 146–7,
156, 177n13, 191n1, 193n8,
195n25, 195n26

Talmud, 66
Tanner, Tony, 90–1
Tarr, Mary Muriel, 29
Ten Lost Tribes, 63, 182n13
Thomas, Keith, 174n21
Thompson, E.P., 55
Thornton, A.P., 193n7
Toland, John, 168n10, 183n17, 187n39
Tompkins, J.M.S., 56, 87, 188n1, 188n2
Trachtenberg, Joshua, 39, 41, 43, 45,
167–8n8, 176n12
Tracy, Robert, 156
transubstantiation, 176n9
Trollope, Anthony, 7, 12
The Way We Live Now (1875), 4, 8,
124, 132
Tschink, Cajetan, 87

Uncanny, 21–5, 91, 172n14
historicization of, 23

usury, 40, 43, 44, 46, 103, 105, 108, 133, 137, 147, 162, 166–7n5, 193n12

vamp, 197n38
see also Bara, Theda
vampirism, 93–4
  as anti-Christ, 121
  and imperialism, 143
  and infection, 116, 121, 126, 147
  and women, 147, 151
Venice, 90, 91, 106
Viereck, George Sylvester, 197n1
Vital, David, 6
Vlad the Impaler, 142, 152
Voltaire, 17, 150, 170n4

Walkowitz, Judith, 121, 154
Walpole, Horace
  The Castle of Otranto (1764), 50, 80
Wandering *Jeu*, 28
Wandering Jew, 23, 34–5, 57, 86, 178n21, 193n12
  as abject figure, 33
  as ambivalent figure, 99
  as anti-Christ figure, 184n26
  as anti-citizen, 28
  conversion of, 89
  demonization of, 5, 88, 158
  and Englishness, 8
  and the Enlightenment, 24
  and epistemology, 28
  legend of, 2, 5, 18, 19, 32, 42, 62, 78, 88–9, 94, 103, 106, 112, 114, 115, 116, 120, 128, 133, 166n1, 166n3, 167–8n8, 179n24, 185n28, 186n34
  as memento mori figure, 89, 102
  in Modernist fiction, 159, 197n1
  in Nazi propaganda, 160
  as psychopathologized type, 145
  in Romantic literature, 5, 28

  secularization of, 88
  as Uncanny figure, 22
  and vampirism, 5, 31, 72
Warner, John, 65
Warwick, Alexandra, 193n9
Webb, Beatrice, 131
Weber, Max, 138
Wegener, Paul, 72, 184n27, 198n4
Wein, Toni, 28, 30, 171n9
Weingrad, Michael, 172n11
Weininger, Otto, 149
Weishaupt, Adam, 60
Wheeler, Michael, 29
White, Sir Arnold
  The Modern Jew (1899), 129–30, 156
Whitehall conference, 64
Wiesel, Eli
  Night (1958), 165
Wilde, Oscar
  The Picture of Dorian Gray (1891), 133, 134
Will, P., 188n1
William of Norwich, 40
Williams, Charles
  All Hallow's Eve (1948), 159
Wilson, Colin, 94
Wollstonecraft, Mary, 109
Wordsworth, William
  Preface to the Lyrical Ballads (1802), 56

Yates, Frances, 69
Young, Robert J.C., 172n13

Zanger, Jules, 174n20, 192n5
Zatlin, Linda Gertner, 192n5
Zevi, Sabbatai, 71–3, 184n24
  see also Jewish messianism
Zionism, 1, 13, 131
Žižek , Slavoj, 31
Zohar, 113